AC114 Accounting I
Kaplan University

Warren~Reeve~Duchac

THOMSON
TM

Australia · Canada · Mexico · Singapore · Spain · United Kingdom · United States

Warren~Reeve~Duchac
AC114 Accounting I - Kaplan University

Executive Editors:
Michele Baird, Maureen Staudt &
Michael Stranz

Project Development Manager:
Linda deStefano

Sr. Marketing Coordinators:
Lindsay Annett and Sara Mercurio

Production/Manufacturing Manager:
Donna M. Brown

Production Editorial Manager:
Dan Plofchan

Pre-Media Services Supervisor:
Becki Walker

Rights and Permissions Specialist:
Kalina Ingham Hintz

Cover Image
Getty Images*

The Adaptable Courseware Program consists of products and additions to existing Thomson products that are produced from camera-ready copy. Peer review, class testing, and accuracy are primarily the responsibility of the author(s).

Title: AC114 Accounting I - Kaplan University
Author: Warren~Reeve~Duchac

ISBN-13: 978-0-324-62499-1
ISBN-10: 0-324-62499-9

International Divisions List

Asia (Including India):
Thomson Learning
(a division of Thomson Asia Pte Ltd)
5 Shenton Way #01-01
UIC Building
Singapore 068808
Tel: (65) 6410-1200
Fax: (65) 6410-1208

Australia/New Zealand:
Thomson Learning Australia
102 Dodds Street
Southbank, Victoria 3006
Australia

Latin America:
Thomson Learning
Seneca 53
Colonia Polano
11560 Mexico, D.F., Mexico
Tel (525) 281-2906
Fax (525) 281-2656

Canada:
Thomson Nelson
1120 Birchmount Road
Toronto, Ontario
Canada M1K 5G4
Tel (416) 752-9100
Fax (416) 752-8102

UK/Europe/Middle East/Africa:
Thomson Learning
High Holborn House
50-51 Bedford Row
London, WC1R 4LS
United Kingdom
Tel 44 (020) 7067-2500
Fax 44 (020) 7067-2600

Spain (Includes Portugal):
Thomson Paraninfo
Calle Magallanes 25
28015 Madrid
España
Tel 34 (0)91 446-3350
Fax 34 (0)91 445-6218

Custom Contents

Introduction to Accounting and Business

objectives

After studying this chapter, you should be able to:

1. *Describe the nature of a business and the role of ethics and accounting in business.*

2. *Summarize the development of accounting principles and relate them to practice.*

3. *State the accounting equation and define each element of the equation.*

4. *Describe and illustrate how business transactions can be recorded in terms of the resulting change in the basic elements of the accounting equation.*

5. *Describe the financial statements of a proprietorship and explain how they interrelate.*

Google™

When two teams pair up for a game of football, there is often a lot of noise. The band plays, the fans cheer, and fireworks light up the scoreboard. Obviously, the fans are committed and care about the outcome of the game. Just like fans at a football game, the owners of a business want their business to "win" against their competitors in the marketplace. While having our football team win can be a source of pride, winning in the marketplace goes beyond pride and has many tangible benefits. Companies that are winners are better able to serve customers, to provide good jobs for employees, and to make more money for the owners.

One such successful company is Google, one of the most visible companies on the Internet. Many of us cannot visit the Web without first stopping at Google to get a search listing. As one writer said, "Google is the closest thing the Web has to an ultimate answer machine."[1] And yet, Google is a free tool—no one asks for your credit card when you use any of Google's search tools. So, do you think Google has been a successful company? Does it make money? How would you know? Accounting helps to answer these questions. Google's accounting information tells us that Google is a very successful company that makes a lot of money, but not from you and me. Google makes its money from advertisers.

In this textbook, we will introduce you to accounting, the language of business. In this chapter, we begin by discussing what a business is, how it operates, and the role that accounting plays.

Nature of Business and Accounting

You can probably list some examples of companies like Google with which you have recently done business. Your examples might be large companies, such as The Coca-Cola Company, Dell Inc., or Amazon.com. They might be local companies, such as gas stations or grocery stores, or perhaps employers. They might be restaurants, law firms, or medical offices. What do all these examples have in common that identify them as businesses?

In general, a **business**[2] is an organization in which basic resources (inputs), such as materials and labor, are assembled and processed to provide goods or services (outputs) to customers. Businesses come in all sizes, from a local coffee house to a DaimlerChrysler, which sells several billion dollars worth of cars and trucks each year. A business's customers are individuals or other businesses who purchase goods or services in exchange for money or other items of value. In contrast, a church is not a business, because those who receive its services are not legally obligated to pay for them.

The objective of most businesses is to maximize profits. **Profit** is the difference between the amounts received from customers for goods or services provided and the amounts paid for the inputs used to provide the goods or services. Some businesses operate with an objective other than to maximize profits. The objective of such not-for-profit businesses is to provide some benefit to society, such as medical research or conservation of natural resources. In other cases, governmental units such as cities operate water works or sewage treatment plants on a nonprofit basis. We will focus in this text on businesses operating to earn a profit. Keep in mind, though, that many of the same concepts and principles apply to not-for-profit businesses as well.

---

1 As quoted on Google's Web site.
2 A complete glossary of terms appears at the end of the text.

TYPES OF BUSINESSES

There are three different types of businesses that are operated for profit: service, merchandising, and manufacturing businesses. Each type of business has unique characteristics.

Service businesses provide services rather than products to customers. Examples of service businesses and the types of services they offer are shown below.

Service Business	Service
The Walt Disney Company	Entertainment
Delta Air Lines	Transportation
Marriott International, Inc.	Hospitality and lodging
Bank of America Corporation	Financial services
XM Satellite Radio	Satellite radio

Merchandising businesses sell products they purchase from other businesses to customers. In this sense, merchandisers bring products and customers together. Examples of merchandising businesses and some of the products they sell are shown below.

Merchandising Business	Product
Wal-Mart	General merchandise
GameStop Corporation	Video games and accessories
Best Buy	Consumer electronics
Gap Inc.	Apparel
Amazon.com	Internet books, music, videos

Manufacturing businesses change basic inputs into products that are sold to individual customers. Examples of manufacturing businesses and some of their products are as follows:

Manufacturing Business	Product
General Motors Corporation	Cars, trucks, vans
Samsung	Cell phones
Dell Inc.	Personal computers
NIKE	Athletic shoes and apparel
The Coca-Cola Company	Beverages
Sony Corporation	Stereos and televisions

TYPES OF BUSINESS ORGANIZATIONS

The common forms of business organization are proprietorship, partnership, corporation, or limited liability company. Each of these forms and their major characteristics are listed below.

- A **proprietorship** is owned by one individual and
  - Comprises 70% of business organizations in the United States.
  - Cost of organizing is low.
  - Is limited to financial resources of the owner.
  - Is used by small businesses.
- A **partnership** is similar to a proprietorship except that it is owned by two or more individuals and
  - Comprises 10% of business organizations in the United States.
  - Combines the skills and resources of more than one person.
- A **corporation** is organized under state or federal statutes as a separate legal taxable entity and
  - Generates 90% of the total dollars of business receipts received.
  - Comprises 20% of the business organizations in the United States.

- Includes ownership divided into shares of stock, sold to shareholders (stockholders).
- Is able to obtain large amounts of resources by issuing stock.
- Is used by large businesses.

■ A **limited liability company (LLC)** combines attributes of a partnership and a corporation in that it is organized as a corporation. However, an LLC can elect to be taxed as a partnership and
- Is a popular alternative to a partnership.
- Has tax and liability advantages to the owners.

> Service, merchandising, and manufacturing businesses are commonly organized as either proprietorships, partnerships, corporations, or limited liability companies.

The three types of businesses we discussed earlier—service, merchandising, and manufacturing—may be organized as either proprietorships, partnerships, corporations, or limited liability companies. Because of the large amount of resources required to operate a manufacturing business, most manufacturing businesses are corporations. Likewise, most large retailers such as Wal-Mart, Home Depot, and JCPenney are corporations.

BUSINESS STAKEHOLDERS

A **business stakeholder** is a person or entity that has an interest in the economic performance and well-being of a business. For example, owners, suppliers, customers, and employees are all stakeholders in a business. Business stakeholders can be classified into one of the four categories illustrated in Exhibit 1.

Capital market stakeholders provide the major financing for the business in order for the business to begin and continue its operations. Banks and other long-term creditors have an economic interest in recovering the amount they loaned the business plus interest. Owners want to maximize the economic value of their investments and thus also have an economic interest in the business.

Product or service market stakeholders include customers who purchase the business's products or services as well as the vendors who supply inputs to the business. Customers have an economic interest in the continued success of the business. For example, customers who purchase advance tickets from Southwest Airlines Co. have an economic interest in whether Southwest will stay in business. Similarly, suppliers are stakeholders in the continued success of their customers as a source of business.

Government stakeholders have an interest in the economic performance of businesses. As a result, city and state governments often provide incentives for businesses to locate in their jurisdictions. City, county, state, and federal governments collect taxes from businesses within their jurisdictions. In addition, workers are taxed on their wages. The better a business does, the more taxes the government can collect.

Internal stakeholders include individuals employed by the business. The managers are those individuals whom the owners have authorized to operate the business. Managers are primarily evaluated on the economic performance of the business. Thus, managers have an incentive to maximize the economic value of the business. Owners may offer managers salary contracts that are tied directly to how well the business performs. For example, a manager might receive a percentage of the profits or a percentage of the increase in profits. Employees provide services to the company they work for in exchange for pay. Thus, employees have an interest in the economic performance of the business, because their jobs depend upon it.

REAL WORLD

The state of Alabama offered DaimlerChrysler millions of dollars in incentives to locate a Mercedes plant in Alabama.

ROLE OF ETHICS IN BUSINESS

The moral principles that guide the conduct of individuals are called **ethics**. Unfortunately, business managers can be pressured to violate personal ethics. Such was the case for a number of companies listed in Exhibit 2, on page 6, that engaged in fraudulent business practices and accounting coverups in the early 2000s.

EXHIBIT 1   Business Stakeholders

Business Stakeholder	Interest in the Business	Examples
Capital market stakeholders	Providers of major financing for the business	Banks and owners
Product or service market stakeholders	Buyers of products or services and vendors to the business	Customers and suppliers
Government stakeholders	Collect taxes and fees from the business and its employees	Federal, state, and local governments
Internal stakeholders	Individuals employed by the business	Employees and managers

Stakeholders

Employees/Managers

Customers

Suppliers

Bank and/or Owners

Business

Government

The companies listed in Exhibit 2 were caught in the midst of ethical lapses that led to fines, firings, and criminal and/or civil prosecution. The second column of Exhibit 2 identifies the nature of scandal. The third column of the table identifies some of the results of these events. In most cases, senior and mid-level executives lost their jobs and were sued by upset investors. In some cases, the executives were also criminally prosecuted and are serving prison terms.

What went wrong for these companies and executives? The answer to this question involves the following three factors:

1. Individual character
2. Firm culture
3. Laws and enforcement

REAL WORLD

Most colleges and universities publish a Student Code of Conduct that sets forth the ethical conduct expected of students.

Individual Character An ethical businessperson displays character by embracing honesty, integrity, and fairness in the face of pressure to hide the truth. Executives often face pressures from senior managers to meet company and analysts' expectations. In many of the cases in Exhibit 2, executives initially justified small violations to avoid such pressures. However, these small lies became big lies as the company's financial problems became worse. By the time the abuses were discovered, the misstatements became sufficient to ruin businesses and wreck lives. For example, David Myers, the former controller

EXHIBIT 2   Accounting and Business Fraud in the 2000s

Company	Nature of Accounting or Business Fraud	Result
Adelphia Communications	Rigas family treated the company assets as their own.	Bankruptcy. Rigas family members found guilty of fraud and lost their investment in the company.
American International Group, Inc. (AIG)	Used sham accounting transactions to inflate performance.	CEO resigned. Executives indicted. AIG paid $126 million in fines.
America Online, Inc. and PurchasePro	Artificially inflated their financial results.	Civil charges filed against senior executives of both companies. $500 million fine.
Computer Associates International, Inc.	Fraudulently inflated its financial results.	CEO and senior executives indicted. Five executives plead guilty. $225 million fine.
Enron	Fraudulently inflated its financial results.	Bankrupcty. Criminal charges against senior executives, over $60 billion in stock market losses.
Fannie Mae	Improperly shifted financial performance between periods.	CEO and CFO fired. Company made a $9 billion correction to previously reported earnings.
HealthSouth	Overstated performance by $4 billion in false entries.	Senior executives criminally indicted.
Qwest Communications International, Inc.	Improperly recognized $3 billion in false receipts.	CEO and six other executives charged with "massive financial fraud." $250 million SEC fine.
Tyco International, Ltd.	Failed to disclose secret loans to executives that were subsequently forgiven.	CEO forced to resign and subjected to frozen asset order and criminal proceedings.
WorldCom	Misstated financial results by nearly $9 billion.	Bankruptcy. Criminal conviction of CEO and CFO. Over $100 billion in stock market losses. Directors forced to pay $18 million.
Xerox Corporation	Recognized $3 billion in revenue prior to when it should have been.	$10 million fine to SEC. Six executives forced to pay $22 million.

of WorldCom, in testifying about his recording of improper transactions stated the following:

> "I didn't think that it was the right thing to do, but I had been asked by Scott (Sullivan, the VP of Finance) to do it. . . ."[3]

Nonetheless, David Myers was criminally convicted and was sentenced to prison.

Firm Culture By their behavior and attitude, senior managers of a company set the firm culture. As explained by one author, when the leader of a company is put on a pedestal, "they begin to believe they and their organizations are one-of-a-kind, that they're changing the face of the industry. They desire rewards and benefits beyond any other CEOs (chief executive officers)."[4] In most of the firms shown in Exhibit 2, the senior managers created a culture of greed and indifference to the truth. This

---

3 Susan Pulliam, "Crossing the Line: At Center of Fraud, WorldCom Official Sees Life Unravel," *The Wall Street Journal*, March 24, 2005, p. A1.
4 Tim Race, "New Economy Executives Are Smitten, and Undone by Their Own Images," *The New York Times*, July 7, 2002. Quote attributed to Professor Jay A. Conger.

Integrity, Objectivity, and Ethics in Business

ETHICS

DOING THE RIGHT THING

Time Magazine named three women as "Persons of the Year 2002." Each of these not-so-ordinary women had the courage, determination, and integrity to do the right thing. Each risked their personal careers to expose shortcomings in their organizations. Sherron Watkins, an Enron vice president, wrote a letter to Enron's chairman, Kenneth Lay, warning him of improper accounting that eventually led to Enron's collapse. Cynthia Cooper, an internal accountant, informed WorldCom's Board of Directors of phony accounting that allowed WorldCom to cover up over $3 billion in losses and forced WorldCom into bankruptcy. Coleen Rowley, an FBI staff attorney, wrote a memo to FBI Director Robert Mueller, exposing how the Bureau brushed off her pleas to investigate Zacarias Moussaoui, who was indicted as a co-conspirator in the September 11 terrorist attacks.

REAL WORLD

Stanley James Cardiges, the former top U.S. sales representative for American Honda, admitted to receiving $2 million to $5 million in illegal kickbacks from dealers. After being sentenced to five years in prison, he admitted to falling into a pattern of unethical behavior early in his career.

culture flowed down to lower-level managers, creating an environment of short cuts, greed, and lies that ultimately resulted in financial fraud.

Laws and Enforcement Many blamed the lack of laws and enforcement for contributing to the financial reporting abuses described in Exhibit 2. For example, Eliot Spitzer, the attorney general of New York, stated the following:

". . . a key lesson from the recent scandals is that the checks on the system simply have not worked. The honor code among CEOs didn't work. Board oversight didn't work. Self-regulation was a complete failure."[5]

As a result, new laws were enacted by Congress, and enforcement efforts have increased since the early 2000s. For example, the Sarbanes-Oxley Act of 2002 (SOX) was enacted. SOX established a new oversight body for the accounting profession called the Public Company Accounting Oversight Board (PCAOB). In addition, SOX established standards for independence, corporate responsibility, enhanced financial disclosures, and corporate accountability.

THE ROLE OF ACCOUNTING IN BUSINESS

What is the role of accounting in business? The simplest answer to this question is that accounting provides information for managers to use in operating the business. In addition, accounting provides information to other stakeholders to use in assessing the economic performance and condition of the business.

In a general sense, **accounting** can be defined as an information system that provides reports to stakeholders about the economic activities and condition of a business. As we indicated earlier in this chapter, we will focus our discussions on accounting and its role in business. However, many of the concepts in this text apply also to individuals, governments, and other types of organizations.

You may think of accounting as the "language of business." This is because accounting is the means by which business information is communicated to the stakeholders. For example, accounting reports summarizing the profitability of a new product help The Coca-Cola Company's management decide whether to continue selling the product. Likewise, financial analysts use accounting reports in deciding whether to recommend the purchase of Coca-Cola's stock. Banks use accounting reports in determining the amount

> Accounting is an information system that provides reports to stakeholders about the economic activities and condition of a business.

---

5 Eliot Spitzer, "Strong Law Enforcement Is Good for the Economy," *The Wall Street Journal*, April 5, 2005, p. A18.

of credit to extend to Coca-Cola. Suppliers use accounting reports in deciding whether to offer credit for Coca-Cola's purchases of supplies and raw materials. State and federal governments use accounting reports as a basis for assessing taxes on Coca-Cola.

The process by which accounting provides information to business stakeholders is as follows.

1. Identify stakeholders.
2. Assess stakeholders' informational needs.
3. Design the accounting information system to meet stakeholders' needs.
4. Record economic data about business activities and events.
5. Prepare accounting reports for stakeholders.

As illustrated in Exhibit 3, stakeholders use accounting reports as a primary, although not the only, source of information on which they base their decisions. Stakeholders use other information as well. For example, in deciding whether to extend credit to a local retail store, a banker would not only use the store's accounting reports, but might also visit the store and inquire about the owner's reputation in the business community.

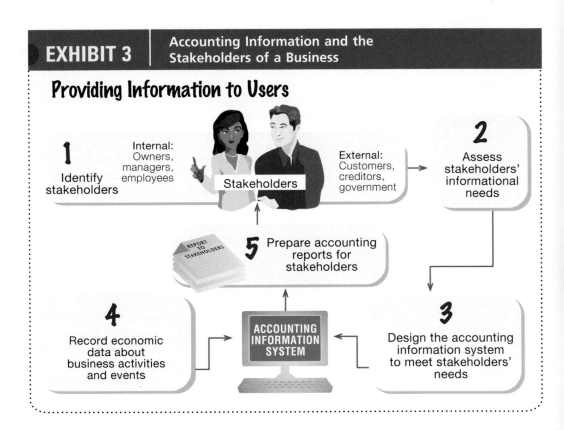

EXHIBIT 3 | Accounting Information and the Stakeholders of a Business

PROFESSION OF ACCOUNTING

You may think that all accounting is the same. However, you will find several specialized fields of accounting in practice. The two most common are financial accounting and managerial accounting. Other fields include cost accounting, environmental accounting, tax accounting, accounting systems, international accounting, not-for-profit accounting, and social accounting.

Financial accounting is primarily concerned with the recording and reporting of economic data and activities for a business. Although such reports provide useful information for managers, they are the primary reports for owners, creditors, governmental agencies, and the public. For example, if you wanted to buy some stock in PepsiCo, Inc., American Airlines, or McDonald's, how would you know in which company to invest? One way is to review financial reports and compare the financial performance and condition of each company. The purpose of financial accounting is to provide such reports.

Managerial accounting, or **management accounting**, uses both financial accounting and estimated data to aid management in running day-to-day operations and in planning future operations. Management accountants gather and report information that is relevant and timely to the decision-making needs of management. For example, management might need information on alternative ways to finance the construction of a new building. Alternatively, management might need information on whether to expand its operations into a new product line. Thus, reports to management can differ widely in form and content.

Whether they are engaged in financial accounting or managerial accounting, accountants are employed in either private accounting or public accounting as shown in Exhibit 4. Accountants employed by a business firm or a not-for-profit organization are said to be employed in **private accounting**. Accountants and their staff who provide services on a fee basis are said to be employed in **public accounting**.

Private accountants have a variety of possible career options inside the firm. Some of these career options are shown in Exhibit 4 along with their starting salaries. The phrase "audit services" may be new to you. Individuals who provide audit services, called auditors, verify the accuracy of financial records, accounts, and systems. Several private accounting careers have certification options. The Institute of Management Accountants (IMA) sponsors the **Certified Management Accountant (CMA)** program. The CMA certificate is evidence of competence in management accounting. Becoming a CMA requires a college degree, two years of experience, and successful completion of a two-day examination. Additional certifications in private accounting include the Certified Internal Auditor (CIA), sponsored by The Institute of Internal Auditors, the Certified Information Systems Auditor (CISA), sponsored by the Information Systems Audit and Control Association, and the Certified Payroll Professional (CPP), sponsored by the American Payroll Association.

EXHIBIT 4 Accounting Career Paths and Salaries

Accounting Career Track	Description	Career Options	Annual Starting Salaries[1]	Certification
Private Accounting	Accountants employed by companies, government, and not-for-profit entities.	Bookkeeper	$28,500	
		Payroll clerk	$30,875	Certified Payroll Professional (CPP)
		General accountant	$35,750	
		Budget analyst	$36,750	
		Cost accountant	$37,375	Certified Management Accountant (CMA)
		Internal auditor	$41,500	Certified Internal Auditor (CIA)
		Information technology auditor	$72,500	Certified Information Systems Auditor (CISA)
Public Accounting	Accountants employed individually or within a public accounting firm in tax or audit services.	Local firms	$36,625	Certified Public Accountant (CPA)
		National firms	$44,375	Certified Public Accountant (CPA)

Source: Robert Half 2006 Salary Guide (Finance and Accounting), Robert Half International, Inc.
[1]Median salaries of a reported range. Private accounting salaries are reported for large companies. Information technology auditor salary is for all company sizes and experience levels combined. Salaries may vary by region.

In public accounting, an accountant may practice as an individual or as a member of a public accounting firm. Public accountants who have met a state's education, experience, and examination requirements may become **Certified Public Accountants (CPAs)**. CPAs generally perform general accounting, audit, or tax services. As can be seen in Exhibit 4, CPAs have slightly better starting salaries than private accountants. Career statistics indicate, however, that these salary differences tend to disappear over time.

The requirements for obtaining a CPA certificate differ among the various states. All states require a college education in accounting, and most states require 150 semester hours of college credit. In addition, a candidate must pass an examination prepared by the American Institute of Certified Public Accountants (AICPA). Because all functions within a business use accounting information, experience in private or public accounting provides a solid foundation for a career. Many positions in industry and in government agencies are held by individuals with accounting backgrounds.

Generally Accepted Accounting Principles

objective   2

Summarize the development of accounting principles and relate them to practice.

If a company's management could record and report financial data as it saw fit, comparisons among companies would be difficult, if not impossible. Thus, financial accountants follow **generally accepted accounting principles (GAAP)** in preparing reports. These reports allow investors and other stakeholders to compare one company to another.

To illustrate the importance of generally accepted accounting principles, assume that each sports conference in college football used different rules for counting touchdowns. For example, assume that the Pacific Athletic Conference (PAC 10) counted a touchdown as six points and the Atlantic Coast Conference (ACC) counted a touchdown as two points. It would be difficult to evaluate the teams under such different scoring systems. A standard set of rules and a standard scoring system help fans compare teams across conferences. Likewise, a standard set of generally accepted accounting principles allows for the comparison of financial performance and condition across companies.

Accounting principles and concepts develop from research, accepted accounting practices, and pronouncements of authoritative bodies. Currently, the **Financial Accounting Standards Board (FASB)** is the authoritative body having the primary responsibility for developing accounting principles. The FASB publishes *Statements of Financial Accounting Standards* as well as *Interpretations* of these Standards.

Because generally accepted accounting principles impact how companies report and what they report, all stakeholders are interested in the setting of these principles. Thus, standards are established according to a process that seeks and considers input from all affected parties. The standard-setting activities of the FASB are published and made available at **http://www.fasb.org.**

In this chapter and throughout this text, we emphasize accounting principles and concepts. It is through this emphasis on the "why" of accounting as well as the "how"

Integrity, Objectivity, and Ethics in Business   ETHICS

ACCOUNTING REFORM

The financial accounting and reporting failures of Enron, WorldCom, Tyco, Xerox, and others shocked the investing public. The disclosure that some of the nation's largest and best-known corporations had overstated profits and misled investors raised the question: Where were the CPAs?

In response, Congress passed the Investor Protection, Auditor Reform, and Transparency Act of 2002, called the Sarbanes-Oxley Act. The Act establishes a Public Company

Accounting Oversight Board to regulate the portion of the accounting profession that has public companies as clients. In addition, the Act prohibits auditors (CPAs) from providing certain types of nonaudit services, such as investment banking or legal services, to their clients, prohibits employment of auditors by clients for one year after they last audited the client, and increases penalties for the reporting of misleading financial statements.

that you will gain an understanding of the full significance of accounting. In the following paragraphs, we discuss the business entity concept and the cost concept.

BUSINESS ENTITY CONCEPT

The individual business unit is the business entity for which economic data are needed. This entity could be an automobile dealer, a department store, or a grocery store. The business entity must be identified, so that the accountant can determine which economic data should be analyzed, recorded, and summarized in reports.

> Under the business entity concept, the activities of a business are recorded separately from the activities of the stakeholders.

The **business entity concept** is important because it limits the economic data in the accounting system to data related directly to the activities of the business. In other words, the business is viewed as an entity separate from its owners, creditors, or other stakeholders. For example, the accountant for a business with one owner (a proprietorship) would record the activities of the business only, not the personal activities, property, or debts of the owner.

THE COST CONCEPT

If a building is bought for $150,000, that amount should be entered into the buyer's accounting records. The seller may have been asking $170,000 for the building up to the time of the sale. The buyer may have initially offered $130,000 for the building. The building may have been assessed at $125,000 for property tax purposes. The buyer may have received an offer of $175,000 for the building the day after it was acquired. These latter amounts have no effect on the accounting records because they did not result in an exchange of the building from the seller to the buyer. The **cost concept** is the basis for entering the *exchange price, or cost, of $150,000* into the accounting records for the building.

Continuing the illustration, the $175,000 offer received by the buyer the day after the building was acquired indicates that it was a bargain purchase at $150,000. To use $175,000 in the accounting records, however, would record an illusory or unrealized profit. If, after buying the building, the buyer accepts the offer and sells the building for $175,000, a profit of $25,000 is then realized and recorded. The new owner would record $175,000 as the cost of the building.

Using the cost concept involves two other important accounting concepts—objectivity and the unit of measure. The **objectivity concept** requires that the accounting records and reports be based upon objective evidence. In exchanges between a buyer and a seller, both try to get the best price. Only the final agreed-upon amount is objective enough for accounting purposes. If the amounts at which properties were recorded were constantly being revised upward and downward based on offers, appraisals, and opinions, accounting reports could soon become unstable and unreliable.

The **unit of measure concept** requires that economic data be recorded in dollars. Money is a common unit of measurement for reporting uniform financial data and reports.

Example Exercise 1-1 objective

On August 25, Gallatin Repair Service extended an offer of $125,000 for land that had been priced for sale at $150,000. On September 3, Gallatin Repair Service accepted the seller's counteroffer of $137,000. On October 20, the land was assessed at a value of $98,000 for property tax purposes. On December 4, Gallatin Repair Service was offered $160,000 for the land by a national retail chain. At what value should the land be recorded in Gallatin Repair Service's records?

Follow My Example 1-1

$137,000. Under the cost concept, the land should be recorded at the cost to Gallatin Repair Service.

For Practice: PE 1-1A, PE 1-1B

The Accounting Equation

objective **3**

State the accounting equation and define each element of the equation.

The resources owned by a business are its **assets**. Examples of assets include cash, land, buildings, and equipment. The rights or claims to the properties are normally divided into two principal types: (1) the rights of creditors and (2) the rights of owners. The rights of creditors represent debts of the business and are called **liabilities**. The rights of the owners are called **owner's equity**. The relationship between the two may be stated in the form of an equation, as follows:

$$\text{Assets} = \text{Liabilities} + \text{Owner's Equity}$$

This equation is known as the **accounting equation**. Liabilities usually are shown before owner's equity in the accounting equation because creditors have first rights to the assets. The claim of the owners is sometimes given greater emphasis by transposing liabilities to the other side of the equation, which yields:

$$\text{Assets} - \text{Liabilities} = \text{Owner's Equity}$$

To illustrate, if the assets owned by a business amount to $100,000 and the liabilities amount to $30,000, the owner's equity is equal to $70,000, as shown below.

Assets	−	Liabilities	=	Owner's Equity
$100,000	−	$30,000	=	$70,000

Example Exercise 1-2
objective **3**

John Joos is the owner and operator of You're A Star, a motivational consulting business. At the end of its accounting period, December 31, 2007, You're A Star has assets of $800,000 and liabilities of $350,000. Using the accounting equation, determine the following amounts:

a. Owner's equity, as of December 31, 2007.
b. Owner's equity, as of December 31, 2008, assuming that assets increased by $130,000 and liabilities decreased by $25,000 during 2008.

Follow My Example 1-2

a. $\qquad$ Assets = Liabilities + Owner's Equity
$\qquad\quad$ $800,000 = $350,000 + Owner's Equity
$\quad$ Owner's Equity = $450,000

b. First, determine the change in Owner's Equity during 2008 as follows:

$\qquad$ Assets = Liabilities + Owner's Equity
$\qquad\quad$ $130,000 = −$25,000 + Owner's Equity
$\quad$ Owner's Equity = $155,000

Next, add the change in Owner's Equity on December 31, 2007 to arrive at Owner's Equity on December 31, 2008, as shown below:

Owner's Equity on December 31, 2008 =
$605,000 = $450,000 + $155,000

For Practice: PE 1-2A, PE 1-2B

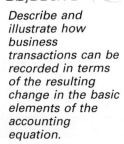

---

objective **4**

Describe and illustrate how business transactions can be recorded in terms of the resulting change in the basic elements of the accounting equation.

Business Transactions and the Accounting Equation

Paying a monthly telephone bill of $168 affects a business's financial condition because it now has less cash on hand. Such an economic event or condition that directly changes an entity's financial condition or directly affects its results of operations is a **business transaction**. For example, purchasing land for $50,000 is a business transaction. In contrast, a change in a business's credit rating does not directly affect cash or any other element of its financial condition.

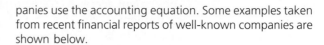

Business Connections

THE ACCOUNTING EQUATION

The accounting equation serves as the basic foundation for the accounting systems of all companies. From the smallest business, such as the local convenience store, to the largest business, such as Ford Motor Company, companies use the accounting equation. Some examples taken from recent financial reports of well-known companies are shown below.

Company	Assets*	=	Liabilities	+	Owner's Equity
The Coca-Cola Company	$ 31,327	=	$15,392	+	$15,935
Circuit City Stores, Inc.	3,709	=	1,795	+	1,914
Dell Inc.	22,874	=	18,053	+	4,821
eBay Inc.	9,626	=	1,599	+	8,027
Hilton Hospitality, Inc.	8,242	=	5,674	+	2,568
McDonald's	27,844	=	13,328	+	14,516
Microsoft Corporation	71,462	=	23,135	+	48,327
Southwest Airlines Co.	11,337	=	5,813	+	5,524
Wal-Mart	124,765	=	77,044	+	47,721

*Amounts are shown in millions of dollars.

All business transactions can be stated in terms of changes in the elements of the accounting equation. You will see how business transactions affect the accounting equation by studying some typical transactions. As a basis for illustration, we will use a business organized by Chris Clark.

Assume that on November 1, 2007, Chris Clark begins a business that will be known as NetSolutions. The first phase of Chris's business plan is to operate NetSolutions as a service business that provides assistance to individuals and small businesses in developing Web pages and in configuring and installing application software. Chris expects this initial phase of the business to last one to two years. During this period, Chris will gather information on the software and hardware needs of customers. During the second phase of the business plan, Chris plans to expand NetSolutions into a personalized retailer of software and hardware for individuals and small businesses.

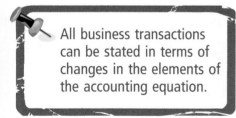

All business transactions can be stated in terms of changes in the elements of the accounting equation.

Each transaction or group of similar transactions during NetSolutions' first month of operations is described in the following paragraphs. The effect of each transaction on the accounting equation is then shown.

@netsolutions   **Transaction a**   Chris Clark deposits $25,000 in a bank account in the name of NetSolutions. The effect of this transaction is to increase the asset cash (on the left side of the equation) by $25,000. To balance the equation, the owner's equity (on the right side of the equation) is increased by the same amount. The equity of the owner is referred to by using the owner's name and "Capital," such as "Chris Clark, Capital." The effect of this transaction on NetSolutions' accounting equation is shown below.

Assets	=	Owner's Equity
Cash	=	Chris Clark, Capital
a. 25,000		25,000

Note that since Chris Clark is the sole owner, NetSolutions is a proprietorship. Note, too, that the accounting equation shown above relates only to the business, NetSolutions. Under the business entity concept, Chris Clark's personal assets, such as a home or personal bank account, and personal liabilities are excluded from the equation.

Transaction b If you purchased this textbook by paying cash, you entered into a transaction in which you exchanged one asset for another. That is, you exchanged cash for the textbook. Businesses often enter into similar transactions. NetSolutions, for example, exchanged $20,000 cash for land. The land is located in a new business park with convenient access to transportation facilities. Chris Clark plans to rent office space and equipment during the first phase of the business plan. During the second phase, Chris plans to build an office and a warehouse on the land.

The purchase of the land changes the makeup of the assets but does not change the total assets. The items in the equation prior to this transaction and the effect of the transaction are shown next, as well as the new amounts, or *balances*, of the items.

	Assets		=	Owner's Equity
	Cash +	Land		Chris Clark, Capital
Bal.	25,000			25,000
b.	−20,000	+20,000		
Bal.	5,000	20,000		25,000

Transaction c You have probably used a credit card to buy clothing or other merchandise. In this type of transaction, you received clothing for a promise to pay your credit card bill in the future. That is, you received an asset and incurred a liability to pay a future bill. During the month, NetSolutions entered into a similar transaction, buying supplies for $1,350 and agreeing to pay the supplier in the near future. This type of transaction is called a purchase *on account*. The liability created is called an **account payable**. Items such as supplies that will be used in the business in the future are called **prepaid expenses**, which are assets. The effect of this transaction is to increase assets and liabilities by $1,350, as follows:

Other examples of common prepaid expenses include insurance and rent. Businesses often report these assets together as a single item, prepaid expenses.

	Assets			=	Liabilities + Owner's Equity	
					Accounts	Chris Clark,
	Cash +	Supplies +	Land		Payable +	Capital
Bal.	5,000		20,000			25,000
c.		+1,350			+1,350	
Bal.	5,000	1,350	20,000		1,350	25,000

Transaction d You may have earned money by painting houses or mowing lawns. If so, you received money for rendering services to a customer. Likewise, a business earns money by selling goods or services to its customers. This amount is called **revenue**.

During its first month of operations, NetSolutions provided services to customers, earning fees of $7,500 and receiving the amount in cash. The receipt of cash increases NetSolutions' assets and also increases Chris Clark's equity in the business. In order to aid in the preparation of financial statements, the revenues of $7,500 are recorded in a separate column to the right of Chris Clark, Capital. This is done so that the effects on owner's capital can be separately identified and summarized. Thus, this transaction is recorded as an increase in Cash and Fees Earned of $7,500 as shown below.

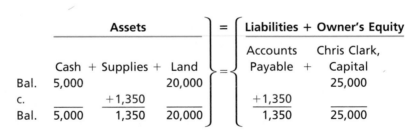

	Assets			=	Liabilities +	Owner's Equity	
					Accounts	Chris Clark,	Fees
	Cash +	Supplies +	Land		Payable +	Capital	+ Earned
Bal.	5,000	1,350	20,000		1,350	25,000	
d.	+7,500						+7,500
Bal.	12,500	1,350	20,000		1,350	25,000	7,500

Special terms may be used to describe certain kinds of revenue, such as **sales** for the sale of merchandise. Revenue from providing services is called **fees earned**. For example, a physician would record fees earned for services to patients. Other examples include **rent revenue** (money received for rent) and **interest revenue** (money received for interest).

Instead of requiring the payment of cash at the time services are provided or goods are sold, a business may accept payment at a later date. Such revenues are called *fees on account* or *sales on account*. In such cases, the firm has an **account receivable**, which is a claim against the customer. An account receivable is an asset, and the revenue is earned as if cash had been received. When customers pay their accounts, there is an exchange of one asset for another. Cash increases, while accounts receivable decreases.

Transaction e If you painted houses to earn money, you probably used your own ladders and brushes. NetSolutions also spent cash or used up other assets in earning revenue. The amounts used in this process of earning revenue are called **expenses**. Expenses include supplies used, wages of employees, and other assets and services used in operating the business.

NetSolutions paid the following expenses during the month: wages, $2,125; rent, $800; utilities, $450; and miscellaneous, $275. Miscellaneous expenses include small amounts paid for such items as postage, coffee, and magazine subscriptions. The effect of this group of transactions is the opposite of the effect of revenues. These transactions reduce cash and owner's equity. Like fees earned, the expenses are recorded in separate columns to the right of Chris Clark, Capital. However, since expenses reduce owner's equity, the expenses are entered as negative amounts.

	Assets			=	Liabilities +			Owner's Equity			
	Cash	+ Supplies +	Land		Accounts Payable +	Chris Clark, Capital	+ Fees Earned	− Wages Expense	− Rent Expense	− Utilities Expense	− Misc. Expense
Bal.	12,500	1,350	20,000		1,350	25,000	7,500				
e.	−3,650							−2,125	−800	−450	−275
Bal.	8,850	1,350	20,000		1,350	25,000	7,500	−2,125	−800	−450	−275

Businesses usually record each revenue and expense transaction separately as it occurs. However, to simplify this illustration, we have summarized NetSolutions' revenues and expenses for the month in transactions (d) and (e).

Transaction f When you pay your monthly credit card bill, you decrease the cash in your checking account and also decrease the amount you owe to the credit card company. Likewise, when NetSolutions pays $950 to creditors during the month, it reduces both assets and liabilities, as shown below.

	Assets			=	Liabilities +			Owner's Equity			
	Cash	+ Supplies +	Land		Accounts Payable +	Chris Clark, Capital	+ Fees Earned	− Wages Expense	− Rent Expense	− Utilities Expense	− Misc. Expense
Bal.	8,850	1,350	20,000		1,350	25,000	7,500	−2,125	−800	−450	−275
f.	−950				−950						
Bal.	7,900	1,350	20,000		400	25,000	7,500	−2,125	−800	−450	−275

You should note that paying an amount on account is different from paying an amount for an expense. The payment of an expense reduces owner's equity, as illustrated in transaction (e). Paying an amount on account reduces the amount owed on a liability.

Transaction g At the end of the month, the cost of the supplies on hand (not yet used) is $550. The remainder of the supplies ($1,350 − $550) was used in the operations of the business and is treated as an expense. This decrease of $800 in supplies and owner's equity is shown as follows:

	Assets			=	Liabilities +			Owner's Equity					
					Accounts	Chris Clark,	Fees	Wages	Rent	Supplies	Utilities	Misc.
	Cash	+ Supplies +	Land	=	Payable +	Capital	+ Earned −	Exp. −	Exp. −	Exp.	− Exp. −	Exp.
Bal.	7,900	1,350	20,000		400	25,000	7,500	−2,125	−800		−450	−275
g.		−800								−800		
Bal.	7,900	550	20,000		400	25,000	7,500	−2,125	−800	−800	−450	−275

Transaction h At the end of the month, Chris Clark withdraws $2,000 in cash from the business for personal use. This transaction is the exact opposite of an investment in the business by the owner. You should be careful not to confuse withdrawals by the owner with expenses. Withdrawals *do not* represent assets or services used in the process of earning revenues. Instead, withdrawals are considered a distribution of capital to the owner. Owner withdrawals are identified by the owner's name followed by *Drawing*. For example, Chris Clark's withdrawal would be identified as Chris Clark, Drawing. Like expenses, withdrawals are recorded in a separate column to the right of Chris Clark, Capital. The effect of the $2,000 withdrawal is shown as follows:

	Assets			=	Liabilities +				Owner's Equity					
					Accounts	Chris Clark,	Chris Clark,	Fees	Wages	Rent	Supplies	Utilities	Misc.
	Cash	+ Supp. +	Land	=	Payable +	Capital	− Drawing	+ Earned −	Exp. −	Exp. −	Exp. −	Exp. −	Exp.
Bal.	7,900	550	20,000		400	25,000		7,500	−2,125	−800	−800	−450	−275
h.	−2,000						−2,000						
Bal.	5,900	550	20,000		400	25,000	−2,000	7,500	−2,125	−800	−800	−450	−275

Summary The transactions of NetSolutions are summarized as follows. They are identified by letter, and the balance of each item is shown after each transaction.

	Assets			= Liabilities +			Owner's Equity						
				Accounts	Chris Clark,	Chris Clark,	Fees	Wages	Rent	Supplies	Utilities	Misc.
	Cash	+ Supp. +	Land	= Payable +	Capital	− Drawing	+ Earned −	Exp. −	Exp. −	Exp. −	Exp. −	Exp.
a.	+25,000				+25,000							
b.	−20,000		+20,000									
Bal.	5,000		20,000		25,000							
c.		+1,350		+1,350								
Bal.	5,000	1,350	20,000	1,350	25,000							
d.	+ 7,500						+7,500					
Bal.	12,500	1,350	20,000	1,350	25,000		7,500					
e.	− 3,650							−2,125	−800		−450	−275
Bal.	8,850	1,350	20,000	1,350	25,000		7,500	−2,125	−800		−450	−275
f.	− 950			− 950								
Bal.	7,900	1,350	20,000	400	25,000		7,500	−2,125	−800		−450	−275
g.		− 800								−800		
Bal.	7,900	550	20,000	400	25,000		7,500	−2,125	−800	−800	−450	−275
h.	− 2,000					−2,000						
Bal.	5,900	550	20,000	400	25,000	−2,000	7,500	−2,125	−800	−800	−450	−275

In reviewing the preceding summary, you should note the following, which apply to all types of businesses:

1. The effect of every transaction is *an increase or a decrease in one or more of the accounting equation elements.*
2. The two sides of the accounting equation are *always equal.*
3. The owner's equity is *increased by amounts invested by the owner* and is *decreased by withdrawals by the owner.* In addition, the owner's equity is *increased by revenues* and is *decreased by expenses.*

The effects of these four types of transactions on owner's equity are illustrated in Exhibit 5.

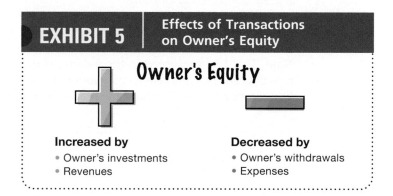

| EXHIBIT 5 | Effects of Transactions on Owner's Equity |

Owner's Equity

Increased by	Decreased by
• Owner's investments	• Owner's withdrawals
• Revenues	• Expenses

Example Exercise 1-3

objective 4

Salvo Delivery Service is owned and operated by Joel Salvo. The following selected transactions were completed by Salvo Delivery Service during February:

1. Received cash from owner as additional investment, $35,000.
2. Paid creditors on account, $1,800.
3. Billed customers for delivery services on account, $11,250.
4. Received cash from customers on account, $6,740.
5. Paid cash to owner for personal use, $1,000.

Indicate the effect of each transaction on the accounting equation elements (Assets, Liabilities, Owner's Equity, Drawing, Revenue, and Expense) by listing the numbers identifying the transactions, (1) through (5). Also, indicate the specific item within the accounting equation element that is affected. To illustrate, the answer to (1) is shown below.

(1) Asset (Cash) increases by $35,000; Owner's Equity (Joel Salvo, Capital) increases by $35,000.

Follow My Example 1-3

(2) Asset (Cash) decreases by $1,800; Liability (Accounts Payable) decreases by $1,800.
(3) Asset (Accounts Receivable) increases by $11,250; Revenue (Delivery Service Fees) increases by $11,250.
(4) Asset (Cash) increases by $6,740; Asset (Accounts Receivable) decreases by $6,740.
(5) Asset (Cash) decreases by $1,000; Drawing (Joel Salvo, Drawing) increases by $1,000.

For Practice: PE 1-3A, PE 1-3B

Financial Statements

objective 5

Describe the financial statements of a proprietorship and explain how they interrelate.

After transactions have been recorded and summarized, reports are prepared for users. The accounting reports that provide this information are called **financial statements**. The principal financial statements of a proprietorship are the income statement, the statement of owner's equity, the balance sheet, and the statement of cash flows. The order in which the statements are normally prepared and the nature of the data presented in each statement are as follows:

- **Income statement**—A summary of the revenue and expenses *for a specific period of time*, such as a month or a year.
- **Statement of owner's equity**—A summary of the changes in the owner's equity that have occurred *during a specific period of time*, such as a month or a year.
- **Balance sheet**—A list of the assets, liabilities, and owner's equity *as of a specific date*, usually at the close of the last day of a month or a year.
- **Statement of cash flows**—A summary of the cash receipts and cash payments *for a specific period of time*, such as a month or a year.

@netsolutions

The basic features of the four statements and their interrelationships are illustrated in Exhibit 6, on page 20. The data for the statements were taken from the summary of transactions of NetSolutions.

All financial statements should be identified by the name of the business, the title of the statement, and the *date* or *period of time*. The data presented in the income statement, the statement of owner's equity, and the statement of cash flows are for a period of time. The data presented in the balance sheet are for a specific date.

You should note the use of indents, captions, dollar signs, and rulings in the financial statements. They aid the reader by emphasizing the sections of the statements.

REAL WORLD

When you buy something at a store, you may *match* the cash register total with the amount you paid the cashier and with the amount of change, if any, you received.

INCOME STATEMENT

The income statement reports the revenues and expenses for a period of time, based on the **matching concept**. This concept is applied by *matching* the expenses with the revenue generated during a period by those expenses. The income statement also reports the excess of the revenue over the expenses incurred. This excess of the revenue over the expenses is called **net income** or **net profit**. If the expenses exceed the revenue, the excess is a **net loss**.

The effects of revenue earned and expenses incurred during the month for NetSolutions were shown in the equation as separate increases and decreases in each item. Net income for a period has the effect of increasing owner's equity (capital) for the period, whereas a net loss has the effect of decreasing owner's equity (capital) for the period.

The revenue, expenses, and the net income of $3,050 for NetSolutions are reported in the income statement in Exhibit 6, on page 20. The order in which the expenses are listed in the income statement varies among businesses. One method is to list them in order of size, beginning with the larger items. Miscellaneous expense is usually shown as the last item, regardless of the amount.

Example Exercise 1-4   objective 5

The assets and liabilities of Chickadee Travel Service at April 30, 2008, the end of the current year, and its revenue and expenses for the year are listed below. The capital of the owner, Adam Cellini, was $80,000 at May 1, 2007, the beginning of the current year.

Accounts payable	$ 12,200	Miscellaneous expense	$ 12,950
Accounts receivable	31,350	Office expense	63,000
Cash	53,050	Supplies	3,350
Fees earned	263,200	Wages expense	131,700
Land	80,000		

Prepare an income statement for the current year ended April 30, 2008.

(continued)

Follow My Example 1-4

CHICKADEE TRAVEL SERVICE
INCOME STATEMENT
For the Year Ended April 30, 2008

Fees earned		$263,200
Expenses:		
Wages expense	$131,700	
Office expense	63,000	
Miscellaneous expense	12,950	
Total expenses		207,650
Net income		$ 55,550

For Practice: PE 1-4A, PE 1-4B

STATEMENT OF OWNER'S EQUITY

The statement of owner's equity reports the changes in the owner's equity for a period of time. It is prepared *after* the income statement because the net income or net loss for the period must be reported in this statement. Similarly, it is prepared *before* the balance sheet, since the amount of owner's equity at the end of the period must be reported on the balance sheet. Because of this, the statement of owner's equity is often viewed as the connecting link between the income statement and balance sheet.

Three types of transactions affected owner's equity for NetSolutions during November: (1) the original investment of $25,000, (2) the revenue and expenses that resulted in net income of $3,050 for the month, and (3) a withdrawal of $2,000 by the owner. This information is summarized in the statement of owner's equity in Exhibit 6.

Example Exercise 1-5   **objective** 5

Using the data for Chickadee Travel Service shown in Example Exercise 1-4, prepare a statement of owner's equity for the current year ended April 30, 2008. Adam Cellini invested an additional $50,000 in the business during the year and withdrew cash of $30,000 for personal use.

Follow My Example 1-5

CHICKADEE TRAVEL SERVICE
STATEMENT OF OWNER'S EQUITY
For the Year Ended April 30, 2008

Adam Cellini, capital, May 1, 2007		$ 80,000
Additional investment by owner during year	$ 50,000	
Net income for the year	55,550	
	$105,550	
Less withdrawals	30,000	
Increase in owner's equity		75,550
Adam Cellini, capital, April 30, 2008		$155,550

For Practice: PE 1-5A, PE 1-5B

EXHIBIT 6

Financial Statements
for NetSolutions

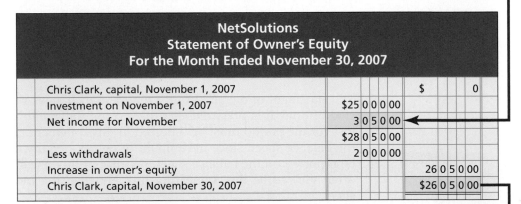

NetSolutions
Income Statement
For the Month Ended November 30, 2007

Fees earned		$7 5 0 0 00
Expenses:		
Wages expense	$2 1 2 5 00	
Rent expense	8 0 0 00	
Supplies expense	8 0 0 00	
Utilities expense	4 5 0 00	
Miscellaneous expense	2 7 5 00	
Total expenses		4 4 5 0 00
Net income		$3 0 5 0 00

NetSolutions
Statement of Owner's Equity
For the Month Ended November 30, 2007

Chris Clark, capital, November 1, 2007		$ 0
Investment on November 1, 2007	$25 0 0 0 00	
Net income for November	3 0 5 0 00	
	$28 0 5 0 00	
Less withdrawals	2 0 0 0 00	
Increase in owner's equity		26 0 5 0 00
Chris Clark, capital, November 30, 2007		$26 0 5 0 00

NetSolutions
Balance Sheet
November 30, 2007

Assets			Liabilities		
Cash	$ 5 9 0 0 00		Accounts payable	$ 4 0 0 00	
Supplies	5 5 0 00		**Owner's Equity**		
Land	20 0 0 0 00		Chris Clark, capital	26 0 5 0 00	
			Total liabilities and		
Total assets	$26 4 5 0 00		owner's equity	$26 4 5 0 00	

NetSolutions
Statement of Cash Flows
For the Month Ended November 30, 2007

Cash flows from operating activities:		
Cash received from customers	$ 7 5 0 0 00	
Deduct cash payments for expenses and		
payments to creditors	4 6 0 0 00	
Net cash flow from operating activities		$ 2 9 0 0 00
Cash flows from investing activities:		
Cash payments for purchase of land		(20 0 0 0 00)
Cash flows from financing activities:		
Cash received as owner's investment	$25 0 0 0 00	
Deduct cash withdrawal by owner	2 0 0 0 00	
Net cash flow from financing activities		23 0 0 0 00
Net cash flow and November 30, 2007, cash balance		$ 5 9 0 0 00

BALANCE SHEET

The balance sheet in Exhibit 6 reports the amounts of NetSolutions' assets, liabilities, and owner's equity at the end of November. The asset and liability amounts are taken from the last line of the summary of transactions presented earlier. Chris Clark, Capital as of November 30, 2007, is taken from the statement of owner's equity. The form of balance sheet shown in Exhibit 6 is called the **account form** because it resembles the basic format of the accounting equation, with assets on the left side and the liabilities and owner's equity sections on the right side. We illustrate an alternative form of balance sheet, called the **report form**, in a later chapter. It presents the liabilities and owner's equity sections below the assets section.

The assets section of the balance sheet normally presents assets in the order that they will be converted into cash or used in operations. Cash is presented first, followed by receivables, supplies, prepaid insurance, and other assets. The assets of a more permanent nature are shown next, such as land, buildings, and equipment.

In the liabilities section of the balance sheet in Exhibit 6, accounts payable is the only liability. When there are two or more categories of liabilities, each should be listed and the total amount of liabilities presented as follows:

Liabilities		
Accounts payable	$12,900	
Wages payable	2,570	
Total liabilities		$15,470

Example Exercise 1-6   objective 5

Using the data for Chickadee Travel Service shown in Example Exercises 1-4 and 1-5, prepare the balance sheet as of April 30, 2008.

Follow My Example 1-6

CHICKADEE TRAVEL SERVICE
BALANCE SHEET
April 30, 2008

Assets		Liabilities	
Cash	$ 53,050	Accounts payable	$ 12,200
Accounts receivable	31,350		
Supplies	3,350	Owner's Equity	
Land	80,000	Adam Cellini, capital	155,550
Total assets	$167,750	Total liabilities and owner's equity	$167,750

For Practice: PE 1-6A, PE 1-6B

STATEMENT OF CASH FLOWS

The statement of cash flows consists of three sections, as we see in Exhibit 6: (1) operating activities, (2) investing activities, and (3) financing activities. Each of these sections is briefly described below.

Cash Flows from Operating Activities This section reports a summary of cash receipts and cash payments from operations. The net cash flow from operating activities will normally differ from the amount of net income for the period. In Exhibit 6, NetSolutions reported net cash flows from operating activities of $2,900 and net income of $3,050. This difference occurs because revenues and expenses may not be recorded at the same time that cash is received from customers or paid to creditors.

Cash Flows from Investing Activities This section reports the cash transactions for the acquisition and sale of relatively permanent assets. Exhibit 6 reports that NetSolutions paid $20,000 for the purchase of land during November.

Cash Flows from Financing Activities This section reports the cash transactions related to cash investments by the owner, borrowings, and cash withdrawals by the owner. Exhibit 6 shows that Chris Clark invested $25,000 in the business and withdrew $2,000 during November.

Preparing the statement of cash flows requires that each of the November cash transactions for NetSolitons be classified as operating, investing, or financing activities. Using the summary of transactions shown on page 16, the November cash transactions for NetSolutions can be classified as follows:

Transaction	Amount	Cash Flow Activity
a.	$25,000	Financing (Investment by Chris Clark)
b.	−20,000	Investing (Purchase of land)
d.	7,500	Operating (Fees earned)
e.	−3,650	Operating (Payment of expenses)
f.	−950	Operating (Payment of account payable)
h.	−2,000	Financing (Withdrawal by Chris Clark)

Transactions (c) and (g) are not listed above since they did not involve a cash receipt or payment. In additon, the payment of accounts payable in transaction (f) is classified as an operating activity since the account payable arose from the purchase of supplies, which are used in operations. Using the preceding classifications of November cash transactions, the statement of cash flows is prepared as shown in Exhibit 6.[6]

The ending cash balance shown on the statement of cash flows also appears on the balance sheet as of the end of the period. To illustrate, the ending cash of $5,900 reported on the November statement of cash flows in Exhibit 6 also appears as the amount of cash on hand in the November 30, 2007, balance sheet.

Since November is NetSolutions' first period of operations, the net cash flow for November and the November 30, 2007, cash balance are the same amount, $5,900, as shown in Exhibit 6. In subsequent periods, NetSolutions will report in its statement of cash flows a beginning cash balance, an increase or a decrease in cash for the period, and an ending cash balance. For example, assume that for December NetSolutions has a decrease in cash of $3,835. The last three lines of NetSolutions' statement of cash flows for December appear as follows:

Decrease in cash	$3,835
Cash as of December 1, 2007	5,900
Cash as of December 31, 2007	$2,065

Example Exercise 1-7   **objective** 5

A summary of cash flows for Chickadee Travel Service for the year ended April 30, 2008, is shown below.

Cash receipts:
Cash received from customers $251,000
Cash received from additional investment of owner 50,000

Cash payments:
Cash paid for expenses 210,000
Cash paid for land 80,000
Cash paid to owner for personal use 30,000

The cash balance as of May 1, 2007, was $72,050.

Prepare a statement of cash flows for Chickadee Travel Service for the year ended April 30, 2008.

(continued)

[6] This method of preparing the statement of cash flows is called the "direct method." This method and the indirect method are discussed further in Chapter 16.

Follow My Example 1-7

CHICKADEE TRAVEL SERVICE
STATEMENT OF CASH FLOWS
For the Year Ended April 30, 2008

Cash flows from operating activities:		
Cash received from customers	$251,000	
Deduct cash payments for expenses	210,000	
Net cash flows from operating activities		$ 41,000
Cash flows from investing activities:		
Cash payments for purchase of land		(80,000)
Cash flows from financing activities:		
Cash received from owner as investment	$ 50,000	
Deduct cash withdrawals by owner	30,000	
Net cash flows from financing activities		20,000
Net decrease in cash during year		$(19,000)
Cash as of May 1, 2007		72,050
Cash as of April 30, 2008		$ 53,050

For Practice: PE 1-7A, PE 1-7B

INTERRELATIONSHIPS AMONG FINANCIAL STATEMENTS

As we mentioned earlier, financial statements are prepared in the order of the income statement, statement of owner's equity, balance sheet, and statement of cash flows. Preparing them in this order is important because the financial statements are interrelated. Using the financial statements of NetSolutions as an example, these interrelationships are shown in Exhibit 6 as follows:[7]

1. The income statement and the statement of owner's equity are interrelated. The net income or net loss appears on the income statement and also on the statement of owner's equity as either an addition (net income) to or deduction (net loss) from the beginning owner's equity and any additional investments by the owner during the period. To illustrate, NetSolutions' net income of $3,050 for November is added to Chris Clark's investment of $25,000 in the statement of owner's equity as shown in Exhibit 6.
2. The statement of owner's equity and the balance sheet are interrelated. The owner's capital at the end of the period on the statement of owner's equity also appears on the balance sheet as owner's capital. To illustrate, Chris Clark, Capital of $26,050 as of November 30, 2007, on the statement of owner's equity also appears on the November 30, 2007, balance sheet as shown in Exhibit 6.
3. The balance sheet and the statement of cash flows are interrelated. The cash on the balance sheet also appears as the end-of-period cash on the statement of cash flows. To illustrate, the cash of $5,900 reported on NetSolutions' balance sheet as of November 30, 2007, is also reported on NetSolutions' November statement of cash flows as the end-of-period cash as shown in Exhibit 6.

The preceding interrelationships shown in Exhibit 6 are important in analyzing financial statements and the impact of transactions on a business. In addition, these interrelationships serve as a check on whether the financial statements have been prepared correctly. For example, if the ending cash on the statement of cash flows doesn't agree with the balance sheet cash, then an error has occurred.

---

7 Depending upon the method of preparing the cash flows from operating activities section of the statement of cash flows, net income (or net loss) may also appear on the statement of cash flows. This interrelationship or method of preparing the statement of cash flows, called the "indirect method," is described and illustrated in Chapter 16.

At a Glance

1. Describe the nature of a business and the role of ethics and accounting in business.

Key Points	Key Learning Outcomes	Example Exercises	Practice Exercises
A business provides goods or services (outputs) to customers with the objective of maximizing profits. Service, merchandising, and manufacturing businesses may be organized as proprietorships, partnerships, corporations, and limited liability companies.	• Distinguish among service, merchandising, and manufacturing businesses. • Describe the characteristics of a proprietorship, partnership, corporation, and limited liability company.		
A business stakeholder is a person or entity (such as an owner, manager, employee, customer, creditor, or the government) who has an interest in the economic performance of the business.	• List business stakeholders.		
Ethics are moral principles that guide the conduct of individuals. Good ethical conduct depends upon individual character, firm culture, and laws and enforcement.	• Define ethics and list the three factors affecting good ethical conduct.		
Accounting, called the "language of business," is an information system that provides reports to stakeholders about the economic activities and condition of a business.	• Describe the role of accounting in business and explain why accounting is called the "language of business."		
Accountants are engaged in private accounting or public accounting.	• Describe what private and public accounting means.		

2. Summarize the development of accounting principles and relate them to practice.

Key Points	Key Learning Outcomes	Example Exercises	Practice Exercises
Generally accepted accounting principles (GAAP) are used in preparing financial statements so that stakeholders can compare one company to another. Accounting principles and concepts develop from research, practice, and pronouncements of authoritative bodies such as the Financial Accounting Standards Board (FASB).	• Explain what is meant by generally accepted accounting principles. • Describe how generally accepted accounting principles are developed.		
The business entity concept views the business as an entity separate from its owners, creditors, or other stakeholders. The cost concept requires that properties and services bought by a business be recorded in terms of actual cost. The objectivity concept requires that the accounting records and reports be based upon objective evidence. The unit of measure concept requires that economic data be recorded in dollars.	• Describe and give an example of what is meant by the business entity concept. • Describe and give an example of what is meant by the cost concept. • Describe and give an example of what is meant by the objectivity concept. • Describe and give an example of what is meant by the unit of measure concept.	1-1	1-1A, 1-1B

3. State the accounting equation and define each element of the equation.

Key Points	Key Learning Outcomes	Example Exercises	Practice Exercises
The resources owned by a business and the rights or claims to these resources may be stated in the form of an equation, as follows: Assets = Liabilities + Owner's Equity	• State the accounting equation. • Define assets, liabilities, and owner's equity. • Given two elements of the accounting equation, solve for the third element.	1-2	1-2A, 1-2B

4. Describe and illustrate how business transactions can be recorded in terms of the resulting change in the basic elements of the accounting equation.

Key Points	Key Learning Outcomes	Example Exercises	Practice Exercises
All business transactions can be stated in terms of the change in one or more of the three elements of the accounting equation.	• Define a business transaction. • Using the accounting equation as a framework, record transactions.	1-3	1-3A, 1-3B

5. Describe the financial statements of a proprietorship and explain how they interrelate.

Key Points	Key Learning Outcomes	Example Exercises	Practice Exercises
The principal financial statements of a proprietorship are the income statement, the statement of owner's equity, the balance sheet, and the statement of cash flows. The income statement reports a period's net income or net loss, which also appears on the statement of owner's equity. The ending owner's capital reported on the statement of owner's equity is also reported on the balance sheet. The ending cash balance is reported on the balance sheet and the statement of cash flows.	• List and describe the financial statements of a proprietorship. • Prepare an income statement. • Prepare a statement of owner's equity. • Prepare a balance sheet. • Prepare a statement of cash flows. • Explain how the financial statements of a proprietorship are interrelated.	1-4 1-5 1-6 1-7	1-4A, 1-4B 1-5A, 1-5B 1-6A, 1-6B 1-7A, 1-7B

Key Terms

account form (21)
account payable (14)
account receivable (15)
accounting (7)
accounting equation (12)
assets (12)
balance sheet (18)
business (2)
business entity concept (11)
business stakeholder (4)
business transaction (12)
Certified Management Accountant (CMA) (9)

Certified Public Accountant (CPA) (10)
corporation (3)
cost concept (11)
ethics (4)
expenses (15)
fees earned (15)
financial accounting (8)
Financial Accounting Standards Board (FASB) (10)
financial statements (17)
generally accepted accounting principles (GAAP) (10)

income statement (18)
interest revenue (15)
liabilities (12)
limited liability company (LLC) (4)
management (or managerial) accounting (9)
manufacturing business (3)
matching concept (18)
merchandising business (3)
net income or net profit (18)
net loss (18)
objectivity concept (11)
owner's equity (12)

Illustrative Problem

Cecil Jameson, Attorney-at-Law, is a proprietorship owned and operated by Cecil Jameson. On July 1, 2007, Cecil Jameson, Attorney-at-Law, has the following assets and liabilities: cash, $1,000; accounts receivable, $3,200; supplies, $850; land, $10,000; accounts payable, $1,530. Office space and office equipment are currently being rented, pending the construction of an office complex on land purchased last year. Business transactions during July are summarized as follows:

a. Received cash from clients for services, $3,928.

b. Paid creditors on account, $1,055.

c. Received cash from Cecil Jameson as an additional investment, $3,700.

d. Paid office rent for the month, $1,200.

e. Charged clients for legal services on account, $2,025.

f. Purchased office supplies on account, $245.

g. Received cash from clients on account, $3,000.

h. Received invoice for paralegal services from Legal Aid Inc. for July (to be paid on August 10), $1,635.

i. Paid the following: wages expense, $850; answering service expense, $250; utilities expense, $325; and miscellaneous expense, $75.

j. Determined that the cost of office supplies on hand was $980; therefore, the cost of supplies used during the month was $115.

k. Jameson withdrew $1,000 in cash from the business for personal use.

Instructions

1. Determine the amount of owner's equity (Cecil Jameson's capital) as of July 1, 2007.
2. State the assets, liabilities, and owner's equity as of July 1 in equation form similar to that shown in this chapter. In tabular form below the equation, indicate the increases and decreases resulting from each transaction and the new balances after each transaction.
3. Prepare an income statement for July, a statement of owner's equity for July, and a balance sheet as of July 31, 2007.
4. (Optional). Prepare a statement of cash flows for July.

Solution

1.

$$\text{Assets} - \text{Liabilities} = \text{Owner's Equity}$$
$$\text{(Cecil Jameson, capital)}$$
$$(\$1,000 + \$3,200 + \$850 + \$10,000) - \$1,530 = \text{Owner's Equity}$$
$$\text{(Cecil Jameson, capital)}$$
$$\$15,050 - \$1,530 = \text{Owner's Equity}$$
$$\text{(Cecil Jameson, capital)}$$
$$\$13,520 = \text{Owner's Equity}$$
$$\text{(Cecil Jameson, capital)}$$

2.

	Cash	+	Accts. Rec.	+	Supp.	+	Land	=	Accts. Pay.	+	Cecil Jameson, Capital	−	Cecil Jameson, Drawing	+	Fees Earned	−	Paralegal Exp.	−	Wages Exp.	−	Rent Exp.	−	Utilities Exp.	−	Answering Service Exp.	−	Supp. Exp.	−	Misc. Exp.
Bal.	1,000		3,200		850		10,000		1,530		13,520																		
a.	+3,928														3,928														
Bal.	4,928		3,200		850		10,000		1,530		13,520																		
b.	−1,055								−1,055																				
Bal.	3,873		3,200		850		10,000		475		13,520				3,928														
c.	+3,700										+3,700																		
Bal.	7,573		3,200		850		10,000		475		17,220				3,928														
d.	−1,200																				−1,200								
Bal.	6,373		3,200		850		10,000		475		17,220				3,928						−1,200								
e.			+2,025												+2,025														
Bal.	6,373		5,225		850		10,000		475		17,220				5,953						−1,200								
f.					+ 245				+ 245																				
Bal.	6,373		5,225		1,095		10,000		720		17,220				5,953						−1,200								
g.	+3,000		−3,000																										
Bal.	9,373		2,225		1,095		10,000		720		17,220				5,953						−1,200								
h.									+1,635								−1,635												
Bal.	9,373		2,225		1,095		10,000		2,355		17,220				5,953		−1,635				−1,200								
i.	−1,500																		−850				−325		−250				−75
Bal.	7,873		2,225		1,095		10,000		2,355		17,220				5,953		−1,635		−850		−1,200		−325		−250				−75
j.					− 115																						−115		
Bal.	7,873		2,225		980		10,000		2,355		17,220				5,953		−1,635		−850		−1,200		−325		−250		−115		−75
k.	−1,000												−1,000																
Bal.	6,873		2,225		980		10,000		2,355		17,220		−1,000		5,953		−1,635		−850		−1,200		−325		−250		−115		−75

3.

Cecil Jameson, Attorney-at-Law
Income Statement
For the Month Ended July 31, 2007

Fees earned		$5,953
Expenses:		
Paralegal expense	$1,635	
Rent expense	1,200	
Wages expense	850	
Utilities expense	325	
Answering service expense	250	
Supplies expense	115	
Miscellaneous expense	75	
Total expenses		4,450
Net income		$1,503

Cecil Jameson, Attorney-at-Law
Statement of Owner's Equity
For the Month Ended July 31, 2007

Cecil Jameson, capital, July 1, 2007		$13,520
Additional investment by owner	$3,700	
Net income for the month	1,503	
	$5,203	
Less withdrawals	1,000	
Increase in owner's equity		4,203
Cecil Jameson, capital, July 31, 2007		$17,723

(continued)

Cecil Jameson, Attorney-at-Law
Balance Sheet
July 31, 2007

Assets		Liabilities	
Cash	$ 6,873	Accounts payable	$ 2,355
Accounts receivable	2,225	**Owner's Equity**	
Supplies	980	Cecil Jameson, capital	17,723
Land	10,000	Total liabilities and	
Total assets	$20,078	owner's equity	$20,078

4. Optional.

Cecil Jameson, Attorney-at-Law
Statement of Cash Flows
For the Month Ended July 31, 2007

Cash flows from operating activities:		
Cash received from customers	$6,928*	
Deduct cash payments for operating expenses	3,755**	
Net cash flows from operating activities		$3,173
Cash flows from investing activities		—
Cash flows from financing activities:		
Cash received from owner as investment	$3,700	
Deduct cash withdrawals by owner	1,000	
Net cash flows from financing activities		2,700
Net increase in cash during year		$5,873
Cash as of July 1, 2007		1,000
Cash as of July 31, 2007		$6,873

*$6,928 = $3,928 + $3,000
**$3,755 = $1,055 + $1,200 + $1,500

Self-Examination Questions

(Answers at End of Chapter)

1. A profit-making business operating as a separate legal entity and in which ownership is divided into shares of stock is known as a:
   A. proprietorship.   C. partnership.
   B. service business.   D. corporation.

2. The resources owned by a business are called:
   A. assets.   C. the accounting equation.
   B. liabilities.   D. owner's equity.

3. A listing of a business entity's assets, liabilities, and owner's equity as of a specific date is a(n):
   A. balance sheet.
   B. income statement.
   C. statement of owner's equity.
   D. statement of cash flows.

4. If total assets increased $20,000 during a period and total liabilities increased $12,000 during the same period, the amount and direction (increase or decrease) of the change in owner's equity for that period is a(n):
   A. $32,000 increase.   C. $8,000 increase.
   B. $32,000 decrease.   D. $8,000 decrease.

5. If revenue was $45,000, expenses were $37,500, and the owner's withdrawals were $10,000, the amount of net income or net loss would be:
   A. $45,000 net income.   C. $37,500 net loss.
   B. $7,500 net income.   D. $2,500 net loss.

Eye Openers

1. What is the objective of most businesses?
2. What is the difference between a manufacturing business and a service business? Is a restaurant a manufacturing business, a service business, or both?

3. Why are most large companies like Microsoft, PepsiCo, Caterpillar, and AutoZone organized as corporations?
4. Who are normally included as the stakeholders of a business?
5. What is the role of accounting in business?
6. Rebecca Olson is the owner of Aquarius Delivery Service. Recently, Rebecca paid interest of $1,850 on a personal loan of $30,000 that she used to begin the business. Should Aquarius Delivery Service record the interest payment? Explain.
7. On February 3, Dependable Repair Service extended an offer of $80,000 for land that had been priced for sale at $90,000. On March 6, Dependable Repair Service accepted the seller's counteroffer of $88,000. Describe how Dependable Repair Service should record the land.
8. a. Land with an assessed value of $250,000 for property tax purposes is acquired by a business for $375,000. Seven years later, the plot of land has an assessed value of $400,000 and the business receives an offer of $725,000 for it. Should the monetary amount assigned to the land in the business records now be increased?
   b. Assuming that the land acquired in (a) was sold for $725,000, how would the various elements of the accounting equation be affected?
9. Describe the difference between an account receivable and an account payable.
10. A business had revenues of $420,000 and operating expenses of $565,000. Did the business (a) incur a net loss or (b) realize net income?
11. A business had revenues of $919,500 and operating expenses of $738,600. Did the business (a) incur a net loss or (b) realize net income?
12. What particular item of financial or operating data appears on both the income statement and the statement of owner's equity? What item appears on both the balance sheet and the statement of owner's equity? What item appears on both the balance sheet and the statement of cash flows?

Practice Exercises

PE 1-1A
Cost concept
obj. 2

On November 15, Johnson Repair Service extended an offer of $35,000 for land that had been priced for sale at $43,000. On December 8, Johnson Repair Service accepted the seller's counteroffer of $37,000. On December 30, the land was assessed at a value of $50,000 for property tax purposes. On April 1, Johnson Repair Service was offered $60,000 for the land by a national retail chain. At what value should the land be recorded in Johnson Repair Service's records?

PE 1-1B
Cost concept
obj. 2

On February 2, Duck Repair Service extended an offer of $90,000 for land that had been priced for sale at $115,000. On February 16, Duck Repair Service accepted the seller's counteroffer of $100,000. On April 29, the land was assessed at a value of $110,000 for property tax purposes. On August 30, Duck Repair Service was offered $130,000 for the land by a national retail chain. At what value should the land be recorded in Duck Repair Service's records?

PE 1-2A
Accounting equation
obj. 3

Daryl Wallin is the owner and operator of Pima LLC, a motivational consulting business. At the end of its accounting period, December 31, 2007, Pima has assets of $617,000 and liabilities of $382,000. Using the accounting equation, determine the following amounts:

a. Owner's equity, as of December 31, 2007.
b. Owner's equity, as of December 31, 2008, assuming that assets increased by $114,000 and liabilities decreased by $29,000 during 2008.

PE 1-2B
Accounting equation
obj. 3

Kristen Hagan is the owner and operator of You're Cool, a motivational consulting business. At the end of its accounting period, December 31, 2007, You're Cool has assets of $336,000 and liabilities of $172,500. Using the accounting equation, determine the following amounts:

a. Owner's equity, as of December 31, 2007.
b. Owner's equity, as of December 31, 2008, assuming that assets increased by $75,000 and liabilities increased by $15,000 during 2008.

PE 1-3A
Transactions
obj. **4**

Mime Delivery Service is owned and operated by Pamela Kolp. The following selected transactions were completed by Mime Delivery Service during October:

1. Received cash from owner as additional investment, $7,500.
2. Paid creditors on account, $815.
3. Billed customers for delivery services on account, $3,250.
4. Received cash from customers on account, $1,150.
5. Paid cash to owner for personal use, $500.

Indicate the effect of each transaction on the accounting equation elements (Assets, Liabilities, Owner's Equity, Drawing, Revenue, and Expense) by listing the numbers identifying the transactions, (1) through (5). Also, indicate the specific item within the accounting equation element that is affected. To illustrate, the answer to (1) is shown below.

(1) Asset (Cash) increases by $7,500; Owner's Equity (Pamela Kolp, Capital) increases by $7,500.

PE 1-3B
Transactions
obj. **4**

Quicken Delivery Service is owned and operated by Zoey Tucker. The following selected transactions were completed by Quicken Delivery Service during July:

1. Received cash from owner as additional investment, $9,000.
2. Paid advertising expense, $674.
3. Purchased supplies on account, $280.
4. Billed customers for delivery services on account, $4,800.
5. Received cash from customers on account, $1,150.

Indicate the effect of each transaction on the accounting equation elements (Assets, Liabilities, Owner's Equity, Drawing, Revenue, and Expense) by listing the numbers identifying the transactions, (1) through (5). Also, indicate the specific item within the accounting equation element that is affected. To illustrate, the answer to (1) is shown below.

(1) Asset (Cash) increases by $9,000; Owner's Equity (Zoey Tucker, Capital) increases by $9,000.

PE 1-4A
Income statement
obj. **5**

The assets and liabilities of Herat Travel Service at June 30, 2008, the end of the current year, and its revenue and expenses for the year are listed below. The capital of the owner, Lola Stahn, was $75,000 at July 1, 2007, the beginning of the current year.

Accounts payable	$ 15,300	Miscellaneous expense	$ 3,150
Accounts receivable	24,350	Office expense	91,350
Cash	70,800	Supplies	5,350
Fees earned	378,200	Wages expense	181,500
Land	100,000		

Prepare an income statement for the current year ended June 30, 2008.

PE 1-4B
Income statement
obj. **5**

The assets and liabilities of Leotard Travel Service at February 28, 2008, the end of the current year, and its revenue and expenses for the year are listed below. The capital of the owner, Harry Thompson, was $190,000 at March 1, 2007, the beginning of the current year.

Accounts payable	$ 21,000	Miscellaneous expense	$ 6,350
Accounts receivable	37,750	Office expense	156,650
Cash	22,700	Supplies	2,550
Fees earned	377,000	Wages expense	225,000
Land	145,000		

Prepare an income statement for the current year ended February 28, 2008.

PE 1-5A
Statement of owner's equity
obj. **5**

Using the data for Herat Travel Service shown in Practice Exercise 1-4A, prepare a statement of owner's equity for the current year ended June 30, 2008. Lola Stahn invested an additional $20,000 in the business during the year and withdrew cash of $12,000 for personal use.

PE 1-5B
Statement of owner's equity
obj. 5

Using the data for Leotard Travel Service shown in Practice Exercise 1-4B, prepare a statement of owner's equity for the current year ended February 28, 2008. Harry Thompson invested an additional $18,000 in the business during the year and withdrew cash of $10,000 for personal use.

PE 1-6A
Balance sheet
obj. 5

Using the data for Herat Travel Service shown in Practice Exercise 1-4A and 1-5A, prepare the balance sheet as of June 30, 2008.

PE 1-6B
Balance sheet
obj. 5

Using the data for Leotard Travel Service shown in Practice Exercise 1-4B and 1-5B, prepare the balance sheet as of February 28, 2008.

PE 1-7A
Statement of cash flows
obj. 5

A summary of cash flows for Herat Travel Service for the year ended June 30, 2008, is shown below.

Cash receipts:	
Cash received from customers	$350,000
Cash received from additional investment of owner	20,000
Cash payments:	
Cash paid for operating expenses	270,000
Cash paid for land	60,000
Cash paid to owner for personal use	12,000

The cash balance as of July 1, 2007, was $42,800.

Prepare a statement of cash flows for Herat Travel Service for the year ended June 30, 2008.

PE 1-7B
Statement of cash flows
obj. 5

A summary of cash flows for Leotard Travel Service for the year ended February 28, 2008, is shown below.

Cash receipts:	
Cash received from customers	$350,000
Cash received from additional investment of owner	18,000
Cash payments:	
Cash paid for operating expenses	365,000
Cash paid for land	27,000
Cash paid to owner for personal use	10,000

The cash balance as of March 1, 2007, was $56,700.

Prepare a statement of cash flows for Leotard Travel Service for the year ended February 28, 2008.

Exercises

EX 1-1
Types of businesses
obj. 1

Indicate whether each of the following companies is primarily a service, merchandise, or manufacturing business. If you are unfamiliar with the company, use the Internet to locate the company's home page or use the finance Web site of Yahoo.com.

1. H&R Block
2. eBay Inc.
3. Wal-Mart Stores, Inc.
4. Ford Motor Company
5. Citigroup
6. Boeing
7. First Union Corporation
8. Alcoa Inc.
9. Procter & Gamble
10. FedEx
11. Gap Inc.
12. Hilton Hospitality, Inc.
13. CVS
14. Caterpillar
15. The Dow Chemical Company

EX 1-2
Professional ethics
obj. 1

ETHICS

A fertilizer manufacturing company wants to relocate to Collier County. A 13-year-old report from a fired researcher at the company says the company's product is releasing toxic by-products. The company has suppressed that report. A second report commissioned by the company shows there is no problem with the fertilizer.
> Should the company's chief executive officer reveal the context of the unfavorable report in discussions with Collier County representatives? Discuss.

EX 1-3
Business entity concept
obj. 2

Frontier Sports sells hunting and fishing equipment and provides guided hunting and fishing trips. Frontier Sports is owned and operated by Wally Schnee, a well-known sports enthusiast and hunter. Wally's wife, Helen, owns and operates Blue Sky Boutique, a women's clothing store. Wally and Helen have established a trust fund to finance their children's college education. The trust fund is maintained by First Bank in the name of the children, Anna and Conner.

For each of the following transactions, identify which of the entities listed should record the transaction in its records.

Entities

F	Frontier Sports
B	First Bank Trust Fund
S	Blue Sky Boutique
X	None of the above

1. Wally paid a breeder's fee for an English springer spaniel to be used as a hunting guide dog.
2. Helen paid her dues to the YWCA.
3. Helen purchased two dozen spring dresses from a Denver designer for a special spring sale.
4. Helen deposited a $3,500 personal check in the trust fund at First Bank.
5. Wally paid for an advertisement in a hunters' magazine.
6. Helen authorized the trust fund to purchase mutual fund shares.
7. Wally paid for dinner and a movie to celebrate their tenth wedding anniversary.
8. Helen donated several dresses from inventory for a local charity auction for the benefit of a women's abuse shelter.
9. Wally received a cash advance from customers for a guided hunting trip.
10. Wally paid a local doctor for his annual physical, which was required by the workmen's compensation insurance policy carried by Frontier Sports.

EX 1-4
Accounting equation
obj. 3

REAL WORLD

✓ Coca-Cola, $15,935

The total assets and total liabilities of Coca-Cola and PepsiCo are shown below.

	Coca-Cola (in millions)	PepsiCo (in millions)
Assets	$31,327	$27,987
Liabilities	15,392	14,415

Determine the owners' equity of each company.

EX 1-5
Accounting equation
obj. 3

REAL WORLD

✓ eBay, $6,728

The total assets and total liabilities of eBay and Google are shown below.

	eBay (in millions)	Google (in millions)
Assets	$7,991	$3,313
Liabilities	1,263	384

Determine the owners' equity of each company.

EX 1-6
Accounting equation
obj. 3
✓ a. $300,600

Determine the missing amount for each of the following:

	Assets	=	Liabilities	+	Owner's Equity
a.	X	=	$85,000	+	$215,600
b.	$93,500	=	X	+	6,150
c.	42,500	=	11,275	+	X

EX 1-7
Accounting equation
objs. 3, 4
✓ b. $710,000

Hector Lopez is the owner and operator of Centillion, a motivational consulting business. At the end of its accounting period, December 31, 2007, Centillion has assets of $950,000 and liabilities of $300,000. Using the accounting equation and considering each case independently, determine the following amounts:

a. Hector Lopez, capital, as of December 31, 2007.
b. Hector Lopez, capital, as of December 31, 2008, assuming that assets increased by $150,000 and liabilities increased by $90,000 during 2008.
c. Hector Lopez, capital, as of December 31, 2008, assuming that assets decreased by $75,000 and liabilities increased by $27,000 during 2008.
d. Hector Lopez, capital, as of December 31, 2008, assuming that assets increased by $125,000 and liabilities decreased by $48,000 during 2008.
e. Net income (or net loss) during 2008, assuming that as of December 31, 2008, assets were $1,200,000, liabilities were $195,000, and there were no additional investments or withdrawals.

EX 1-8
Asset, liability, owner's equity items
obj. 3

Indicate whether each of the following is identified with (1) an asset, (2) a liability, or (3) owner's equity:

a. land
b. wages expense
c. accounts payable
d. fees earned
e. supplies
f. cash

EX 1-9
Effect of transactions on accounting equation
obj. 4

Describe how the following business transactions affect the three elements of the accounting equation.

a. Purchased supplies on account.
b. Purchased supplies for cash.
c. Paid for utilities used in the business.
d. Received cash for services performed.
e. Invested cash in business.

EX 1-10
Effect of transactions on accounting equation
obj. 4
✓ a. (1) increase $70,000

a. A vacant lot acquired for $75,000 is sold for $145,000 in cash. What is the effect of the sale on the total amount of the seller's (1) assets, (2) liabilities, and (3) owner's equity?
b. Assume that the seller owes $40,000 on a loan for the land. After receiving the $145,000 cash in (a), the seller pays the $40,000 owed. What is the effect of the payment on the total amount of the seller's (1) assets, (2) liabilities, and (3) owner's equity?

EX 1-11
Effect of transactions on owner's equity
obj. 4

Indicate whether each of the following types of transactions will either (a) increase owner's equity or (b) decrease owner's equity:

1. revenues
2. expenses
3. owner's investments
4. owner's withdrawals

EX 1-12
Transactions
obj. 4

The following selected transactions were completed by Pilgrim Delivery Service during July:

1. Received cash from owner as additional investment, $115,000.
2. Received cash for providing delivery services, $58,000.
3. Paid advertising expense, $2,000.
4. Paid creditors on account, $4,800.
5. Billed customers for delivery services on account, $31,250.
6. Purchased supplies for cash, $800.
7. Paid rent for July, $3,000.   *(continued)*

8. Received cash from customers on account, $10,740.
9. Determined that the cost of supplies on hand was $135; therefore, $665 of supplies had been used during the month.
10. Paid cash to owner for personal use, $1,500.

Indicate the effect of each transaction on the accounting equation by listing the numbers identifying the transactions, (1) through (10), in a column, and inserting at the right of each number the appropriate letter from the following list:

a. Increase in an asset, decrease in another asset.
b. Increase in an asset, increase in a liability.
c. Increase in an asset, increase in owner's equity.
d. Decrease in an asset, decrease in a liability.
e. Decrease in an asset, decrease in owner's equity.

EX 1-13
Nature of transactions
obj. 4
✓ *d. $26,500*

Otto Egan operates his own catering service. Summary financial data for August are presented in equation form as follows. Each line designated by a number indicates the effect of a transaction on the equation. Each increase and decrease in owner's equity, except transaction (5), affects net income.

	Assets			= Liabilities +		Owner's Equity		
	Cash +	Supplies +	Land =	Accounts Payable +	Otto Egan, Capital −	Otto Egan, Drawing +	Fees Earned −	Expenses
Bal.	27,000	3,000	100,000	15,000	115,000			
1.	+45,000						45,000	
2.	−20,000		+20,000					
3.	−16,000							−16,000
4.		+3,000		+ 3,000				
5.	− 5,000					−5,000		
6.	−12,000			−12,000				
7.		−2,500						−2,500
Bal.	19,000	3,500	120,000	6,000	115,000	−5,000	45,000	−18,500

a. Describe each transaction.
b. What is the amount of net decrease in cash during the month?
c. What is the amount of net increase in owner's equity during the month?
d. What is the amount of the net income for the month?
e. How much of the net income for the month was retained in the business?

EX 1-14
Net income and owner's withdrawals
obj. 5

The income statement of a proprietorship for the month of July indicates a net income of $117,800. During the same period, the owner withdrew $150,000 in cash from the business for personal use.

Would it be correct to say that the business incurred a net loss of $32,200 during the month? Discuss.

EX 1-15
Net income and owner's equity for four businesses
obj. 5
✓ *Charlie: Net income, $180,000*

Four different proprietorships, Alpha, Bravo, Charlie, and Delta, show the same balance sheet data at the beginning and end of a year. These data, exclusive of the amount of owner's equity, are summarized as follows:

	Total Assets	Total Liabilities
Beginning of the year	$1,350,000	$540,000
End of the year	2,160,000	900,000

On the basis of the above data and the following additional information for the year, determine the net income (or loss) of each company for the year. (*Hint:* First determine the amount of increase or decrease in owner's equity during the year.)

Alpha: The owner had made no additional investments in the business and had made no withdrawals from the business.
Bravo: The owner had made no additional investments in the business but had withdrawn $120,000.

Charlie:	The owner had made an additional investment of $270,000 but had made no withdrawals.
Delta:	The owner had made an additional investment of $270,000 and had withdrawn $120,000.

EX 1-16
Balance sheet items
obj. 5

From the following list of selected items taken from the records of Maya Appliance Service as of a specific date, identify those that would appear on the balance sheet:

1. Accounts Payable
2. Cash
3. Fees Earned
4. Ishmael Maya, Capital
5. Land
6. Supplies
7. Supplies Expense
8. Utilities Expense
9. Wages Expense
10. Wages Payable

EX 1-17
Income statement items
obj. 5

Based on the data presented in Exercise 1-16, identify those items that would appear on the income statement.

EX 1-18
Statement of owner's equity
obj. 5

✓ *Lynn Jepsen, capital, June 30, 2008: $864,250*

Financial information related to Pickerel Company, a proprietorship, for the month ended June 30, 2008, is as follows:

Net income for June	$196,350
Lynn Jepsen's withdrawals during June	15,000
Lynn Jepsen, capital, June 1, 2008	682,900

Prepare a statement of owner's equity for the month ended June 30, 2008.

EX 1-19
Income statement
obj. 5

✓ *Net income: $91,330*

Giblet Services was organized on February 1, 2008. A summary of the revenue and expense transactions for February follows:

Fees earned	$479,280
Wages expense	310,600
Rent expense	60,000
Supplies expense	6,200
Miscellaneous expense	11,150

Prepare an income statement for the month ended February 28.

EX 1-20
Missing amounts from balance sheet and income statement data
obj. 5

✓ *(a) $117,225*

One item is omitted in each of the following summaries of balance sheet and income statement data for the following four different proprietorships:

	Oscar	Papa	Quebec	Romeo
Beginning of the year:				
Assets	$540,000	$125,000	$200,000	(d)
Liabilities	324,000	65,000	152,000	$120,000
End of the year:				
Assets	670,500	175,000	180,000	248,000
Liabilities	292,500	55,000	160,000	136,000
During the year:				
Additional investment in				
the business	(a)	25,000	20,000	40,000
Withdrawals from the				
business	36,000	8,000	(c)	60,000
Revenue	177,975	(b)	230,000	112,000
Expenses	97,200	32,000	245,000	128,000

Determine the missing amounts, identifying them by letter. (*Hint:* First determine the amount of increase or decrease in owner's equity during the year.)

EX 1-21
Balance sheets, net income
obj. 5

✓ b. $54,510

Financial information related to the proprietorship of Burst Interiors for March and April 2008 is as follows:

	March 31, 2008	April 30, 2008
Accounts payable	$18,480	$ 19,920
Accounts receivable	40,800	46,950
Gary Deming, capital	?	?
Cash	72,000	122,400
Supplies	3,600	3,000

a. Prepare balance sheets for Burst Interiors as of March 31 and as of April 30, 2008.
b. Determine the amount of net income for April, assuming that the owner made no additional investments or withdrawals during the month.
c. Determine the amount of net income for April, assuming that the owner made no additional investments but withdrew $15,000 during the month.

EX 1-22
Financial statements
obj. 5

Each of the following items is shown in the financial statements of Exxon Mobil Corporation. Identify the financial statement (balance sheet or income statement) in which each item would appear.

a. Accounts payable
b. Cash equivalents
c. Crude oil inventory
d. Equipment
e. Exploration expenses
f. Income taxes payable
g. Investments
h. Long-term debt
i. Marketable securities
j. Notes and loans payable
k. Notes receivable
l. Operating expenses
m. Prepaid taxes
n. Sales
o. Selling expenses

EX 1-23
Statement of cash flows
obj. 5

Indicate whether each of the following activities would be reported on the statement of cash flows as (a) an operating activity, (b) an investing activity, or (c) a financing activity:

1. Cash received as owner's investment
2. Cash received from fees earned
3. Cash paid for land
4. Cash paid for expenses

EX 1-24
Statement of cash flows
obj. 5

A summary of cash flows for Webster Consulting Group for the year ended July 31, 2008, is shown below.

Cash receipts:
Cash received from customers $495,000
Cash received from additional investment of owner 20,000
Cash payments:
Cash paid for operating expenses 371,500
Cash paid for land 40,000
Cash paid to owner for personal use 9,000

The cash balance as of August 1, 2007, was $46,750.
    Prepare a statement of cash flows for Webster Consulting Group for the year ended July 31, 2008.

EX 1-25
Financial statements
obj. 5

Galaxy Realty, organized October 1, 2008, is owned and operated by Ora Tasker. How many errors can you find in the following financial statements for Galaxy Realty, prepared after its second month of operations?

✓ Correct amount of
total assets is $39,200

Galaxy Realty
Income Statement
November 30, 2008

Sales commissions		$103,800
Expenses:		
Office salaries expense	$64,800	
Rent expense	22,000	
Automobile expense	5,000	
Miscellaneous expense	1,600	
Supplies expense	600	
Total expenses		94,000
Net income		$ 29,800

Ora Tasker
Statement of Owner's Equity
November 30, 2007

Ora Tasker, capital, November 1, 2008	$20,800
Less withdrawals during November	4,000
	$16,800
Additional investment during November	5,000
	$21,800
Net income for the month	29,800
Ora Tasker, capital, November 30, 2008	$51,600

Balance Sheet
For the Month Ended November 30, 2008

Assets		Liabilities	
Cash	$ 6,600	Accounts receivable	$28,600
Accounts payable	7,600	Supplies	4,000
		Owner's Equity	
		Ora Tasker, capital	51,600
Total assets	$14,200	Total liabilities and owner's equity	$84,200

Problems Series A

PR 1-1A
Transactions

obj. 4

✓ *Cash bal. at end of June: $24,620*

On June 1 of the current year, Doni Gilmore established a business to manage rental property. She completed the following transactions during June:

a. Opened a business bank account with a deposit of $25,000 from personal funds.
b. Purchased supplies (pens, file folders, and copy paper) on account, $1,150.
c. Received cash from fees earned for managing rental property, $4,500.
d. Paid rent on office and equipment for the month, $1,500.
e. Paid creditors on account, $600.
f. Billed customers for fees earned for managing rental property, $2,250.
g. Paid automobile expenses (including rental charges) for month, $400, and miscellaneous expenses, $180.
h. Paid office salaries, $1,200.
i. Determined that the cost of supplies on hand was $380; therefore, the cost of supplies used was $770.
j. Withdrew cash for personal use, $1,000.

Instructions

1. Indicate the effect of each transaction and the balances after each transaction, using the following tabular headings:

(continued)

Assets			= Liabilities +		Owner's Equity							
Cash	+ Accounts Receivable	+ Supplies	= Accounts Payable	+ Doni Gilmore, Capital	− Doni Gilmore, Drawing	+ Fees Earned	− Rent Expense	− Salaries Expense	− Supplies Expense	− Auto Expense	− Misc. Expense

2. Briefly explain why the owner's investment and revenues increased owner's equity, while withdrawals and expenses decreased owner's equity.

PR 1-2A
Financial statements
obj. 5

✔ *1. Net income: $137,500*

Following are the amounts of the assets and liabilities of Pedigree Travel Agency at December 31, 2008, the end of the current year, and its revenue and expenses for the year. The capital of Shiann Ott, owner, was $115,000 on January 1, 2008, the beginning of the current year. During the current year, Shiann withdrew $40,000.

Accounts payable	$ 12,500	Rent expense	$25,000
Accounts receivable	42,300	Supplies	2,700
Cash	180,000	Supplies expense	2,800
Fees earned	250,000	Utilities expense	18,200
Miscellaneous expense	1,500	Wages expense	65,000

Instructions
1. Prepare an income statement for the current year ended December 31, 2008.
2. Prepare a statement of owner's equity for the current year ended December 31, 2008.
3. Prepare a balance sheet as of December 31, 2008.

PR 1-3A
Financial statements
obj. 5

✔ *1. Net income: $23,665*

Barry Kimm established Mariner Financial Services on January 1, 2008. Mariner Financial Services offers financial planning advice to its clients. The effect of each transaction and the balances after each transaction for January are shown at the bottom of the page.

Instructions
1. Prepare an income statement for the month ended January 31, 2008.
2. Prepare a statement of owner's equity for the month ended January 31, 2008.
3. Prepare a balance sheet as of January 31, 2008.
4. (Optional). Prepare a statement of cash flows for the month ending January 31, 2008.

	Assets			= Liabilities +		Owner's Equity						
	Cash	+ Accounts Receivable	+ Supplies	= Accounts Payable	+ Barry Kimm, Capital	− Barry Kimm, Drawing	+ Fees Earned	− Salaries Expense	− Rent Expense	− Auto Expense	− Supplies Expense	− Misc. Expense
a.	+25,000				+25,000							
b.		+1,180		+1,180								
Bal.	25,000	1,180		1,180	25,000							
c.	− 580			− 580								
Bal.	24,420	1,180		600	25,000							
d.	+42,000						+42,000					
Bal.	66,420	1,180		600	25,000		42,000					
e.	− 7,500								−7,500			
Bal.	58,920	1,180		600	25,000		42,000		−7,500			
f.	− 5,780									−4,500		−1,280
Bal.	53,140	1,180		600	25,000		42,000		−7,500	−4,500		−1,280
g.	−15,000							−15,000				
Bal.	38,140	1,180		600	25,000		42,000	−15,000	−7,500	−4,500		−1,280
h.			− 455								−455	
Bal.	38,140		725	600	25,000		42,000	−15,000	−7,500	−4,500	−455	−1,280
i.		+10,400					+10,400					
Bal.	38,140	10,400	725	600	25,000		52,400	−15,000	−7,500	−4,500	−455	−1,280
j.	− 9,000					−9,000						
Bal.	29,140	10,400	725	600	25,000	−9,000	52,400	−15,000	−7,500	−4,500	−455	−1,280

PR 1-4A
Transactions; financial statements

objs. 4, 5

✓2. Net income: $16,850

On March 1, 2008, Ginny Tyler established Seltzer Realty. Ginny completed the following transactions during the month of March:

a. Opened a business bank account with a deposit of $30,000 from personal funds.
b. Purchased supplies (pens, file folders, paper, etc.) on account, $2,650.
c. Paid creditor on account, $1,500.
d. Earned sales commissions, receiving cash, $36,750.
e. Paid rent on office and equipment for the month, $5,200.
f. Withdrew cash for personal use, $8,000.
g. Paid automobile expenses (including rental charge) for month, $2,500, and miscellaneous expenses, $1,200.
h. Paid office salaries, $9,250.
i. Determined that the cost of supplies on hand was $900; therefore, the cost of supplies used was $1,750.

Instructions

1. Indicate the effect of each transaction and the balances after each transaction, using the following tabular headings:

Assets		=	Liabilities	+	Owner's Equity						
Cash + Supplies =			Accounts Payable +		Ginny Tyler, Capital −	Ginny Tyler, Drawing +	Sales Commissions −	Office Salaries Expense −	Rent Expense −	Auto Expense −	Supplies Expense −	Misc. Expense

2. Prepare an income statement for March, a statement of owner's equity for March, and a balance sheet as of March 31.

PR 1-5A
Transactions; financial statements

objs. 4, 5

✓3. Net income: $9,445

Argon Dry Cleaners is owned and operated by Kerry Ulman. A building and equipment are currently being rented, pending expansion to new facilities. The actual work of dry cleaning is done by another company at wholesale rates. The assets and the liabilities of the business on July 1, 2008, are as follows: Cash, $8,500; Accounts Receivable, $15,500; Supplies, $1,600; Land, $18,000; Accounts Payable, $5,200. Business transactions during July are summarized as follows:

a. Kerry Ulman invested additional cash in the business with a deposit of $30,000 in the business bank account.
b. Paid $22,000 for the purchase of land as a future building site.
c. Received cash from cash customers for dry cleaning sales, $17,900.
d. Paid rent for the month, $3,000.
e. Purchased supplies on account, $1,550.
f. Paid creditors on account, $4,950.
g. Charged customers for dry cleaning sales on account, $12,350.
h. Received monthly invoice for dry cleaning expense for July (to be paid on August 10), $7,880.
i. Paid the following: wages expense, $5,100; truck expense, $1,200; utilities expense, $800; miscellaneous expense, $950.
j. Received cash from customers on account, $13,200.
k. Determined that the cost of supplies on hand was $1,275; therefore, the cost of supplies used during the month was $1,875.
l. Withdrew $5,000 cash for personal use.

Instructions

1. Determine the amount of Kerry Ulman's capital as of July 1 of the current year.
2. State the assets, liabilities, and owner's equity as of July 1 in equation form similar to that shown in this chapter. In tabular form below the equation, indicate increases and decreases resulting from each transaction and the new balances after each transaction.
3. Prepare an income statement for July, a statement of owner's equity for July, and a balance sheet as of July 31.
4. (Optional). Prepare a statement of cash flows for July.

PR 1-6A
Missing amounts from financial statements

obj. 5

✓ k. $120,000

The financial statements at the end of Cayenne Realty's first month of operations are shown below.

Cayenne Realty
Income Statement
For the Month Ended June 30, 2008

Fees earned		$ (a)
Expenses:		
Wages expense	$34,000	
Rent expense	12,800	
Supplies expense	(b)	
Utilities expense	7,200	
Miscellaneous expense	4,400	
Total expenses		70,400
Net income		$49,600

Cayenne Realty
Statement of Owner's Equity
For the Month Ended June 30, 2008

Andrea Merkel, capital, June 1, 2008		$ (c)
Investment on June 1, 2008	$160,000	49600
Net income for June	(d) 110,400	
	(e) 49600	
Less withdrawals	24,000	
Increase in owner's equity		73600 (f)
Andrea Merkel, capital, June 30, 2008		(g)
		123,200

Cayenne Realty
Balance Sheet
June 30, 2008

Assets		Liabilities	
Cash	$ 17,800	Accounts payable	$ 6,400
Supplies	14,200	**Owner's Equity**	
Land	160,000	Andrea Merkel, capital	(i)
		Total liabilities and	
Total assets	(h)	owner's equity	(j)

Cayenne Realty
Statement of Cash Flows
For the Month Ended June 30, 2008

Cash flows from operating activities:		
Cash received from customers	$ (k)	
Deduct cash payments for expenses and		
payments to creditors	78,200	
Net cash flow from operating activities		$ (l)
Cash flows from investing activities:		
Cash payments for acquisition of land		(m)
Cash flows from financing activities:		
Cash received as owner's investment	(n)	
Deduct cash withdrawal by owner	(o)	
Net cash flow from financing activities		(p)
Net cash flow and June 30, 2008, cash balance		(q)

Instructions

By analyzing the interrelationships among the four financial statements, determine the proper amounts for (a) through (q).

Problems Series B

PR 1-1B
Transactions
obj. 4

✓ *Cash bal. at end of March: $37,550*

Ana Urbin established an insurance agency on March 1 of the current year and completed the following transactions during March:

a. Opened a business bank account with a deposit of $40,000 from personal funds.
b. Purchased supplies on account, $1,500.
c. Paid creditors on account, $800.
d. Received cash from fees earned on insurance commissions, $7,250.
e. Paid rent on office and equipment for the month, $2,500.
f. Paid automobile expenses for month, $1,000, and miscellaneous expenses, $400.
g. Paid office salaries, $2,000.
h. Determined that the cost of supplies on hand was $400; therefore, the cost of supplies used was $1,100.
i. Billed insurance companies for sales commissions earned, $9,350.
j. Withdrew cash for personal use, $3,000.

Instructions

1. Indicate the effect of each transaction and the balances after each transaction, using the following tabular headings:

Assets			=	Liabilities	+			Owner's Equity					
Cash	+ Accounts Receivable	+ Supplies	=	Accounts Payable	+	Ana Urbin, Capital	− Ana Urbin, Drawing	+ Fees Earned	− Rent Expense	− Salaries Expense	− Supplies Expense	− Auto Expense	− Misc. Expense

2. ▬▬▶ Briefly explain why the owner's investment and revenues increased owner's equity, while withdrawals and expenses decreased owner's equity.

PR 1-2B
Financial statements
obj. 5

✓ *1. Net income: $130,000*

The amounts of the assets and liabilities of Abyss Travel Service at June 30, 2008, the end of the current year, and its revenue and expenses for the year are listed below. The capital of Megan Koch, owner, was $60,000 at July 1, 2007, the beginning of the current year, and the owner withdrew $50,000 during the current year.

Accounts payable	$ 12,500	Supplies	$ 4,250
Accounts receivable	48,750	Supplies expense	8,250
Cash	99,500	Taxes expense	6,400
Fees earned	375,000	Utilities expense	31,200
Miscellaneous expense	3,150	Wages expense	145,400
Rent expense	50,600		

Instructions

1. Prepare an income statement for the current year ended June 30, 2008.
2. Prepare a statement of owner's equity for the current year ended June 30, 2008.
3. Prepare a balance sheet as of June 30, 2008.

PR 1-3B
Financial statements
obj. 5

✓ *1. Net income: $14,875*

Kelly Cassidy established Firefly Computer Services on May 1, 2008. The effect of each transaction and the balances after each transaction for May are shown at the top of the following page.

Instructions

1. Prepare an income statement for the month ended May 31, 2008.
2. Prepare a statement of owner's equity for the month ended May 31, 2008.
3. Prepare a balance sheet as of May 31, 2008.
4. (Optional). Prepare a statement of cash flows for the month ending May 31, 2008.

(continued)

	Assets			= Liabilities +	Owner's Equity							
	Cash	+ Accounts Receivable	+ Supplies =	Accounts Payable	+ Kelly Cassidy, Capital	− Kelly Cassidy, Drawing	+ Fees Earned	− Salaries Expense	− Rent Expense	− Auto Expense	− Supplies Expense	− Misc. Expense
a.	+25,000				+25,000							
b.			+3,600	+3,600								
Bal.	25,000		3,600	3,600	25,000							
c.	+22,500						+22,500					
Bal.	47,500		3,600	3,600	25,000		22,500					
d.	− 9,000								−9,000			
Bal.	38,500		3,600	3,600	25,000		22,500		−9,000			
e.	− 1,250			−1,250								
Bal.	37,250		3,600	2,350	25,000		22,500		−9,000			
f.		+18,750					+18,750					
Bal.	37,250	18,750	3,600	2,350	25,000		41,250		−9,000			
g.	− 5,750									−3,875		−1,875
Bal.	31,500	18,750	3,600	2,350	25,000		41,250		−9,000	−3,875		−1,875
h.	−10,000							−10,000				
Bal.	21,500	18,750	3,600	2,350	25,000		41,250	−10,000	−9,000	−3,875		−1,875
i.			−1,625								−1,625	
Bal.	21,500	18,750	1,975	2,350	25,000		41,250	−10,000	−9,000	−3,875	−1,625	−1,875
j.	− 5,000					−5,000						
Bal.	16,500	18,750	1,975	2,350	25,000	−5,000	41,250	−10,000	−9,000	−3,875	−1,625	−1,875

PR 1-4B

Transactions; financial statements

objs. 4, 5

✓ 2. Net income: $12,990

On April 1, 2008, Britt Quinn established Uptown Realty. Britt completed the following transactions during the month of April:

a. Opened a business bank account with a deposit of $30,000 from personal funds.
b. Paid rent on office and equipment for the month, $2,200.
c. Paid automobile expenses (including rental charge) for month, $1,200, and miscellaneous expenses, $650.
d. Purchased supplies (pens, file folders, and copy paper) on account, $200.
e. Earned sales commissions, receiving cash, $20,800.
f. Paid creditor on account, $150.
g. Paid office salaries, $3,600.
h. Withdrew cash for personal use, $1,500.
i. Determined that the cost of supplies on hand was $40; therefore, the cost of supplies used was $160.

Instructions

1. Indicate the effect of each transaction and the balances after each transaction, using the following tabular headings:

	Assets		= Liabilities +	Owner's Equity							
	Cash	+ Supplies =	Accounts Payable	+ Britt Quinn, Capital	− Britt Quinn, Drawing	+ Sales Commissions	− Office Salaries Expense	− Rent Expense	− Auto Expense	− Supplies Expense	− Misc. Expense

2. Prepare an income statement for April, a statement of owner's equity for April, and a balance sheet as of April 30.

PR 1-5B

Transactions; financial statements

objs. 4, 5

✓ 3. Net income: $2,320

Skivvy Dry Cleaners is owned and operated by Jean Potts. A building and equipment are currently being rented, pending expansion to new facilities. The actual work of dry cleaning is done by another company at wholesale rates. The assets and the liabilities of the business on November 1, 2008, are as follows: Cash, $17,200; Accounts Receivable, $19,000; Supplies, $3,750; Land, $30,000; Accounts Payable, $8,200. Business transactions during November are summarized as follows:

a. Jean Potts invested additional cash in the business with a deposit of $50,000 in the business bank account.

b. Purchased land for use as a parking lot, paying cash of $45,000.

c. Paid rent for the month, $4,500.

d. Charged customers for dry cleaning sales on account, $15,250.

e. Paid creditors on account, $5,800.

f. Purchased supplies on account, $3,200.

g. Received cash from cash customers for dry cleaning sales, $22,900.

h. Received cash from customers on account, $17,250.

i. Received monthly invoice for dry cleaning expense for November (to be paid on December 10), $16,380.

j. Paid the following: wages expense, $6,200; truck expense, $1,875; utilities expense, $1,575; miscellaneous expense, $850.

k. Determined that the cost of supplies on hand was $2,500; therefore, the cost of supplies used during the month was $4,450.

l. Withdrew $6,000 for personal use.

Instructions

1. Determine the amount of Jean Potts's capital as of November 1.

2. State the assets, liabilities, and owner's equity as of November 1 in equation form similar to that shown in this chapter. In tabular form below the equation, indicate increases and decreases resulting from each transaction and the new balances after each transaction.

3. Prepare an income statement for November, a statement of owner's equity for November, and a balance sheet as of November 30.

4. (Optional). Prepare a statement of cash flows for November.

PR 1-6B

Missing amounts from financial statements

obj. **5**

✓ i. $60,660

The financial statements at the end of Harp Realty's first month of operations are shown below and on the next page.

Harp Realty
Income Statement
For the Month Ended April 30, 2008

Fees earned		$28,200
Expenses:		
Wages expense	$ (a)	
Rent expense	2,880	
Supplies expense	2,400	
Utilities expense	1,620	
Miscellaneous expense	990	
Total expenses		14,340
Net income		(b)

Harp Realty
Statement of Owner's Equity
For the Month Ended April 30, 2008

Iris Sigrist, capital, April 1, 2008		$ (c)
Investment on April 1, 2008	$ (d)	
Net income for April	(e)	
	(f)	
Less withdrawals	(g)	
Increase in owner's equity		(h)
Iris Sigrist, capital, April 30, 2008		(i)

Harp Realty
Balance Sheet
April 30, 2008

Assets		Liabilities	
Cash	$17,700	Accounts payable	$1,440
Supplies	1,200	**Owner's Equity**	
Land	(j)	Iris Sigrist, capital	(l)
		Total liabilities and	
Total assets	(k)	owner's equity	(m)

(continued)

Harp Realty
Statement of Cash Flows
For the Month Ended April 30, 2008

Cash flows from operating activities:		
Cash received from customers	$ (n)	
Deduct cash payments for expenses and		
payments to creditors	14,100	
Net cash flow from operating activities		$ (o)
Cash flows from investing activities:		
Cash payments for acquisition of land		(43,200)
Cash flows from financing activities:		
Cash received as owner's investment	$54,000	
Deduct cash withdrawal by owner	7,200	
Net cash flow from financing activities		(p)
Net cash flow and April 30, 2008, cash balance		(q)

Instructions

By analyzing the interrelationships among the four financial statements, determine the proper amounts for (a) through (q).

Continuing Problem

✓ *2. Net income: $730*

Kris Payne enjoys listening to all types of music and owns countless CDs and tapes. Over the years, Kris has gained a local reputation for knowledge of music from classical to rap and the ability to put together sets of recordings that appeal to all ages.

During the last several months, Kris served as a guest disc jockey on a local radio station. In addition, Kris has entertained at several friends' parties as the host deejay.

On April 1, 2008, Kris established a proprietorship known as Dancin Music. Using an extensive collection of CDs and tapes, Kris will serve as a disc jockey on a fee basis for weddings, college parties, and other events. During April, Kris entered into the following transactions:

April 1. Deposited $10,000 in a checking account in the name of Dancin Music.
2. Received $2,500 from a local radio station for serving as the guest disc jockey for April.
2. Agreed to share office space with a local real estate agency, Cash Realty. Dancin Music will pay one-fourth of the rent. In addition, Dancin Music agreed to pay a portion of the salary of the receptionist and to pay one-fourth of the utilities. Paid $1,000 for the rent of the office.
4. Purchased supplies (blank CDs, poster board, extension cords, etc.) from Richt Office Supply Co. for $350. Agreed to pay $100 within 10 days and the remainder by May 3, 2008.
6. Paid $750 to a local radio station to advertise the services of Dancin Music twice daily for two weeks.
8. Paid $800 to a local electronics store for renting digital recording equipment.
12. Paid $300 (music expense) to Rocket Music for the use of its current music demos to make various music sets.
13. Paid Richt Office Supply Co. $100 on account.
16. Received $350 from a dentist for providing two music sets for the dentist to play for her patients.
22. Served as disc jockey for a wedding party. The father of the bride agreed to pay $1,350 the 1st of May.
25. Received $500 from a friend for serving as the disc jockey for a cancer charity ball hosted by the local hospital.
29. Paid $240 (music expense) to Score Music for the use of its library of music demos.
30. Received $1,000 for serving as disc jockey for a local club's monthly dance.
30. Paid Cash Realty $400 for Dancin Music's share of the receptionist's salary for April.

30. Paid Cash Realty $350 for Dancin Music's share of the utilities for April.

30. Determined that the cost of supplies on hand is $170. Therefore, the cost of supplies used during the month was $180.

30. Paid for miscellaneous expenses, $150.

30. Paid $800 royalties (music expense) to Federated Clearing for use of various artists' music during the month.

30. Withdrew $300 of cash from Dancin Music for personal use.

Instructions

1. Indicate the effect of each transaction and the balances after each transaction, using the following tabular headings:

Assets			= Liabilities +						Owner's Equity						
Cash	Accounts Receivable	Supplies	Accounts Payable	Kris Payne, Capital	Kris Payne, Drawing	Fees Earned	Music Expense	Office Rent Expense	Equipment Rent Expense	Advertising Expense	Wages Expense	Utilities Expense	Supplies Expense	Misc. Expense

2. Prepare an income statement for Dancin Music for the month ended April 30, 2008.

3. Prepare a statement of owner's equity for Dancin Music for the month ended April 30, 2008.

4. Prepare a balance sheet for Dancin Music as of April 30, 2008.

Special Activities

SA 1-1
Ethics and professional conduct in business

Group Project

ETHICS

Chester Hunter, president of Jackrabbit Enterprises, applied for a $250,000 loan from Belgrade National Bank. The bank requested financial statements from Jackrabbit Enterprises as a basis for granting the loan. Chester has told his accountant to provide the bank with a balance sheet. Chester has decided to omit the other financial statements because there was a net loss during the past year.

In groups of three or four, discuss the following questions:

1. Is Chester behaving in a professional manner by omitting some of the financial statements?

2. a. What types of information about their businesses would owners be willing to provide bankers? What types of information would owners not be willing to provide?

   b. What types of information about a business would bankers want before extending a loan?

   c. What common interests are shared by bankers and business owners?

SA 1-2
Net income

On July 7, 2007, Dr. Jennifer Dejong established Second Opinion, a medical practice organized as a proprietorship. The following conversation occurred the following January between Dr. Dejong and a former medical school classmate, Dr. James Tomlin, at an American Medical Association convention in Paris.

Dr. Tomlin: Jennifer, good to see you again. Why didn't you call when you were in Chicago? We could have had dinner together.

Dr. Dejong: Actually, I never made it to Chicago this year. My husband and kids went up to our Aspen condo twice, but I got stuck in Boston. I opened a new consulting practice this July and haven't had any time for myself since.

Dr. Tomlin: I heard about it . . . Second . . . something . . . right?

Dr. Dejong: Yes, Second Opinion. My husband chose the name.

Dr. Tomlin: I've thought about doing something like that. Are you making any money? I mean, is it worth your time?

Dr. Dejong: You wouldn't believe it. I started by opening a bank account with $50,000, and my December bank statement has a balance of $140,000. Not bad for six months—all pure profit.

Dr. Tomlin: Maybe I'll try it in Chicago! Let's have breakfast together tomorrow and you can fill me in on the details.

➤ Comment on Dr. Dejong's statement that the difference between the opening bank balance ($50,000) and the December statement balance ($140,000) is pure profit.

SA 1-3
Transactions and financial statements

Kathy Hoss, a junior in college, has been seeking ways to earn extra spending money. As an active sports enthusiast, Kathy plays tennis regularly at the Racquet Club, where her family has a membership. The president of the club recently approached Kathy with the proposal that she manage the club's tennis courts. Kathy's primary duty would be to supervise the operation of the club's four indoor and six outdoor courts, including court reservations.

In return for her services, the club would pay Kathy $150 per week, plus Kathy could keep whatever she earned from lessons and the fees from the use of the ball machine. The club and Kathy agreed to a one-month trial, after which both would consider an arrangement for the remaining two years of Kathy's college career. On this basis, Kathy organized Advantage. During June 2007, Kathy managed the tennis courts and entered into the following transactions:

a. Opened a business account by depositing $1,500.
b. Paid $250 for tennis supplies (practice tennis balls, etc.).
c. Paid $160 for the rental of videotape equipment to be used in offering lessons during June.
d. Arranged for the rental of two ball machines during June for $200. Paid $140 in advance, with the remaining $60 due July 1.
e. Received $1,600 for lessons given during June.
f. Received $350 in fees from the use of the ball machines during June.
g. Paid $600 for salaries of part-time employees who answered the telephone and took reservations while Kathy was giving lessons.
h. Paid $150 for miscellaneous expenses.
i. Received $600 from the club for managing the tennis courts during June.
j. Determined that the cost of supplies on hand at the end of the month totaled $150; therefore, the cost of supplies used was $100.
k. Withdrew $500 for personal use on June 30.

As a friend and accounting student, you have been asked by Kathy to aid her in assessing the venture.

1. Indicate the effect of each transaction and the balances after each transaction, using the following tabular headings:

Assets		=	Liabilities	+	Owner's Equity					
Cash	+ Supplies	=	Accounts Payable	+	Kathy Hoss, Capital	– Kathy Hoss, Drawing	+ Service Revenue	– Salary Expense	– Rent Expense	– Supplies Expense	– Misc. Expense

2. Prepare an income statement for June.
3. Prepare a statement of owner's equity for June.
4. Prepare a balance sheet as of June 30.
5. a. Assume that Kathy Hoss could earn $8 per hour working 30 hours a week as a waitress. Evaluate which of the two alternatives, working as a waitress or operating Advantage, would provide Kathy with the most income per month.
   b. ➤ Discuss any other factors that you believe Kathy should consider before discussing a long-term arrangement with the Racquet Club.

SA 1-4
Certification requirements for accountants

Internet Project

By satisfying certain specific requirements, accountants may become certified as public accountants (CPAs), management accountants (CMAs), or internal auditors (CIAs). Find the certification requirements for one of these accounting groups by accessing the appropriate Internet site listed below.

Site	Description
http://www.ais-cpa.com	This site lists the address and/or Internet link for each state's board of accountancy. Find your state's requirements.
http://www.imanet.org	This site lists the requirements for becoming a CMA.
http://www.theiia.org	This site lists the requirements for becoming a CIA.

SA 1-5
Cash flows

Amazon.com, an Internet retailer, was incorporated and began operation in the mid-90s. On the statement of cash flows, would you expect Amazon.com's net cash flows from operating, investing, and financing activities to be positive or negative for its first three years of operations? Use the following format for your answers, and briefly explain your logic.

	First Year	Second Year	Third Year
Net cash flows from operating activities	negative		
Net cash flows from investing activities			
Net cash flows from financing activities			

SA 1-6
*Financial analysis of
Enron Corporation*

Internet Project

The now defunct Enron Corporation, once headquartered in Houston, Texas, provided products and services for natural gas, electricity, and communications to wholesale and retail customers. Enron's operations were conducted through a variety of subsidiaries and affiliates that involved transporting gas through pipelines, transmitting electricity, and managing energy commodities. The following data were taken from Enron's financial statements.

	In millions
Total revenues	$100,789
Total costs and expenses	98,836
Operating income	1,953
Net income	979
Total assets	65,503
Total liabilities	54,033
Total owners' equity	11,470
Net cash flows from operating activities	4,779
Net cash flows from investing activities	(4,264)
Net cash flows from financing activities	571
Net increase in cash	1,086

The market price of Enron's stock was approximately $83 per share when the prior financial statement data were taken. However, eventually Enron's stock was selling for $0.22 per share. Review the preceding financial statement data and search the Internet for articles on Enron Corporation. Briefly explain why Enron's stock dropped so dramatically.

Answers to Self-Examination Questions

1. **D** A corporation, organized in accordance with state or federal statutes, is a separate legal entity in which ownership is divided into shares of stock (answer D). A proprietorship (answer A) is an unincorporated business owned by one individual. A service business (answer B) provides services to its customers. It can be organized as a proprietorship, partnership, corporation, or limited liability company. A partnership (answer C) is an unincorporated business owned by two or more individuals.
2. **A** The resources owned by a business are called assets (answer A). The debts of the business are called liabilities (answer B), and the equity of the owners is called owner's equity (answer D). The relationship between assets, liabilities, and owner's equity is expressed as the accounting equation (answer C).
3. **A** The balance sheet is a listing of the assets, liabilities, and owner's equity of a business at a specific date (answer A). The income statement (answer B) is a summary of the revenue and expenses of a business for a specific period of time. The statement of owner's equity (answer C) summarizes the changes in owner's

equity for a proprietorship or partnership during a specific period of time. The statement of cash flows (answer D) summarizes the cash receipts and cash payments for a specific period of time.

4. **C** The accounting equation is:

$$\text{Assets} = \text{Liabilities} + \text{Owner's Equity}$$

Therefore, if assets increased by $20,000 and liabilities increased by $12,000, owner's equity must have increased by $8,000 (answer C), as indicated in the following computation:

Assets	= Liabilities + Owner's Equity
+$20,000	= +$12,000 + Owner's Equity
+$20,000 − $12,000 =	Owner's Equity
+$8,000	= Owner's Equity

5. **B** Net income is the excess of revenue over expenses, or $7,500 (answer B). If expenses exceed revenue, the difference is a net loss. Withdrawals by the owner are the opposite of the owner's investing in the business and do not affect the amount of net income or net loss.

Analyzing Transactions

© BODYWEDGE 21/PRNEWSFOTO (AP TOPIC GALLERY)

objectives

After studying this chapter, you should be able to:

1 *Describe the characteristics of an account and record transactions using a chart of accounts and journal.*

2 *Describe and illustrate the posting of journal entries to accounts.*

3 *Prepare an unadjusted trial balance and explain how it can be used to discover errors.*

4 *Discover and correct errors in recording transactions.*

Gold's Gym International, Inc.

You can organize your digital music within your MP3 player or IPod® according to various playlists, according to your favorite songs, genre, artist, or album. Your playlists allow you to quickly retrieve music for listening. Computer files are organized within folders for the same reason. Information, like music or digital files, is organized into categories to simplify retrieval and reporting. In the same way that you organize your digital information, a business also needs to organize its transactions. For example, when you shop at **Wal-Mart** or **Target**, or buy groceries at **Kroger** or **SUPERVALU**, you enter into a transaction that is processed and recorded by the business. A company such as **Gold's Gym**, the largest co-ed gym chain in the world, must also process, record, and summarize its transactions. For example, Gold's would want to record all its cash transactions so that they can be summarized as a single category, called "cash." This is much the same way you would summarize the cash transactions in the check register of your checkbook.

In Chapter 1, we analyzed and recorded this kind of information by using the accounting equation, Assets = Liabilities + Owner's Equity. However, such a format is not practical for most businesses, and in this chapter we will study more efficient methods of recording transactions. We will conclude this chapter by discussing how accounting errors may occur and how they may be detected and corrected by the accounting process.

Using Accounts to Record Transactions

objective 1

Describe the characteristics of an account and record transactions using a chart of accounts and journal.

In Chapter 1, we recorded the November transactions for NetSolutions using the accounting equation format shown in Exhibit 1. However, this format is not efficient or practical for companies that have to record and summarize thousands or millions of transactions daily. As a result, accounting systems are designed to show the increases and decreases in each financial statement item as a separate record. This record is called an **account**.

To illustrate, the Cash column of Exhibit 1 records the increases and decreases in cash. Likewise, the other columns in Exhibit 1 record the increases and decreases in Supplies; Land; Accounts Payable; Chris Clark, Capital; Chris Clark, Drawing; Fees Earned; Wages Expense; Rent Expense; Supplies Expense; Utilities Expense; and Miscellaneous Expense. As we illustrate next, each of these columns can be organized into a separate account that more efficiently records and summarizes transactions.

An account, in its simplest form, has three parts. First, each account has a title, which is the name of the item recorded in the account. Second, each account has a space for recording increases in the amount of the item. Third, each account has a space for recording decreases in the amount of the item. The account form presented below is called a **T account** because it resembles the letter T. The left side of the account is called the *debit* side, and the right side is called the *credit* side.[1]

Title	
Left side	Right side
debit	*credit*
~~increase~~	~~decrease~~

---

1 The terms *debit* and *credit* are derived from the Latin *debere* and *credere*.

► **EXHIBIT 1**   **NetSolutions November Transactions**   @**netsolutions**

	Assets			= Liabilities +	Owner's Equity						
				Accounts	Chris Clark,	Chris Clark,	Fees	Wages	Rent	Supplies	Utilities	Misc.
	Cash +	Supp. +	Land =	Payable +	Capital −	Drawing +	Earned −	Exp. −	Exp. −	Exp. −	Exp. −	Exp.
a.	+25,000				+25,000							
b.	−20,000		+20,000									
Bal.	5,000		20,000		25,000							
c.		+1,350		+1,350								
Bal.	5,000	1,350	20,000	1,350	25,000							
d.	+ 7,500						+7,500					
Bal.	12,500	1,350	20,000	1,350	25,000		7,500					
e.	− 3,650							−2,125	−800		−450	−275
Bal.	8,850	1,350	20,000	1,350	25,000		7,500	−2,125	−800		−450	−275
f.	− 950			− 950								
Bal.	7,900	1,350	20,000	400	25,000		7,500	−2,125	−800		−450	−275
g.		− 800								−800		
Bal.	7,900	550	20,000	400	25,000		7,500	−2,125	−800	−800	−450	−275
h.	− 2,000					−2,000						
Bal.	5,900	550	20,000	400	25,000	−2,000	7,500	−2,125	−800	−800	−450	−275

> Amounts entered on the left side of an account are debits, and amounts entered on the right side of an account are credits.

Amounts entered on the left side of an account, regardless of the account title, are called **debits** to the account. When debits are entered in an account, the account is said to be *debited*. Amounts entered on the right side of an account are called **credits**, and the account is said to be *credited*. Debits and credits are sometimes abbreviated as *Dr.* and *Cr.*

The cash account shown below illustrates how NetSolutions' November cash transactions shown in the first column of Exhibit 1 would be recorded in an account. Transactions involving receipts of cash are listed on the debit side of the account. For example, the receipt of $25,000 from Chris Clark in transaction (a) is entered on the debit side of the account. The letter or date of the transaction is also entered into the account. This is done so that if any questions later arise related to the entry, the entry can be traced back to the underlying transaction data. The transactions involving cash payments are listed on the credit side. For example, the payment of $20,000 to purchase land in transaction (b) is entered on the credit side of the account.

If at any time the total of the cash receipts is needed, the entries on the debit side of the account may be added. For NetSolutions, the total receipts is $32,500 ($25,000 + $7,500). Likewise, the total cash payments of $26,600 ($20,000 + $3,650 + $950 + $2,000) may be determined by adding the entries on the credit side of the account. Subtracting the smaller sum from the larger, $32,500 − $26,600, identifies the amount of cash on hand, $5,900. This amount is called the **balance of the account** and is inserted in the

Many times when accountants analyze complex transactions, they use T accounts to simplify the thought process. In the same way, you will find T accounts a useful device in this and later accounting courses.

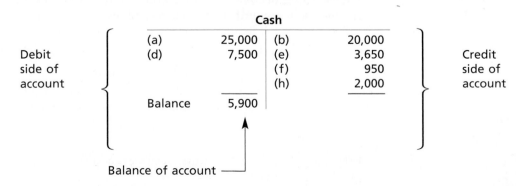

		Cash			
Debit side of account	(a)	25,000	(b)	20,000	Credit side of account
	(d)	7,500	(e)	3,650	
			(f)	950	
			(h)	2,000	
	Balance	5,900			

Balance of account

account, in the debit column. In this way, the balance is identified as a debit balance.[2] This balance is reported on the balance sheet for NetSolutions as of November 30, 2007, shown in Exhibit 6 of Chapter 1. Each of the columns in Exhibit 1 can be converted into an account form in a similar manner as was done for the cash column of Exhibit 1. We illustrate each of these accounts later in this chapter.

CHART OF ACCOUNTS

A group of accounts for a business entity is called a **ledger**. A list of the accounts in the ledger is called a **chart of accounts**. The accounts are normally listed in the order in which they appear in the financial statements. The balance sheet accounts are usually listed first, in the order of assets, liabilities, and owner's equity. The income statement accounts are then listed in the order of revenues and expenses. Each of these major account classifications is briefly described below.

Assets are resources owned by the business entity. These resources can be physical items, such as cash and supplies, or intangibles that have value, such as patent rights. Some other examples of assets include accounts receivable, prepaid expenses (such as insurance), buildings, equipment, and land.

Liabilities are debts owed to outsiders (creditors). Liabilities are often identified on the balance sheet by titles that include the word *payable*. Examples of liabilities include accounts payable, notes payable, and wages payable. Cash received before services are delivered creates a liability to perform the services. These future service commitments are often called *unearned revenues*. Examples of unearned revenues are magazine subscriptions received by a publisher and tuition received by a college at the beginning of a term.

Owner's equity is the owner's right to the assets of the business. For a proprietorship, the owner's equity on the balance sheet is represented by the balance of the owner's *capital* account. A **drawing** account represents the amount of withdrawals made by the owner.

Revenues are increases in owner's equity as a result of selling services or products to customers. Examples of revenues include fees earned, fares earned, commissions revenue, and rent revenue.

Expenses result from using up assets or consuming services in the process of generating revenues. Examples of typical expenses include wages expense, rent expense, utilities expense, supplies expense, and miscellaneous expense.

A chart of accounts is designed to meet the information needs of a company's managers and other users of its financial statements. The accounts within the chart of accounts are numbered for use as references. A flexible numbering system is normally used, so that new accounts can be added without affecting other account numbers.

Exhibit 2 is NetSolutions' chart of accounts that we will be using in this chapter. Additional accounts will be introduced in later chapters. In Exhibit 2, each account number has two digits. The first digit indicates the major classification of the ledger in which the account is located. Accounts beginning with 1 represent assets; 2, liabilities; 3, owner's equity; 4, revenue; and 5, expenses. The second digit indicates the location of the account within its class. You should note that each of the columns in Exhibit 1 has been assigned an account number in the chart of accounts shown in Exhibit 2. In addition, we have added accounts for Accounts Receivable, Prepaid Insurance, Office Equipment, and Unearned Rent. These accounts will be used in recording NetSolutions' December transactions later in this chapter.

ANALYZING AND SUMMARIZING TRANSACTIONS IN ACCOUNTS

Every business transaction affects at least two accounts. To illustrate how transactions are analyzed and summarized in accounts, we will use the NetSolutions transactions from Chapter 1, with dates added. First, we illustrate how transactions (a), (b), (c), and

REAL WORLD

Procter & Gamble's account numbers have over 30 digits to reflect P&G's many different operations and regions.

---

2 The totals of the debit and credit columns may be shown separately in an account. When this is done, these amounts should be identified in some way so that they are not mistaken for entries or the ending balance of the account.

EXHIBIT 2   Analysis and Recording of Transactions Using Accounts

Balance Sheet Accounts		Income Statement Accounts	
1. Assets		**4. Revenue**	
11	Cash	41	Fees Earned
12	Accounts Receivable		**5. Expenses**
14	Supplies	51	Wages Expense
15	Prepaid Insurance	52	Rent Expense
17	Land	54	Utilities Expense
18	Office Equipment	55	Supplies Expense
	2. Liabilities	59	Miscellaneous Expense
21	Accounts Payable		
23	Unearned Rent		
	3. Owner's Equity		
31	Chris Clark, Capital		
32	Chris Clark, Drawing		

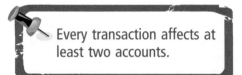

Every transaction affects at least two accounts.

(f) are analyzed and summarized in balance sheet accounts (assets, liabilities, and owner's equity). Next, we illustrate how transactions (d), (e), and (g) are analyzed and summarized in income statement accounts (revenues and expenses). Finally, we illustrate how the withdrawal of cash by Chris Clark, transaction (h), is analyzed and summarized in the accounts.

Balance Sheet Accounts Chris Clark's first transaction, (a), was to deposit $25,000 in a bank account in the name of NetSolutions. The effect of this November 1 transaction on the balance sheet is to increase assets and owner's equity, as shown below.

November 1 Transaction

NetSolutions
Balance Sheet
November 1, 2007

Assets		Owner's Equity	
Cash	$25 0 0 0 00	Chris Clark, capital	$25 0 0 0 00

This transaction is initially entered in a record called a **journal**. The title of the account to be debited is listed first, followed by the amount to be debited. The title of the account to be credited is listed below and to the right of the debit, followed by the amount to be credited. This process of recording a transaction in the journal is called **journalizing**. This form of recording a transaction is called a **journal entry**.

The journal entry for transaction (a) is shown below.

JOURNAL   Page 1

	Date		Description	Post. Ref.	Debit	Credit	
1	2007 Nov.	1	Cash		25 0 0 0 00		1
2			Chris Clark, Capital			25 0 0 0 00	2
3			Invested cash in NetSolutions.				3

A journal can be thought of as being similar to an individual's diary of significant day-to-day life events.

The increase in the asset (Cash), which is reported on the left side of the balance sheet, is debited to the cash account. The increase in owner's equity, which is reported on the right side of the balance sheet, is credited to the Chris Clark, capital account. As other assets are acquired, the increases are also recorded as debits to asset accounts. Likewise, other increases in owner's equity will be recorded as credits to owner's equity accounts.

The effects of this transaction are shown in the accounts by transferring the amount and date of the journal entry to the left (debit) side of Cash and to the right (credit) side of Chris Clark, Capital, as follows:

Cash		Chris Clark, Capital	
Nov. 1	25,000	Nov. 1	25,000

November 5 Transaction

On November 5 [transaction (b)], NetSolutions bought land for $20,000, paying cash. This transaction increases one asset account and decreases another. It is entered in the journal as a $20,000 increase (debit) to Land and a $20,000 decrease (credit) to Cash, as shown below.

4					4
5	5	Land	20 0 0 0 00		5
6		Cash		20 0 0 0 00	6
7		Purchased land for building site.			7

The effect of this entry is shown in the accounts of NetSolutions as follows:

Cash		Land		Chris Clark, Capital	
Nov. 1 25,000	Nov. 5 20,000	Nov. 5 20,000			Nov. 1 25,000

November 10 Transaction

On November 10 [transaction (c)], NetSolutions purchased supplies on account for $1,350. This transaction increases an asset account and increases a liability account. It is entered in the journal as a $1,350 increase (debit) to Supplies and a $1,350 increase (credit) to Accounts Payable, as shown below. To simplify the illustration, the effect of entry (c) and the remaining journal entries for NetSolutions will be shown in the accounts later.

8					8
9	10	Supplies	1 3 5 0 00		9
10		Accounts Payable		1 3 5 0 00	10
11		Purchased supplies on account.			11

November 30 Transaction

On November 30 [transaction (f)], NetSolutions paid creditors on account, $950. This transaction decreases a liability account and decreases an asset account. It is entered in the journal as a $950 decrease (debit) to Accounts Payable and a $950 decrease (credit) to Cash, as shown below.

23					23
24	30	Accounts Payable	9 5 0 00		24
25		Cash		9 5 0 00	25
26		Paid creditors on account.			26

> The left side of all accounts is the debit side, and the right side is the credit side.

In the preceding examples, you should observe that the left side of asset accounts is used for recording increases, and the right side is used for recording decreases. Also, the right side of liability and owner's equity accounts is used to record increases, and the left side of such accounts is used to record decreases. The left side of all accounts, whether asset, liability, or owner's equity, is the debit side, and the right side is the credit side. Thus, a debit may be either an increase or a decrease, depending on the account affected. Likewise, a credit may be either an increase or a decrease, depending on the account.

The general rules of debit and credit for balance sheet accounts may be stated as follows:

	Debit	Credit
Asset accounts	Increase (+)	Decrease (−)
Liability accounts	Decrease (−)	Increase (+)
Owner's equity (capital) accounts	Decrease (−)	Increase (+)

The rules of debit and credit may also be stated in relationship to the accounting equation, as shown below. The side of the account for recording increases is shown in green.

Balance Sheet Accounts

ASSETS Asset Accounts			LIABILITIES Liability Accounts			OWNER'S EQUITY Owner's Equity Accounts	
Debit for increases(+)	Credit for decreases(−)	=	Debit for decreases(−)	Credit for increases(+)	+	Debit for decreases(−)	Credit for increases(+)

Example Exercise 2-1 — objective 1

Prepare a journal entry for the purchase of a truck on June 3 for $42,500, paying $8,500 cash and the remainder on account.

Follow My Example 2-1

June 3	Truck	42,500	
	Cash		8,500
	Accounts Payable		34,000

For Practice: PE 2-1A, PE 2-1B

Income Statement Accounts The analysis of revenue and expense transactions focuses on how each transaction affects owner's equity. Transactions that increase revenue will increase owner's equity. Just as increases in owner's equity are recorded as credits, so, too, are increases in revenue accounts. Transactions that increase expense will decrease owner's equity. Just as decreases in owner's equity are recorded as debits, increases in expense accounts are recorded as debits.

November 18 Transaction We will use NetSolutions' transactions (d), (e), and (g) to illustrate the analysis of transactions and the rules of debit and credit for revenue and expense accounts. On November 18 [transaction (d)], NetSolutions received fees of $7,500 from customers for services provided. This transaction increases an asset account and increases a revenue account. It is entered in the journal as a $7,500 increase (debit) to Cash and a $7,500 increase (credit) to Fees Earned, as shown below [transaction (d)].

12					12
13	18	Cash	7 5 0 0 00		13
14		Fees Earned		7 5 0 0 00	14
15		Received fees from customers.			15

Business Connections

REAL WORLD

THE HIJACKING RECEIVABLE

A company's chart of accounts should reflect the basic nature of its operations. Occasionally, however, transactions take place that give rise to unusual accounts. The following is a story of one such account.

During the early 1970s, before strict airport security was implemented across the United States, several airlines experienced hijacking incidents. One such incident occurred on November 10, 1972, when a **Southern Airways** DC-9 en route from Memphis to Miami was hijacked during a stopover in Birmingham, Alabama. The three hijackers boarded the plane in Birmingham armed with handguns and hand grenades. At gunpoint, the hijackers took the plane, the plane's crew of four, and 27 passengers to nine American cities, Toronto, and eventually to Havana, Cuba.

During the long flight, the hijackers threatened to crash the plane into the Oak Ridge, Tennessee, nuclear facilities, insisted on talking with President Nixon, and demanded a ransom of $10 million. **Southern Airways**, however, was only able to come up with $2 million. Even-

tually, the pilot talked the hijackers into settling for the $2 million when the plane landed in Chattanooga for refueling.

Upon landing in Havana, the Cuban authorities arrested the hijackers and, after a brief delay, sent the plane, passengers, and crew back to the United States. The hijackers and $2 million stayed in Cuba.

How did Southern Airways account for and report the hijacking payment in its subsequent financial statements? As you might have analyzed, the initial entry credited Cash for $2 million. The debit was to an account entitled "Hijacking Payment." This account was reported as a type of receivable under "other assets" on Southern's balance sheet. The company maintained that it would be able to collect the cash from the Cuban government and that, therefore, a receivable existed. In fact, in August 1975, Southern Airways was repaid $2 million by the Cuban government, which was, at that time, attempting to improve relations with the United States.

November 30 Transaction   Throughout the month, NetSolutions incurred the following expenses: wages, $2,125; rent, $800; utilities, $450; and miscellaneous, $275. To simplify the illustration, the entry to journalize the payment of these expenses is recorded on November 30 [transaction (e)], as shown below. This transaction increases various expense accounts and decreases an asset account.

16					16
17	30	Wages Expense	2 1 2 5 00		17
18		Rent Expense	8 0 0 00		18
19		Utilities Expense	4 5 0 00		19
20		Miscellaneous Expense	2 7 5 00		20
21		Cash		3 6 5 0 00	21
22		Paid expenses.			22

You should note that regardless of the number of accounts, the sum of the debits is always equal to the sum of the credits in a journal entry.

November 30 Transaction   On November 30, NetSolutions recorded the amount of supplies used in the operations during the month [transaction (g)]. This transaction increases an expense account and decreases an asset account. The journal entry for transaction (g) is shown below.

27					27
28	30	Supplies Expense	8 0 0 00		28
29		Supplies		8 0 0 00	29
30		Supplies used during November.			30

The general rules of debit and credit for analyzing transactions affecting income statement accounts are stated as shown at the top of the following page.

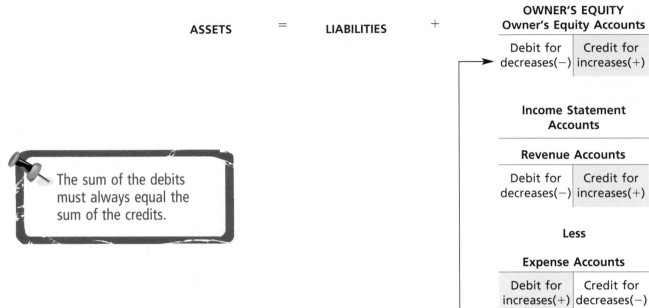

	Debit	Credit
Revenue accounts	Decrease (−)	Increase (+)
Expense accounts	Increase (+)	Decrease (−)

The rules of debit and credit for income statement accounts may also be summarized in relationship to the accounting equation, owner's equity accounts, and net income or net loss as shown below.

> The sum of the debits must always equal the sum of the credits.

ASSETS = LIABILITIES +

OWNER'S EQUITY
Owner's Equity Accounts

Debit for decreases(−)	Credit for increases(+)

Income Statement Accounts

Revenue Accounts

Debit for decreases(−)	Credit for increases(+)

Less

Expense Accounts

Debit for increases(+)	Credit for decreases(−)

Equals

Net Income
Revenues exceed expenses
Increases owner's equity (capital)

or

Net Loss
Expenses exceed revenues
Decreases owner's equity (capital)

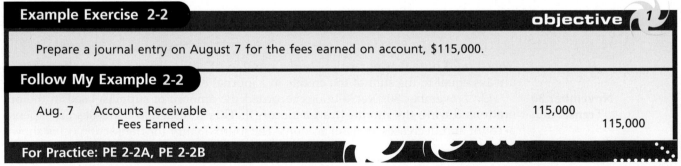

Example Exercise 2-2   **objective** 1

Prepare a journal entry on August 7 for the fees earned on account, $115,000.

Follow My Example 2-2

Aug. 7	Accounts Receivable	115,000	
	Fees Earned		115,000

For Practice: PE 2-2A, PE 2-2B

Drawing Account The owner of a proprietorship may withdraw cash from the business for personal use. This is common practice for owners devoting full time to the business, since the business may be the owner's main source of income. Such withdrawals have the effect of decreasing owner's equity. Just as decreases in owner's equity are recorded as debits, increases in withdrawals are recorded as debits. Withdrawals are debited to an account with the owner's name followed by *Drawing* or *Personal*.

November 30   In transaction (h), Chris Clark withdrew $2,000 in cash from NetSolutions for per-
Transaction sonal use. The effect of this transaction is to increase the drawing account and decrease the cash account. The journal entry for transaction (h) is shown on the next page.

	2007							
1	Nov.	30	Chris Clark, Drawing		2 0 0 0 00			1
2			Cash			2 0 0 0 00		2
3			Chris Clark withdrew cash for					3
4			personal use.					4

Example Exercise 2-3

 objective 1

Prepare a journal entry on December 29 for the payment of $12,000 to the owner of Smartstaff Consulting Services, Dominique Walsh, for personal use.

Follow My Example 2-3

Dec. 29   Dominique Walsh, Drawing   12,000
                    Cash   12,000

For Practice: PE 2-3A, PE 2-3B

NORMAL BALANCES OF ACCOUNTS

The sum of the increases recorded in an account is usually equal to or greater than the sum of the decreases recorded in the account. For this reason, the normal balances of all accounts are positive rather than negative. For example, the total debits (increases) in an asset account will ordinarily be greater than the total credits (decreases). Thus, asset accounts normally have debit balances.

The rules of debit and credit and the normal balances of the various types of accounts are summarized in Exhibit 3. In Exhibit 3, the side of the account for recording increases and the normal balance is shown in green.

When an account normally having a debit balance actually has a credit balance, or vice versa, an error may have occurred or an unusual situation may exist. For example, a credit balance in the office equipment account could result only from an error. On the other hand, a debit balance in an accounts payable account could result from an overpayment.

Example Exercise 2-4

 objective 1

State for each account whether it is likely to have (a) debit entries only, (b) credit entries only, or (c) both debit and credit entries. Also, indicate its normal balance.

1. Amber Saunders, Drawing
2. Accounts Payable
3. Cash
4. Fees Earned
5. Supplies
6. Utilities Expense

Follow My Example 2-4

1. Debit entries only; normal debit balance
2. Debit and credit entries; normal credit balance
3. Debit and credit entries; normal debit balance
4. Credit entries only; normal credit balance
5. Debit and credit entries; normal debit balance
6. Debit entries only; normal debit balance

For Practice: PE 2-4A, PE 2-4B

Integrity, Objectivity, and Ethics in Business

 ETHICS

WILL JOURNALIZING PREVENT FRAUD?

While journalizing transactions reduces the possibility of fraud, it by no means eliminates it. For example, embezzlement can be hidden within the double-entry bookkeeping system by creating fictitious suppliers to whom checks are issued.

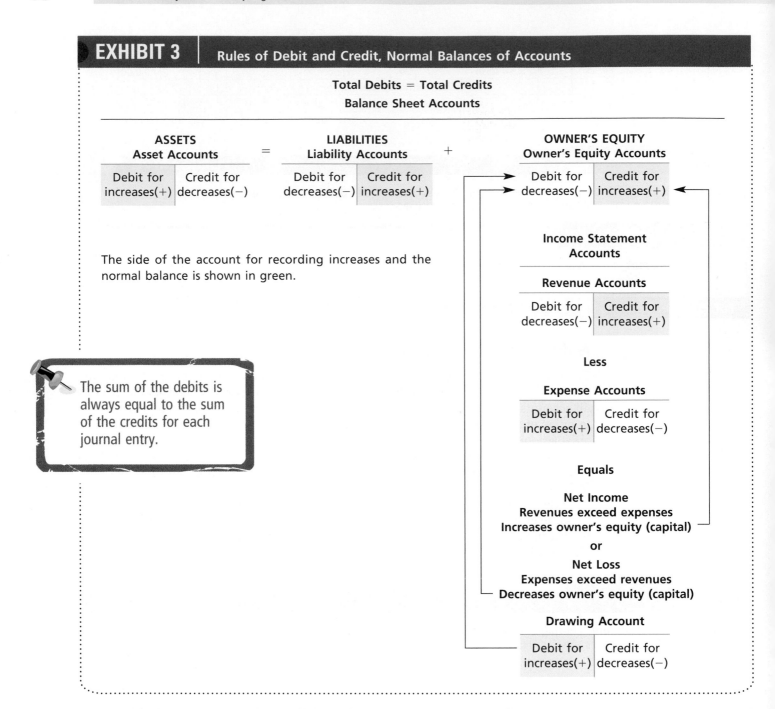

| EXHIBIT 3 | Rules of Debit and Credit, Normal Balances of Accounts |

Total Debits = Total Credits
Balance Sheet Accounts

ASSETS Asset Accounts			LIABILITIES Liability Accounts			OWNER'S EQUITY Owner's Equity Accounts	
Debit for increases(+)	Credit for decreases(−)	=	Debit for decreases(−)	Credit for increases(+)	+	Debit for decreases(−)	Credit for increases(+)

The side of the account for recording increases and the normal balance is shown in green.

Income Statement Accounts

Revenue Accounts

Debit for decreases(−)	Credit for increases(+)

Less

Expense Accounts

Debit for increases(+)	Credit for decreases(−)

Equals

Net Income
Revenues exceed expenses
Increases owner's equity (capital)

or

Net Loss
Expenses exceed revenues
Decreases owner's equity (capital)

Drawing Account

Debit for increases(+)	Credit for decreases(−)

The sum of the debits is always equal to the sum of the credits for each journal entry.

Double-Entry Accounting System

In 1494, Luca Pacioli, a Franciscan monk, invented the double-entry accounting system that is still used today.

In the preceding paragraphs, we illustrated the rules of debit and credit for recording transactions in accounts using journal entries. In doing so, the sum of the debits is always equal to the sum of the credits for each journal entry. As shown in Exhibit 3, this equality of debits and credits for each transaction is built into the accounting equation: Assets = Liabilities + Owner's Equity. Because of this double equality, this system of recording transactions is called the **double-entry accounting system**.

As we illustrate in the remainder of this text, the double-entry accounting system is a very powerful tool in analyzing the effects of transactions. Using this system to analyze transactions is summarized below and in Exhibit 4.

1. Carefully read the description of the transaction to determine whether an asset, liability, owner's equity, revenue, expense, or drawing account is affected by the transaction.

EXHIBIT 4	Recording Transactions Using Double-Entry Accounting

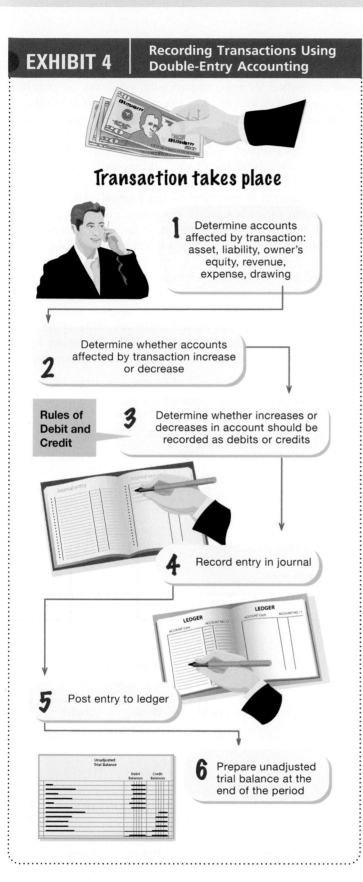

Transaction takes place

1 Determine accounts affected by transaction: asset, liability, owner's equity, revenue, expense, drawing

2 Determine whether accounts affected by transaction increase or decrease

Rules of Debit and Credit

3 Determine whether increases or decreases in account should be recorded as debits or credits

4 Record entry in journal

5 Post entry to ledger

6 Prepare unadjusted trial balance at the end of the period

2. For each account affected by the transaction, determine whether the account increases or decreases.
3. Determine whether each increase or decrease should be recorded as a debit or a credit, following the rules of debit and credit shown in Exhibit 3.
4. Record the transaction using a journal entry.
5. Periodically post journal entries to the accounts in the ledger.
6. Prepare an unadjusted trial balance at the end of the period.

We have described and illustrated steps 1–4 in the preceding paragraphs. In the remainder of this chapter, we describe and illustrate steps 5 and 6.

2 objective

Describe and illustrate the posting of journal entries to accounts.

Posting Journal Entries to Accounts

As we discussed in the preceding section, a transaction is first recorded in a journal. Periodically, the journal entries are transferred to the accounts in the ledger (step 5 in Exhibit 4). The ledger is a history of transactions by account. The process of transferring the debits and credits from the journal entries to the accounts is called **posting**.

In practice, businesses use a variety of formats for recording journal entries. A business may use one all-purpose journal, sometimes called a **two-column journal**, or it may use several journals. In the latter case, each journal is used to record different types of transactions, such as cash receipts or cash payments. The journals may be part of either a manual accounting system or a computerized accounting system.[3]

As a review of the analysis and recording of transactions and to illustrate posting in a manual accounting system, we will use the December transactions of NetSolutions. The first transaction in December occurred on December 1.

---

3 The use of special journals and computerized accounting systems is discussed in Chapter 5, after the basics of accounting systems have been covered.

December 1
Transaction
NetSolutions paid a premium of $2,400 for a comprehensive insurance policy covering liability, theft, and fire. The policy covers a one-year period.

Analysis   When you purchase insurance for your automobile, you may be required to pay the insurance premium in advance. In this case, your transaction is similar to NetSolutions. Advance payments of expenses such as insurance are prepaid expenses, which are assets. For NetSolutions, the asset acquired for the cash payment is insurance protection for 12 months. The asset Prepaid Insurance increases and is debited for $2,400. The asset Cash decreases and is credited for $2,400. The recording and posting of this transaction is shown in Exhibit 5.

Note where the date of the transaction is recorded in the journal. Also note that the entry is explained as the payment of an insurance premium. Such explanations should be brief. For unusual and complex transactions, such as a long-term rental arrangement, the journal entry explanation may include a reference to the rental agreement or other business document.

You will note that the T account form is not used in this illustration. Although the T account clearly separates debit and credit entries, in practice, the T account is usually replaced with the standard form shown in Exhibit 5.

The debits and credits for each journal entry are posted to the accounts in the order in which they occur in the journal. To illustrate, the debit portion of the December 1 journal entry is posted to the prepaid account in Exhibit 5 using the following four steps:

Step 1: The date (Dec. 1) is entered in the Date Column of Prepaid Insurance;

EXHIBIT 5

Diagram of the Recording and Posting of a Debit and a Credit

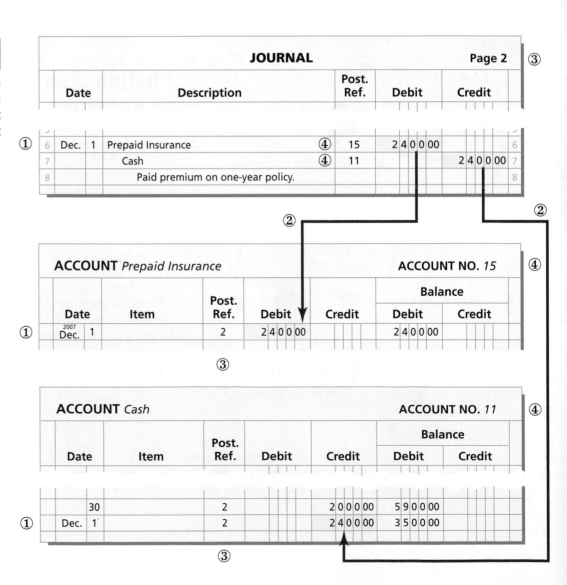

Step 2: The amount (2,400) is entered into the Debit Column of Prepaid Insurance;

Step 3: The journal page number (2) is entered in the Posting Reference (Post. Ref.) Column of Prepaid Insurance;

Step 4: The account number (15) is entered in the Posting Reference (Post. Ref.) Column in the journal.

As shown in Exhibit 5, the credit portion of the December 1 journal entry is posted to the cash account in a similar manner.

The remaining December transactions for NetSolutions are analyzed in the following paragraphs. These transactions are posted to the ledger in Exhibit 6, shown later. To simplify and reduce repetition, some of the December transactions are stated in summary form. For example, cash received for services is normally recorded on a daily basis. In this example, however, only summary totals are recorded at the middle and end of the month. Likewise, all fees earned on account during December are recorded at the middle and end of the month. In practice, each fee earned is recorded separately.

December 1 Transaction

NetSolutions paid rent for December, $800. The company from which NetSolutions is renting its store space now requires the payment of rent on the first of each month, rather than at the end of the month.

Analysis You may pay monthly rent on an apartment on the first of each month. Your rent transaction is similar to NetSolutions. The advance payment of rent is an asset, much like the advance payment of the insurance premium in the preceding transaction. Unlike the insurance premium, this prepaid rent will expire in one month. When an asset that is purchased will be used up in a short period of time, such as a month, it is normal to debit an expense account initially. This avoids having to transfer the balance from an asset account (Prepaid Rent) to an expense account (Rent Expense) at the end of the month. Thus, when the rent for December is prepaid at the beginning of the month, Rent Expense is debited for $800, and Cash is credited for $800.

10	1	Rent Expense	52	8 0 0 00	10
11		Cash	11		8 0 0 00	11
12		Paid rent for December.			12

December 1 Transaction

NetSolutions received an offer from a local retailer to rent the land purchased on November 5. The retailer plans to use the land as a parking lot for its employees and customers. NetSolutions agreed to rent the land to the retailer for three months, with the rent payable in advance. NetSolutions received $360 for three months' rent beginning December 1.

Analysis By agreeing to rent the land and accepting the $360, NetSolutions has incurred an obligation (liability) to the retailer. This obligation is to make the land available for use for three months and not to interfere with its use. The liability created by receiving the cash in advance of providing the service is called **unearned revenue**. Thus, the $360 received is an increase in an asset and is debited to Cash. The liability account Unearned Rent increases and is credited for $360. As time passes, the unearned rent liability will decrease and will become revenue.

14	1	Cash	11	3 6 0 00	14
15		Unearned Rent	23		3 6 0 00	15
16		Received advance payment for			16
17		three months' rent on land.			17

Magazines that receive subscriptions in advance must record the receipts as unearned revenues. Likewise, airlines that receive ticket payments in advance must record the receipts as unearned revenues until the passengers use the tickets.

December 4 Transaction

NetSolutions purchased office equipment on account from Executive Supply Co. for $1,800.

Analysis   The asset account Office Equipment increases and is therefore debited for $1,800. The liability account Accounts Payable increases and is credited for $1,800.

18					18
19	4	Office Equipment	18	1 8 0 0 00	19
20		Accounts Payable	21	1 8 0 0 00	20
21		Purchased office equipment			21
22		on account.			22

December 6 Transaction

NetSolutions paid $180 for a newspaper advertisement.

Analysis   An expense increases and is debited for $180. The asset Cash decreases and is credited for $180. Expense items that are expected to be minor in amount are normally included as part of the miscellaneous expense. Thus, Miscellaneous Expense is debited for $180.

23					23
24	6	Miscellaneous Expense	59	1 8 0 00	24
25		Cash	11	1 8 0 00	25
26		Paid for newspaper ad.			26

December 11 Transaction

NetSolutions paid creditors $400.

Analysis   This payment decreases the liability account Accounts Payable, which is debited for $400. Cash also decreases and is credited for $400.

27					27
28	11	Accounts Payable	21	4 0 0 00	28
29		Cash	11	4 0 0 00	29
30		Paid creditors on account.			30

December 13 Transaction

NetSolutions paid a receptionist and a part-time assistant $950 for two weeks' wages.

Analysis   This transaction is similar to the December 6 transaction, where an expense account is increased and Cash is decreased. Thus, Wages Expense is debited for $950, and Cash is credited for $950.

In computerized accounting systems, some transactions may be automatically authorized and recorded when certain events occur. For example, the wages of employees may be paid automatically at the end of each pay period.

						JOURNAL					Page 3
	Date		Description	Post. Ref.	Debit			Credit			
1	2007 Dec.	13	Wages Expense	51	9 5 0 00						1
2			Cash	11				9 5 0 00			2
3			Paid two weeks' wages.								3

December 16 Transaction

NetSolutions received $3,100 from fees earned for the first half of December.

Analysis   Cash increases and is debited for $3,100. The revenue account Fees Earned increases and is credited for $3,100.

4					4
5	16	Cash	11	3 1 0 0 00	5
6		Fees Earned	41	3 1 0 0 00	6
7		Received fees from customers.			7

December 16
Transaction

Fees earned on account totaled $1,750 for the first half of December.

Analysis   Assume that you have agreed to take care of a neighbor's dog for a week for $100. At the end of the week, you agree to wait until the first of the next month to receive the $100. Like NetSolutions, you have provided services on account and thus have a right to receive the payment from your neighbor. When a business agrees that payment for services provided or goods sold can be accepted at a later date, the firm has an **account receivable**, which is a claim against the customer. The account receivable is an asset, and the revenue is earned even though no cash has been received. Thus, Accounts Receivable increases and is debited for $1,750. The revenue account Fees Earned increases and is credited for $1,750.

8					8
9	16	Accounts Receivable	12	1 7 5 0 00	9
10		Fees Earned	41	1 7 5 0 00	10
11		Recorded fees earned on account.			11

December 20
Transaction

NetSolutions paid $900 to Executive Supply Co. on the $1,800 debt owed from the December 4 transaction.

Analysis   This is similar to the transaction of December 11.

12					12
13	20	Accounts Payable	21	9 0 0 00	13
14		Cash	11	9 0 0 00	14
15		Paid part of amount owed to			15
16		Executive Supply Co.			16

December 21
Transaction

NetSolutions received $650 from customers in payment of their accounts.

Analysis   When customers pay amounts owed for services they have previously received, one asset increases and another asset decreases. Thus, Cash is debited for $650, and Accounts Receivable is credited for $650.

17					17
18	21	Cash	11	6 5 0 00	18
19		Accounts Receivable	12	6 5 0 00	19
20		Received cash from customers			20
21		on account.			21

December 23
Transaction

NetSolutions paid $1,450 for supplies.

Analysis   The asset account Supplies increases and is debited for $1,450. The asset account Cash decreases and is credited for $1,450.

22					22
23	23	Supplies	14	1 4 5 0 00	23
24		Cash	11	1 4 5 0 00	24
25		Purchased supplies.			25

December 27
Transaction

NetSolutions paid the receptionist and the part-time assistant $1,200 for two weeks' wages.

Analysis   This is similar to the transaction of December 13.

					Post.						
26											26
27		27	Wages Expense		51	1 2 0 0 00					27
28			Cash		11			1 2 0 0 00			28
29			Paid two weeks' wages.								29

December 31
Transaction

NetSolutions paid its $310 telephone bill for the month.

Analysis   You pay a telephone bill each month. Businesses, such as NetSolutions, also must pay monthly utility bills. Such transactions are similar to the transaction of December 6. The expense account Utilities Expense is debited for $310, and Cash is credited for $310.

30											30
31		31	Utilities Expense		54	3 1 0 00					31
32			Cash		11			3 1 0 00			32
33			Paid telephone bill.								33

December 31
Transaction

NetSolutions paid its $225 electric bill for the month.

Analysis   This is similar to the preceding transaction.

JOURNAL   Page 4

	Date		Description	Post. Ref.	Debit	Credit	
1	2007 Dec.	31	Utilities Expense	54	2 2 5 00		1
2			Cash	11		2 2 5 00	2
3			Paid electric bill.				3

December 31
Transaction

NetSolutions received $2,870 from fees earned for the second half of December.

Analysis   This is similar to the transaction of December 16.

4							4
5		31	Cash	11	2 8 7 0 00		5
6			Fees Earned	41		2 8 7 0 00	6
7			Received fees from customers.				7

December 31
Transaction

Fees earned on account totaled $1,120 for the second half of December.

Analysis   This is similar to the transaction of December 16.

8							8
9		31	Accounts Receivable	12	1 1 2 0 00		9
10			Fees Earned	41		1 1 2 0 00	10
11			Recorded fees earned on account.				11

December 31
Transaction

Chris Clark withdrew $2,000 for personal use.

Analysis   This transaction resulted in an increase in the amount of withdrawals and is recorded by a $2,000 debit to Chris Clark, Drawing. The decrease in business cash is recorded by a $2,000 credit to Cash.

12							12
13		31	Chris Clark, Drawing	32	2 0 0 0 00		13
14			Cash	11		2 0 0 0 00	14
15			Chris Clark withdrew cash for				15
16			personal use.				16

Example Exercise 2-5

objective 2

On March 1, the cash account balance was $22,350. During March, cash receipts totaled $241,880 and the March 31 balance was $19,125. Determine the cash payments made during March.

Follow My Example 2-5

Using the following T account, solve for the amount of cash payments (indicated by ? below).

Cash			
Mar. 1 Bal.	22,350	?	Cash payments
Cash receipts	241,880		
Mar. 31 Bal.	19,125		

$19,125 = $22,350 + $241,880 − Cash payments
Cash payments = $22,350 + $241,880 − $19,125 = $245,105

For Practice: PE 2-5A, PE 2-5B

The journal for NetSolutions since it was organized on November 1 is shown in Exhibit 6. Exhibit 6 also shows the ledger after the transactions for both November and December have been posted.

EXHIBIT 6

Journal and Ledger— NetSolutions

JOURNAL
Page 1

	Date		Description	Post. Ref.	Debit	Credit	
1	2007 Nov.	1	Cash	11	25 0 0 0 00		1
2			Chris Clark, Capital	31		25 0 0 0 00	2
3			Invested cash in NetSolutions.				3
4							4
5		5	Land	17	20 0 0 0 00		5
6			Cash	11		20 0 0 0 00	6
7			Purchased land for building site.				7
8							8
9		10	Supplies	14	1 3 5 0 00		9
10			Accounts Payable	21		1 3 5 0 00	10
11			Purchased supplies on account.				11
12							12
13		18	Cash	11	7 5 0 0 00		13
14			Fees Earned	41		7 5 0 0 00	14
15			Received fees from customers.				15
16							16
17		30	Wages Expense	51	2 1 2 5 00		17
18			Rent Expense	52	8 0 0 00		18
19			Utilities Expense	54	4 5 0 00		19
20			Miscellaneous Expense	59	2 7 5 00		20
21			Cash	11		3 6 5 0 00	21
22			Paid expenses.				22
23							23
24		30	Accounts Payable	21	9 5 0 00		24
25			Cash	11		9 5 0 00	25
26			Paid creditors on account.				26
27							27
28		30	Supplies Expense	55	8 0 0 00		28
29			Supplies	14		8 0 0 00	29
30			Supplies used during November.				30

(continued)

EXHIBIT 6

	Date		Description	Post. Ref.	Debit	Credit	
	JOURNAL					Page 2	
1	2007 Nov.	30	Chris Clark, Drawing	32	2 0 0 0 00		1
2			Cash	11		2 0 0 0 00	2
3			Chris Clark withdrew cash for				3
4			personal use.				4
5							5
6	Dec.	1	Prepaid Insurance	15	2 4 0 0 00		6
7			Cash	11		2 4 0 0 00	7
8			Paid premium on one-year policy.				8
9							9
10		1	Rent Expense	52	8 0 0 00		10
11			Cash	11		8 0 0 00	11
12			Paid rent for December.				12
13							13
14		1	Cash	11	3 6 0 00		14
15			Unearned Rent	23		3 6 0 00	15
16			Received advance payment for				16
17			three months' rent on land.				17
18							18
19		4	Office Equipment	18	1 8 0 0 00		19
20			Accounts Payable	21		1 8 0 0 00	20
21			Purchased office equipment				21
22			on account.				22
23							23
24		6	Miscellaneous Expense	59	1 8 0 00		24
25			Cash	11		1 8 0 00	25
26			Paid for newspaper ad.				26
27							27
28		11	Accounts Payable	21	4 0 0 00		28
29			Cash	11		4 0 0 00	29
30			Paid creditors on account.				30

(continued)

EXHIBIT 6

	Date		Description	Post. Ref.	Debit	Credit	
1	2007 Dec.	13	Wages Expense	51	9 5 0 00		1
2			Cash	11		9 5 0 00	2
3			Paid two weeks' wages.				3
4							4
5		16	Cash	11	3 1 0 0 00		5
6			Fees Earned	41		3 1 0 0 00	6
7			Received fees from customers.				7
8							8
9		16	Accounts Receivable	12	1 7 5 0 00		9
10			Fees Earned	41		1 7 5 0 00	10
11			Recorded fees earned on account.				11
12							12
13		20	Accounts Payable	21	9 0 0 00		13
14			Cash	11		9 0 0 00	14
15			Paid part of amount owed to				15
16			Executive Supply Co.				16
17							17
18		21	Cash	11	6 5 0 00		18
19			Accounts Receivable	12		6 5 0 00	19
20			Received cash from customers				20
21			on account.				21
22							22
23		23	Supplies	14	1 4 5 0 00		23
24			Cash	11		1 4 5 0 00	24
25			Purchased supplies.				25
26							26
27		27	Wages Expense	51	1 2 0 0 00		27
28			Cash	11		1 2 0 0 00	28
29			Paid two weeks' wages.				29
30							30
31		31	Utilities Expense	54	3 1 0 00		31
32			Cash	11		3 1 0 00	32
33			Paid telephone bill.				33

JOURNAL Page 3

(continued)

EXHIBIT 6

	JOURNAL					Page 4
	Date	Description	Post. Ref.	Debit	Credit	
1	2007 Dec. 31	Utilities Expense	54	2 2 5 00		1
2		Cash	11		2 2 5 00	2
3		Paid electric bill.				3
4						4
5	31	Cash	11	2 8 7 0 00		5
6		Fees Earned	41		2 8 7 0 00	6
7		Received fees from customers.				7
8						8
9	31	Accounts Receivable	12	1 1 2 0 00		9
10		Fees Earned	41		1 1 2 0 00	10
11		Recorded fees earned on account.				11
12						12
13	31	Chris Clark, Drawing	32	2 0 0 0 00		13
14		Cash	11		2 0 0 0 00	14
15		Chris Clark withdrew cash for				15
16		personal use.				16

LEDGER

ACCOUNT *Cash*   ACCOUNT NO. *11*

Date	Item	Post. Ref.	Debit	Credit	Balance Debit	Balance Credit
2007 Nov. 1		1	25 0 0 0 00		25 0 0 0 00	
5		1		20 0 0 0 00	5 0 0 0 00	
18		1	7 5 0 0 00		12 5 0 0 00	
30		1		3 6 5 0 00	8 8 5 0 00	
30		1		9 5 0 00	7 9 0 0 00	
30		2		2 0 0 0 00	5 9 0 0 00	
Dec. 1		2		2 4 0 0 00	3 5 0 0 00	
1		2		8 0 0 00	2 7 0 0 00	
1		2	3 6 0 00		3 0 6 0 00	
6		2		1 8 0 00	2 8 8 0 00	
11		2		4 0 0 00	2 4 8 0 00	
13		3		9 5 0 00	1 5 3 0 00	
16		3	3 1 0 0 00		4 6 3 0 00	
20		3		9 0 0 00	3 7 3 0 00	
21		3	6 5 0 00		4 3 8 0 00	
23		3		1 4 5 0 00	2 9 3 0 00	
27		3		1 2 0 0 00	1 7 3 0 00	
31		3		3 1 0 00	1 4 2 0 00	
31		4		2 2 5 00	1 1 9 5 00	
31		4	2 8 7 0 00		4 0 6 5 00	
31		4		2 0 0 0 00	2 0 6 5 00	

(continued)

EXHIBIT 6

ACCOUNT *Accounts Receivable*   **ACCOUNT NO.** *12*

Date		Item	Post. Ref.	Debit	Credit	Balance	
						Debit	Credit
2007 Dec.	16		3	1 7 5 0 00		1 7 5 0 00	
	21		3		6 5 0 00	1 1 0 0 00	
	31		4	1 1 2 0 00		2 2 2 0 00	

ACCOUNT *Supplies*   **ACCOUNT NO.** *14*

Date		Item	Post. Ref.	Debit	Credit	Balance	
						Debit	Credit
2007 Nov.	10		1	1 3 5 0 00		1 3 5 0 00	
	30		1		8 0 0 00	5 5 0 00	
Dec.	23		3	1 4 5 0 00		2 0 0 0 00	

ACCOUNT *Prepaid Insurance*   **ACCOUNT NO.** *15*

Date		Item	Post. Ref.	Debit	Credit	Balance	
						Debit	Credit
2007 Dec.	1		2	2 4 0 0 00		2 4 0 0 00	

ACCOUNT *Land*   **ACCOUNT NO.** *17*

Date		Item	Post. Ref.	Debit	Credit	Balance	
						Debit	Credit
2007 Nov.	5		1	20 0 0 0 00		20 0 0 0 00	

ACCOUNT *Office Equipment*   **ACCOUNT NO.** *18*

Date		Item	Post. Ref.	Debit	Credit	Balance	
						Debit	Credit
2007 Dec.	4		2	1 8 0 0 00		1 8 0 0 00	

(continued)

EXHIBIT 6

ACCOUNT *Accounts Payable*   **ACCOUNT NO.** *21*

Date		Item	Post. Ref.	Debit	Credit	Balance Debit	Balance Credit
2007 Nov.	10		1		1 3 5 0 00		1 3 5 0 00
	30		1	9 5 0 00			4 0 0 00
Dec.	4		2		1 8 0 0 00		2 2 0 0 00
	11		2	4 0 0 00			1 8 0 0 00
	20		3	9 0 0 00			9 0 0 00

ACCOUNT *Unearned Rent*   **ACCOUNT NO.** *23*

Date		Item	Post. Ref.	Debit	Credit	Balance Debit	Balance Credit
2007 Dec.	1		2		3 6 0 00		3 6 0 00

ACCOUNT *Chris Clark, Capital*   **ACCOUNT NO.** *31*

Date		Item	Post. Ref.	Debit	Credit	Balance Debit	Balance Credit
2007 Nov.	1		1		25 0 0 0 00		25 0 0 0 00

ACCOUNT *Chris Clark, Drawing*   **ACCOUNT NO.** *32*

Date		Item	Post. Ref.	Debit	Credit	Balance Debit	Balance Credit
2007 Nov.	30		2	2 0 0 0 00		2 0 0 0 00	
Dec.	31		4	2 0 0 0 00		4 0 0 0 00	

ACCOUNT *Fees Earned*   **ACCOUNT NO.** *41*

Date		Item	Post. Ref.	Debit	Credit	Balance Debit	Balance Credit
2007 Nov.	18		1		7 5 0 0 00		7 5 0 0 00
Dec.	16		3		3 1 0 0 00		10 6 0 0 00
	16		3		1 7 5 0 00		12 3 5 0 00
	31		4		2 8 7 0 00		15 2 2 0 00
	31		4		1 1 2 0 00		16 3 4 0 00

(continued)

EXHIBIT 6

ACCOUNT *Wages Expense*   **ACCOUNT NO. 51**

Date		Item	Post. Ref.	Debit	Credit	Balance Debit	Balance Credit
2007 Nov.	30		1	2 1 2 5 00		2 1 2 5 00	
Dec.	13		3	9 5 0 00		3 0 7 5 00	
	27		3	1 2 0 0 00		4 2 7 5 00	

ACCOUNT *Rent Expense*   **ACCOUNT NO. 52**

Date		Item	Post. Ref.	Debit	Credit	Balance Debit	Balance Credit
2007 Nov.	30		1	8 0 0 00		8 0 0 00	
Dec.	1		2	8 0 0 00		1 6 0 0 00	

ACCOUNT *Utilities Expense*   **ACCOUNT NO. 54**

Date		Item	Post. Ref.	Debit	Credit	Balance Debit	Balance Credit
2007 Nov.	30		1	4 5 0 00		4 5 0 00	
Dec.	31		3	3 1 0 00		7 6 0 00	
	31		4	2 2 5 00		9 8 5 00	

ACCOUNT *Supplies Expense*   **ACCOUNT NO. 55**

Date		Item	Post. Ref.	Debit	Credit	Balance Debit	Balance Credit
2007 Nov.	30		1	8 0 0 00		8 0 0 00	

ACCOUNT *Miscellaneous Expense*   **ACCOUNT NO. 59**

Date		Item	Post. Ref.	Debit	Credit	Balance Debit	Balance Credit
2007 Nov.	30		1	2 7 5 00		2 7 5 00	
Dec.	6		2	1 8 0 00		4 5 5 00	

(concluded)

Trial Balance

objective   **3**

Prepare an unadjusted trial balance and explain how it can be used to discover errors.

@netsolutions

How can you be sure that you have not made an error in posting the debits and credits to the ledger? One way is to determine the equality of the debits and credits in the ledger. This equality should be proved at the end of each accounting period, if not more often. Such a proof, called a **trial balance**, may be in the form of a computer printout or in the form shown in Exhibit 7.

The trial balance shown in Exhibit 7 is prepared by first listing the name of the company (NetSolutions), its title (Unadjusted Trial Balance), and the date it is prepared (December 31, 2007). The trial balance shown in Exhibit 7 is titled an unadjusted trial balance. This is to distinguish it from other trial balances that we will be preparing in later chapters. These other trial balances include an adjusted trial balance and a post-closing trial balance.[4]

The account balances in Exhibit 7 are taken from the ledger shown in Exhibit 6. Thus, before the trial balance can be prepared, each account balance in the ledger must be determined. When the standard account form is used, the balance of each account appears in the balance column on the same line as the last posting to the account.

EXHIBIT 7	NetSolutions Unadjusted Trial Balance December 31, 2007		
Trial Balance		Debit Balances	Credit Balances
	Cash	2 0 6 5 00	
	Accounts Receivable	2 2 2 0 00	
	Supplies	2 0 0 0 00	
	Prepaid Insurance	2 4 0 0 00	
	Land	20 0 0 0 00	
	Office Equipment	1 8 0 0 00	
	Accounts Payable		9 0 0 00
	Unearned Rent		3 6 0 00
	Chris Clark, Capital		25 0 0 0 00
	Chris Clark, Drawing	4 0 0 0 00	
	Fees Earned		16 3 4 0 00
	Wages Expense	4 2 7 5 00	
	Rent Expense	1 6 0 0 00	
	Utilities Expense	9 8 5 00	
	Supplies Expense	8 0 0 00	
	Miscellaneous Expense	4 5 5 00	
		42 6 0 0 00	42 6 0 0 00

The trial balance does not provide complete proof of the accuracy of the ledger. It indicates only that the debits and the credits are equal. This proof is of value, however, because errors often affect the equality of debits and credits. If the two totals of a trial balance are not equal, an error has occurred. In the next section of this chapter, we will discuss procedures for discovering and correcting errors.

---

4 The adjusted trial balance is discussed in Chapter 3, and the post-closing trial balance is discussed in Chapter 4.

Example Exercise 2-6

objective **3**

For each of the following errors, considered individually, indicate whether the error would cause the trial balance totals to be unequal. If the error would cause the trial balance total to be unequal, indicate whether the debit or credit total is higher and by how much.

a. Payment of a cash withdrawal of $5,600 was journalized and posted as a debit of $6,500 to Salary Expense and a credit of $6,500 to Cash.

b. A fee of $2,850 earned from a client was debited to Accounts Receivable for $2,580 and credited to Fees Earned for $2,850.

c. A payment of $3,500 to a creditor was posted as a debit of $3,500 to Accounts Payable and a debit of $3,500 to Cash.

Follow My Example 2-6

a. The totals are equal since both the debit and credit entries were journalized and posted for $6,500.

b. The totals are unequal. The credit total is higher by $270 ($2,850 − $2,580).

c. The totals are unequal. The debit total is higher by $7,000 ($3,500 + $3,500).

For Practice: PE 2-6A, PE 2-6B

Discovery and Correction of Errors

objective **4**

Discover and correct errors in recording transactions.

REAL WORLD

Many large corporations such as Microsoft and Quaker Oats round the figures in their financial statements to millions of dollars.

Errors will sometimes occur in journalizing and posting transactions. In some cases, however, an error might not be significant enough to affect the decisions of management or others. In such cases, the **materiality concept** implies that the error may be treated in the easiest possible way. For example, an error of a few dollars in recording an asset as an expense for a business with millions of dollars in assets would be considered immaterial, and a correction would not be necessary. In the remaining paragraphs, we assume that errors discovered are material and should be corrected.

DISCOVERY OF ERRORS

As mentioned previously, preparing the trial balance is one of the primary ways to discover errors in the ledger. However, it indicates only that the debits and credits are equal. If the two totals of the trial balance are not equal, it is probably due to one or more of the errors described in Exhibit 8.

Among the types of errors that will *not* cause the trial balance totals to be unequal are the following:

1. Failure to record a transaction or to post a transaction.
2. Recording the same erroneous amount for both the debit and the credit parts of a transaction.
3. Recording the same transaction more than once.
4. Posting a part of a transaction correctly as a debit or credit but to the wrong account.

It is obvious that care should be used in recording transactions in the journal and in posting to the accounts. The need for accuracy in determining account balances and reporting them on the trial balance is also evident.

Errors in the accounts may be discovered in various ways: (1) through audit procedures, (2) by looking at the trial balance, or (3) by chance. If the two trial balance totals are not equal, the amount of the difference between the totals should be determined before searching for the error.

EXHIBIT 8 | Errors Causing Unequal Trial Balance

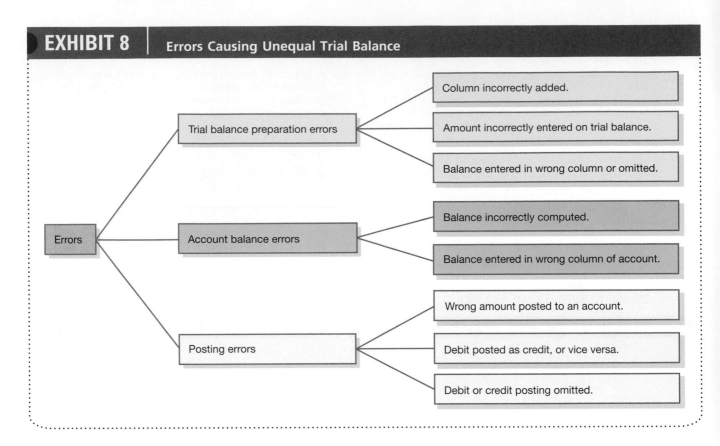

The amount of the difference between the two totals of a trial balance sometimes gives a clue as to the nature of the error or where it occurred. For example, a difference of 10, 100, or 1,000 between two totals is often the result of an error in addition. A difference between totals can also be due to omitting a debit or a credit posting. If the difference can be evenly divided by 2, the error may be due to the posting of a debit as a credit, or vice versa. For example, if the debit total is $20,640 and the credit total is $20,236, the difference of $404 may indicate that a credit posting of $404 was omitted or that a credit of $202 was incorrectly posted as a debit.

Two other common types of errors are known as transpositions and slides. A **transposition** occurs when the order of the digits is changed mistakenly, such as writing $542 as $452 or $524. In a **slide**, the entire number is mistakenly moved one or more spaces to the right or the left, such as writing $542.00 as $54.20 or $5,420.00. If an error of either type has occurred and there are no other errors, the difference between the two trial balance totals can be evenly divided by 9.

If an error is not revealed by the trial balance, the steps in the accounting process must be retraced, beginning with the last step and working back to the entries in the journal. Usually, errors causing the trial balance totals to be unequal will be discovered before all of the steps are retraced.

CORRECTION OF ERRORS

The procedures used to correct an error vary according to the nature of the error, when the error is discovered, and whether a manual or computerized accounting system is used. Oftentimes, an error is discovered as it is being journalized or posted. In such cases, the error is simply corrected. For example, computerized accounting systems automatically verify for each journal entry whether the total debits equal the total credits. If the totals are not equal, an error report is created and the computer program will not proceed until the journal entry is corrected.

Occasionally, however, an error is not discovered until after a journal entry has been recorded and posted to the accounts. Correcting this type of error is more complex. To illustrate, assume that on May 5 a $12,500 purchase of office equipment on account was incorrectly journalized and posted as a debit to Supplies and a credit to Accounts Payable for $12,500. This posting of the incorrect entry is shown in the following T accounts:

	Supplies		Accounts Payable	
Incorrect:	12,500			12,500

Before making a correcting entry, it is best to determine the debit(s) and credit(s) that should have been recorded. These are shown in the following T accounts:

	Office Equipment		Accounts Payable	
Correct:	12,500			12,500

Comparing the two sets of T accounts shows that the incorrect debit to Supplies may be corrected by debiting Office Equipment for $12,500 and crediting Supplies for $12,500. The following correcting entry is then journalized and posted:

Entry to Correct Error:

17							17
18	May	31	Office Equipment	18	12 5 0 0 00		18
19			Supplies	14		12 5 0 0 00	19
20			To correct erroneous debit				20
21			to Supplies on May 5. See invoice				21
22			from Bell Office Equipment Co.				22

Example Exercise 2-7   objective 4

The following errors took place in journalizing and posting transactions:

a. A withdrawal of $6,000 by Cheri Ramey, owner of the business, was recorded as a debit to Office Salaries Expense and a credit to Cash.
b. Utilities Expense of $4,500 paid for the current month was recorded as a debit to Miscellaneous Expense and a credit to Accounts Payable.

Journalize the entries to correct the errors. Omit explanations.

Follow My Example 2-7

a. Cheri Ramey, Drawing 6,000
        Office Salaries Expense   6,000

b. Accounts Payable 4,500
        Miscellaneous Expense   4,500

    Utilities Expense 4,500
        Cash   4,500

Note: The first entry in (b) reverses the incorrect entry, and the second entry records the correct entry. These two entries could also be combined into one entry; however, preparing two entries will make it easier for someone later to understand what had happened and why the entries were necessary.

For Practice: PE 2-7A, PE 2-7B

At a Glance

1. Describe the characteristics of an account and record transactions using a chart of accounts and journal.

Key Points	Key Learning Outcomes	Example Exercises	Practice Exercises
The record used for recording individual transactions is an account. A group of accounts is called a ledger. The system of accounts that make up a ledger is called a chart of accounts. Transactions are initially entered in a record called a journal.	• Prepare a chart of accounts for a proprietorship.		
	• Prepare journal entries.	2-1 2-2 2-3	2-1A, 2-1B 2-2A, 2-2B 2-3A, 2-3B
The simplest form of an account, a T account, has three parts: (1) a title; (2) a left side, called the debit side; and (3) a right side, called the credit side. Amounts entered on the left side of an account are called debits to the account. Amounts entered on the right side of an account are called credits. Periodically, the balance of the account is determined.	• Record entries in T accounts.		
The rules of debit and credit for recording increases or decreases in asset, liability, owner's equity, revenue, expense, and drawing accounts are shown in Exhibit 3. Each transaction is recorded so that the sum of the debits is always equal to the sum of the credits. The normal balance of an account is the side of the account (debit or credit) in which increases are recorded.	• List the rules of debit and credit.	2-4	2-4A, 2-4B
	• Determine the normal balance for accounts.	2-4	2-4A, 2-4B

2. Describe and illustrate the posting of journal entries to accounts.

Key Points	Key Learning Outcomes	Example Exercises	Practice Exercises
The debits and credits for each journal entry are periodically posted to the accounts in the order in which they occur in the journal using the steps illustrated in Exhibit 5.	• Post journal entries to a standard account.		
	• Post journal entries to a T account.	2-5	2-5A, 2-5B

3. Prepare an unadjusted trial balance and explain how it can be used to discover errors.

Key Points	Key Learning Outcomes	Example Exercises	Practice Exercises
A trial balance is prepared by listing the accounts from the ledger and their balances. If the two totals of the trial balance are not equal, an error has occurred.	• Prepare an unadjusted trial balance.	2-6	2-6A, 2-6B

4. Discover and correct errors in recording transactions.

Key Points	Key Learning Outcomes	Example Exercises	Practice Exercises
Errors may be discovered (1) by audit procedures, (2) by looking at the trial balance, or (3) by chance.	• Discover errors in journalizing, posting, or preparing the trial balance. • Prepare correcting entries for errors that have been journalized and posted.	2-7	2-7A, 2-7B

Key Terms

account (49)
account receivable (63)
assets (51)
balance of the account (50)
chart of accounts (51)
credits (50)
debits (50)
double-entry accounting system (58)

drawing (51)
expenses (51)
journal (52)
journal entry (52)
journalizing (52)
ledger (51)
liabilities (51)
materiality concept (73)
owner's equity (51)

posting (59)
revenues (51)
slide (74)
T account (49)
transposition (74)
trial balance (72)
two-column journal (59)
unearned revenue (61)

Illustrative Problem

J. F. Outz, M.D., has been practicing as a cardiologist for three years. During April, 2007, Outz completed the following transactions in her practice of cardiology.

Apr. 1. Paid office rent for April, $800.
3. Purchased equipment on account, $2,100.
5. Received cash on account from patients, $3,150.
8. Purchased X-ray film and other supplies on account, $245.
9. One of the items of equipment purchased on April 3 was defective. It was returned with the permission of the supplier, who agreed to reduce the account for the amount charged for the item, $325.
12. Paid cash to creditors on account, $1,250.
17. Paid cash for renewal of a six-month property insurance policy, $370.
20. Discovered that the balances of the cash account and the accounts payable account as of April 1 were overstated by $200. A payment of that amount to a creditor in March had not been recorded. Journalize the $200 payment as of April 20.
24. Paid cash for laboratory analysis, $545.
27. Paid cash from business bank account for personal and family expenses, $1,250.
30. Recorded the cash received in payment of services (on a cash basis) to patients during April, $1,720.
30. Paid salaries of receptionist and nurses, $1,725.
30. Paid various utility expenses, $360.
30. Recorded fees charged to patients on account for services performed in April, $5,145.
30. Paid miscellaneous expenses, $132.

Outz's account titles, numbers, and balances as of April 1 (all normal balances) are listed as follows: Cash, 11, $4,123; Accounts Receivable, 12, $6,725; Supplies, 13, $290; Prepaid Insurance, 14, $465; Equipment, 18, $19,745; Accounts Payable, 22, $765; J. F. Outz, Capital, 31, $30,583; J. F. Outz, Drawing, 32; Professional Fees, 41; Salary Expense, 51; Rent Expense, 53; Laboratory Expense, 55; Utilities Expense, 56; Miscellaneous Expense, 59.

Instructions

1. Open a ledger of standard four-column accounts for Dr. Outz as of April 1. Enter the balances in the appropriate balance columns and place a check mark (✓) in the posting reference column. (*Hint:* Verify the equality of the debit and credit balances in the ledger before proceeding with the next instruction.)
2. Journalize each transaction in a two-column journal.
3. Post the journal to the ledger, extending the month-end balances to the appropriate balance columns after each posting.
4. Prepare an unadjusted trial balance as of April 30.

Solution

2. and **3.**

JOURNAL Page 27

Date		Description	Post. Ref.	Debit	Credit
2007 Apr.	1	Rent Expense	53	800 00	
		Cash	11		800 00
		Paid office rent for April.			
	3	Equipment	18	2100 00	
		Accounts Payable	22		2100 00
		Purchased equipment on account.			
	5	Cash	11	3150 00	
		Accounts Receivable	12		3150 00
		Received cash on account.			
	8	Supplies	13	245 00	
		Accounts Payable	22		245 00
		Purchased supplies.			
	9	Accounts Payable	22	325 00	
		Equipment	18		325 00
		Returned defective equipment.			
	12	Accounts Payable	22	1250 00	
		Cash	11		1250 00
		Paid creditors on account.			
	17	Prepaid Insurance	14	370 00	
		Cash	11		370 00
		Renewed six-month property policy.			
	20	Accounts Payable	22	200 00	
		Cash	11		200 00
		Recorded March payment			
		to creditor.			

JOURNAL — Page 28

	Date	Description	Post. Ref.	Debit	Credit	
1	2007 Apr. 24	Laboratory Expense	55	5 4 5 00		1
2		Cash	11		5 4 5 00	2
3		Paid for laboratory analysis.				3
4						4
5	27	J. F. Outz, Drawing	32	1 2 5 0 00		5
6		Cash	11		1 2 5 0 00	6
7		J. F. Outz withdrew cash for				7
8		personal use.				8
9						9
10	30	Cash	11	1 7 2 0 00		10
11		Professional Fees	41		1 7 2 0 00	11
12		Received fees from patients.				12
13						13
14	30	Salary Expense	51	1 7 2 5 00		14
15		Cash	11		1 7 2 5 00	15
16		Paid salaries.				16
17						17
18	30	Utilities Expense	56	3 6 0 00		18
19		Cash	11		3 6 0 00	19
20		Paid utilities.				20
21						21
22	30	Accounts Receivable	12	5 1 4 5 00		22
23		Professional Fees	41		5 1 4 5 00	23
24		Recorded fees earned on account.				24
25						25
26	30	Miscellaneous Expense	59	1 3 2 00		26
27		Cash	11		1 3 2 00	27
28		Paid expenses.				28

1. and 3.

ACCOUNT Cash — ACCOUNT NO. 11

Date	Item	Post. Ref.	Debit	Credit	Balance Debit	Balance Credit
2007 Apr. 1	Balance	✓			4 1 2 3 00	
1		27		8 0 0 00	3 3 2 3 00	
5		27	3 1 5 0 00		6 4 7 3 00	
12		27		1 2 5 0 00	5 2 2 3 00	
17		27		3 7 0 00	4 8 5 3 00	
20		27		2 0 0 00	4 6 5 3 00	
24		28		5 4 5 00	4 1 0 8 00	
27		28		1 2 5 0 00	2 8 5 8 00	
30		28	1 7 2 0 00		4 5 7 8 00	
30		28		1 7 2 5 00	2 8 5 3 00	
30		28		3 6 0 00	2 4 9 3 00	
30		28		1 3 2 00	2 3 6 1 00	

ACCOUNT *Accounts Receivable*   **ACCOUNT NO.** *12*

Date		Item	Post. Ref.	Debit	Credit	Balance Debit	Balance Credit
2007 Apr.	1	Balance	✓			6 7 2 5 00	
	5		27		3 1 5 0 00	3 5 7 5 00	
	30		28	5 1 4 5 00		8 7 2 0 00	

ACCOUNT *Supplies*   **ACCOUNT NO.** *13*

Date		Item	Post. Ref.	Debit	Credit	Balance Debit	Balance Credit
2007 Apr.	1	Balance	✓			2 9 0 00	
	8		27	2 4 5 00		5 3 5 00	

ACCOUNT *Prepaid Insurance*   **ACCOUNT NO.** *14*

Date		Item	Post. Ref.	Debit	Credit	Balance Debit	Balance Credit
2007 Apr.	1	Balance	✓			4 6 5 00	
	17		27	3 7 0 00		8 3 5 00	

ACCOUNT *Equipment*   **ACCOUNT NO.** *18*

Date		Item	Post. Ref.	Debit	Credit	Balance Debit	Balance Credit
2007 Apr.	1	Balance	✓			19 7 4 5 00	
	3		27	2 1 0 0 00		21 8 4 5 00	
	9		27		3 2 5 00	21 5 2 0 00	

ACCOUNT *Accounts Payable*   **ACCOUNT NO.** *22*

Date		Item	Post. Ref.	Debit	Credit	Balance Debit	Balance Credit
2007 Apr.	1	Balance	✓				7 6 5 00
	3		27		2 1 0 0 00		2 8 6 5 00
	8		27		2 4 5 00		3 1 1 0 00
	9		27	3 2 5 00			2 7 8 5 00
	12		27	1 2 5 0 00			1 5 3 5 00
	20		27	2 0 0 00			1 3 3 5 00

ACCOUNT *J. F. Outz, Capital*   **ACCOUNT NO.** *31*

Date		Item	Post. Ref.	Debit	Credit	Balance Debit	Balance Credit
2007 Apr.	1	Balance	✓				30 5 8 3 00

ACCOUNT *J. F. Outz, Drawing*   **ACCOUNT NO.** *32*

Date	Item	Post. Ref.	Debit	Credit	Balance Debit	Balance Credit
2007 Apr. 27		28	1 2 5 0 00		1 2 5 0 00	

ACCOUNT *Professional Fees*   **ACCOUNT NO.** *41*

Date	Item	Post. Ref.	Debit	Credit	Balance Debit	Balance Credit
2007 Apr. 30		28		1 7 2 0 00		1 7 2 0 00
30		28		5 1 4 5 00		6 8 6 5 00

ACCOUNT *Salary Expense*   **ACCOUNT NO.** *51*

Date	Item	Post. Ref.	Debit	Credit	Balance Debit	Balance Credit
2007 Apr. 30		28	1 7 2 5 00		1 7 2 5 00	

ACCOUNT *Rent Expense*   **ACCOUNT NO.** *53*

Date	Item	Post. Ref.	Debit	Credit	Balance Debit	Balance Credit
2007 Apr. 1		27	8 0 0 00		8 0 0 00	

ACCOUNT *Laboratory Expense*   **ACCOUNT NO.** *55*

Date	Item	Post. Ref.	Debit	Credit	Balance Debit	Balance Credit
2007 Apr. 24		28	5 4 5 00		5 4 5 00	

ACCOUNT *Utilities Expense*   **ACCOUNT NO.** *56*

Date	Item	Post. Ref.	Debit	Credit	Balance Debit	Balance Credit
2007 Apr. 30		28	3 6 0 00		3 6 0 00	

ACCOUNT *Miscellaneous Expense*   **ACCOUNT NO.** *59*

Date	Item	Post. Ref.	Debit	Credit	Balance Debit	Balance Credit
2007 Apr. 30		28	1 3 2 00		1 3 2 00	

4.

J. F. Outz, M.D.
Unadjusted Trial Balance
April 30, 2007

	Debit Balances	Credit Balances
Cash	2 3 6 1 00	
Accounts Receivable	8 7 2 0 00	
Supplies	5 3 5 00	
Prepaid Insurance	8 3 5 00	
Equipment	21 5 2 0 00	
Accounts Payable		1 3 3 5 00
J. F. Outz, Capital		30 5 8 3 00
J. F. Outz, Drawing	1 2 5 0 00	
Professional Fees		6 8 6 5 00
Salary Expense	1 7 2 5 00	
Rent Expense	8 0 0 00	
Laboratory Expense	5 4 5 00	
Utilities Expense	3 6 0 00	
Miscellaneous Expense	1 3 2 00	
	38 7 8 3 00	38 7 8 3 00

Self-Examination Questions

(Answers at End of Chapter)

1. A debit may signify a(n):
   A. increase in an asset account.
   B. decrease in an asset account.
   C. increase in a liability account.
   D. increase in the owner's capital account.

2. The type of account with a normal credit balance is:
   A. an asset. C. a revenue.
   B. drawing. D. an expense.

3. A debit balance in which of the following accounts would indicate a likely error?
   A. Accounts Receivable
   B. Cash
   C. Fees Earned
   D. Miscellaneous Expense

4. The receipt of cash from customers in payment of their accounts would be recorded by:
   A. a debit to Cash and a credit to Accounts Receivable.
   B. a debit to Accounts Receivable and a credit to Cash.
   C. a debit to Cash and a credit to Accounts Payable.
   D. a debit to Accounts Payable and a credit to Cash.

5. The form listing the titles and balances of the accounts in the ledger on a given date is the:
   A. income statement.
   B. balance sheet.
   C. statement of owner's equity.
   D. trial balance.

Eye Openers

1. What is the difference between an account and a ledger?
2. Do the terms *debit* and *credit* signify increase or decrease or can they signify either? Explain.
3. Explain why the rules of debit and credit are the same for liability accounts and owner's equity accounts.

4. What is the effect (increase or decrease) of a debit to an expense account (a) in terms of owner's equity and (b) in terms of expense?
5. What is the effect (increase or decrease) of a credit to a revenue account (a) in terms of owner's equity and (b) in terms of revenue?
6. Rabun Company adheres to a policy of depositing all cash receipts in a bank account and making all payments by check. The cash account as of January 31 has a credit balance of $2,500, and there is no undeposited cash on hand. (a) Assuming no errors occurred during journalizing or posting, what caused this unusual balance? (b) Is the $2,500 credit balance in the cash account an asset, a liability, owner's equity, a revenue, or an expense?
7. Cortes Company performed services in February for a specific customer, for a fee of $6,000. Payment was received the following March. (a) Was the revenue earned in February or March? (b) What accounts should be debited and credited in (1) February and (2) March?
8. What proof is provided by a trial balance?
9. If the two totals of a trial balance are equal, does it mean that there are no errors in the accounting records? Explain.
10. Assume that a trial balance is prepared with an account balance of $21,360 listed as $21,630 and an account balance of $1,500 listed as $15,000. Identify the transposition and the slide.
11. Assume that when a purchase of supplies of $1,380 for cash was recorded, both the debit and the credit were journalized and posted as $1,830. (a) Would this error cause the trial balance to be out of balance? (b) Would the trial balance be out of balance if the $1,380 entry had been journalized correctly but the credit to Cash had been posted as $1,830?
12. Assume that Hahn Consulting erroneously recorded the payment of $5,000 of owner withdrawals as a debit to Salary Expense. (a) How would this error affect the equality of the trial balance? (b) How would this error affect the income statement, statement of owner's equity, and balance sheet?
13. Assume that Hacienda Realty Co. borrowed $80,000 from Clinton Bank and Trust. In recording the transaction, Hacienda erroneously recorded the receipt as a debit to Cash, $80,000, and a credit to Fees Earned, $80,000. (a) How would this error affect the equality of the trial balance? (b) How would this error affect the income statement, statement of owner's equity, and balance sheet?
14. In journalizing and posting the entry to record the purchase of supplies for cash, the accounts payable account was credited in error. What is the preferred procedure to correct this error?
15. Banks rely heavily upon customers' deposits as a source of funds. Demand deposits normally pay interest to the customer, who is entitled to withdraw at any time without prior notice to the bank. Checking and NOW (negotiable order of withdrawal) accounts are the most common form of demand deposits for banks. Assume that Peachtree Storage has a checking account at Buckhead Savings Bank. What type of account (asset, liability, owner's equity, revenue, expense, drawing) does the account balance of $18,750 represent from the viewpoint of (a) Peachtree Storage and (b) Buckhead Savings Bank?

Practice Exercises

PE 2-1A
Journal entry for purchase of office equipment
obj. 1

Prepare a journal entry for the purchase of office equipment on November 23 for $13,750, paying $5,000 cash and the remainder on account.

PE 2-1B
Journal entry for purchase of office supplies
obj. 1

Prepare a journal entry for the purchase of office supplies on March 13 for $6,500, paying $1,300 cash and the remainder on account.

PE 2-2A
Journal entry for fees earned on account
obj. 1

Prepare a journal entry on February 2 for fees earned on account, $6,300.

PE 2-2B
Journal entry for cash received for services rendered
obj. 1

Prepare a journal entry on January 21 for cash received for services rendered, $1,250.

PE 2-3A
Journal entry for owner's withdrawal
obj. 1

Prepare a journal entry on October 31 for the withdrawal of $4,500 by Amy Sykes for personal use.

PE 2-3B
Journal entry for owner's withdrawal
obj. 1

Prepare a journal entry on July 31 for the withdrawal of $7,250 by Paul Wright for personal use.

PE 2-4A
Rules of debit and credit and normal balances
obj. 1

State for each account whether it is likely to have (a) debit entries only, (b) credit entries only, or (c) both debit and credit entries. Also, indicate its normal balance.

1. Notes Payable	4. Commissions Earned
2. Accounts Receivable	5. Unearned Rent
3. Wages Expense	6. Shinya Mylod, Capital

PE 2-4B
Rules of debit and credit and normal balances
obj. 1

State for each account whether it is likely to have (a) debit entries only, (b) credit entries only, or (c) both debit and credit entries. Also, indicate its normal balance.

1. Prepaid Insurance	4. Miscellaneous Expense
2. Rent Revenue	5. Accounts Payable
3. Li Xu, Drawing	6. Cash

PE 2-5A
Determining cash receipts
obj. 2

On April 1, the cash account balance was $18,750. During April, cash payments totaled $219,140, and the April 30 balance was $22,175. Determine the cash receipts during April.

PE 2-5B
Determining supplies expense
obj. 2

On January 1, the supplies account balance was $1,035. During January, supplies of $2,325 were purchased, and $786 of supplies were on hand as of January 31. Determine supplies expense for January.

PE 2-6A
Effect of errors on a trial balance
obj. 3

For each of the following errors, considered individually, indicate whether the error would cause the trial balance totals to be unequal. If the error would cause the trial balance total to be unequal, indicate whether the debit or credit total is higher and by how much.

a. A payment of $468 on account was debited to Accounts Payable for $486 and credited to Cash for $486.
b. A purchase of supplies of $1,130 was debited to Supplies for $1,130 and debited to Accounts Payable for $1,130.
c. The payment of an insurance premium of $2,450 for a two-year policy was debited to Prepaid Insurance for $2,450 and credited to Cash for $2,540.

PE 2-6B
Effect of errors on a trial balance
obj. 3

For each of the following errors, considered individually, indicate whether the error would cause the trial balance totals to be unequal. If the error would cause the trial balance total to be unequal, indicate whether the debit or credit total is higher and by how much.

a. The receipt of cash on account of $1,312 was recorded as a debit to Cash for $1,012 and a credit to Accounts Receivable for $1,312.
b. The payment of cash for the purchase of office equipment of $4,500 was debited to Land for $4,500 and credited to Cash for $4,500.
c. The payment of $1,420 on account was debited to Accounts Payable for $142 and credited to Cash for $1,420.

PE 2-7A
Correction of errors
obj. 4

The following errors took place in journalizing and posting transactions:

a. The payment of $3,125 from a customer on account was recorded as a debit to Cash and a credit to Accounts Payable.
b. Advertising expense of $1,500 paid for the current month was recorded as a debit to Miscellaneous Expense and a credit to Advertising Expense.

Journalize the entries to correct the errors. Omit explanations.

PE 2-7B
Correction of errors
obj. 4

The following errors took place in journalizing and posting transactions:

a. The purchase of supplies of $2,690 on account was recorded as a debit to Office Equipment and a credit to Supplies.
b. The receipt of $3,750 for services rendered was recorded as a debit to Accounts Receivable and a credit to Fees Earned.

Journalize the entries to correct the errors. Omit explanations.

Exercises

EX 2-1
Chart of accounts
obj. 1

The following accounts appeared in recent financial statements of Continental Airlines:

Accounts Payable	Flight Equipment
Air Traffic Liability	Landing Fees
Aircraft Fuel Expense	Passenger Revenue
Cargo and Mail Revenue	Purchase Deposits for Flight Equipment
Commissions	Spare Parts and Supplies

Identify each account as either a balance sheet account or an income statement account. For each balance sheet account, identify it as an asset, a liability, or owner's equity. For each income statement account, identify it as a revenue or an expense.

EX 2-2
Chart of accounts
obj. 1

Mandalay Interiors is owned and operated by Angie Stowe, an interior decorator. In the ledger of Mandalay Interiors, the first digit of the account number indicates its major account classification (1—assets, 2—liabilities, 3—owner's equity, 4—revenues, 5—expenses). The second digit of the account number indicates the specific account within each of the preceding major account classifications.

Match each account number with its most likely account in the list below. The account numbers are 11, 12, 13, 21, 31, 32, 41, 51, 52, and 53.

Accounts Payable	Fees Earned
Accounts Receivable	Land
Angie Stowe, Capital	Miscellaneous Expense
Angie Stowe, Drawing	Supplies Expense
Cash	Wages Expense

EX 2-3
Chart of accounts
obj. 1

Dazzle School is a newly organized business that teaches people how to inspire and influence others. The list of accounts to be opened in the general ledger is as follows:

Accounts Payable	Miscellaneous Expense	Supplies
Accounts Receivable	Prepaid Insurance	Supplies Expense
Cash	Rebecca Wimmer, Capital	Unearned Rent
Equipment	Rebecca Wimmer, Drawing	Wages Expense
Fees Earned	Rent Expense	

List the accounts in the order in which they should appear in the ledger of Dazzle School and assign account numbers. Each account number is to have two digits: the first digit is to indicate the major classification (1 for assets, etc.), and the second digit is to identify the specific account within each major classification (11 for Cash, etc.).

EX 2-4
Identifying transactions
obj. 1

Eos Co. is a travel agency. The nine transactions recorded by Eos during March 2008, its first month of operations, are indicated in the following T accounts:

Cash		Equipment		Tosha Lewis, Drawing	
(1) 30,000	(2) 1,800	(3) 24,000		(8) 2,500	
(7) 10,000	(3) 9,000				
	(4) 3,050				
	(6) 7,500				
	(8) 2,500				

Accounts Receivable		Accounts Payable		Service Revenue	
(5) 15,000	(7) 10,000	(6) 7,500	(3) 15,000		(5) 15,000

Supplies		Tosha Lewis, Capital		Operating Expenses	
(2) 1,800	(9) 1,050		(1) 30,000	(4) 3,050	
				(9) 1,050	

Indicate for each debit and each credit: (a) whether an asset, liability, owner's equity, drawing, revenue, or expense account was affected and (b) whether the account was increased (+) or decreased (−). Present your answers in the following form, with transaction (1) given as an example:

	Account Debited		Account Credited	
Transaction	Type	Effect	Type	Effect
(1)	asset	+	owner's equity	+

EX 2-5
Journal entries
objs. 1, 2

Based upon the T accounts in Exercise 2-4, prepare the nine journal entries from which the postings were made. Journal entry explanations may be omitted.

EX 2-6
Trial balance
obj. **3**

✓ *Total Debit Column:*
$52,500

Based upon the data presented in Exercise 2-4, prepare an unadjusted trial balance, listing the accounts in their proper order.

EX 2-7
Normal entries for accounts
obj. **1**

During the month, Witherspoon Labs Co. has a substantial number of transactions affecting each of the following accounts. State for each account whether it is likely to have (a) debit entries only, (b) credit entries only, or (c) both debit and credit entries.

1. Accounts Payable
2. Accounts Receivable
3. Cash
4. Fees Earned

5. Insurance Expense
6. Keith Dupree, Drawing
7. Supplies Expense

EX 2-8
Normal balances of accounts
obj. **1**

Identify each of the following accounts of Sydney Services Co. as asset, liability, owner's equity, revenue, or expense, and state in each case whether the normal balance is a debit or a credit.

a. Accounts Payable
b. Accounts Receivable
c. Boyd Magnus, Capital
d. Boyd Magnus, Drawing
e. Cash

f. Fees Earned
g. Office Equipment
h. Rent Expense
i. Supplies
j. Wages Expense

EX 2-9
Rules of debit and credit
obj. **1**

The following table summarizes the rules of debit and credit. For each of the items (a) through (l), indicate whether the proper answer is a debit or a credit.

	Increase	Decrease	Normal Balance
Balance sheet accounts:			
Asset	(a)	Credit	(b)
Liability	(c)	(d)	Credit
Owner's equity:			
Capital	Credit	(e)	(f)
Drawing	(g)	(h)	Debit
Income statement accounts:			
Revenue	(i)	(j)	(k)
Expense	Debit	(l)	Debit

EX 2-10
Capital account balance
obj. **1**

As of January 1, Sarah Bredy, Capital, had a credit balance of $21,800. During the year, withdrawals totaled $1,500, and the business incurred a net loss of $24,000.

a. Calculate the balance of Sarah Bredy, Capital, as of the end of the year.
b. Assuming that there have been no recording errors, will the balance sheet prepared at December 31 balance? Explain.

EX 2-11
Cash account balance
obj. **1**

During the month, Harpoon Co. received $479,250 in cash and paid out $312,380 in cash.

a. Do the data indicate that Harpoon Co. earned $166,870 during the month? Explain.
b. If the balance of the cash account is $241,925 at the end of the month, what was the cash balance at the beginning of the month?

EX 2-12
Account balances
obj. 1
✓ c. $5,100

a. On June 1, the cash account balance was $11,150. During June, cash receipts totaled $72,300 and the June 30 balance was $15,750. Determine the cash payments made during June.

b. On July 1, the accounts receivable account balance was $25,500. During July, $115,000 was collected from customers on account. Assuming the July 31 balance was $27,500, determine the fees billed to customers on account during July.

c. During December, $60,500 was paid to creditors on account, and purchases on account were $77,700. Assuming the December 31 balance of Accounts Payable was $22,300, determine the account balance on December 1.

EX 2-13
Transactions
objs. 1, 2

The Boa Co. has the following accounts in its ledger: Cash; Accounts Receivable; Supplies; Office Equipment; Accounts Payable; Alfonso Finley, Capital; Alfonso Finley, Drawing; Fees Earned; Rent Expense; Advertising Expense; Utilities Expense; Miscellaneous Expense.

Journalize the following selected transactions for October 2007 in a two-column journal. Journal entry explanations may be omitted.

Oct. 1. Paid rent for the month, $2,500.
       3. Paid advertising expense, $1,100.
       4. Paid cash for supplies, $725.
       6. Purchased office equipment on account, $7,500.
      10. Received cash from customers on account, $3,600.
      12. Paid creditor on account, $600.
      20. Withdrew cash for personal use, $1,000.
      27. Paid cash for repairs to office equipment, $500.
      30. Paid telephone bill for the month, $195.
      31. Fees earned and billed to customers for the month, $20,150.
      31. Paid electricity bill for the month, $315.

EX 2-14
Journalizing and posting
objs. 1, 2

On July 27, 2008, Colorcast Co. purchased $1,875 of supplies on account. In Colorcast Co.'s chart of accounts, the supplies account is No. 15, and the accounts payable account is No. 21.

a. Journalize the July 27, 2008, transaction on page 38 of Colorcast Co.'s two-column journal. Include an explanation of the entry.

b. Prepare a four-column account for Supplies. Enter a debit balance of $735 as of July 1, 2008. Place a check mark (✓) in the Posting Reference column.

c. Prepare a four-column account for Accounts Payable. Enter a credit balance of $11,380 as of July 1, 2008. Place a check mark (✓) in the Posting Reference column.

d. Post the July 27, 2008, transaction to the accounts.

EX 2-15
Transactions and T accounts
objs. 1, 2

The following selected transactions were completed during August of the current year:

1. Billed customers for fees earned, $13,750.
2. Purchased supplies on account, $1,325.
3. Received cash from customers on account, $8,150.
4. Paid creditors on account, $800.

a. Journalize the above transactions in a two-column journal, using the appropriate number to identify the transactions. Journal entry explanations may be omitted.

b. Post the entries prepared in (a) to the following T accounts: Cash, Supplies, Accounts Receivable, Accounts Payable, Fees Earned. To the left of each amount posted in the accounts, place the appropriate number to identify the transactions.

EX 2-16
Trial balance
obj. 3

The accounts in the ledger of Matice Co. as of July 31, 2008, are listed in alphabetical order as follows. All accounts have normal balances. The balance of the cash account has been intentionally omitted.

Accounts Payable	$ 56,130	Notes Payable	$120,000
Accounts Receivable	112,500	Prepaid Insurance	9,000
Cash	?	Rent Expense	180,000
Fees Earned	930,000	Supplies	6,300
Insurance Expense	18,000	Supplies Expense	23,700
Land	255,000	Unearned Rent	27,000
Milton Adair, Capital	259,920	Utilities Expense	124,500
Milton Adair, Drawing	60,000	Wages Expense	525,000
Miscellaneous Expense	26,700		

✓ *Total Credit Column:*
$1,393,050

Prepare an unadjusted trial balance, listing the accounts in their proper order and inserting the missing figure for cash.

EX 2-17
Effect of errors on trial balance

obj. 3

Indicate which of the following errors, each considered individually, would cause the trial balance totals to be unequal:

a. A fee of $2,350 earned and due from a client was not debited to Accounts Receivable or credited to a revenue account, because the cash had not been received.

b. A payment of $1,500 to a creditor was posted as a debit of $1,500 to Accounts Payable and a debit of $1,500 to Cash.

c. A payment of $6,000 for equipment purchased was posted as a debit of $600 to Equipment and a credit of $600 to Cash.

d. Payment of a cash withdrawal of $12,000 was journalized and posted as a debit of $21,000 to Salary Expense and a credit of $12,000 to Cash.

e. A receipt of $750 from an account receivable was journalized and posted as a debit of $750 to Cash and a credit of $750 to Fees Earned.

EX 2-18
Errors in trial balance

obj. 3

✓ *Total of Credit Column: $363,200*

The following preliminary unadjusted trial balance of Awesome Co., a sports ticket agency, does not balance:

Awesome Co.
Unadjusted Trial Balance
December 31, 2008

	Debit Balances	Credit Balances
Cash	94,700	
Accounts Receivable	44,200	
Prepaid Insurance		16,000
Equipment	15,000	
Accounts Payable		25,960
Unearned Rent		5,800
Sean Milner, Capital	164,840	
Sean Milner, Drawing	20,000	
Service Revenue		167,500
Wages Expense		84,000
Advertising Expense	14,400	
Miscellaneous Expense		2,850
	353,140	302,110

When the ledger and other records are reviewed, you discover the following: (1) the debits and credits in the cash account total $94,700 and $67,950, respectively; (2) a billing of $5,000 to a customer on account was not posted to the accounts receivable account; (3) a payment of $3,600 made to a creditor on account was not posted to the accounts payable account; (4) the balance of the unearned rent account is $8,500; (5) the correct balance of the equipment account is $150,000; and (6) each account has a normal balance.
    Prepare a corrected unadjusted trial balance.

EX 2-19
Effect of errors on trial balance

obj. 3

The following errors occurred in posting from a two-column journal:

1. A credit of $5,125 to Accounts Payable was not posted.
2. A debit of $675 to Accounts Payable was posted as a credit.
3. A debit of $1,375 to Supplies was posted twice.
4. A debit of $3,575 to Wages Expense was posted as $3,557.
5. An entry debiting Accounts Receivable and crediting Fees Earned for $6,000 was not posted.
6. A credit of $350 to Cash was posted as $530.
7. A debit of $1,000 to Cash was posted to Miscellaneous Expense.

Considering each case individually (i.e., assuming that no other errors had occurred), indicate: (a) by "yes" or "no" whether the trial balance would be out of balance; (b) if answer to (a) is "yes," the amount by which the trial balance totals would differ; and (c) whether the debit or credit column of the trial balance would have the larger total. Answers should be presented in the following form, with error (1) given as an example:

Error	(a) Out of Balance	(b) Difference	(c) Larger Total
1.	yes	$5,125	debit

EX 2-20
Errors in trial balance

obj. 3

✓ *Total of Credit Column: $375,000*

Identify the errors in the following trial balance. All accounts have normal balances.

Hybrid Co.
Unadjusted Trial Balance
For the Month Ending October 31, 2008

	Debit Balances	Credit Balances
Cash	22,500	
Accounts Receivable		49,200
Prepaid Insurance	10,800	
Equipment	150,000	
Accounts Payable	5,550	
Salaries Payable		3,750
Nolan Towns, Capital		129,600
Nolan Towns, Drawing		18,000
Service Revenue		236,100
Salary Expense	98,430	
Advertising Expense		21,600
Miscellaneous Expense	4,470	
	458,250	458,250

EX 2-21
Entries to correct errors

obj. 4

The following errors took place in journalizing and posting transactions:

a. A withdrawal of $20,000 by Joel Goodson, owner of the business, was recorded as a debit to Wages Expense and a credit to Cash.
b. Rent of $3,600 paid for the current month was recorded as a debit to Rent Expense and a credit to Prepaid Rent.

Journalize the entries to correct the errors. Omit explanations.

EX 2-22
Entries to correct errors

obj. 4

The following errors took place in journalizing and posting transactions:

a. A $940 purchase of supplies for cash was recorded as a debit to Supplies Expense and a credit to Accounts Payable.
b. Cash of $2,750 received on account was recorded as a debit to Fees Earned and a credit to Cash.

Journalize the entries to correct the errors. Omit explanations.

Problems Series A

PR 2-1A
Entries into T accounts and trial balance
objs. 1, 2, 3

✓ *3. Total of Debit Column: $51,200*

Hannah Knox, an architect, opened an office on July 1, 2008. During the month, she completed the following transactions connected with her professional practice:

a. Transferred cash from a personal bank account to an account to be used for the business, $25,000.
b. Paid July rent for office and workroom, $2,000.
c. Purchased used automobile for $16,500, paying $1,500 cash and giving a note payable for the remainder.
d. Purchased office and computer equipment on account, $6,500.
e. Paid cash for supplies, $975.
f. Paid cash for annual insurance policies, $1,200.
g. Received cash from client for plans delivered, $3,750.
h. Paid cash for miscellaneous expenses, $240.
i. Paid cash to creditors on account, $2,500.
j. Paid installment due on note payable, $450.
k. Received invoice for blueprint service, due in August, $750.
l. Recorded fee earned on plans delivered, payment to be received in August, $3,150.
m. Paid salary of assistant, $1,500.
n. Paid gas, oil, and repairs on automobile for July, $280.

Instructions
1. Record the above transactions directly in the following T accounts, without journalizing: Cash; Accounts Receivable; Supplies; Prepaid Insurance; Automobiles; Equipment; Notes Payable; Accounts Payable; Hannah Knox, Capital; Professional Fees; Rent Expense; Salary Expense; Automobile Expense; Blueprint Expense; Miscellaneous Expense. To the left of the amount entered in the accounts, place the appropriate letter to identify the transaction.
2. Determine account balances of the T accounts. Accounts containing a single entry only (such as Prepaid Insurance) do not need a balance.
3. Prepare an unadjusted trial balance for Hannah Knox, Architect, as of July 31, 2008.

PR 2-2A
Journal entries and trial balance
objs. 1, 2, 3

✓ *4. c. $6,425*

On March 1, 2008, Kara Frantz established Mudcat Realty, which completed the following transactions during the month:

a. Kara Frantz transferred cash from a personal bank account to an account to be used for the business, $15,000.
b. Paid rent on office and equipment for the month, $2,500.
c. Purchased supplies on account, $850.
d. Paid creditor on account, $400.
e. Earned sales commissions, receiving cash, $15,750.
f. Paid automobile expenses (including rental charge) for month, $2,400, and miscellaneous expenses, $600.
g. Paid office salaries, $3,250.
h. Determined that the cost of supplies used was $575.
i. Withdrew cash for personal use, $1,000.

Instructions
1. Journalize entries for transactions (a) through (i), using the following account titles: Cash; Supplies; Accounts Payable; Kara Frantz, Capital; Kara Frantz, Drawing; Sales Commissions; Office Salaries Expense; Rent Expense; Automobile Expense; Supplies Expense; Miscellaneous Expense. Explanations may be omitted.
2. Prepare T accounts, using the account titles in (1). Post the journal entries to these accounts, placing the appropriate letter to the left of each amount to identify the transactions. Determine the account balances, after all posting is complete. Accounts containing only a single entry do not need a balance.
3. Prepare an unadjusted trial balance as of March 31, 2008.

(continued)

4. Determine the following:
   a. Amount of total revenue recorded in the ledger.
   b. Amount of total expenses recorded in the ledger.
   c. Amount of net income for March.

PR 2-3A
Journal entries and trial balance
objs. 1, 2, 3

✓ *3. Total of Credit Column: $49,825*

On June 1, 2008, Brooks Dodd established an interior decorating business, Coordinated Designs. During the month, Brooks completed the following transactions related to the business:

June 1. Brooks transferred cash from a personal bank account to an account to be used for the business, $18,000.
      5. Paid rent for period of June 5 to end of month, $2,150.
      6. Purchased office equipment on account, $8,500.
      8. Purchased a used truck for $18,000, paying $10,000 cash and giving a note payable for the remainder.
     10. Purchased supplies for cash, $1,200.
     12. Received cash for job completed, $10,500.
     15. Paid annual premiums on property and casualty insurance, $2,400.
     23. Recorded jobs completed on account and sent invoices to customers, $5,950.
     24. Received an invoice for truck expenses, to be paid in July, $1,000.
     29. Paid utilities expense, $1,200.
     29. Paid miscellaneous expenses, $400.
     30. Received cash from customers on account, $3,200.
     30. Paid wages of employees, $2,900.
     30. Paid creditor a portion of the amount owed for equipment purchased on June 6, $2,125.
     30. Withdrew cash for personal use, $1,750.

Instructions
1. Journalize each transaction in a two-column journal, referring to the following chart of accounts in selecting the accounts to be debited and credited. (Do not insert the account numbers in the journal at this time.) Explanations may be omitted.

11	Cash	31	Brooks Dodd, Capital
12	Accounts Receivable	32	Brooks Dodd, Drawing
13	Supplies	41	Fees Earned
14	Prepaid Insurance	51	Wages Expense
16	Equipment	53	Rent Expense
18	Truck	54	Utilities Expense
21	Notes Payable	55	Truck Expense
22	Accounts Payable	59	Miscellaneous Expense

2. Post the journal to a ledger of four-column accounts, inserting appropriate posting references as each item is posted. Extend the balances to the appropriate balance columns after each transaction is posted.
3. Prepare an unadjusted trial balance for Coordinated Designs as of June 30, 2008.

PR 2-4A
Journal entries and trial balance
objs. 1, 2, 3

✓ *4. Total of Debit Column: $430,650*

Passport Realty acts as an agent in buying, selling, renting, and managing real estate. The unadjusted trial balance on October 31, 2008, is shown at the top of the following page.
   The following business transactions were completed by Passport Realty during November 2008:

Nov. 1. Paid rent on office for month, $5,000.
      2. Purchased office supplies on account, $1,750.
      5. Paid annual insurance premiums, $4,800.
     10. Received cash from clients on account, $52,000.
     15. Purchased land for a future building site for $90,000, paying $10,000 in cash and giving a note payable for the remainder.
     17. Paid creditors on account, $7,750.

Passport Realty
Unadjusted Trial Balance
October 31, 2008

		Debit Balances	Credit Balances
11	Cash	26,300	
12	Accounts Receivable	67,500	
13	Prepaid Insurance	3,000	
14	Office Supplies	1,800	
16	Land	—	
21	Accounts Payable		13,020
22	Unearned Rent		—
23	Notes Payable		—
31	Ashley Carnes, Capital		32,980
32	Ashley Carnes, Drawing	2,000	
41	Fees Earned		260,000
51	Salary and Commission Expense	148,200	
52	Rent Expense	30,000	
53	Advertising Expense	17,800	
54	Automobile Expense	5,500	
59	Miscellaneous Expense	3,900	
		306,000	306,000

Nov. 20. Returned a portion of the office supplies purchased on November 2, receiving full credit for their cost, $250.

23. Paid advertising expense, $2,100.

27. Discovered an error in computing a commission; received cash from the salesperson for the overpayment, $700.

28. Paid automobile expense (including rental charges for an automobile), $1,500.

29. Paid miscellaneous expenses, $450.

30. Recorded revenue earned and billed to clients during the month, $48,400.

30. Paid salaries and commissions for the month, $25,000.

30. Withdrew cash for personal use, $8,000.

30. Rented land purchased on November 15 to local merchants association for use as a parking lot in December and January, during a street rebuilding program; received advance payment of $2,500.

Instructions

1. Record the November 1, 2008, balance of each account in the appropriate balance column of a four-column account, write *Balance* in the item section, and place a check mark (✓) in the Posting Reference column.

2. Journalize the transactions for November in a two-column journal. Journal entry explanations may be omitted.

3. Post to the ledger, extending the account balance to the appropriate balance column after each posting.

4. Prepare an unadjusted trial balance of the ledger as of November 30, 2008.

PR 2-5A
Errors in trial balance

objs. 3, 4

✓7. Total of Debit Column: $43,338.10

If the working papers correlating with this textbook are not used, omit Problem 2-5A.

The following records of Mainstay TV Repair are presented in the working papers:

- Journal containing entries for the period July 1–31.
- Ledger to which the July entries have been posted.
- Preliminary trial balance as of July 31, which does not balance.

Locate the errors, supply the information requested, and prepare a corrected trial balance according to the following instructions. The balances recorded in the accounts as of July 1 and the entries in the journal are correctly stated. If it is necessary to correct any posted amounts in the ledger, a line should be drawn through the erroneous figure and the correct amount inserted above. Corrections or notations may be inserted on the preliminary trial balance in any manner desired. It is not necessary to complete all of the instructions if equal trial balance totals can be obtained earlier. However, the requirements of instructions (6) and (7) should be completed in any event.

Instructions

1. Verify the totals of the preliminary trial balance, inserting the correct amounts in the schedule provided in the working papers.
2. Compute the difference between the trial balance totals.
3. Compare the listings in the trial balance with the balances appearing in the ledger, and list the errors in the space provided in the working papers.
4. Verify the accuracy of the balance of each account in the ledger, and list the errors in the space provided in the working papers.
5. Trace the postings in the ledger back to the journal, using small check marks to identify items traced. Correct any amounts in the ledger that may be necessitated by errors in posting, and list the errors in the space provided in the working papers.
6. Journalize as of July 31 the payment of $125 for advertising expense. The bill had been paid on July 31 but was inadvertently omitted from the journal. Post to the ledger. (Revise any amounts necessitated by posting this entry.)
7. Prepare a new unadjusted trial balance.

PR 2-6A
Corrected trial balance

obj. 3

✓ 1. Total of Debit
Column: $200,000

Iberian Carpet has the following unadjusted trial balance as of March 31, 2008.

Iberian Carpet
Unadjusted Trial Balance
March 31, 2008

	Debit Balances	Credit Balances
Cash	4,300	
Accounts Receivable	11,870	
Supplies	2,320	
Prepaid Insurance	880	
Equipment	56,000	
Notes Payable		26,100
Accounts Payable		7,900
Jose Mendrano, Capital		38,400
Jose Mendrano, Drawing	14,500	
Fees Earned		122,700
Wages Expense	70,000	
Rent Expense	16,600	
Advertising Expense	720	
Miscellaneous Expense	1,450	
	178,640	195,100

The debit and credit totals are not equal as a result of the following errors:

a. The balance of cash was understated by $3,000.
b. A cash receipt of $4,500 was posted as a debit to Cash of $5,400.
c. A debit of $1,850 to Accounts Receivable was not posted.
d. A return of $350 of defective supplies was erroneously posted as a $530 credit to Supplies.
e. An insurance policy acquired at a cost of $175 was posted as a credit to Prepaid Insurance.
f. The balance of Notes Payable was understated by $7,500.
g. A credit of $900 in Accounts Payable was overlooked when determining the balance of the account.
h. A debit of $3,500 for a withdrawal by the owner was posted as a credit to Jose Mendrano, Capital.
i. The balance of $7,200 in Advertising Expense was entered as $720 in the trial balance.
j. Gas, Electricity, and Water Expense, with a balance of $6,900, was omitted from the trial balance.

Instructions

1. Prepare a corrected unadjusted trial balance as of March 31, 2008.
2. Does the fact that the unadjusted trial balance in (1) is balanced mean that there are no errors in the accounts? Explain.

Problems Series B

PR 2-1B
Entries into T accounts and trial balance

objs. 1, 2, 3

✓ *3. Total of Debit Column: $47,800*

Lynette Moss, an architect, opened an office on April 1, 2008. During the month, she completed the following transactions connected with her professional practice:

a. Transferred cash from a personal bank account to an account to be used for the business, $22,500.
b. Purchased used automobile for $15,300, paying $4,000 cash and giving a note payable for the remainder.
c. Paid April rent for office and workroom, $2,500.
d. Paid cash for supplies, $1,200.
e. Purchased office and computer equipment on account, $5,200.
f. Paid cash for annual insurance policies on automobile and equipment, $1,600.
g. Received cash from a client for plans delivered, $6,500.
h. Paid cash to creditors on account, $1,800.
i. Paid cash for miscellaneous expenses, $300.
j. Received invoice for blueprint service, due in May, $800.
k. Recorded fee earned on plans delivered, payment to be received in May, $3,500.
l. Paid salary of assistant, $1,500.
m. Paid cash for miscellaneous expenses, $210.
n. Paid installment due on note payable, $200.
o. Paid gas, oil, and repairs on automobile for April, $250.

Instructions

1. Record the above transactions directly in the following T accounts, without journalizing: Cash; Accounts Receivable; Supplies; Prepaid Insurance; Automobiles; Equipment; Notes Payable; Accounts Payable; Lynette Moss, Capital; Professional Fees; Rent Expense; Salary Expense; Blueprint Expense; Automobile Expense; Miscellaneous Expense. To the left of each amount entered in the accounts, place the appropriate letter to identify the transaction.
2. Determine account balances of the T accounts. Accounts containing a single entry only (such as Prepaid Insurance) do not need a balance.
3. Prepare an unadjusted trial balance for Lynette Moss, Architect, as of April 30, 2008.

PR 2-2B
Journal entries and trial balance

objs. 1, 2, 3

✓ *4. c. $5,575*

On July 1, 2008, Bill Bonds established Genesis Realty, which completed the following transactions during the month:

a. Bill Bonds transferred cash from a personal bank account to an account to be used for the business, $18,000.
b. Purchased supplies on account, $1,000.
c. Earned sales commissions, receiving cash, $14,600.
d. Paid rent on office and equipment for the month, $3,000.
e. Paid creditor on account, $600.
f. Withdrew cash for personal use, $1,500.
g. Paid automobile expenses (including rental charge) for month, $2,000, and miscellaneous expenses, $500.
h. Paid office salaries, $2,800.
i. Determined that the cost of supplies used was $725.

Instructions

1. Journalize entries for transactions (a) through (i), using the following account titles: Cash; Supplies; Accounts Payable; Bill Bonds, Capital; Bill Bonds, Drawing; Sales Commissions; Rent Expense; Office Salaries Expense; Automobile Expense; Supplies Expense; Miscellaneous Expense. Journal entry explanations may be omitted.

(continued)

2. Prepare T accounts, using the account titles in (1). Post the journal entries to these accounts, placing the appropriate letter to the left of each amount to identify the transactions. Determine the account balances, after all posting is complete. Accounts containing only a single entry do not need a balance.
3. Prepare an unadjusted trial balance as of July 31, 2008.
4. Determine the following:
   a. Amount of total revenue recorded in the ledger.
   b. Amount of total expenses recorded in the ledger.
   c. Amount of net income for July.

PR 2-3B
Journal entries and trial balance
objs. 1, 2, 3

✓ *3. Total of Credit Column: $47,675*

On October 1, 2008, Kristy Gomez established an interior decorating business, Ultimate Designs. During the month, Kristy Gomez completed the following transactions related to the business:

Oct. 1. Kristy transferred cash from a personal bank account to an account to be used for the business, $20,000.
  3. Paid rent for period of October 3 to end of month, $1,600.
  10. Purchased a truck for $15,000, paying $5,000 cash and giving a note payable for the remainder.
  13. Purchased equipment on account, $4,500.
  14. Purchased supplies for cash, $1,100.
  15. Paid annual premiums on property and casualty insurance, $2,800.
  15. Received cash for job completed, $6,100.
  21. Paid creditor a portion of the amount owed for equipment purchased on October 13, $2,400.
  24. Recorded jobs completed on account and sent invoices to customers, $8,600.
  26. Received an invoice for truck expenses, to be paid in November, $875.
  27. Paid utilities expense, $900.
  27. Paid miscellaneous expenses, $315.
  29. Received cash from customers on account, $4,100.
  30. Paid wages of employees, $2,500.
  31. Withdrew cash for personal use, $3,000.

Instructions
1. Journalize each transaction in a two-column journal, referring to the following chart of accounts in selecting the accounts to be debited and credited. (Do not insert the account numbers in the journal at this time.) Journal entry explanations may be omitted.

11 Cash	31 Kristy Gomez, Capital
12 Accounts Receivable	32 Kristy Gomez, Drawing
13 Supplies	41 Fees Earned
14 Prepaid Insurance	51 Wages Expense
16 Equipment	53 Rent Expense
18 Truck	54 Utilities Expense
21 Notes Payable	55 Truck Expense
22 Accounts Payable	59 Miscellaneous Expense

2. Post the journal to a ledger of four-column accounts, inserting appropriate posting references as each item is posted. Extend the balances to the appropriate balance columns after each transaction is posted.
3. Prepare an unadjusted trial balance for Ultimate Designs as of October 31, 2008.

PR 2-4B
Journal entries and trial balance
objs. 1, 2, 3

✓ *4. Total of Debit Column: $375,230*

Equity Realty acts as an agent in buying, selling, renting, and managing real estate. The unadjusted trial balance on July 31, 2008, is shown at the top of the following page.
  The following business transactions were completed by Equity Realty during August 2008:

Aug. 1. Purchased office supplies on account, $1,500.
  2. Paid rent on office for month, $2,500.
  3. Received cash from clients on account, $28,720.
  5. Paid annual insurance premiums, $3,600.

Equity Realty
Unadjusted Trial Balance
July 31, 2008

		Debit Balances	Credit Balances
11	Cash	21,200	
12	Accounts Receivable	35,750	
13	Prepaid Insurance	4,500	
14	Office Supplies	1,000	
16	Land	—	
21	Accounts Payable		6,200
22	Unearned Rent		—
23	Notes Payable		—
31	Jody Craft, Capital		31,550
32	Jody Craft, Drawing	16,000	
41	Fees Earned		220,000
51	Salary and Commission Expense	140,000	
52	Rent Expense	17,500	
53	Advertising Expense	14,300	
54	Automobile Expense	6,400	
59	Miscellaneous Expense	1,100	
		257,750	257,750

Aug. 9. Returned a portion of the office supplies purchased on August 1, receiving full credit for their cost, $250.

17. Paid advertising expense, $3,450.

23. Paid creditors on account, $2,670.

29. Paid miscellaneous expenses, $500.

30. Paid automobile expense (including rental charges for an automobile), $1,500.

31. Discovered an error in computing a commission; received cash from the salesperson for the overpayment, $1,000.

31. Paid salaries and commissions for the month, $17,400.

31. Recorded revenue earned and billed to clients during the month, $51,900.

31. Purchased land for a future building site for $75,000, paying $10,000 in cash and giving a note payable for the remainder.

31. Withdrew cash for personal use, $5,000.

31. Rented land purchased on August 31 to a local university for use as a parking lot during football season (September, October, and November); received advance payment of $2,000.

Instructions

1. Record the August 1 balance of each account in the appropriate balance column of a four-column account, write *Balance* in the item section, and place a check mark (✓) in the Posting Reference column.

2. Journalize the transactions for August in a two-column journal. Journal entry explanations may be omitted.

3. Post to the ledger, extending the account balance to the appropriate balance column after each posting.

4. Prepare an unadjusted trial balance of the ledger as of August 31, 2008.

PR 2-5B
Errors in trial balance

objs. 3, 4

If the working papers correlating with this textbook are not used, omit Problem 2-5B.

The following records of Mainstay TV Repair are presented in the working papers:

- Journal containing entries for the period July 1–31.
- Ledger to which the July entries have been posted.
- Preliminary trial balance as of July 31, which does not balance.

Locate the errors, supply the information requested, and prepare a corrected trial balance according to the following instructions. The balances recorded in the accounts as of July 1

✓ 7. Total of Credit
Column: $43,338.10

and the entries in the journal are correctly stated. If it is necessary to correct any posted amounts in the ledger, a line should be drawn through the erroneous figure and the correct amount inserted above. Corrections or notations may be inserted on the preliminary trial balance in any manner desired. It is not necessary to complete all of the instructions if equal trial balance totals can be obtained earlier. However, the requirements of instructions (6) and (7) should be completed in any event.

Instructions
1. Verify the totals of the preliminary trial balance, inserting the correct amounts in the schedule provided in the working papers.
2. Compute the difference between the trial balance totals.
3. Compare the listings in the trial balance with the balances appearing in the ledger, and list the errors in the space provided in the working papers.
4. Verify the accuracy of the balance of each account in the ledger, and list the errors in the space provided in the working papers.
5. Trace the postings in the ledger back to the journal, using small check marks to identify items traced. Correct any amounts in the ledger that may be necessitated by errors in posting, and list the errors in the space provided in the working papers.
6. Journalize as of July 31 the payment of $110 for gas and electricity. The bill had been paid on July 31 but was inadvertently omitted from the journal. Post to the ledger. (Revise any amounts necessitated by posting this entry.)
7. Prepare a new unadjusted trial balance.

PR 2-6B
Corrected trial balance

obj. 3

✓ 1. Total of Debit
Column: $234,000

Epic Video has the following unadjusted trial balance as of July 31, 2008:

Epic Video
Unadjusted Trial Balance
July 31, 2008

	Debit Balances	Credit Balances
Cash	6,250	
Accounts Receivable	12,520	
Supplies	2,232	
Prepaid Insurance	710	
Equipment	54,000	
Notes Payable		22,500
Accounts Payable		4,980
Carlton Dey, Capital		30,400
Carlton Dey, Drawing	11,500	
Fees Earned		178,020
Wages Expense	102,000	
Rent Expense	20,850	
Advertising Expense	9,540	
Gas, Electricity, and Water Expense	5,670	
	225,272	235,900

The debit and credit totals are not equal as a result of the following errors:

a. The balance of cash was overstated by $5,000.
b. A cash receipt of $3,200 was posted as a credit to Cash of $2,300.
c. A debit of $2,780 to Accounts Receivable was not posted.
d. A return of $235 of defective supplies was erroneously posted as a $253 credit to Supplies.
e. An insurance policy acquired at a cost of $500 was posted as a credit to Prepaid Insurance.
f. The balance of Notes Payable was overstated by $4,500.
g. A credit of $600 in Accounts Payable was overlooked when the balance of the account was determined.

h. A debit of $2,000 for a withdrawal by the owner was posted as a debit to Carlton Dey, Capital.

i. The balance of $9,450 in Advertising Expense was entered as $9,540 in the trial balance.

j. Miscellaneous Expense, with a balance of $2,520, was omitted from the trial balance.

Instructions

1. Prepare a corrected unadjusted trial balance as of July 31 of the current year.

2. ━━━▶ Does the fact that the unadjusted trial balance in (1) is balanced mean that there are no errors in the accounts? Explain.

Continuing Problem

✓ *4. Total of Debit Column: $37,800*

The transactions completed by Dancin Music during April 2008 were described at the end of Chapter 1. The following transactions were completed during May, the second month of the business's operations:

May 1. Kris Payne made an additional investment in Dancin Music by depositing $2,500 in Dancin Music's checking account.

1. Instead of continuing to share office space with a local real estate agency, Kris decided to rent office space near a local music store. Paid rent for May, $1,600.

1. Paid a premium of $3,360 for a comprehensive insurance policy covering liability, theft, and fire. The policy covers a one-year period.

2. Received $1,350 on account.

3. On behalf of Dancin Music, Kris signed a contract with a local radio station, KPRG, to provide guest spots for the next three months. The contract requires Dancin Music to provide a guest disc jockey for 80 hours per month for a monthly fee of $2,400. Any additional hours beyond 80 will be billed to KPRG at $40 per hour. In accordance with the contract, Kris received $4,800 from KPRG as an advance payment for the first two months.

3. Paid $250 on account.

4. Paid an attorney $300 for reviewing the May 3rd contract with KPRG. (Record as Miscellaneous Expense.)

5. Purchased office equipment on account from One-Stop Office Mart, $5,000.

8. Paid for a newspaper advertisement, $180.

11. Received $750 for serving as a disc jockey for a college fraternity party.

13. Paid $500 to a local audio electronics store for rental of digital recording equipment.

14. Paid wages of $1,000 to receptionist and part-time assistant.

16. Received $1,500 for serving as a disc jockey for a wedding reception.

18. Purchased supplies on account, $750.

21. Paid $325 to Rocket Music for use of its current music demos in making various music sets.

22. Paid $800 to a local radio station to advertise the services of Dancin Music twice daily for the remainder of May.

23. Served as disc jockey for a party for $2,500. Received $750, with the remainder due June 4, 2008.

27. Paid electric bill, $560.

28. Paid wages of $1,000 to receptionist and part-time assistant.

29. Paid miscellaneous expenses, $150.

30. Served as a disc jockey for a charity ball for $1,500. Received $400, with the remainder due on June 9, 2008.

31. Received $2,800 for serving as a disc jockey for a party.

31. Paid $900 royalties (music expense) to Federated Clearing for use of various artists' music during May.

31. Withdrew $1,000 cash from Dancin Music for personal use.

Dancin Music's chart of accounts and the balance of accounts as of May 1, 2008 (all normal balances), are as follows:

11	Cash	$ 9,160	41	Fees Earned	$5,700
12	Accounts Receivable	1,350	50	Wages Expense	400
14	Supplies	170	51	Office Rent Expense	1,000
15	Prepaid Insurance	—	52	Equipment Rent Expense	800
17	Office Equipment	—	53	Utilities Expense	350
21	Accounts Payable	250	54	Music Expense	1,340
23	Unearned Revenue	—	55	Advertising Expense	750
31	Kris Payne, Capital	10,000	56	Supplies Expense	180
32	Kris Payne, Drawing	300	59	Miscellaneous Expense	150

Instructions

1. Enter the May 1, 2008, account balances in the appropriate balance column of a four-column account. Write *Balance* in the Item column, and place a check mark (✓) in the Posting Reference column. (*Hint:* Verify the equality of the debit and credit balances in the ledger before proceeding with the next instruction.)
2. Analyze and journalize each transaction in a two-column journal, omitting journal entry explanations.
3. Post the journal to the ledger, extending the account balance to the appropriate balance column after each posting.
4. Prepare an unadjusted trial balance as of May 31, 2008.

Special Activities

SA 2-1
Ethics and professional conduct in business

ETHICS

At the end of the current month, Tomas Lott prepared a trial balance for AAA Rescue Service. The credit side of the trial balance exceeds the debit side by a significant amount. Tomas has decided to add the difference to the balance of the miscellaneous expense account in order to complete the preparation of the current month's financial statements by a 5 o'clock deadline. Tomas will look for the difference next week when he has more time.

▸ Discuss whether Tomas is behaving in a professional manner.

SA 2-2
Account for revenue

Ennis College requires students to pay tuition each term before classes begin. Students who have not paid their tuition are not allowed to enroll or to attend classes.

What journal entry do you think Ennis College would use to record the receipt of the students' tuition payments? Describe the nature of each account in the entry.

SA 2-3
Record transactions

The following discussion took place between Mary Louden, the office manager of Zoomworks Data Company, and a new accountant, Allen Jarvis.

Allen: I've been thinking about our method of recording entries. It seems that it's inefficient.
Mary: In what way?
Allen: Well—correct me if I'm wrong—it seems like we have unnecessary steps in the process. We could easily develop a trial balance by posting our transactions directly into the ledger and bypassing the journal altogether. In this way, we could combine the recording and posting process into one step and save ourselves a lot of time. What do you think?
Mary: We need to have a talk.

▸ What should Mary say to Allen?

SA 2-4
Debits and credits

Group Project

The following excerpt is from a conversation between Shelley Ryan, the president and chief operating officer of Diamond Construction Company, and her neighbor, Miguel Jimenez.

Miguel: Shelley, I'm taking a course in night school, "Intro to Accounting." I was wondering—could you answer a couple of questions for me?

Shelley: Well, I will if I can.

Miguel: Okay, our instructor says that it's critical we understand the basic concepts of accounting, or we'll never get beyond the first test. My problem is with those rules of debit and credit . . . you know, assets increase with debits, decrease with credits, etc.

Shelley: Yes, pretty basic stuff. You just have to memorize the rules. It shouldn't be too difficult.

Miguel: Sure, I can memorize the rules, but my problem is I want to be sure I understand the basic concepts behind the rules. For example, why can't assets be increased with credits and decreased with debits like revenue? As long as everyone did it that way, why not? It would seem easier if we had the same rules for all increases and decreases in accounts. Also, why is the left side of an account called the debit side? Why couldn't it be called something simple . . . like the "LE" for Left Entry? The right side could be called just "RE" for Right Entry. Finally, why are there just two sides to an entry? Why can't there be three or four sides to an entry?

In a group of four or five, select one person to play the role of Shelley and one person to play the role of Miguel.

1. ◖▭▭▭▷ After listening to the conversation between Shelley and Miguel, help Shelley answer Miguel's questions.
2. What information (other than just debit and credit journal entries) could the accounting system gather that might be useful to Shelley in managing Diamond Construction Company?

SA 2-5
Transactions and income statement

Shane Raburn is planning to manage and operate Birdie Caddy Service at Biloxi Golf and Country Club during June through August 2008. Shane will rent a small maintenance building from the country club for $500 per month and will offer caddy services, including cart rentals, to golfers. Shane has had no formal training in record keeping.

Shane keeps notes of all receipts and expenses in a shoe box. An examination of Shane's shoe box records for June revealed the following:

June 1. Withdrew $2,000 from personal bank account to be used to operate the caddy service.

1. Paid rent to Biloxi Golf and Country Club, $500.
2. Paid for golf supplies (practice balls, etc.), $650.
3. Arranged for the rental of 40 regular (pulling) golf carts and 10 gasoline-driven carts for $1,500 per month. Paid $750 in advance, with the remaining $750 due June 20.
7. Purchased supplies, including gasoline, for the golf carts on account, $350. Biloxi Golf and Country Club has agreed to allow Shane to store the gasoline in one of its fuel tanks at no cost.
15. Received cash for services from June 1–15, $3,150.
17. Paid cash to creditors on account, $350.
20. Paid remaining rental on golf carts, $750.
22. Purchased supplies, including gasoline, on account, $200.
25. Accepted IOUs from customers on account, $850.
28. Paid miscellaneous expenses, $180.
30. Received cash for services from June 16–30, $3,200.
30. Paid telephone and electricity (utilities) expenses, $160.
30. Paid wages of part-time employees, $450.
30. Received cash in payment of IOUs on account, $550.
30. Determined the amount of supplies on hand at the end of June, $390.

Shane has asked you several questions concerning his financial affairs to date, and he has asked you to assist with his record keeping and reporting of financial data.

a. To assist Shane with his record keeping, prepare a chart of accounts that would be appropriate for Birdie Caddy Service.

b. Prepare an income statement for June in order to help Shane assess the profitability of Birdie Caddy Service. For this purpose, the use of T accounts may be helpful in analyzing the effects of each June transaction.

c. Based on Shane's records of receipts and payments, calculate the amount of cash on hand on June 30. For this purpose, a T account for cash may be useful.

d. ⬤▬▬▶ A count of the cash on hand on June 30 totaled $4,980. Briefly discuss the possible causes of the difference between the amount of cash computed in (c) and the actual amount of cash on hand.

SA 2-6
Opportunities for accountants

>>> Internet Project <<<

The increasing complexity of the current business and regulatory environment has created an increased demand for accountants who can analyze business transactions and interpret their effects on the financial statements. In addition, a basic ability to analyze the effects of transactions is necessary to be successful in all fields of business as well as in other disciplines, such as law. To better understand the importance of accounting in today's environment, search the Internet or your local newspaper for job opportunities. One possible Internet site is **http://www.monster.com**. Then do one of the following:

1. Print a listing of at least two ads for accounting jobs. Alternatively, bring to class at least two newspaper ads for accounting jobs.

2. Print a listing of at least two ads for nonaccounting jobs for which some knowledge of accounting is preferred or necessary. Alternatively, bring to class at least two newspaper ads for such jobs.

Answers to Self-Examination Questions

1. **A**   A debit may signify an increase in an asset account (answer A) or a decrease in a liability or owner's capital account. A credit may signify a decrease in an asset account (answer B) or an increase in a liability or owner's capital account (answers C and D).

2. **C**   Liability, capital, and revenue (answer C) accounts have normal credit balances. Asset (answer A), drawing (answer B), and expense (answer D) accounts have normal debit balances.

3. **C**   Accounts Receivable (answer A), Cash (answer B), and Miscellaneous Expense (answer D) would all normally have debit balances. Fees Earned should normally have a credit balance. Hence, a debit balance in Fees Earned (answer C) would indicate a likely error in the recording process.

4. **A**   The receipt of cash from customers on account increases the asset Cash and decreases the asset Accounts Receivable, as indicated by answer A. Answer B has the debit and credit reversed, and answers C and D involve transactions with creditors (accounts payable) and not customers (accounts receivable).

5. **D**   The trial balance (answer D) is a listing of the balances and the titles of the accounts in the ledger on a given date, so that the equality of the debits and credits in the ledger can be verified. The income statement (answer A) is a summary of revenue and expenses for a period of time. The balance sheet (answer B) is a presentation of the assets, liabilities, and owner's equity on a given date. The statement of owner's equity (answer C) is a summary of the changes in owner's equity for a period of time.

The Adjusting Process

© JEFF KRAVITZ/ASSOCIATED PRESS

objectives

After studying this chapter, you should be able to:

1 *Describe the nature of the adjusting process.*

2 *Journalize entries for accounts requiring adjustment.*

3 *Summarize the adjustment process.*

4 *Prepare an adjusted trial balance.*

Marvel Entertainment, Inc.

Do you subscribe to any magazines? Most of us subscribe to one or more magazines such as *Cosmopolitan*, *Sports Illustrated*, *Golf Digest*, *Newsweek*, or *Rolling Stone*. Magazines usually require you to prepay the yearly subscription price before you receive any issues. When should the magazine company record revenue from the subscriptions? As we discussed in Chapter 2, sometimes revenues are earned and expenses are incurred at the point cash is received or paid. For transactions such as magazine subscriptions, the revenue is earned when the magazine is delivered, not when the cash is received. Most companies are required to account for revenues and expenses when the benefit is substantially provided or consumed, which may not be when cash is received or paid.

One company that records revenue from subscriptions is Marvel Entertainment, Inc. Marvel began in 1939 as a comic book publishing company, establishing such popular comic book characters as Spider-Man®, X-Men®, Fantastic Four®, and the Avengers®. From these humble beginnings, Marvel has grown into a full-line, multi-billion-dollar entertainment company. Marvel not only publishes comic books, but it has also added feature films, such as the *Spider-Man* movies, video games, and toys to its product offerings.

Most companies, like Marvel Entertainment, are required to update their accounting records for items such as revenues earned from magazine subscriptions before preparing their financial statements. In this chapter, we describe and illustrate this updating process.

Nature of the Adjusting Process

objective 1

Describe the nature of the adjusting process.

REAL WORLD

American Airlines uses the accrual basis of accounting. Revenues are recognized when passengers take flights, not when the passenger makes the reservation or pays for the ticket.

When accountants prepare financial statements, they assume that the economic life of the business can be divided into time periods. Using this **accounting period concept**, accountants must determine in which period the revenues and expenses of the business should be reported. To determine the proper period, accountants use generally accepted accounting principles, which require the use of the accrual basis of accounting.

Under the **accrual basis of accounting**, revenues are reported in the income statement in the period in which they are earned. For example, revenue is reported when the services are provided to customers. Cash may or may not be received from customers during this period. The accounting concept that supports this reporting of revenues is called the **revenue recognition concept**.

Under the accrual basis, expenses are reported in the same period as the revenues to which they relate. For example, employee wages are reported as an expense in the period in which the employees provided services to customers, and not necessarily when the wages are paid. The accounting concept that supports reporting revenues and related expenses in the same period is called the **matching concept**, or **matching principle**. By matching revenues and expenses, net income or loss for the period will be properly reported on the income statement.

Although generally accepted accounting principles require the accrual basis of accounting, some businesses use the **cash basis of accounting**. Under the cash basis of accounting, revenues and expenses are reported in the income statement in the period in which cash is received or paid. For example, fees are recorded when cash is received from clients, and wages are recorded when cash is paid to employees. The net income (or net loss) is the difference between the cash receipts (revenues) and the cash payments (expenses).

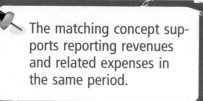

The matching concept supports reporting revenues and related expenses in the same period.

Small service businesses may use the cash basis, because they have few receivables and payables. For example, attorneys, physicians, and real estate agents often use the cash basis. For them, the cash basis will yield financial statements similar to those prepared under the accrual basis. For most large businesses, the cash basis will not provide accurate financial statements for user needs. For this reason, we will emphasize the accrual basis in this text.

THE ADJUSTING PROCESS

At the end of an accounting period, many of the balances of accounts in the ledger can be reported, without change, in the financial statements. For example, the balances of the cash and land accounts are normally the amount reported on the balance sheet.

Under the accrual basis, however, some accounts in the ledger require updating.[1] For example, the balances listed for prepaid expenses are normally overstated because the use of these assets is not recorded on a day-to-day basis. The balance of the supplies account usually represents the cost of supplies at the beginning of the period plus the cost of supplies acquired during the period. To record the daily use of supplies would require many entries with small amounts. In addition, the total amount of supplies is small relative to other assets, and managers usually do not require day-to-day information about supplies.

All adjusting entries affect at least one income statement account and one balance sheet account.

The analysis and updating of accounts at the end of the period before the financial statements are prepared is called the **adjusting process**. The journal entries that bring the accounts up to date at the end of the accounting period are called **adjusting entries**. All adjusting entries affect at least one income statement account and one balance sheet account. Thus, an adjusting entry will *always* involve a revenue or an expense account *and* an asset or a liability account. In the next section, we describe how to determine if an account needs adjusting.

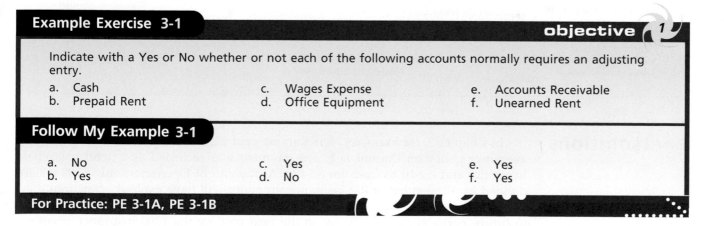

Example Exercise 3-1   objective **1**

Indicate with a Yes or No whether or not each of the following accounts normally requires an adjusting entry.

a. Cash
b. Prepaid Rent
c. Wages Expense
d. Office Equipment
e. Accounts Receivable
f. Unearned Rent

Follow My Example 3-1

a. No
b. Yes
c. Yes
d. No
e. Yes
f. Yes

For Practice: PE 3-1A, PE 3-1B

TYPES OF ACCOUNTS REQUIRING ADJUSTMENT

Is there an easy way to know when an adjusting entry is needed? Yes, four basic types of accounts require adjusting entries. These accounts are prepaid expenses, unearned revenues, accrued revenues, and accrued expenses.

---

1 Under the cash basis of accounting, accounts do not require adjusting. This is because transactions are recorded only when cash is received or paid. Thus, the matching concept is not used under the cash basis.

The tuition you pay at the beginning of each term is an example of a prepaid expense to you, as a student.

Prepaid expenses, sometimes referred to as *deferred expenses*, are items that have been initially recorded as assets but are expected to become expenses over time or through the normal operations of the business. Supplies and prepaid insurance are two examples of prepaid expenses that may require adjustment at the end of an accounting period. Other examples include prepaid advertising and prepaid interest.

Unearned revenues, sometimes referred to as *deferred revenues*, are items that have been initially recorded as liabilities but are expected to become revenues over time or through the normal operations of the business. An example of unearned revenue is unearned rent. Other examples include tuition received in advance by a school, an annual retainer fee received by an attorney, premiums received in advance by an insurance company, and magazine subscriptions received in advance by a publisher.

Prepaid expenses and unearned revenues are created from transactions that involve the receipt or payment of cash. In both cases, the recording of the related expense or revenue is delayed until the end of the period or to a future period as illustrated in Exhibit 1.

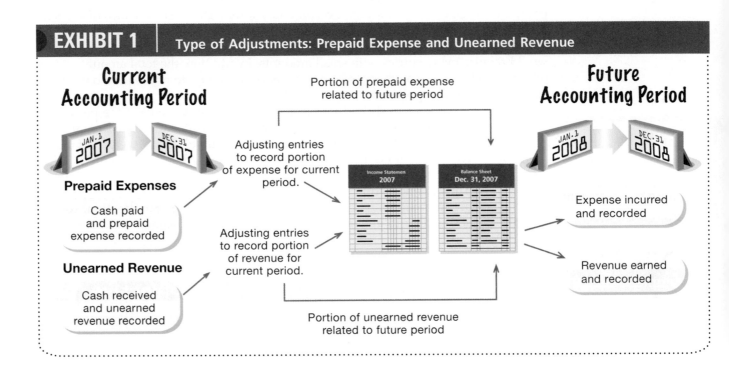

EXHIBIT 1 | Type of Adjustments: Prepaid Expense and Unearned Revenue

@netsolutions

In Chapter 2, for example, NetSolutions paid $2,400 as a premium on a one-year insurance policy on December 1. The payment was recorded as a debit to Prepaid Insurance and credit to Cash for $2,400. At the end of December, only $200 ($2,400 divided by 12 months) of the insurance premium will have expired as insurance expense, and the recording of the remaining $2,200 of insurance expense will be delayed to future periods. As we will see in the next section, the $200 insurance premium expiring in December will be recorded as insurance expense at the end of December, using an adjusting entry.

Accrued revenues, sometimes referred to as *accrued assets*, are revenues that have been earned but have not been recorded in the accounts. An example of an accrued revenue is fees for services that an attorney has provided but hasn't billed to the client at the end of the period. Other examples include unbilled commissions by a travel agent, accrued interest on notes receivable, and accrued rent on property rented to others.

Accrued expenses, sometimes referred to as *accrued liabilities*, are expenses that have been incurred but have not been recorded in the accounts. An example of an accrued expense is accrued wages owed to employees at the end of a period. Other examples include accrued interest on notes payable and accrued taxes.

Accrued revenues and expenses are created by an unrecorded revenue that has been earned or an unrecorded expense that has been incurred. For example, in the next section, we will record accrued revenues and accrued wages expense for NetSolutions at the end of December by using adjusting entries. Prior to recording the adjusting entries, neither accrued revenues nor accrued wages have been recorded. The nature of accrued revenues and expenses is illustrated in Exhibit 2.

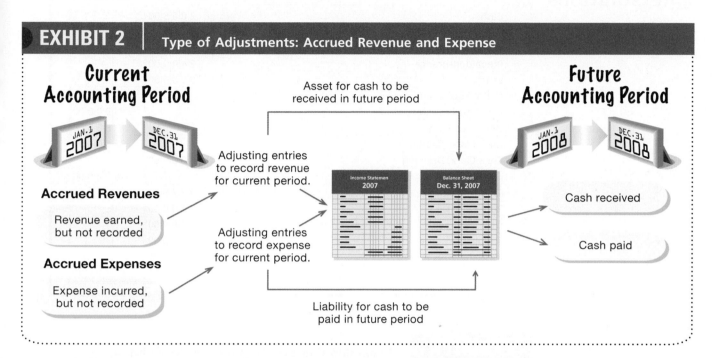

EXHIBIT 2 | Type of Adjustments: Accrued Revenue and Expense

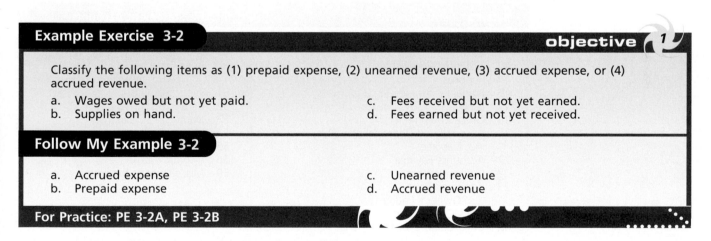

Example Exercise 3-2   objective 1

Classify the following items as (1) prepaid expense, (2) unearned revenue, (3) accrued expense, or (4) accrued revenue.

a. Wages owed but not yet paid.   c. Fees received but not yet earned.
b. Supplies on hand.   d. Fees earned but not yet received.

Follow My Example 3-2

a. Accrued expense   c. Unearned revenue
b. Prepaid expense   d. Accrued revenue

For Practice: PE 3-2A, PE 3-2B

Recording Adjusting Entries

objective 2

Journalize entries for accounts requiring adjustment.

The examples of adjusting entries in the following paragraphs are based on the ledger of NetSolutions as reported in the December 31, 2007, unadjusted trial balance in Exhibit 3.

An expanded chart of accounts for NetSolutions is shown in Exhibit 4. The additional accounts that will be used in this chapter are shown in color. In addition, the adjusting entries are shown in color in T accounts to separate them from other transactions.

EXHIBIT 3

Unadjusted Trial
Balance for
NetSolutions

@netsolutions

NetSolutions
Unadjusted Trial Balance
December 31, 2007

	Debit Balances	Credit Balances
Cash	2 0 6 5 00	
Accounts Receivable	2 2 2 0 00	
Supplies	2 0 0 0 00	
Prepaid Insurance	2 4 0 0 00	
Land	20 0 0 0 00	
Office Equipment	1 8 0 0 00	
Accounts Payable		9 0 0 00
Unearned Rent		3 6 0 00
Chris Clark, Capital		25 0 0 0 00
Chris Clark, Drawing	4 0 0 0 00	
Fees Earned		16 3 4 0 00
Wages Expense	4 2 7 5 00	
Rent Expense	1 6 0 0 00	
Utilities Expense	9 8 5 00	
Supplies Expense	8 0 0 00	
Miscellaneous Expense	4 5 5 00	
	42 6 0 0 00	42 6 0 0 00

EXHIBIT 4   **Expanded Chart of Accounts for NetSolutions**

Balance Sheet Accounts		Income Statement Accounts	
	1. Assets		4. Revenue
11	Cash	41	Fees Earned
12	Accounts Receivable	42	Rent Revenue
14	Supplies		5. Expenses
15	Prepaid Insurance	51	Wages Expense
17	Land	52	Rent Expense
18	Office Equipment	53	Depreciation Expense
19	Accumulated Depreciation—Equipment	54	Utilities Expense
	2. Liabilities	55	Supplies Expense
21	Accounts Payable	56	Insurance Expense
22	Wages Payable	59	Miscellaneous Expense
23	Unearned Rent		
	3. Owner's Equity		
31	Chris Clark, Capital		
32	Chris Clark, Drawing		

PREPAID EXPENSES

The concept of adjusting accounting records was introduced in Chapters 1 and 2 in the illustration for NetSolutions. In that illustration, supplies were purchased on November 10 [transaction (c)]. The supplies used during November were recorded on November 30 [transaction (g)].

The balance in NetSolutions' supplies account on December 31 is $2,000. Some of these supplies (CDs, paper, envelopes, etc.) were used during December, and some are still on hand (not used). If either amount is known, the other can be determined. It is normally easier to determine the cost of the supplies on hand at the end of the month than it is to keep a daily record of those used. Assuming that on December 31 the amount of supplies on hand is $760, the amount to be transferred from the asset account to the expense account is $1,240, computed as follows:

2860

Supplies available during December (balance of account)	$2,000	*124S*
Supplies on hand, December 31	760	*1349*
Supplies used (amount of adjustment)	$1,240	

As we discussed in Chapter 2, increases in expense accounts are recorded as debits and decreases in asset accounts are recorded as credits. At the end of December, the supplies expense account should be debited for $1,240, and the supplies account should be credited for $1,240 to record the supplies used during December. The adjusting journal entry and T accounts for Supplies and Supplies Expense are as follows:

2007 Dec.	31	Supplies Expense	55	1 2 4 0 00	
		Supplies	14		1 2 4 0 00
		Supplies used ($2,000 − $760).			

Supplies

Bal.	2,000	Dec. 31	1,240
Adj. Bal.	760		

Supplies Expense

Bal.	800
Dec. 31	1,240
Adj. Bal.	2,040

After the adjustment has been recorded and posted, the supplies account has a debit balance of $760. This balance represents an asset that will become an expense in a future period.

The debit balance of $2,400 in NetSolutions' prepaid insurance account represents a December 1 prepayment of insurance for 12 months. At the end of December, the insurance expense account should be increased (debited), and the prepaid insurance account should be decreased (credited) by $200, the insurance for one month. The adjusting journal entry and T accounts for Prepaid Insurance and Insurance Expense are as follows:

	31	Insurance Expense	56	2 0 0 00	
		Prepaid Insurance	15		2 0 0 00
		Insurance expired ($2,400/12).			

Prepaid Insurance

Bal.	2,400	Dec. 31	200
Adj. Bal.	2,200		

Insurance Expense

Dec. 31	200

Integrity, Objectivity, and Ethics in Business

FREE ISSUE

Office supplies are often available to employees on a "free issue" basis. This means that employees do not have to "sign" for the release of office supplies but merely obtain the necessary supplies from a local storage area as needed. Just because supplies are easily available, however, doesn't mean they can be taken for personal use. There are many instances where employees have been terminated for taking supplies home for personal use.

> The adjusted balance of a prepaid expense is an asset that will become an expense in a future period.

After the adjustment has been recorded and posted, the prepaid insurance account has a debit balance of $2,200. This balance represents an asset that will become an expense in future periods. The insurance expense account has a debit balance of $200, which is an expense of the current period.

What is the effect of omitting adjusting entries? If the preceding adjustments for supplies ($1,240) and insurance ($200) are not recorded, the financial statements prepared as of December 31 will be misstated. On the income statement, Supplies Expense and Insurance Expense will be understated by a total of $1,440, and net income will be overstated by $1,440. On the balance sheet, Supplies and Prepaid Insurance will be overstated by a total of $1,440. Since net income increases owner's equity, Chris Clark, Capital will also be overstated by $1,440 on the balance sheet. The effects of omitting these adjusting entries on the income statement and balance sheet are as follows:

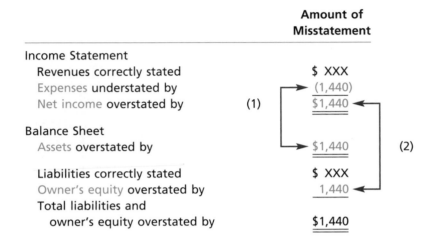

Arrow (1) indicates the effect of the understated expenses on assets. Arrow (2) indicates the effect of the overstated net income on owner's equity.

Prepayments of expenses are sometimes made at the beginning of the period in which they will be *entirely consumed*. On December 1, for example, NetSolutions paid rent of $800 for the month. On December 1, the rent payment represents the asset prepaid rent. The prepaid rent expires daily, and at the end of December, the entire amount has become an expense (rent expense). In cases such as this, the initial payment is recorded as an expense rather than as an asset. Thus, if the payment is recorded as a debit to Rent Expense, no adjusting entry is needed at the end of the period.[2]

Example Exercise 3-3   objective 2

The prepaid insurance account had a beginning balance of $6,400 and was debited for $3,600 of premiums paid during the year. Journalize the adjusting entry required at the end of the year assuming the amount of unexpired insurance related to future periods is $3,250.

Follow My Example 3-3

Insurance Expense 6,750
    Prepaid Insurance 6,750
      Insurance expired ($6,400 + $3,600 − $3,250).

For Practice: PE 3-3A, PE 3-3B

---

2 This alternative treatment of recording the cost of supplies, rent, and other prepayments of expenses is discussed in an appendix that can be downloaded from the book's companion Web site.

UNEARNED REVENUES

According to NetSolutions' trial balance on December 31, the balance in the unearned rent account is $360. This balance represents the receipt of three months' rent on December 1 for December, January, and February. At the end of December, the unearned rent account should be decreased (debited) by $120, and the rent revenue account should be increased (credited) by $120. The $120 represents the rental revenue for one month ($360/3). The adjusting journal entry and T accounts are shown below.

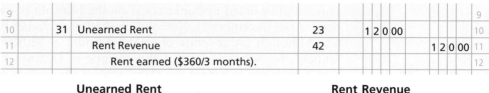

9						9
10	31	Unearned Rent	23	1 2 0 00		10
11		Rent Revenue	42		1 2 0 00	11
12		Rent earned ($360/3 months).				12

Unearned Rent				**Rent Revenue**		
Dec. 31	120	Bal.	360		Dec. 31	120
		Adj. Bal.	240			

After the adjustment has been recorded and posted, the unearned rent account, which is a liability, has a credit balance of $240. This amount represents a deferral that will become revenue in a future period. The rent revenue account has a balance of $120, which is revenue of the current period.[3]

If the preceding adjustment of unearned rent and rent revenue is not recorded, the financial statements prepared on December 31 will be misstated. On the income statement, Rent Revenue and the net income will be understated by $120. On the balance sheet, Unearned Rent will be overstated by $120, and Chris Clark, Capital will be understated by $120. The effects of omitting this adjusting entry are shown below.

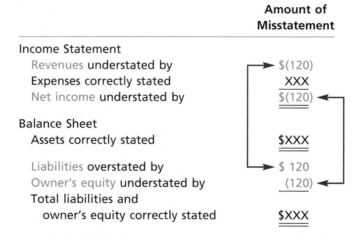

	Amount of Misstatement
Income Statement	
Revenues **understated by**	$(120)
Expenses **correctly stated**	XXX
Net income **understated by**	$(120)
Balance Sheet	
Assets **correctly stated**	$XXX
Liabilities **overstated by**	$ 120
Owner's equity **understated by**	(120)
Total liabilities and owner's equity **correctly stated**	$XXX

Example Exercise 3-4   objective 2

The balance in the unearned fees account, before adjustment at the end of the year, is $44,900. Journalize the adjusting entry required if the amount of unearned fees at the end of the year is $22,300.

Follow My Example 3-4

Unearned Fees	22,600	
Fees Earned		22,600
Fees earned ($44,900 − $22,300).		

For Practice: PE 3-4A, PE 3-4B

---

3 An alternative treatment of recording revenues received in advance of their being earned is discussed in an appendix that can be downloaded from the book's companion Web site (www.thomsonedu.com/accounting/warren).

ACCRUED REVENUES

During an accounting period, some revenues are recorded only when cash is received. Thus, at the end of an accounting period, there may be items of revenue that have been earned *but have not been recorded*. In such cases, the amount of the revenue should be recorded by debiting an asset account and crediting a revenue account.

To illustrate, assume that NetSolutions signed an agreement with Dankner Co. on December 15. The agreement provides that NetSolutions will be on call to answer computer questions and render assistance to Dankner Co.'s employees. The services provided will be billed to Dankner Co. on the fifteenth of each month at a rate of $20 per hour. As of December 31, NetSolutions had provided 25 hours of assistance to Dankner Co. Although the revenue of $500 (25 hours × $20) will be billed and collected in January, NetSolutions earned the revenue in December. The adjusting journal entry and T accounts to record the claim against the customer (an account receivable) and the fees earned in December are shown below.

RadioShack Corporation is engaged in consumer electronics retailing. RadioShack accrues revenue for finance charges, late charges, and returned check fees related to its credit operations.

14	31	Accounts Receivable	12	500 00	14
15		Fees Earned	41		500 00 15
16		Accrued fees (25 hrs. × $20)			16

Accounts Receivable

Bal.	2,220
Dec. 31	500
Adj. Bal.	2,720

Fees Earned

Bal.	16,340
Dec. 31	500
Adj. Bal.	16,840

If the adjustment for the accrued asset ($500) is not recorded, Fees Earned and the net income will be understated by $500 on the income statement. On the balance sheet, Accounts Receivable and Chris Clark, Capital will be understated by $500. The effects of omitting this adjusting entry are shown below.

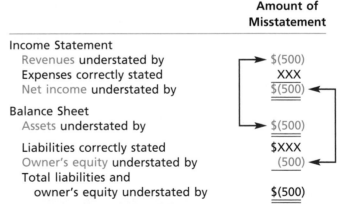

	Amount of Misstatement
Income Statement	
Revenues understated by	$(500)
Expenses correctly stated	XXX
Net income understated by	$(500)
Balance Sheet	
Assets understated by	$(500)
Liabilities correctly stated	$XXX
Owner's equity understated by	(500)
Total liabilities and	
owner's equity understated by	$(500)

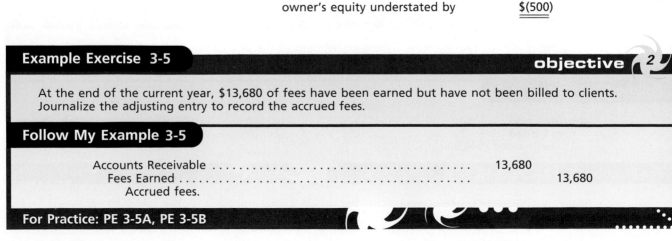

Example Exercise 3-5   **objective 2**

At the end of the current year, $13,680 of fees have been earned but have not been billed to clients. Journalize the adjusting entry to record the accrued fees.

Follow My Example 3-5

Accounts Receivable	13,680	
Fees Earned		13,680
Accrued fees.		

For Practice: PE 3-5A, PE 3-5B

ACCRUED EXPENSES

Some types of services, such as insurance, are normally paid for *before* they are used. These prepayments are deferrals. Other types of services are paid for *after* the service has been performed. For example, wages expense accumulates or *accrues* hour by hour and day by day, but payment may be made only weekly, biweekly, or monthly. The amount of such an accrued but unpaid item at the end of the accounting period is both an expense and a liability. In the case of wages expense, if the last day of a pay period is not the last day of the accounting period, the accrued wages expense and the related liability must be recorded in the accounts by an adjusting entry. This adjusting entry is necessary so that expenses are properly matched to the period in which they were incurred.

At the end of December, accrued wages for NetSolutions were $250. This amount is an additional expense of December and is debited to the wages expense account. It is also a liability as of December 31 and is credited to Wages Payable. The adjusting journal entry and T accounts are as follows:

17					17
18	31	Wages Expense	51	2 5 0 00	18
19		Wages Payable	22	2 5 0 00	19
20		Accrued wages.			20

Wages Expense		Wages Payable	
Bal.	4,275		
Dec. 31	250 ←	Dec. 31 →	250
Adj. Bal.	4,525		

Callaway Golf Company, a manufacturer of such innovative golf clubs as the "Big Bertha" driver, reports accrued warranty expense on its balance sheet.

After the adjustment has been recorded and posted, the debit balance of the wages expense account is $4,525, which is the wages expense for the two months, November and December. The credit balance of $250 in Wages Payable is the amount of the liability for wages owed as of December 31.

The accrual of the wages expense for NetSolutions is summarized in Exhibit 5, on page 114. Note that NetSolutions paid wages of $950 on December 13 and $1,200 on December 27. These payments covered the biweekly pay periods that ended on those days. The wages of $250 incurred for Monday and Tuesday, December 30 and 31, are accrued at December 31. The wages paid on January 10 totaled $1,275, which included the $250 accrued wages of December 31. The payment of the January 10 wages is recorded by debiting Wages Expense for $1,025, debiting Wages Payable for $250, and crediting Cash for $1,275, as shown below.[4]

21						21
22	Jan.	10	Wages Expense	1 0 2 5 00		22
23			Wages Payable	2 5 0 00		23
24			Cash		1 2 7 5 00	24

What would be the effect on the financial statements if the adjustment for wages ($250) is not recorded? On the income statement, Wages Expense will be understated by $250, and the net income will be overstated by $250. On the balance sheet, Wages

---

4 To simplify the subsequent recording of the following period's transactions, some accountants use what is known as reversing entries for certain types of adjustments. Reversing entries are discussed and illustrated in an appendix at the end of the textbook.

EXHIBIT 5

Accrued Wages

1. Wages are paid on the second and fourth Fridays for the two-week periods ending on those Fridays. The payments were $950 on December 13 and $1,200 on December 27.

2. The wages accrued for Monday and Tuesday, December 30 and 31, are $250.

3. Wages paid on Friday, January 10, total $1,275.

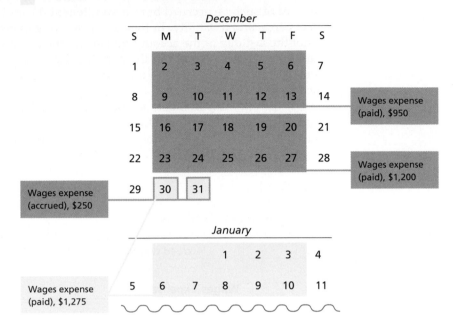

Payable will be understated by $250, and Chris Clark, Capital will be overstated by $250. The effects of omitting this adjusting entry are shown as follows:

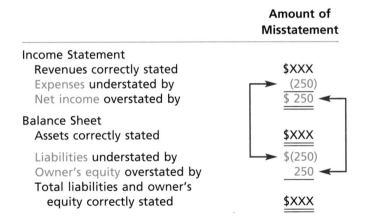

	Amount of Misstatement
Income Statement	
Revenues correctly stated	$XXX
Expenses **understated** by	(250)
Net income **overstated** by	$ 250
Balance Sheet	
Assets correctly stated	$XXX
Liabilities **understated** by	$(250)
Owner's equity **overstated** by	250
Total liabilities and owner's equity correctly stated	$XXX

Example Exercise 3-6   objective 2

Sanregret Realty Co. pays weekly salaries of $12,500 on Friday for a five-day week ending on that day. Journalize the necessary adjusting entry at the end of the accounting period, assuming that the period ends on Thursday.

Follow My Example 3-6

Salaries Expense	10,000	
Salaries Payable		10,000
Accrued salaries [($12,500/5 days) × 4 days].		

For Practice: PE 3-6A, PE 3-6B

DEPRECIATION EXPENSE

Physical resources that are owned and used by a business and are permanent or have a long life are called **fixed assets**, or **plant assets**. In a sense, fixed assets are a type of long-term prepaid expense. Because of their nature and long life, they are discussed separately from other prepaid expenses, such as supplies and prepaid insurance.

NetSolutions' fixed assets include office equipment, which is used much like supplies are used to generate revenue. Unlike supplies, however, there is no visible reduction in the quantity of the equipment. Instead, as time passes, the equipment loses its ability to provide useful services. This decrease in usefulness is called **depreciation**.

All fixed assets, except land, lose their usefulness. Decreases in the usefulness of assets that are used in generating revenue are recorded as expenses. However, such decreases for fixed assets are difficult to measure. For this reason, a portion of the cost of a fixed asset is recorded as an expense each year of its useful life. This periodic expense is called **depreciation expense**. Methods of computing depreciation expense are discussed and illustrated in a later chapter.

Lowe's Companies, Inc., reported land, buildings, and store equipment at a cost of over $18 billion and accumulated depreciation of over $4.1 billion.

The adjusting entry to record depreciation is similar to the adjusting entry for supplies used. The account debited is a depreciation expense account. However, the asset account Office Equipment is not credited because both the original cost of a fixed asset and the amount of depreciation recorded since its purchase are normally reported on the balance sheet. The account credited is an **accumulated depreciation** account. Accumulated depreciation accounts are called **contra accounts**, or **contra asset accounts**, because they are deducted from the related asset accounts on the balance sheet. The normal balance of a contra account is opposite to the account from which it is deducted. Thus, the normal balance for Accumulated Depreciation is a credit.

Normal titles for fixed asset accounts and their related contra asset accounts are as follows:

Fixed Asset	Contra Asset
Land	None—Land is not depreciated.
Buildings	Accumulated Depreciation—Buildings
Store Equipment	Accumulated Depreciation—Store Equipment
Office Equipment	Accumulated Depreciation—Office Equipment

The adjusting entry to record depreciation for December for NetSolutions is illustrated in the following journal entry and T accounts. The estimated amount of depreciation for the month is assumed to be $50.

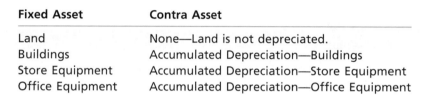

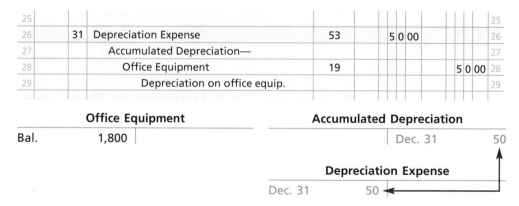

The $50 increase in the accumulated depreciation account is subtracted from the $1,800 cost recorded in the related fixed asset account. The difference between the two balances is the $1,750 cost that has not yet been depreciated. This amount ($1,750) is called the **book value of the asset** (or **net book value**), which may be presented on the balance sheet in the following manner:

Office equipment	$1,800	
Less accumulated depreciation	50	$1,750

You should note that the market value of a fixed asset usually differs from its book value. This is because depreciation is an *allocation* method, not a *valuation* method. That is, depreciation allocates the cost of a fixed asset to expense over its estimated life. Depreciation does not attempt to measure changes in market values, which may vary significantly from year to year.

If the previous adjustment for depreciation ($50) is not recorded, Depreciation Expense on the income statement will be understated by $50, and the net income will be overstated by $50. On the balance sheet, the book value of Office Equipment and Chris Clark, Capital will be overstated by $50. The effects of omitting the adjustment for depreciation are shown below.

	Amount of Misstatement
Income Statement	
Revenues correctly stated	$XX
Expenses understated by	(50)
Net income overstated by	$ 50
Balance Sheet	
Assets overstated by	$ 50
Liabilities correctly stated	$XX
Owner's equity overstated by	50
Total liabilities and owner's equity overstated by	$ 50

Example Exercise 3-7   objective 2

The estimated amount of depreciation on equipment for the current year is $4,250. Journalize the adjusting entry to record the depreciation.

Follow My Example 3-7

Depreciation Expense	4,250	
Accumulated Depreciation—Equipment		4,250
Depreciation on equipment.		

For Practice: PE 3-7A, PE 3-7B

Summary of Adjustment Process

objective 3

Summarize the adjustment process.

@netsolutions

We have described and illustrated the basic types of adjusting entries in the preceding section. A summary of these basic adjustments, including the type of adjustment, the adjusting entry, and the effect of the adjustment on the financial statements, is shown in Exhibit 6. As Exhibit 6 illustrates, each adjustment affects the income statement and balance sheet.

The adjusting entries for NetSolutions that we illustrated in this chapter are shown in Exhibit 7, on page 118. The adjusting entries are dated as of the last day of the period. However, because some time may be needed for collecting the adjustment information, the entries are usually recorded at a later date. Each adjusting entry is normally supported by an explanation. These adjusting entries have been posted to the ledger for NetSolutions shown in Exhibit 8, on pages 119–120. The adjustments are shown in color in Exhibit 8 to distinguish them from other transactions.

EXHIBIT 6 Summary of Adjustments

Financial Statement Effect of Adjustment
Increase (Decrease)

Type of Adjustment	Adjusting Entry			Revenues	− Expenses	= Income	Assets	= Liabilities	+ Owner's Equity
				Income Statement		Net	Balance Sheet		Owner's
Prepaid Expenses									
Supplies	Supplies Exp.	1,240			1,240	(1,240)			
	Supplies		1,240				(1,240)		(1,240)
Prepaid Insurance	Insurance Exp.	200			200	(200)			
	Prepaid Ins.		200				(200)		(200)
Unearned Revenue									
Unearned Rent	Unearned Rent	120						(120)	120
	Rent Revenue		120	120		120			
Accrued Revenue									
Accrued Fees	Accts. Receivable	500					500		500
	Fees Earned		500	500		500			
Accrued Expense									
Accrued Wages	Wages Expense	250			250	(250)			
	Wages Payable		250					250	(250)
Depreciation Expense									
Office Equipment	Depreciation Exp.	50			50	(50)			
	Acc. Dep. —								
	Office Equip.		50				(50)		(50)

Example Exercise 3-8

objective 3

For the year ending December 31, 2008, Mann Medical Co. mistakenly omitted adjusting entries for (1) $8,600 of unearned revenue that was earned, (2) earned revenue that was not billed of $12,500, and (3) accrued wages of $2,900. Indicate the combined effect of the errors on (a) revenues, (b) expenses, and (c) net income for 2008.

Follow My Example 3-8

a. Revenues were understated by $21,100 ($8,600 + $12,500).
b. Expenses were understated by $2,900.
c. Net income was understated by $18,200 ($8,600 + $12,500 − $2,900).

For Practice: PE 3-8A, PE 3-8B

EXHIBIT 7

Adjusting Entries—
NetSolutions

	Date		Description	Post. Ref.	Debit	Credit	
1			Adjusting Entries				1
2	2007 Dec.	31	Supplies Expense	55	1 2 4 0 00		2
3			Supplies	14		1 2 4 0 00	3
4			Supplies used ($2,000 − $760).				4
5							5
6		31	Insurance Expense	56	2 0 0 00		6
7			Prepaid Insurance	15		2 0 0 00	7
8			Insurance expired ($2,400/12 months).				8
9							9
10		31	Unearned Rent	23	1 2 0 00		10
11			Rent Revenue	42		1 2 0 00	11
12			Rent earned ($360/3 months).				12
13							13
14		31	Accounts Receivable	12	5 0 0 00		14
15			Fees Earned	41		5 0 0 00	15
16			Accrued fees (25 hrs. × $20).				16
17							17
18		31	Wages Expense	51	2 5 0 00		18
19			Wages Payable	22		2 5 0 00	19
20			Accrued wages.				20
21							21
22		31	Depreciation Expense	53	5 0 00		22
23			Accum. Depr.—Office Equip.	19		5 0 00	23
24			Depreciation on office equip.				24
25							25

JOURNAL   Page 5

REAL WORLD

One way for an accountant to check whether all adjustments have been made is to compare the current period's adjustments with those of the prior period.

Business Connections

REAL WORLD

Microsoft Corporation develops, manufactures, licenses, and supports a wide range of computer software products, including Windows XP®, Windows NT®, Word®, Excel®, and the Xbox® gaming system. When Microsoft sells its products, it incurs an obligation to support its software with technical support and periodic updates. As a result, not all the revenue is earned on the date of sale; some of the revenue on the date of sale is unearned. The portion of revenue related to support services, such as updates and technical support, is earned as time passes and support is provided to customers. Thus, each year Microsoft makes adjusting entries transferring some of its unearned revenue to revenue. The following excerpts were taken from Microsoft's 2005 financial statements.

The percentage of revenue recorded as unearned . . . ranges from approximately 15% to 25% of the sales price for Windows XP Home, approximately 5% to 15% of the sales price for Windows XP Professional, and approximately 1% to 15% of the sales price for desktop applications . . .

Unearned Revenue:

	June 30, 2005	June 30, 2004
Unearned revenue (in millions)	$9,167	$8,177

During the year ending June 30, 2006, Microsoft expects to record over $7,500 million of unearned revenue as revenue.

At the same time, Microsoft will record additional unearned revenue from current period sales.

Source: Taken from Microsoft's June 30, 2005, annual report.

EXHIBIT 8   Ledger with Adjusting Entries—NetSolutions

ACCOUNT *Cash*   **ACCOUNT NO.** *11*

Date	Item	Post. Ref.	Debit	Credit	Balance Debit	Balance Credit
2007 Nov. 1		1	25,000		25,000	
5		1		20,000	5,000	
18		1	7,500		12,500	
30		1		3,650	8,850	
30		1		950	7,900	
30		2		2,000	5,900	
Dec. 1		2		2,400	3,500	
1		2		800	2,700	
1		2	360		3,060	
6		2		180	2,880	
11		2		400	2,480	
13		3		950	1,530	
16		3	3,100		4,630	
20		3		900	3,730	
21		3	650		4,380	
23		3		1,450	2,930	
27		3		1,200	1,730	
31		3		310	1,420	
31		4		225	1,195	
31		4	2,870		4,065	
31		4		2,000	2,065	

ACCOUNT *Accounts Receivable*   **ACCOUNT NO.** *12*

Date	Item	Post. Ref.	Debit	Credit	Balance Debit	Balance Credit
2007 Dec. 16		3	1,750		1,750	
21		3		650	1,100	
31		4	1,120		2,220	
31	Adjusting	5	500		2,720	

ACCOUNT *Supplies*   **ACCOUNT NO.** *14*

Date	Item	Post. Ref.	Debit	Credit	Balance Debit	Balance Credit
2007 Nov. 10		1	1,350		1,350	
30		1		800	550	
Dec. 23		3	1,450		2,000	
31	Adjusting	5		1,240	760	

ACCOUNT *Prepaid Insurance*   **ACCOUNT NO.** *15*

Date	Item	Post. Ref.	Debit	Credit	Balance Debit	Balance Credit
2007 Dec. 1		2	2,400		2,400	
31	Adjusting	5		200	2,200	

ACCOUNT *Land*   **ACCOUNT NO.** *17*

Date	Item	Post. Ref.	Debit	Credit	Balance Debit	Balance Credit
2007 Nov. 5		1	20,000		20,000	

ACCOUNT *Office Equipment*   **ACCOUNT NO.** *18*

Date	Item	Post. Ref.	Debit	Credit	Balance Debit	Balance Credit
2007 Dec. 4		2	1,800		1,800	

ACCOUNT *Acc. Depr.—Equipment*   **ACCOUNT NO.** *19*

Date	Item	Post. Ref.	Debit	Credit	Balance Debit	Balance Credit
2007 Dec. 31	Adjusting	5		50		50

ACCOUNT *Accounts Payable*   **ACCOUNT NO.** *21*

Date	Item	Post. Ref.	Debit	Credit	Balance Debit	Balance Credit
2007 Nov. 10		1		1,350		1,350
30		1	950			400
Dec. 4		2		1,800		2,200
11		2	400			1,800
20		3	900			900

ACCOUNT *Wages Payable*   **ACCOUNT NO.** *22*

Date	Item	Post. Ref.	Debit	Credit	Balance Debit	Balance Credit
2007 Dec. 31	Adjusting	5		250		250

ACCOUNT *Unearned Rent*   **ACCOUNT NO.** *23*

Date	Item	Post. Ref.	Debit	Credit	Balance Debit	Balance Credit
2007 Dec. 1		2		360		360
31	Adjusting	5	120			240

ACCOUNT *Chris Clark, Capital*   **ACCOUNT NO.** *31*

Date	Item	Post. Ref.	Debit	Credit	Balance Debit	Balance Credit
2007 Nov. 1		1		25,000		25,000

(continued)

EXHIBIT 8

ACCOUNT Chris Clark, Drawing		ACCOUNT NO. 32				
Date	Item	Post. Ref.	Debit	Credit	Balance Debit	Balance Credit
2007 Nov. 30		2	2,000		2,000	
Dec. 31		4	2,000		4,000	

ACCOUNT Fees Earned		ACCOUNT NO. 41				
Date	Item	Post. Ref.	Debit	Credit	Balance Debit	Balance Credit
2007 Nov. 18		1		7,500		7,500
Dec. 16		3		3,100		10,600
16		3		1,750		12,350
31		4		2,870		15,220
31		4		1,120		16,340
31	Adjusting	5		500		16,840

ACCOUNT Rent Revenue		ACCOUNT NO. 42				
Date	Item	Post. Ref.	Debit	Credit	Balance Debit	Balance Credit
2007 Dec. 31	Adjusting	5		120		120

ACCOUNT Wages Expense		ACCOUNT NO. 51				
Date	Item	Post. Ref.	Debit	Credit	Balance Debit	Balance Credit
2007 Nov. 30		1	2,125		2,125	
Dec. 13		3	950		3,075	
27		3	1,200		4,275	
31	Adjusting	5	250		4,525	

ACCOUNT Rent Expense		ACCOUNT NO. 52				
Date	Item	Post. Ref.	Debit	Credit	Balance Debit	Balance Credit
2007 Nov. 30		1	800		800	
Dec. 1		2	800		1,600	

ACCOUNT Depreciation Expense		ACCOUNT NO. 53				
Date	Item	Post. Ref.	Debit	Credit	Balance Debit	Balance Credit
2007 Dec. 31	Adjusting	5	50		50	

ACCOUNT Utilities Expense		ACCOUNT NO. 54				
Date	Item	Post. Ref.	Debit	Credit	Balance Debit	Balance Credit
2007 Nov. 30		1	450		450	
Dec. 31		3	310		760	
31		4	225		985	

ACCOUNT Supplies Expense		ACCOUNT NO. 55				
Date	Item	Post. Ref.	Debit	Credit	Balance Debit	Balance Credit
2007 Nov. 30		1	800		800	
Dec. 31	Adjusting	5	1,240		2,040	

ACCOUNT Insurance Expense		ACCOUNT NO. 56				
Date	Item	Post. Ref.	Debit	Credit	Balance Debit	Balance Credit
2007 Dec. 31	Adjusting	5	200		200	

ACCOUNT Miscellaneous Expense		ACCOUNT NO. 59				
Date	Item	Post. Ref.	Debit	Credit	Balance Debit	Balance Credit
2007 Nov. 30		1	275		275	
Dec. 6		2	180		455	

Adjusted Trial Balance

objective **4**

Prepare an adjusted trial balance.

After all the adjusting entries have been posted, another trial balance, called the **adjusted trial balance**, is prepared. The purpose of the adjusted trial balance is to verify the equality of the total debit balances and total credit balances before we prepare the financial statements. If the adjusted trial balance does not balance, an error has occurred. However, as we discussed in Chapter 2, errors may have occurred even though the adjusted trial balance totals agree. For example, the adjusted trial balance totals would agree if an adjusting entry has been omitted.

@netsolutions

Exhibit 9 shows the adjusted trial balance for NetSolutions as of December 31, 2007. In Chapter 4, we discuss how financial statements, including a classified balance sheet, can be prepared from an adjusted trial balance. We also discuss the use of an end-of-period spreadsheet (work sheet) as an aid in summarizing the data for preparing adjusting entries and financial statements.

EXHIBIT 9

Adjusted Trial Balance

NetSolutions
Adjusted Trial Balance
December 31, 2007

	Debit Balances	Credit Balances
Cash	2 0 6 5 00	
Accounts Receivable	2 7 2 0 00	
Supplies	7 6 0 00	
Prepaid Insurance	2 2 0 0 00	
Land	20 0 0 0 00	
Office Equipment	1 8 0 0 00	
Accumulated Depreciation—Equipment		5 0 00
Accounts Payable		9 0 0 00
Wages Payable		2 5 0 00
Unearned Rent		2 4 0 00
Chris Clark, Capital		25 0 0 0 00
Chris Clark, Drawing	4 0 0 0 00	
Fees Earned		16 8 4 0 00
Rent Revenue		1 2 0 00
Wages Expense	4 5 2 5 00	
Rent Expense	1 6 0 0 00	
Depreciation Expense	5 0 00	
Utilities Expense	9 8 5 00	
Supplies Expense	2 0 4 0 00	
Insurance Expense	2 0 0 00	
Miscellaneous Expense	4 5 5 00	
	43 4 0 0 00	43 4 0 0 00

Example Exercise 3-9

objective 4

For each of the following errors, considered individually, indicate whether the error would cause the adjusted trial balance totals to be unequal. If the error would cause the adjusted trial balance totals to be unequal, indicate whether the debit or credit total is higher and by how much.
a. The adjustment for accrued fees of $5,340 was journalized as a debit to Accounts Payable for $5,340 and a credit to Fees Earned of $5,340.
b. The adjustment for depreciation of $3,260 was journalized as a debit to Depreciation Expense for $3,620 and a credit to Accumulated Depreciation for $3,260.

Follow My Example 3-9

a. The totals are equal even though the debit should have been to Accounts Receivable instead of Accounts Payable.
b. The totals are unequal. The debit total is higher by $360 ($3,620 − $3,260).

For Practice: PE 3-9A, PE 3-9B

At a Glance

1. Describe the nature of the adjusting process.

Key Points	Key Learning Outcomes	Example Exercises	Practice Exercises
The accrual basis of accounting requires that revenues are reported in the period in which they are earned and expenses matched with the revenues they generate. The updating of accounts at the end of the accounting period is called the adjusting process. Each adjusting entry affects an income statement and balance sheet account. The four types of accounts requiring adjusting entries are prepaid expenses, unearned revenues, accrued revenues, and accrued expenses.	• Explain why accrual accounting requires adjusting entries. • List accounts that do and do NOT require adjusting entries at the end of the accounting period. • Give an example of a prepaid expense, unearned revenue, accrued revenue, and accrued expense.	3-1 3-2	3-1A, 3-1B 3-2A, 3-2B

2. Journalize entries for accounts requiring adjustment.

Key Points	Key Learning Outcomes	Example Exercises	Practice Exercises
Adjusting entries illustrated in this chapter include prepaid expenses, unearned revenues, accrued revenues, and accrued expenses. In addition, the adjusting entry necessary to record depreciation on fixed assets was illustrated.	• Prepare an adjusting entry for a prepaid expense. • Prepare an adjusting entry for an unearned revenue. • Prepare an adjusting entry for an accrued revenue. • Prepare an adjusting entry for an accrued expense. • Prepare an adjusting entry for depreciation expense.	3-3 3-4 3-5 3-6 3-7	3-3A, 3-3B 3-4A, 3-4B 3-5A, 3-5B 3-6A, 3-6B 3-7A, 3-7B

3. Summarize the adjustment process.

Key Points	Key Learning Outcomes	Example Exercises	Practice Exercises
A summary of adjustments, including the type of adjustment, the adjusting entry, and the effect of omitting an adjustment on the financial statements, is shown in Exhibit 6.	• Determine the effect on the income statement and balance sheet of omitting an adjusting entry for prepaid expense, unearned revenue, accrued revenue, accrued expense, and depreciation.	3-8	3-8A, 3-8B

4. Prepare an adjusted trial balance.

Key Points	Key Learning Outcomes	Example Exercises	Practice Exercises
After all the adjusting entries have been posted, the equality of the total debit balances and total credit balances is verified by an adjusted trial balance.	• Prepare an adjusted trial balance. • Determine the effect of errors on the equality of the adjusted trial balance.	3-9	3-9A, 3-9B

Key Terms

accounting period concept (104)
accrual basis of accounting (104)
accrued expenses (106)
accrued revenues (106)
accumulated depreciation (115)
adjusted trial balance (120)
adjusting entries (105)

adjusting process (105)
book value of the asset (or net book value) (115)
cash basis of accounting (104)
contra account (or contra asset account) (115)
depreciation (115)

depreciation expense (115)
fixed assets (or plant assets) (115)
matching concept (or matching principle) (104)
prepaid expenses (106)
revenue recognition concept (104)
unearned revenues (106)

Illustrative Problem

Three years ago, T. Roderick organized Harbor Realty. At July 31, 2008, the end of the current year, the unadjusted trial balance of Harbor Realty appears as shown below.

Harbor Realty
Unadjusted Trial Balance
July 31, 2008

	Debit Balances	Credit Balances
Cash	3 4 2 5 00	
Accounts Receivable	7 0 0 0 00	
Supplies	1 2 7 0 00	
Prepaid Insurance	6 2 0 00	
Office Equipment	51 6 5 0 00	
Accumulated Depreciation		9 7 0 0 00
Accounts Payable		9 2 5 00
Wages Payable		0 00
Unearned Fees		1 2 5 0 00
T. Roderick, Capital		29 0 0 0 00
T. Roderick, Drawing	5 2 0 0 00	
Fees Earned		59 1 2 5 00
Wages Expense	22 4 1 5 00	
Depreciation Expense	0 00	
Rent Expense	4 2 0 0 00	
Utilities Expense	2 7 1 5 00	
Supplies Expense	0 00	
Insurance Expense	0 00	
Miscellaneous Expense	1 5 0 5 00	
	100 0 0 0 00	100 0 0 0 00

The data needed to determine year-end adjustments are as follows:

a. Supplies on hand at July 31, 2008, $380.
b. Insurance premiums expired during the year, $315.
c. Depreciation of equipment during the year, $4,950.
d. Wages accrued but not paid at July 31, 2008, $440.
e. Accrued fees earned but not recorded at July 31, 2008, $1,000.
f. Unearned fees on July 31, 2008, $750.

Instructions

1. Prepare the necessary adjusting journal entries. Include journal entry explanations.
2. Determine the balance of the accounts affected by the adjusting entries, and prepare an adjusted trial balance.

Solution   **1.**

JOURNAL

	Date		Description	Post. Ref.	Debit	Credit	
1	2008 July	31	Supplies Expense		8 9 0 00		1
2			Supplies			8 9 0 00	2
3			Supplies used ($1,270 − $380).				3
4							4
5		31	Insurance Expense		3 1 5 00		5
6			Prepaid Insurance			3 1 5 00	6
7			Insurance expired.				7
8							8
9		31	Depreciation Expense		4 9 5 0 00		9
10			Accumulated Depreciation			4 9 5 0 00	10
11			Depreciation expense.				11
12							12
13		31	Wages Expense		4 4 0 00		13
14			Wages Payable			4 4 0 00	14
15			Accrued wages.				15
16							16
17		31	Accounts Receivable		1 0 0 0 00		17
18			Fees Earned			1 0 0 0 00	18
19			Accrued fees.				19
20							20
21		31	Unearned Fees		5 0 0 00		21
22			Fees Earned			5 0 0 00	22
23			Fees earned ($1,250 − $750).				23

2.

Harbor Realty
Adjusted Trial Balance
July 31, 2008

	Debit Balances	Credit Balances
Cash	3 4 2 5 00	
Accounts Receivable	8 0 0 0 00	
Supplies	3 8 0 00	
Prepaid Insurance	3 0 5 00	
Office Equipment	51 6 5 0 00	
Accumulated Depreciation		14 6 5 0 00
Accounts Payable		9 2 5 00
Wages Payable		4 4 0 00
Unearned Fees		7 5 0 00
T. Roderick, Capital		29 0 0 0 00
T. Roderick, Drawing	5 2 0 0 00	
Fees Earned		60 6 2 5 00
Wages Expense	22 8 5 5 00	
Depreciation Expense	4 9 5 0 00	
Rent Expense	4 2 0 0 00	
Utilities Expense	2 7 1 5 00	
Supplies Expense	8 9 0 00	
Insurance Expense	3 1 5 00	
Miscellaneous Expense	1 5 0 5 00	
	106 3 9 0 00	106 3 9 0 00

Self-Examination Questions

(Answers at End of Chapter)

1. Which of the following items represents a deferral?
   A. Prepaid insurance
   B. Wages payable
   C. Fees earned
   D. Accumulated depreciation

2. If the supplies account, before adjustment on May 31, indicated a balance of $2,250, and supplies on hand at May 31 totaled $950, the adjusting entry would be:
   A. debit Supplies, $950; credit Supplies Expense, $950.
   B. debit Supplies, $1,300; credit Supplies Expense, $1,300.
   C. debit Supplies Expense, $950; credit Supplies, $950.
   D. debit Supplies Expense, $1,300; credit Supplies, $1,300.

3. The balance in the unearned rent account for Jones Co. as of December 31 is $1,200. If Jones Co. failed to record the adjusting entry for $600 of rent earned during December, the effect on the balance sheet and income statement for December would be:
   A. assets understated $600; net income overstated $600.
   B. liabilities understated $600; net income understated $600.

C. liabilities overstated $600; net income understated $600.
D. liabilities overstated $600; net income overstated $600.

4. If the estimated amount of depreciation on equipment for a period is $2,000, the adjusting entry to record depreciation would be:
   A. debit Depreciation Expense, $2,000; credit Equipment, $2,000.
   B. debit Equipment, $2,000; credit Depreciation Expense, $2,000.
   C. debit Depreciation Expense, $2,000; credit Accumulated Depreciation, $2,000.
   D. debit Accumulated Depreciation, $2,000; credit Depreciation Expense, $2,000.

5. If the equipment account has a balance of $22,500 and its accumulated depreciation account has a balance of $14,000, the book value of the equipment would be:
   A. $36,500.   C. $14,000.
   B. $22,500.   D. $8,500.

Eye Openers

1. How are revenues and expenses reported on the income statement under (a) the cash basis of accounting and (b) the accrual basis of accounting?
2. Fees for services provided are billed to a customer during 2007. The customer remits the amount owed in 2008. During which year would the revenues be reported on the income statement under (a) the cash basis? (b) the accrual basis?
3. Employees performed services in 2007, but the wages were not paid until 2008. During which year would the wages expense be reported on the income statement under (a) the cash basis? (b) the accrual basis?
4. Is the matching concept related to (a) the cash basis of accounting or (b) the accrual basis of accounting?
5. Is the balance listed for cash on the trial balance, before the accounts have been adjusted, the amount that should normally be reported on the balance sheet? Explain.
6. Is the balance listed for supplies on the trial balance, before the accounts have been adjusted, the amount that should normally be reported on the balance sheet? Explain.
7. Why are adjusting entries needed at the end of an accounting period?
8. What is the difference between *adjusting entries* and *correcting entries*?
9. Identify the four different categories of adjusting entries frequently required at the end of an accounting period.
10. If the effect of the credit portion of an adjusting entry is to increase the balance of a liability account, which of the following statements describes the effect of the debit portion of the entry?
    a. Increases the balance of a revenue account.
    b. Increases the balance of an expense account.
    c. Increases the balance of an asset account.
11. If the effect of the debit portion of an adjusting entry is to increase the balance of an asset account, which of the following statements describes the effect of the credit portion of the entry?
    a. Increases the balance of a revenue account.
    b. Increases the balance of an expense account.
    c. Increases the balance of a liability account.

12. Does every adjusting entry have an effect on determining the amount of net income for a period? Explain.

13. What is the nature of the balance in the prepaid insurance account at the end of the accounting period (a) before adjustment? (b) after adjustment?

14. On October 1 of the current year, a business paid the October rent on the building that it occupies. (a) Do the rights acquired at October 1 represent an asset or an expense? (b) What is the justification for debiting Rent Expense at the time of payment?

15. (a) Explain the purpose of the two accounts: Depreciation Expense and Accumulated Depreciation. (b) What is the normal balance of each account? (c) Is it customary for the balances of the two accounts to be equal in amount? (d) In what financial statements, if any, will each account appear?

Practice Exercises

PE 3-1A
Accounts requiring adjustment
obj. 1

Indicate with a Yes or No whether or not each of the following accounts normally requires an adjusting entry.

a. Salaries Payable
b. Land
c. Dana Cates, Drawing
d. Accumulated Depreciation
e. Unearned Rent
f. Supplies

PE 3-1B
Accounts requiring adjustment
obj. 1

Indicate with a Yes or No whether or not each of the following accounts normally requires an adjusting entry.

a. Mary Elizabeth Rebok, Capital
b. Building
c. Prepaid Insurance
d. Cash
e. Interest Payable
f. Miscellaneous Expense

PE 3-2A
Type of adjustment
obj. 1

Classify the following items as (1) prepaid expense, (2) unearned revenue, (3) accrued revenue, or (4) accrued expense.

a. Cash received for services not yet rendered
b. Salaries owed but not yet paid
c. Insurance paid
d. Rent revenue earned but not received

PE 3-2B
Type of adjustment
obj. 1

Classify the following items as (1) prepaid expense, (2) unearned revenue, (3) accrued revenue, or (4) accrued expense.

a. Rent expense owed but not yet paid
b. Fees earned but not received
c. Supplies on hand
d. Cash received for use of land next month

PE 3-3A
Adjustment for supplies used
obj. 2

The supplies account had a beginning balance of $1,245 and was debited for $2,860 for supplies purchased during the year. Journalize the adjusting entry required at the end of the year assuming the amount of supplies on hand is $1,349.

PE 3-3B
Adjustment for insurance expired
obj. 2

The prepaid insurance account had a beginning balance of $4,800 and was debited for $5,850 of premiums paid during the year. Journalize the adjusting entry required at the end of the year assuming the amount of unexpired insurance related to future periods is $4,125.

PE 3-4A
Adjustment for unearned fees
obj. 2

The balance in the unearned fees account, before adjustment at the end of the year, is $23,676. Journalize the adjusting entry required assuming the amount of unearned fees at the end of the year is $7,388.

PE 3-4B
Adjustment for unearned rent
obj. 2

On August 1, 2007, Myopic Co. received $6,900 for the rent of land for 12 months. Journalize the adjusting entry required for unearned rent on December 31, 2007.

PE 3-5A
Adjustment for accrued fees
obj. 2

At the end of the current year, $7,234 of fees have been earned but have not been billed to clients. Journalize the adjusting entry to record the accrued fees.

PE 3-5B
Adjustment for accrued fees
obj. 2

At the end of the current year, $1,772 of fees have been earned but have not been billed to clients. Journalize the adjusting entry to record the accrued fees.

PE 3-6A
Adjustment for salaries payable
obj. 2

Yarbrough Realty Co. pays weekly salaries of $11,875 on Friday for a five-day workweek ending on that day. Journalize the necessary adjusting entry at the end of the accounting period assuming that the period ends on Tuesday.

PE 3-6B
Adjustment for salaries payable
obj. 2

Hobbs Realty Co. pays weekly salaries of $24,840 on Monday for a six-day workweek ending the preceding Saturday. Journalize the necessary adjusting entry at the end of the accounting period assuming that the period ends on Thursday.

PE 3-7A
Adjustment for depreciation
obj. 2

The estimated amount of depreciation on equipment for the current year is $6,450. Journalize the adjusting entry to record the depreciation.

PE 3-7B
Adjustment for depreciation
obj. 2

The estimated amount of depreciation on equipment for the current year is $1,820. Journalize the adjusting entry to record the depreciation.

PE 3-8A
Effect of omitting adjustments
obj. 3

For the year ending February 28, 2007, Miracle Medical Co. mistakenly omitted adjusting entries for (1) depreciation of $2,276, (2) fees earned that were not billed of $9,638, and (3) accrued wages of $780. Indicate the combined effect of the errors on (a) revenues, (b) expenses, and (c) net income for the year ended February 28, 2007.

PE 3-8B
Effect of omitting adjustments
obj. 3

For the year ending June 30, 2008, Ambulatory Medical Services Co. mistakenly omitted adjusting entries for (1) $1,034 of supplies that were used, (2) unearned revenue of $6,481 that was earned, and (3) insurance of $7,500 that expired. Indicate the combined effect of the errors on (a) revenues, (b) expenses, and (c) net income for the year ended June 30, 2008.

PE 3-9A
Effect of errors on adjusted trial balance
obj. 4

For each of the following errors, considered individually, indicate whether the error would cause the adjusted trial balance totals to be unequal. If the error would cause the adjusted trial balance totals to be unequal, indicate whether the debit or credit total is higher and by how much.

a. The adjustment of depreciation of $3,500 was omitted from the end-of-period adjusting entries.

b. The adjustment of $2,565 for accrued fees earned was journalized as a debit to Accounts Receivable for $2,565 and a credit to Fees Earned for $2,556.

PE 3-9B
Effect of errors on adjusted trial balance
obj. 4

For each of the following errors, considered individually, indicate whether the error would cause the adjusted trial balance totals to be unequal. If the error would cause the adjusted trial balance totals to be unequal, indicate whether the debit or credit total is higher and by how much.

a. The entry for $460 of supplies used during the period was journalized as a debit to Supplies Expense of $460 and a credit to Supplies of $640.

b. The adjustment for accrued wages of $1,240 was journalized as a debit to Wages Expense for $1,240 and a credit to Accounts Payable for $1,240.

Exercises

EX 3-1
Classifying types of adjustments
obj. 1

Classify the following items as (a) prepaid expense, (b) unearned revenue, (c) accrued revenue, or (d) accrued expense.

1. Fees earned but not yet received.
2. Taxes owed but payable in the following period.
3. Utilities owed but not yet paid.
4. Salary owed but not yet paid.
5. Supplies on hand.
6. Fees received but not yet earned.
7. A two-year premium paid on a fire insurance policy.
8. Subscriptions received in advance by a magazine publisher.

EX 3-2
Classifying adjusting entries
obj. 1

The following accounts were taken from the unadjusted trial balance of Hartford Co., a congressional lobbying firm. Indicate whether or not each account would normally require an adjusting entry. If the account normally requires an adjusting entry, use the following notation to indicate the type of adjustment:

AE—Accrued Expense
AR—Accrued Revenue
PE—Prepaid Expense
UR—Unearned Revenue

To illustrate, the answer for the first account is shown below.

Account	Answer
Accounts Receivable	Normally requires adjustment (AR).
Cash	
Charmaine Hollis, Drawing	
Interest Payable	
Interest Receivable	
Land	
Office Equipment	
Prepaid Rent	
Supplies	
Unearned Fees	
Wages Expense	

EX 3-3
Adjusting entry for supplies
obj. 2

The balance in the supplies account, before adjustment at the end of the year, is $2,975. Journalize the adjusting entry required if the amount of supplies on hand at the end of the year is $614.

EX 3-4
Determining supplies purchased
obj. 2

The supplies and supplies expense accounts at December 31, after adjusting entries have been posted at the end of the first year of operations, are shown in the following T accounts:

Supplies		Supplies Expense	
Bal.	279	Bal.	1,261

Determine the amount of supplies purchased during the year.

EX 3-5
Effect of omitting adjusting entry
obj. 2

At December 31, the end of the first month of operations, the usual adjusting entry transferring prepaid insurance expired to an expense account is omitted. Which items will be incorrectly stated, because of the error, on (a) the income statement for December and (b) the balance sheet as of December 31? Also indicate whether the items in error will be overstated or understated.

EX 3-6
Adjusting entries for prepaid insurance
obj. 2

The balance in the prepaid insurance account, before adjustment at the end of the year, is $6,175. Journalize the adjusting entry required under each of the following *alternatives* for determining the amount of the adjustment: (a) the amount of insurance expired during the year is $4,180; (b) the amount of unexpired insurance applicable to future periods is $1,995.

EX 3-7
Adjusting entries for prepaid insurance
obj. 2

The prepaid insurance account had a balance of $3,600 at the beginning of the year. The account was debited for $4,800 for premiums on policies purchased during the year. Journalize the adjusting entry required at the end of the year for each of the following situations: (a) the amount of unexpired insurance applicable to future periods is $2,950; (b) the amount of insurance expired during the year is $5,450.

EX 3-8
Adjusting entries for unearned fees
obj. 2

✓ *Amount of entry: $22,320*

The balance in the unearned fees account, before adjustment at the end of the year, is $49,500. Journalize the adjusting entry required if the amount of unearned fees at the end of the year is $27,180.

EX 3-9
Effect of omitting adjusting entry
obj. 2

At the end of August, the first month of the business year, the usual adjusting entry transferring rent earned to a revenue account from the unearned rent account was omitted. Indicate which items will be incorrectly stated, because of the error, on (a) the income statement for August and (b) the balance sheet as of August 31. Also indicate whether the items in error will be overstated or understated.

EX 3-10
Adjusting entry for accrued fees
obj. 2

At the end of the current year, $17,600 of fees have been earned but have not been billed to clients.

a. Journalize the adjusting entry to record the accrued fees.
b. If the cash basis rather than the accrual basis had been used, would an adjusting entry have been necessary? Explain.

EX 3-11
Adjusting entries for unearned and accrued fees
obj. 2

The balance in the unearned fees account, before adjustment at the end of the year, is $39,750. Of these fees, $12,300 have been earned. In addition, $7,100 of fees have been earned but have not been billed. Journalize the adjusting entries (a) to adjust the unearned fees account and (b) to record the accrued fees.

EX 3-12
Effect on financial statements of omitting adjusting entry
obj. 2

The adjusting entry for accrued fees was omitted at December 31, the end of the current year. Indicate which items will be in error, because of the omission, on (a) the income statement for the current year and (b) the balance sheet as of December 31. Also indicate whether the items in error will be overstated or understated.

EX 3-13
Adjusting entries for accrued salaries
obj. 2

✓ a. Amount of entry: $12,375

Ash Realty Co. pays weekly salaries of $20,625 on Friday for a five-day workweek ending on that day. Journalize the necessary adjusting entry at the end of the accounting period assuming that the period ends (a) on Wednesday and (b) on Thursday.

EX 3-14
Determining wages paid
obj. 2

The wages payable and wages expense accounts at March 31, after adjusting entries have been posted at the end of the first month of operations, are shown in the following T accounts:

Wages Payable		Wages Expense	
	Bal. 6,480	Bal. 72,150	

Determine the amount of wages paid during the month.

EX 3-15
Effect of omitting adjusting entry
obj. 2

Accrued salaries of $3,910 owed to employees for December 30 and 31 are not considered in preparing the financial statements for the year ended December 31. Indicate which items will be erroneously stated, because of the error, on (a) the income statement for the year and (b) the balance sheet as of December 31. Also indicate whether the items in error will be overstated or understated.

EX 3-16
Effect of omitting adjusting entry
obj. 2

Assume that the error in Exercise 3-15 was not corrected and that the $3,910 of accrued salaries was included in the first salary payment in January. Indicate which items will be erroneously stated, because of failure to correct the initial error, on (a) the income statement for the month of January and (b) the balance sheet as of January 31.

EX 3-17
Adjusting entries for prepaid and accrued taxes
obj. 2

✓ b. $18,675

Pisces Financial Services was organized on April 1 of the current year. On April 2, Pisces prepaid $3,000 to the city for taxes (license fees) for the *next* 12 months and debited the prepaid taxes account. Pisces is also required to pay in January an annual tax (on property) for the *previous* calendar year. The estimated amount of the property tax for the current year (April 1 to December 31) is $16,425.

a. Journalize the two adjusting entries required to bring the accounts affected by the two taxes up to date as of December 31, the end of the current year.
b. What is the amount of tax expense for the current year?

EX 3-18
Adjustment for depreciation
obj. 2

The estimated amount of depreciation on equipment for the current year is $3,275. Journalize the adjusting entry to record the depreciation.

EX 3-19
Determining fixed asset's book value
obj. 2

The balance in the equipment account is $678,950, and the balance in the accumulated depreciation—equipment account is $262,200.

a. What is the book value of the equipment?
b. Does the balance in the accumulated depreciation account mean that the equipment's loss of value is $262,200? Explain.

EX 3-20
Book value of fixed assets
objs. 2, 3

In a recent balance sheet, Microsoft Corporation reported *Property, Plant, and Equipment* of $6,078 million and *Accumulated Depreciation* of $3,855 million.

a. What was the book value of the fixed assets?
b. Would the book value of Microsoft Corporation's fixed assets normally approximate their fair market values?

EX 3-21
Effects of errors on financial statements
objs. 2, 3

For a recent period, Circuit City Stores, Inc., reported accrued expenses and other current liabilities of $228,966,000. For the same period, Circuit City reported earnings of $95,789,000 before income taxes. If accrued expenses and other current liabilities had not been recorded, what would have been the earnings (loss) before income taxes?

EX 3-22
Effects of errors on financial statements
objs. 2, 3

For a recent year, the balance sheet for The Campbell Soup Company includes accrued liabilities of $606,000,000. The income before taxes for The Campbell Soup Company for the year was $1,030,000,000.

a. If the accruals had not been recorded at the end of the year, by how much would income before taxes have been misstated?
b. What is the percentage of the misstatement in (a) to the reported income of $1,030,000,000? Round to one decimal place.

EX 3-23
Effects of errors on financial statements
objs. 2, 3

The accountant for Cyprus Medical Co., a medical services consulting firm, mistakenly omitted adjusting entries for (a) unearned revenue earned during the year ($12,450) and (b) accrued wages ($7,280). Indicate the effect of each error, considered individually, on the income statement for the current year ended August 31. Also indicate the effect of each error on the August 31 balance sheet. Set up a table similar to the following, and record your

✓1. a. Revenue
understated, $12,450

answers by inserting the dollar amount in the appropriate spaces. Insert a zero if the error does not affect the item.

	Error (a)		Error (b)	
	Over-stated	Under-stated	Over-stated	Under-stated
1. Revenue for the year would be	$ ___	$ ___	$ ___	$ ___
2. Expenses for the year would be	$ ___	$ ___	$ ___	$ ___
3. Net income for the year would be	$ ___	$ ___	$ ___	$ ___
4. Assets at August 31 would be	$ ___	$ ___	$ ___	$ ___
5. Liabilities at August 31 would be	$ ___	$ ___	$ ___	$ ___
6. Owner's equity at August 31 would be	$ ___	$ ___	$ ___	$ ___

EX 3-24
Effects of errors on financial statements
objs. 2, 3

If the net income for the current year had been $262,800 in Exercise 3-23, what would have been the correct net income if the proper adjusting entries had been made?

EX 3-25
Adjusting entries for depreciation; effect of error
objs. 2, 3

On December 31, a business estimates depreciation on equipment used during the first year of operations to be $18,100.

a. Journalize the adjusting entry required as of December 31.
b. If the adjusting entry in (a) were omitted, which items would be erroneously stated on (1) the income statement for the year and (2) the balance sheet as of December 31?

EX 3-26
Adjusting entries from trial balances
obj. 4

The unadjusted and adjusted trial balances for Tomahawk Services Co. on July 31, 2008, are shown below.

Tomahawk Services Co.
Trial Balance
July 31, 2008

	Unadjusted		Adjusted	
	Debit Balances	Credit Balances	Debit Balances	Credit Balances
Cash	48		48	
Accounts Receivable	114		126	
Supplies	36		27	
Prepaid Insurance	60		36	
Land	78		78	
Equipment	120		120	
Accumulated Depreciation—Equipment		24		39
Accounts Payable		78		78
Wages Payable		0		3
Cleo Dexter, Capital		276		276
Cleo Dexter, Drawing	24		24	
Fees Earned		222		234
Wages Expense	72		75	
Rent Expense	24		24	
Insurance Expense	0		24	
Utilities Expense	12		12	
Depreciation Expense	0		15	
Supplies Expense	0		9	
Miscellaneous Expense	12		12	
	600	600	630	630

Journalize the five entries that adjusted the accounts at July 31, 2008. None of the accounts were affected by more than one adjusting entry.

EX 3-27
Adjusting entries from trial balances
obj. 4

✓ *Corrected trial balance totals, $310,950*

The accountant for Sweetwater Laundry prepared the following unadjusted and adjusted trial balances. Assume that all balances in the unadjusted trial balance and the amounts of the adjustments are correct. Identify the errors in the accountant's adjusting entries.

Sweetwater Laundry
Trial Balance
October 31, 2008

	Unadjusted Debit Balances	Unadjusted Credit Balances	Adjusted Debit Balances	Adjusted Credit Balances
Cash	7,500		7,500	
Accounts Receivable	18,250		22,000	
Laundry Supplies	3,750		5,500	
Prepaid Insurance*	5,200		1,400	
Laundry Equipment	140,000		134,000	
Accumulated Depreciation		48,000		48,000
Accounts Payable		9,600		9,600
Wages Payable				1,200
Mattie Ivy, Capital		60,300		60,300
Mattie Ivy, Drawing	28,775		28,775	
Laundry Revenue		182,100		182,100
Wages Expense	49,200		49,200	
Rent Expense	25,575		25,575	
Utilities Expense	18,500		18,500	
Depreciation Expense			6,000	
Laundry Supplies Expense			1,750	
Insurance Expense			800	
Miscellaneous Expense	3,250		3,250	
	300,000	300,000	304,250	301,200

*$3,800 of insurance expired during the year.

Problems Series A

PR 3-1A
Adjusting entries
obj. 2

On July 31, 2008, the following data were accumulated to assist the accountant in preparing the adjusting entries for Fremont Realty:

a. The supplies account balance on July 31 is $1,975. The supplies on hand on July 31 are $625.
b. The unearned rent account balance on July 31 is $3,750, representing the receipt of an advance payment on July 1 of three months' rent from tenants.
c. Wages accrued but not paid at July 31 are $1,000.
d. Fees accrued but unbilled at July 31 are $12,275.
e. Depreciation of office equipment is $850.

Instructions
1. Journalize the adjusting entries required at July 31, 2008.
2. Briefly explain the difference between adjusting entries and entries that would be made to correct errors.

PR 3-2A
Adjusting entries
obj. 2

Selected account balances before adjustment for Foxboro Realty at December 31, 2008, the end of the current year, are as follows:

	Debits	Credits
Accounts Receivable	$18,250	
Equipment	72,500	
Accumulated Depreciation		$ 11,900
Prepaid Rent	7,500	
Supplies	2,050	
Wages Payable		—
Unearned Fees		8,500
Fees Earned		187,950
Wages Expense	60,100	
Rent Expense	—	
Depreciation Expense	—	
Supplies Expense	—	

Data needed for year-end adjustments are as follows:

a. Unbilled fees at December 31, $1,650.
b. Supplies on hand at December 31, $200.
c. Rent expired, $5,000.
d. Depreciation of equipment during year, $1,150.
e. Unearned fees at December 31, $1,500.
f. Wages accrued but not paid at December 31, $3,150.

Instructions
Journalize the six adjusting entries required at December 31, based upon the data presented.

PR 3-3A
Adjusting entries
obj. 2

Iron River Company, an electronics repair store, prepared the unadjusted trial balance at the end of its first year of operations shown below.

Iron River Company
Unadjusted Trial Balance
April 30, 2008

	Debit Balances	Credit Balances
Cash	3,450	
Accounts Receivable	22,500	
Supplies	5,400	
Equipment	113,700	
Accounts Payable		5,250
Unearned Fees		6,000
Walker Kellogg, Capital		78,000
Walker Kellogg, Drawing	4,500	
Fees Earned		135,750
Wages Expense	31,500	
Rent Expense	24,000	
Utilities Expense	17,250	
Miscellaneous Expense	2,700	
	225,000	225,000

For preparing the adjusting entries, the following data were assembled:

a. Fees earned but unbilled on April 30 were $1,775.
b. Supplies on hand on April 30 were $1,200.
c. Depreciation of equipment was estimated to be $4,100 for the year.
d. The balance in unearned fees represented the April 1 receipt in advance for services to be provided. Only $1,750 of the services was provided between April 1 and April 30.
e. Unpaid wages accrued on April 30 were $600.

Instructions
Journalize the adjusting entries necessary on April 30, 2008.

PR 3-4A
Adjusting entries
objs. 2, 3, 4

Danville Company specializes in the repair of music equipment and is owned and operated by Harry Nagel. On April 30, 2008, the end of the current year, the accountant for Danville Company prepared the following trial balances:

Danville Company
Trial Balance
April 30, 2008

	Unadjusted		Adjusted	
	Debit Balances	Credit Balances	Debit Balances	Credit Balances
Cash	12,750		12,750	
Accounts Receivable	36,500		36,500	
Supplies	3,750		900	
Prepaid Insurance	4,750		1,500	
Equipment	120,150		120,150	
Accumulated Depreciation—Equipment		31,500		34,000
Automobiles	36,500		36,500	
Accumulated Depreciation—Automobiles		18,250		20,400
Accounts Payable		8,310		8,800
Salaries Payable		—		2,000
Unearned Service Fees		6,000		2,900
Harry Nagel, Capital		131,340		131,340
Harry Nagel, Drawing	25,000		25,000	
Service Fees Earned		244,600		247,700
Salary Expense	172,300		174,300	
Rent Expense	18,000		18,000	
Supplies Expense	—		2,850	
Depreciation Expense—Equipment	—		2,500	
Depreciation Expense—Automobiles	—		2,150	
Utilities Expense	4,300		4,790	
Taxes Expense	2,725		2,725	
Insurance Expense	—		3,250	
Miscellaneous Expense	3,275		3,275	
	440,000	440,000	447,140	447,140

Instructions

Journalize the seven entries that adjusted the accounts at April 30. None of the accounts were affected by more than one adjusting entry.

PR 3-5A
Adjusting entries and adjusted trial balances
objs. 2, 3, 4

✓ *2. Total of Debit Column: $765,000*

Cambridge Company is a small editorial services company owned and operated by Dave Maier. On December 31, 2008, the end of the current year, Cambridge Company's accounting clerk prepared the unadjusted trial balance shown at the top of the following page.

The data needed to determine year-end adjustments are as follows:

a. Unexpired insurance at December 31, $2,700.
b. Supplies on hand at December 31, $480.
c. Depreciation of building for the year, $1,600.
d. Depreciation of equipment for the year, $4,400.
e. Rent unearned at December 31, $3,250.
f. Accrued salaries and wages at December 31, $2,800.
g. Fees earned but unbilled on December 31, $6,200.

Instructions

1. Journalize the adjusting entries. Add additional accounts as needed.
2. Determine the balances of the accounts affected by the adjusting entries, and prepare an adjusted trial balance.

Cambridge Company
Unadjusted Trial Balance
December 31, 2008

	Debit Balances	Credit Balances
Cash	5,550	
Accounts Receivable	28,350	
Prepaid Insurance	7,200	
Supplies	1,980	
Land	112,500	
Building	212,250	
Accumulated Depreciation—Building		137,550
Equipment	135,300	
Accumulated Depreciation—Equipment		97,950
Accounts Payable		12,150
Unearned Rent		6,750
Dave Maier, Capital		201,000
Dave Maier, Drawing	15,000	
Fees Earned		294,600
Salaries and Wages Expense	143,370	
Utilities Expense	42,375	
Advertising Expense	22,800	
Repairs Expense	17,250	
Miscellaneous Expense	6,075	
	750,000	750,000

PR 3-6A
Adjusting entries and errors

obj. 3

✓ *2. Corrected Net Income: $157,600*

At the end of June, the first month of operations, the following selected data were taken from the financial statements of Teryse Weire, an attorney:

Net income for June	$155,000
Total assets at June 30	350,000
Total liabilities at June 30	120,000
Total owner's equity at June 30	230,000

In preparing the financial statements, adjustments for the following data were overlooked:

a. Supplies used during June, $1,800.
b. Unbilled fees earned at June 30, $11,600.
c. Depreciation of equipment for June, $4,950.
d. Accrued wages at June 30, $2,250.

Instructions

1. Journalize the entries to record the omitted adjustments.
2. Determine the correct amount of net income for June and the total assets, liabilities, and owner's equity at June 30. In addition to indicating the corrected amounts, indicate the effect of each omitted adjustment by setting up and completing a columnar table similar to the following. Adjustment (a) is presented as an example.

	Net Income	Total Assets	Total Liabilities	Total Owner's Equity
Reported amounts	$155,000	$350,000	$120,000	$230,000
Corrections:				
Adjustment (a)	−1,800	−1,800	0	−1,800
Adjustment (b)				
Adjustment (c)				
Adjustment (d)				
Corrected amounts				

Problems Series B

PR 3-1B
Adjusting entries
obj. 2

On October 31, 2008, the following data were accumulated to assist the accountant in preparing the adjusting entries for Twin Bluffs Realty:

a. Fees accrued but unbilled at October 31 are $11,385.
b. The supplies account balance on October 31 is $2,973. The supplies on hand at October 31 are $740.
c. Wages accrued but not paid at October 31 are $1,500.
d. The unearned rent account balance at October 31 is $9,450, representing the receipt of an advance payment on October 1 of three months' rent from tenants.
e. Depreciation of office equipment is $2,650.

Instructions
1. Journalize the adjusting entries required at October 31, 2008.
2. Briefly explain the difference between adjusting entries and entries that would be made to correct errors.

PR 3-2B
Adjusting entries
obj. 2

Selected account balances before adjustment for Green Lake Realty at August 31, 2008, the end of the current year, are shown below.

	Debits	Credits
Accounts Receivable	$38,250	
Accumulated Depreciation		$ 26,900
Depreciation Expense	—	
Equipment	90,500	
Fees Earned		275,500
Prepaid Rent	9,750	
Rent Expense	—	
Supplies	2,145	
Supplies Expense	—	
Unearned Fees		6,175
Wages Expense	81,500	
Wages Payable		—

Data needed for year-end adjustments are as follows:

a. Supplies on hand at August 31, $500.
b. Depreciation of equipment during year, $1,375.
c. Rent expired during year, $4,525.
d. Wages accrued but not paid at August 31, $2,200.
e. Unearned fees at August 31, $1,500.
f. Unbilled fees at August 31, $6,780.

Instructions
Journalize the six adjusting entries required at August 31, based upon the data presented.

PR 3-3B
Adjusting entries
obj. 2

Lander Outfitters Co., an outfitter store for fishing treks, prepared the unadjusted trial balance shown on the following page at the end of its first year of operations.
   For preparing the adjusting entries, the following data were assembled:

a. Supplies on hand on June 30 were $300.
b. Fees earned but unbilled on June 30 were $2,310.
c. Depreciation of equipment was estimated to be $1,500 for the year.

d. Unpaid wages accrued on June 30 were $475.

e. The balance in unearned fees represented the June 1 receipt in advance for services to be provided. Only $1,000 of the services was provided between June 1 and June 30.

Lander Outfitters Co.
Unadjusted Trial Balance
June 30, 2008

	Debit Balances	Credit Balances
Cash	6,610	
Accounts Receivable	21,900	
Supplies	1,820	
Equipment	37,860	
Accounts Payable		3,050
Unearned Fees		4,800
Tim Hudson, Capital		55,700
Tim Hudson, Drawing	2,500	
Fees Earned		71,450
Wages Expense	38,210	
Rent Expense	13,790	
Utilities Expense	10,050	
Miscellaneous Expense	2,260	
	135,000	135,000

Instructions

Journalize the adjusting entries necessary on June 30.

PR 3-4B
Adjusting entries
objs. 2, 3, 4

Elkton Company specializes in the maintenance and repair of signs, such as billboards. On July 31, 2008, the accountant for Elkton Company prepared the following trial balances.

Elkton Company
Trial Balance
July 31, 2008

	Unadjusted Debit Balances	Unadjusted Credit Balances	Adjusted Debit Balances	Adjusted Credit Balances
Cash	4,750		4,750	
Accounts Receivable	17,400		17,400	
Supplies	3,600		975	
Prepaid Insurance	5,650		1,200	
Land	50,000		50,000	
Buildings	120,000		120,000	
Accumulated Depreciation—Buildings		49,500		53,100
Trucks	75,000		75,000	
Accumulated Depreciation—Trucks		11,800		13,300
Accounts Payable		6,920		7,520
Salaries Payable		—		1,180
Unearned Service Fees		7,400		5,100
Mario Salas, Capital		146,700		146,700
Mario Salas, Drawing	5,000		5,000	
Service Fees Earned		152,680		154,980
Salary Expense	73,600		74,780	
Depreciation Expense—Trucks	—		1,500	
Rent Expense	9,600		9,600	
Supplies Expense	—		2,625	
Utilities Expense	6,200		6,800	
Depreciation Expense—Buildings	—		3,600	
Taxes Expense	1,720		1,720	
Insurance Expense	—		4,450	
Miscellaneous Expense	2,480		2,480	
	375,000	375,000	381,880	381,880

Instructions

Journalize the seven entries that adjusted the accounts at July 31. None of the accounts were affected by more than one adjusting entry.

PR 3-5B
*Adjusting entries and
adjusted trial balances*
objs. 2, 3, 4

✓ *2. Total of Debit
Column: $285,150*

Lincoln Service Co., which specializes in appliance repair services, is owned and operated by Molly Jordan. Lincoln Service Co.'s accounting clerk prepared the following unadjusted trial balance at December 31, 2008, shown below.

Lincoln Service Co.
Unadjusted Trial Balance
December 31, 2008

	Debit Balances	Credit Balances
Cash	2,100	
Accounts Receivable	10,300	
Prepaid Insurance	3,000	
Supplies	1,725	
Land	50,000	
Building	80,750	
Accumulated Depreciation—Building		37,850
Equipment	44,000	
Accumulated Depreciation—Equipment		17,650
Accounts Payable		3,750
Unearned Rent		3,600
Molly Jordan, Capital		83,550
Molly Jordan, Drawing	2,500	
Fees Earned		128,600
Salaries and Wages Expense	50,900	
Utilities Expense	14,100	
Advertising Expense	7,500	
Repairs Expense	6,100	
Miscellaneous Expense	2,025	
	275,000	275,000

The data needed to determine year-end adjustments are as follows:

a. Depreciation of building for the year, $3,500.
b. Depreciation of equipment for the year, $2,300.
c. Accrued salaries and wages at December 31, $1,100.
d. Unexpired insurance at December 31, $750.
e. Fees earned but unbilled on December 31, $3,250.
f. Supplies on hand at December 31, $525.
g. Rent unearned at December 31, $1,500.

Instructions

1. Journalize the adjusting entries. Add additional accounts as needed.
2. Determine the balances of the accounts affected by the adjusting entries and prepare an adjusted trial balance.

PR 3-6B
*Adjusting entries and
errors*
obj. 3

✓ *2. Corrected Net
Income: $97,755*

At the end of October, the first month of operations, the following selected data were taken from the financial statements of Lauren Powell, an attorney:

Net income for October	$ 99,480
Total assets at October 31	400,000
Total liabilities at October 31	100,000
Total owner's equity at October 31	300,000

In preparing the financial statements, adjustments for the following data were overlooked:

a. Unbilled fees earned at October 31, $8,000.
b. Depreciation of equipment for October, $5,500.
c. Accrued wages at October 31, $2,500.
d. Supplies used during October, $1,725.

Instructions
1. Journalize the entries to record the omitted adjustments.
2. Determine the correct amount of net income for October and the total assets, liabilities, and owner's equity at October 31. In addition to indicating the corrected amounts, indicate the effect of each omitted adjustment by setting up and completing a columnar table similar to the following. Adjustment (a) is presented as an example.

	Net Income	Total Assets	Total Liabilities	Total Owner's Equity
Reported amounts	$99,480	$400,000	$100,000	$300,000
Corrections:				
Adjustment (a)	+8,000	+8,000	0	+8,000
Adjustment (b)	_____	_____	_____	_____
Adjustment (c)	_____	_____	_____	_____
Adjustment (d)	_____	_____	_____	_____
Corrected amounts	_____	_____	_____	_____

Continuing Problem

✓ *3. Total of Debit Column: $39,500*

The unadjusted trial balance that you prepared for Dancin Music at the end of Chapter 2 should appear as follows:

Dancin Music
Unadjusted Trial Balance
May 31, 2008

	Debit Balances	Credit Balances
Cash	12,085	
Accounts Receivable	2,850	
Supplies	920	
Prepaid Insurance	3,360	
Office Equipment	5,000	
Accounts Payable		5,750
Unearned Revenue		4,800
Kris Payne, Capital		12,500
Kris Payne, Drawing	1,300	
Fees Earned		14,750
Wages Expense	2,400	
Office Rent Expense	2,600	
Equipment Rent Expense	1,300	
Utilities Expense	910	
Music Expense	2,565	
Advertising Expense	1,730	
Supplies Expense	180	
Miscellaneous Expense	600	
	37,800	37,800

The data needed to determine adjustments for the two-month period ending May 31, 2008, are as follows:

a. During May, Dancin Music provided guest disc jockeys for KPRG for a total of 115 hours. For information on the amount of the accrued revenue to be billed to KPRG, see the contract described in the May 3, 2008, transaction at the end of Chapter 2.
b. Supplies on hand at May 31, $160.
c. The balance of the prepaid insurance account relates to the May 1, 2008, transaction at the end of Chapter 2.
d. Depreciation of the office equipment is $100.

e. The balance of the unearned revenue account relates to the contract between Dancin Music and KPRG, described in the May 3, 2008, transaction at the end of Chapter 2.

f. Accrued wages as of May 31, 2008, were $200.

Instructions

1. Prepare adjusting journal entries. You will need the following additional accounts:

   18 Accumulated Depreciation—Office Equipment
   22 Wages Payable
   57 Insurance Expense
   58 Depreciation Expense

2. Post the adjusting entries, inserting balances in the accounts affected.
3. Prepare an adjusted trial balance.

Special Activities

SA 3-1
Ethics and professional conduct in business

ETHICS

Annette Kagel opened Harre Real Estate Co. on January 1, 2007. At the end of the first year, the business needed additional capital. On behalf of Harre Real Estate, Annette applied to Lake County State Bank for a loan of $200,000. Based on Harre Real Estate's financial statements, which had been prepared on a cash basis, the Lake County State Bank loan officer rejected the loan as too risky.

After receiving the rejection notice, Annette instructed her accountant to prepare the financial statements on an accrual basis. These statements included $31,500 in accounts receivable and $10,200 in accounts payable. Annette then instructed her accountant to record an additional $10,000 of accounts receivable for commissions on property for which a contract had been signed on December 28, 2007, but which would not be formally "closed" and the title transferred until January 5, 2008.

Annette then applied for a $200,000 loan from First National Bank, using the revised financial statements. On this application, Annette indicated that she had not previously been rejected for credit.

Discuss the ethical and professional conduct of Annette Kagel in applying for the loan from First National Bank.

SA 3-2
Accrued expense

REAL WORLD

On December 30, 2008, you buy a Ford Expedition. It comes with a three-year, 36,000-mile warranty. On March 5, 2009, you return the Expedition to the dealership for some basic repairs covered under the warranty. The cost of the repairs to the dealership is $1,560. In what year, 2008 or 2009, should Ford Motor Company recognize the cost of the warranty repairs as an expense?

SA 3-3
Accrued revenue

REAL WORLD

The following is an excerpt from a conversation between Sybil Towns and Greg Gibbs just before they boarded a flight to London on American Airlines. They are going to London to attend their company's annual sales conference.

Sybil: Greg, aren't you taking an introductory accounting course at college?
Greg: Yes, I decided it's about time I learned something about accounting. You know, our annual bonuses are based upon the sales figures that come from the accounting department.
Sybil: I guess I never really thought about it.
Greg: You should think about it! Last year, I placed a $500,000 order on December 28. But when I got my bonus, the $500,000 sale wasn't included. They said it hadn't been shipped until January 3, so it would have to count in next year's bonus.
Sybil: A real bummer!
Greg: Right! I was counting on that bonus including the $500,000 sale.
Sybil: Did you complain?

Greg: Yes, but it didn't do any good. Ashley, the head accountant, said something about matching revenues and expenses. Also, something about not recording revenues until the sale is final. I figure I'd take the accounting course and find out whether she's just jerking me around.

Sybil: I never really thought about it. When do you think American Airlines will record its revenues from this flight?

Greg: Mmm . . . I guess it could record the revenue when it sells the ticket . . . or . . . when the boarding passes are taken at the door . . . or . . . when we get off the plane . . . or when our company pays for the tickets . . . or . . . I don't know. I'll ask my accounting instructor.

Discuss when American Airlines should recognize the revenue from ticket sales to properly match revenues and expenses.

SA 3-4
Adjustments and financial statements

Several years ago, your brother opened Pomona Television Repair. He made a small initial investment and added money from his personal bank account as needed. He withdrew money for living expenses at irregular intervals. As the business grew, he hired an assistant. He is now considering adding more employees, purchasing additional service trucks, and purchasing the building he now rents. To secure funds for the expansion, your brother submitted a loan application to the bank and included the most recent financial statements (shown below) prepared from accounts maintained by a part-time bookkeeper.

Pomona Television Repair
Income Statement
For the Year Ended July 31, 2008

Service revenue		$90,000
Less: Rent paid	$30,000	
Wages paid	28,500	
Supplies paid	5,100	
Utilities paid	3,175	
Insurance paid	2,400	
Miscellaneous payments	3,600	72,775
Net income		$17,225

Pomona Television Repair
Balance Sheet
July 31, 2008

Assets

Cash	$10,600
Amounts due from customers	12,500
Truck	36,900
Total assets	$60,000

Equities

Owner's capital	$60,000

After reviewing the financial statements, the loan officer at the bank asked your brother if he used the accrual basis of accounting for revenues and expenses. Your brother responded that he did and that is why he included an account for "Amounts Due from Customers." The loan officer then asked whether or not the accounts were adjusted prior to the preparation of the statements. Your brother answered that they had not been adjusted.

a. Why do you think the loan officer suspected that the accounts had not been adjusted prior to the preparation of the statements?
b. Indicate possible accounts that might need to be adjusted before an accurate set of financial statements could be prepared.

SA 3-5
Codes of ethics
Group Project

ETHICS

Obtain a copy of your college or university's student code of conduct. In groups of three or four, answer the following question.

1. Compare this code of conduct with the accountant's Codes of Professional Conduct, which is linked to the text Web site at **www.thomsonedu.com/accounting/warren**.
2. One of your classmates asks you for permission to copy your homework, which your instructor will be collecting and grading for part of your overall term grade. Although your instructor has not stated whether one student may or may not copy another student's homework, is it ethical for you to allow your classmate to copy your homework? Is it ethical for your classmate to copy your homework?

Answers to Self-Examination Questions

1. **A** A deferral is the delay in recording an expense already paid, such as prepaid insurance (answer A). Wages payable (answer B) is considered an accrued expense or accrued liability. Fees earned (answer C) is a revenue item. Accumulated depreciation (answer D) is a contra account to a fixed asset.

2. **D** The balance in the supplies account, before adjustment, represents the amount of supplies available. From this amount ($2,250) is subtracted the amount of supplies on hand ($950) to determine the supplies used ($1,300). Since increases in expense accounts are recorded by debits and decreases in asset accounts are recorded by credits, answer D is the correct entry.

3. **C** The failure to record the adjusting entry debiting Unearned Rent, $600, and crediting Rent Revenue, $600, would have the effect of overstating liabilities by $600 and understating net income by $600 (answer C).

4. **C** Since increases in expense accounts (such as depreciation expense) are recorded by debits and it is customary to record the decreases in usefulness of fixed assets as credits to accumulated depreciation accounts, answer C is the correct entry.

5. **D** The book value of a fixed asset is the difference between the balance in the asset account and the balance in the related accumulated depreciation account, or $22,500 − $14,000, as indicated by answer D ($8,500).

chapter
4

Completing the Accounting Cycle

© ERIC RISBERG/ASSOCIATED PRESS

objectives

After studying this chapter, you should be able to:

1 *Describe the flow of accounting information from the unadjusted trial balance into the adjusted trial balance and financial statements.*

2 *Prepare financial statements from adjusted account balances.*

3 *Prepare closing entries.*

4 *Describe the accounting cycle.*

5 *Illustrate the accounting cycle for one period.*

6 *Explain what is meant by the fiscal year and the natural business year.*

Electronic Arts Inc.

Most of us have had to file a personal tax return. At the beginning of the year, you estimate your upcoming income and decide whether you need to increase your payroll tax withholdings or perhaps pay estimated taxes. During the year, you earn income and enter into tax-related transactions, such as making charitable contributions. At the end of the year, your employer sends you a tax withholding information form (W-2) form, and you collect the tax records needed for completing your yearly tax forms. As the next year begins, you start the cycle all over again.

Businesses also go through a cycle of activities. For example, Electronic Arts Inc., the world's largest developer and marketer of electronic game software, begins its cycle by developing new or revised game titles, such as Madden NFL Football®, Need for Speed®, Tiger Woods PGA Tour®, The Sims®, and The Lord of the Rings®. These games are marketed and sold throughout the year. During the year, operating transactions of the business are recorded. For Electronic Arts, such transactions include the salaries for game developers, advertising expenditures, costs for producing and packaging games, and game revenues. At the end of the year, financial statements are prepared that summarize the operating activities for the year. Electronic Arts publishes these statements on its Web site at **http://www.investor.ea.com**. Finally, before the start of the next year, the accounts are readied for recording the operations of the next year.

As we saw in Chapter 1, the initial cycle for NetSolutions began with Chris Clark's investment in the business on November 1, 2007. The cycle continued with recording NetSolutions' transactions for November and December, as we discussed and illustrated in Chapters 1 and 2. In Chapter 3, the cycle continued when the adjusting entries for the two months ending December 31, 2007, were recorded. In this chapter, we complete the cycle for NetSolutions by preparing financial statements and getting the accounts ready for recording transactions of the next period.

Flow of Accounting Information

objective 1

Describe the flow of accounting information from the unadjusted trial balance into the adjusted trial balance and financial statements.

@netsolutions

Many companies use Microsoft's Excel® software to prepare end-of-period spreadsheets (work sheets).

The end-of-period process by which accounts are adjusted and the financial statements are prepared is one of the most important in accounting. Using our illustration of NetSolutions from Chapters 1–3, this process is summarized in spreadsheet form in Exhibit 1.

Exhibit 1 begins with the unadjusted trial balance as of the end of the period. The unadjusted trial balance serves as a control to verify that the total of the debit balances equals the total of the credit balances. If the trial balance totals are unequal, an error has occurred, which must be found and corrected before the end-of-period process can continue.

The adjustments that we explained and illustrated for NetSolutions in Chapter 3 are shown in the Adjustments columns of Exhibit 1. Cross-referencing (by letters) the debit and credit of each adjustment is useful in reviewing the impact of the adjustments on the unadjusted account balances. The order of the adjustments on the spreadsheet is not important, and the adjustments are normally entered in the order in which the data are assembled. When the titles of the accounts to be adjusted do not appear in the unadjusted trial balance, the accounts are inserted in the Account Title column, below the unadjusted trial balance totals. The total of the Adjustments columns is a control to verify the mathematical accuracy of the adjustment data and adjusting entries. The total of the Debit column must equal the total of the Credit column.

The adjustment data are added to or subtracted from the amounts in the Unadjusted Trial Balance columns to arrive at the Adjusted Trial Balance columns. In this way, the Adjusted Trial Balance columns of Exhibit 1 illustrate the impact of the adjusting entries

EXHIBIT 1   End-of-Period Spreadsheet (Work Sheet)

NetSolutions
End-of-Period Spreadsheet (Work Sheet)
For the Two Months Ended December 31, 2007

	A	B	C	D	E	F	G	H	I	J	K	
		Unadjusted Trial Balance		Adjustments		Adjusted Trial Balance		Income Statement		Balance Sheet		
	Account Title	Dr.	Cr.	Dr.	Cr.	Dr.	Cr.	Dr.	Cr.	Dr.	Cr.	
1	Cash	2,065				2,065				2,065		1
2	Accounts Receivable	2,220		(d) 500		2,720				2,720		2
3	Supplies	2,000			(a) 1,240	760				760		3
4	Prepaid Insurance	2,400			(b) 200	2,200				2,200		4
5	Land	20,000				20,000				20,000		5
6	Office Equipment	1,800				1,800				1,800		6
7	Accounts Payable		900				900				900	7
8	Unearned Rent		360	(c) 120			240				240	8
9	Chris Clark, Capital		25,000				25,000				25,000	9
10	Chris Clark, Drawing	4,000				4,000				4,000		10
11	Fees Earned		16,340		(d) 500		16,840		16,840			11
12	Wages Expense	4,275		(e) 250		4,525		4,525				12
13	Rent Expense	1,600				1,600		1,600				13
14	Utilities Expense	985				985		985				14
15	Supplies Expense	800		(a) 1,240		2,040		2,040				15
16	Miscellaneous Expense	455				455		455				16
17		42,600	42,600									17
18	Insurance Expense			(b) 200		200		200				18
19	Rent Revenue				(c) 120		120		120			19
20	Wages Payable				(e) 250		250				250	20
21	Depreciation Expense			(f) 50		50		50				21
22	Accumulated Depreciation				(f) 50		50				50	22
23				2,360	2,360	43,400	43,400	9,855	16,960	33,545	26,440	23
24	Net income							7,105			7,105	24
25								16,960	16,960	33,545	33,545	25

on the unadjusted accounts. The totals of the Adjusted Trial Balance columns prove the equality of the totals of the debit and credit balances after adjustment.

Exhibit 1 also illustrates the flow of the accounts from the adjusted trial balance into the financial statements. The revenue and expense accounts are extended to the Income Statement columns. At the bottom of the Income Statement columns, the net income or net loss for the period is shown. For example, Exhibit 1 shows that NetSolutions had net income of $7,105 for the period. Likewise, the assets, liabilities, owner's capital, and drawing accounts are extended to the Balance Sheet columns. Since net income increases owner's capital, NetSolutions' net income of $7,105 is also shown in the Balance Sheet Cr. column. As we will describe and illustrate in the next section, the financial statements can be prepared directly from Exhibit 1.

To summarize, Exhibit 1 illustrates the end-of-period process by which accounts are adjusted and how the adjusted accounts flow into the financial statements. The spreadsheet shown in Exhibit 1 is not a required part of the accounting process. However, many accountants prepare such a spreadsheet, often called a work sheet, in manual or electronic form, as part of their normal end-of-period process. The primary advantage in doing so is that it allows managers and accountants to see the impact of the adjustments on the financial statements. This is especially useful for adjustments that depend upon estimates. We discuss such estimates and their impact on the financial statements in later chapters.[1]

---

1 The appendix to this chapter describes and illustrates how to prepare the end-of-period spreadsheet (work sheet) shown in Exhibit 1.

Example Exercise 4-1

objective

The balances for the accounts listed below appear in the Adjusted Trial Balance columns of the end-of-period spreadsheet (work sheet). Indicate whether each balance should be extended to (a) an Income Statement column or (b) a Balance Sheet column.

1. Amber Bablock, Drawing
2. Utilities Expense
3. Accumulated Depreciation—Equipment
4. Unearned Rent

5. Fees Earned
6. Accounts Payable
7. Rent Revenue
8. Supplies

Follow My Example 4-1

1. Balance Sheet column
2. Income Statement column
3. Balance Sheet column
4. Balance Sheet column

5. Income Statement column
6. Balance Sheet column
7. Income Statement column
8. Balance Sheet column

For Practice: PE 4-1A, PE 4-1B

Financial Statements

objective 2

Prepare financial statements from adjusted account balances.

Using Exhibit 1, the financial statements for NetSolutions can be prepared. The income statement, the statement of owner's equity, and the balance sheet are shown in Exhibit 2, on page 148. In the following paragraphs, we discuss each of these financial statements and how they are prepared.

INCOME STATEMENT

@netsolutions

The income statement is prepared directly from the Income Statement or Adjusted Trial Balance columns of Exhibit 1 beginning with fees earned of $16,840. The order of the expenses may change, however, from that listed in Exhibit 1. As we did in Chapter 1, we list the expenses in the income statement in Exhibit 2 in order of size, beginning with the larger items. Miscellaneous expense is the last item, regardless of its amount.

STATEMENT OF OWNER'S EQUITY

The first item presented on the statement of owner's equity is the balance of the owner's capital account at the beginning of the period. In Exhibit 1, however, the

Example Exercise 4-2

objective

In the Balance Sheet columns of the end-of-period spreadsheet (work sheet) for Dimple Consulting Co. for the current year, the Debit column total is $678,450, and the Credit column total is $599,750 before the amount for net income or net loss has been included. In preparing the income statement from the end-of-period spreadsheet (work sheet), what is the amount of net income or net loss?

Follow My Example 4-2

A net income of $78,700 ($678,450 − $599,750) would be reported. When the Debit column of the Balance Sheet columns is more than the Credit column, net income is reported. If the Credit column exceeds the Debit column, a net loss is reported.

For Practice: PE 4-2A, PE 4-2B

EXHIBIT 2   Financial Statements Prepared from Work Sheet

NetSolutions
Income Statement
For the Two Months Ended December 31, 2007

Fees earned	$16 8 4 0 00	
Rent revenue	1 2 0 00	
Total revenues		$16 9 6 0 00
Expenses:		
Wages expense	$ 4 5 2 5 00	
Supplies expense	2 0 4 0 00	
Rent expense	1 6 0 0 00	
Utilities expense	9 8 5 00	
Insurance expense	2 0 0 00	
Depreciation expense	5 0 00	
Miscellaneous expense	4 5 5 00	
Total expenses		9 8 5 5 00
Net income		$ 7 1 0 5 00

NetSolutions
Statement of Owner's Equity
For the Two Months Ended December 31, 2007

Chris Clark, capital, November 1, 2007		$ 0
Investment on November 1, 2007	$25 0 0 0 00	
Net income for November and December	7 1 0 5 00	
	$32 1 0 5 00	
Less withdrawals	4 0 0 0 00	
Increase in owner's equity		28 1 0 5 00
Chris Clark, capital, December 31, 2007		$28 1 0 5 00

NetSolutions
Balance Sheet
December 31, 2007

Assets			Liabilities		
Current assets:			Current liabilities:		
Cash	$ 2 0 6 5 00		Accounts payable	$ 9 0 0 00	
Accounts receivable	2 7 2 0 00		Wages payable	2 5 0 00	
Supplies	7 6 0 00		Unearned rent	2 4 0 00	
Prepaid insurance	2 2 0 0 00		Total liabilities		$ 1 3 9 0 00
Total current assets		$ 7 7 4 5 00			
Property, plant, and equipment:					
Land	$20 0 0 0 00				
Office equipment $1,800					
Less accum. depr. 50	1 7 5 0 00		**Owner's Equity**		
Total property, plant,			Chris Clark, capital		28 1 0 5 00
and equipment		21 7 5 0 00	Total liabilities and		
Total assets		$29 4 9 5 00	owner's equity		$29 4 9 5 00

Integrity, Objectivity, and Ethics in Business

THE ROUND TRIP

A common type of fraud involves artificially inflating revenue. One fraudulent method of inflating revenue is called "round tripping." Under this scheme, a selling company (S) "lends" money to a customer company (C). The money is then used by C to purchase a product from S. Thus, S sells product to C and is paid with the money just loaned to C! This looks like a sale in the accounting records, but in reality, S is shipping free product. The fraud is exposed when it is determined that there was no intent to repay the original loan.

amount listed as owner's capital is not always the account balance at the beginning of the period. The owner may have invested additional assets in the business during the period. Thus, for the beginning balance and any additional investments, it is necessary to refer to the owner's capital account in the ledger. These amounts, along with the net income (or net loss) and the drawing account balance shown on the adjusted trial balance, are used to determine the ending owner's capital account balance.

The basic form of the statement of owner's equity is shown in Exhibit 2. For NetSolutions, the amount of drawings by the owner was less than the net income. If the owner's withdrawals had exceeded the net income, the order of the net income and the withdrawals would have been reversed. The difference between the two items would then be deducted from the beginning capital account balance. Other factors, such as additional investments or a net loss, also require some change in the form, as shown in the following example:

Allan Johnson, capital, January 1, 2007	$39,000	
Additional investment during the year	6,000	
Total		$45,000
Net loss for the year	$ 5,600	
Withdrawals	9,500	
Decrease in owner's equity		15,100
Allan Johnson, capital, December 31, 2007		$29,900

Example Exercise 4-3   objective 2

Zack Gaddis owns and operates Gaddis Employment Services. On January 1, 2007, Zack Gaddis, Capital had a balance of $186,000. During the year, Zack invested an additional $40,000 and withdrew $25,000. For the year ended December 31, 2007, Gaddis Employment Services reported a net income of $18,750. Prepare a statement of owner's equity for the year ended December 31, 2007.

Follow My Example 4-3

GADDIS EMPLOYMENT SERVICES
STATEMENT OF OWNER'S EQUITY
For the Year Ended December 31, 2007

Zack Gaddis, capital, January 1, 2007	$186,000	
Additional investment during 2007	40,000	
Total		$226,000
Withdrawals	$ 25,000	
Less net income	18,750	
Decrease in owner's equity		6,250
Zack Gaddis, capital, December 31, 2007		$219,750

For Practice: PE 4-3A, PE 4-3B

BALANCE SHEET

The balance sheet is prepared directly from the Balance Sheet or Adjusted Trial Balance columns of Exhibit 1 beginning with Cash of $2,065.

The balance sheet in Exhibit 2 was expanded by adding subsections for current assets; property, plant, and equipment; and current liabilities. Such a balance sheet is a *classified balance sheet*. In the following paragraphs, we describe some of the sections and subsections that may be used in a balance sheet. We will introduce additional sections in later chapters.

> Two common classes of assets are current assets and property, plant, and equipment.

Assets Assets are commonly divided into classes for presentation on the balance sheet. Two of these classes are (1) current assets and (2) property, plant, and equipment.

Current Assets Cash and other assets that are expected to be converted to cash or sold or used up usually within one year or less, through the normal operations of the business, are called **current assets**. In addition to cash, the current assets usually owned by a service business are notes receivable, accounts receivable, supplies, and other prepaid expenses.

Notes receivable are amounts that customers owe. They are written promises to pay the amount of the note and possibly interest at an agreed rate. Accounts receivable are also amounts customers owe, but they are less formal than notes and do not provide for interest. Accounts receivable normally result from providing services or selling merchandise on account. Notes receivable and accounts receivable are current assets because they will usually be converted to cash within one year or less.

Property, Plant, and Equipment The property, plant, and equipment section may also be described as **fixed assets** or **plant assets**. These assets include equipment, machinery, buildings, and land. With the exception of land, as we discussed in Chapter 3, fixed assets depreciate over a period of time. The cost, accumulated depreciation, and book value of each major type of fixed asset are normally reported on the balance sheet or in accompanying notes.

> Two common classes of liabilities are current liabilities and long-term liabilities.

Liabilities Liabilities are the amounts the business owes to creditors. The two most common classes of liabilities are (1) current liabilities and (2) long-term liabilities.

Current Liabilities Liabilities that will be due within a short time (usually one year or less) and that are to be paid out of current assets are called **current liabilities**. The most common liabilities in this group are notes payable and accounts payable. Other current liability accounts commonly found in the ledger are Wages Payable, Interest Payable, Taxes Payable, and Unearned Fees.

Long-Term Liabilities Liabilities that will not be due for a long time (usually more than one year) are called **long-term liabilities**. If NetSolutions had long-term liabilities, they would be reported below the current liabilities. As long-term liabilities come due and are to be paid within one year, they are classified as current liabilities. If they are to be renewed rather than paid, they would continue to be classified as long term. When an asset is pledged as security for a liability, the obligation may be called a *mortgage note payable* or a *mortgage payable*.

Owner's Equity The owner's right to the assets of the business is presented on the balance sheet below the liabilities section. The owner's equity is added to the total liabilities, and this total must be equal to the total assets.

Example Exercise 4-4

objective 2

The following accounts appear in an adjusted trial balance of Hindsight Consulting. Indicate whether each account would be reported in the (a) current asset; (b) property, plant, and equipment; (c) current liability; (d) long-term liability; or (e) owner's equity section of the December 31, 2007, balance sheet of Hindsight Consulting.

1. Jason Corbin, Capital
2. Notes Receivable (due in 6 months)
3. Notes Payable (due in 2009)
4. Land

5. Cash
6. Unearned Rent (3 months)
7. Accumulated Depreciation—Equipment
8. Accounts Payable

Follow My Example 4-4

1. Owner's equity
2. Current asset
3. Long-term liability
4. Property, plant, and equipment

5. Current asset
6. Current liability
7. Property, plant, and equipment
8. Current liability

For Practice: PE 4-4A, PE 4-4B

Business Connections

 REAL WORLD

INTERNATIONAL DIFFERENCES

Financial statements prepared under accounting practices in other countries often differ from those prepared under generally accepted accounting principles found in the United States. This is to be expected, since cultures and market structures differ from country to country.

To illustrate, **BMW Group** prepares its financial statements under German law and German accounting principles. In doing so, BMW's balance sheet reports fixed assets first, followed by current assets. It also reports owner's equity before the liabilities. In contrast, balance sheets prepared under U.S. accounting principles report current assets followed by fixed assets and current liabilities followed by long-term liabilities and owner's equity. The U.S.

form of balance sheet is organized to emphasize creditor interpretation and analysis. For example, current assets and current liabilities are presented first to facilitate their interpretation and analysis by creditors. Likewise, to emphasize their importance, liabilities are reported before owner's equity.

Regardless of these differences, the basic principles underlying the accounting equation and the double-entry accounting system are the same in Germany and the United States. Even though differences in recording and reporting exist, the accounting equation holds true: the total assets still equal the total liabilities and owner's equity.

Closing Entries

 objective 3

Prepare closing entries.

@netsolutions

As we discussed in Chapter 3, the adjusting entries are recorded in the journal at the end of the accounting period. For NetSolutions, the adjusting entries are shown in Exhibit 7 of Chapter 3.

After the adjusting entries have been posted to NetSolutions' ledger, shown in Exhibit 6 (on pages 155–159), the ledger is in agreement with the data reported on the financial statements. The balances of the accounts reported on the balance sheet are carried forward from year to year. Because they are relatively permanent, these accounts are called **real accounts**. The balances of the accounts reported on the income statement are not carried forward from year to year. Likewise, the balance of the owner's withdrawal account, which is reported on the statement of owner's equity, is

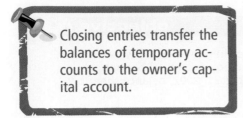

Closing entries transfer the balances of temporary accounts to the owner's capital account.

not carried forward. Because these accounts report amounts for only one period, they are called **temporary accounts** or **nominal accounts**.

To report amounts for only one period, temporary accounts should have zero balances at the beginning of a period. How are these balances converted to zero? The revenue and expense account balances are transferred to an account called **Income Summary**. The balance of Income Summary is then transferred to the owner's capital account. The balance of the owner's drawing account is also transferred to the owner's capital account. The entries that transfer these balances are called **closing entries**. The transfer process is called the **closing process**. Exhibit 3 is a diagram of this process.

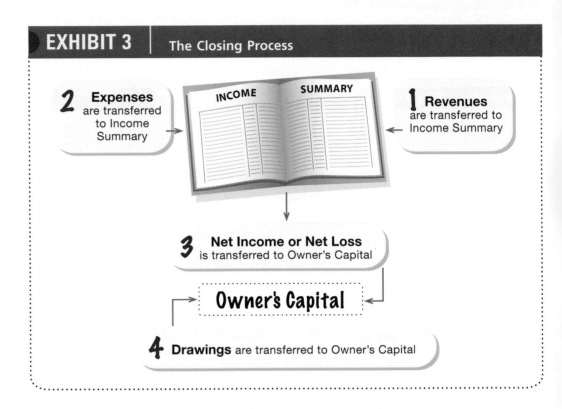

EXHIBIT 3 | The Closing Process

2 Expenses are transferred to Income Summary

INCOME   SUMMARY

1 Revenues are transferred to Income Summary

3 Net Income or Net Loss is transferred to Owner's Capital

Owner's Capital

4 Drawings are transferred to Owner's Capital

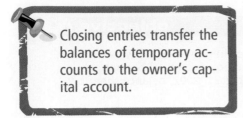

The income summary account does not appear on the financial statements.

You should note that Income Summary is used only at the end of the period. At the beginning of the closing process, Income Summary has no balance. During the closing process, Income Summary will be debited and credited for various amounts. At the end of the closing process, Income Summary will again have no balance. Because Income Summary has the effect of clearing the revenue and expense accounts of their balances, it is sometimes called a **clearing account**. Other titles used for this account include Revenue and Expense Summary, Profit and Loss Summary, and Income and Expense Summary.

It is possible to close the temporary revenue and expense accounts without using a clearing account such as Income Summary. In this case, the balances of the revenue and expense accounts are closed directly to the owner's capital account. This process is automatic in a computerized accounting system. In a manual system, the use of an income summary account aids in detecting and correcting errors.

JOURNALIZING AND POSTING CLOSING ENTRIES

Four closing entries are required at the end of an accounting period, as outlined in Exhibit 3. The account titles and balances needed in preparing these entries may be obtained from the end-of-period spreadsheet (work sheet), the adjusted trial balance, the income statement, the statement of owner's equity, or the ledger.

A flowchart of the closing entries for NetSolutions is shown in Exhibit 4. The balances in the accounts are those shown in the adjusted trial balance columns of the end-of-period spreadsheet (work sheet) shown in Exhibit 1.

EXHIBIT 4 | Flowchart of Closing Entries for NetSolutions

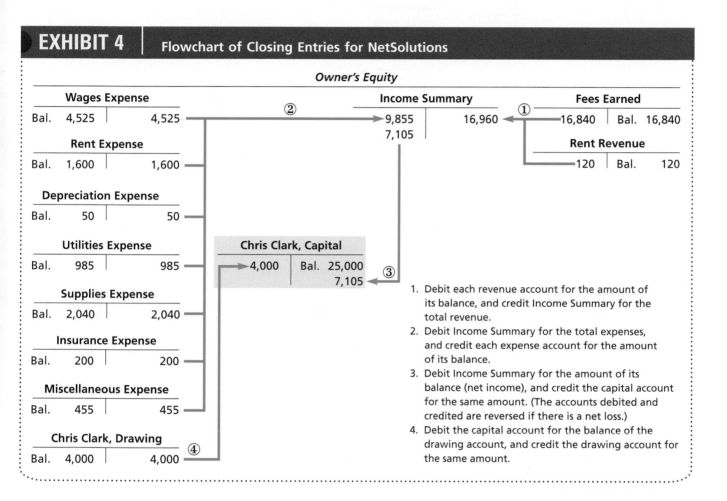

The closing entries for NetSolutions are shown in Exhibit 5. After the closing entries have been posted to the ledger, as shown in Exhibit 6 (on pages 155–159), the balance in the capital account will agree with the amount reported on the statement of owner's equity and the balance sheet. In addition, the revenue, expense, and drawing accounts will have zero balances.

After the entry to close an account has been posted, a line should be inserted in both balance columns opposite the final entry. The next period's transactions for the revenue, expense, and drawing accounts will be posted directly below the closing entry.

EXHIBIT 5

Closing Entries for
NetSolutions

			JOURNAL			Page 6	
	Date		Description	Post. Ref.	Debit	Credit	
1			Closing Entries				1
2	2007 Dec.	31	Fees Earned	41	16 8 4 0 00		2
3			Rent Revenue	42	1 2 0 00		3
4			Income Summary	33		16 9 6 0 00	4
5							5
6		31	Income Summary	33	9 8 5 5 00		6
7			Wages Expense	51		4 5 2 5 00	7
8			Rent Expense	52		1 6 0 0 00	8
9			Depreciation Expense	53		5 0 00	9
10			Utilities Expense	54		9 8 5 00	10
11			Supplies Expense	55		2 0 4 0 00	11
12			Insurance Expense	56		2 0 0 00	12
13			Miscellaneous Expense	59		4 5 5 00	13
14							14
15		31	Income Summary	33	7 1 0 5 00		15
16			Chris Clark, Capital	31		7 1 0 5 00	16
17							17
18		31	Chris Clark, Capital	31	4 0 0 0 00		18
19			Chris Clark, Drawing	32		4 0 0 0 00	19

Example Exercise 4-5   objective **3**

After the accounts have been adjusted at July 31, the end of the fiscal year, the following balances are taken from the ledger of Cabriolet Services Co.:

Terry Lambert, Capital	$615,850
Terry Lambert, Drawing	25,000
Fees Earned	380,450
Wages Expense	250,000
Rent Expense	65,000
Supplies Expense	18,250
Miscellaneous Expense	6,200

Journalize the four entries required to close the accounts.

Follow My Example 4-5

July	31	Fees Earned	380,450	
		Income Summary		380,450
	31	Income Summary	339,450	
		Wages Expense		250,000
		Rent Expense		65,000
		Supplies Expense		18,250
		Miscellaneous Expense		6,200
	31	Income Summary	41,000	
		Terry Lambert, Capital		41,000
	31	Terry Lambert, Capital	25,000	
		Terry Lambert, Drawing		25,000

For Practice: PE 4-5A, PE 4-5B

POST-CLOSING TRIAL BALANCE

The last accounting procedure for a period is to prepare a trial balance after the closing entries have been posted. The purpose of the post-closing (after closing) trial balance is to make sure that the ledger is in balance at the beginning of the next period. The accounts and amounts should agree exactly with the accounts and amounts listed on the balance sheet at the end of the period. The post-closing trial balance for NetSolutions is shown in Exhibit 7, on page 159.

Instead of preparing a formal post-closing trial balance, it is possible to list the accounts directly from the ledger, using a computer. The computer printout, in effect, becomes the post-closing trial balance.

EXHIBIT 6

Ledger for NetSolutions

LEDGER

ACCOUNT Cash   **ACCOUNT NO. 11**

Date		Item	Post. Ref.	Debit	Credit	Balance Debit	Balance Credit
2007 Nov.	1		1	25 000 00		25 000 00	
	5		1		20 000 00	5 000 00	
	18		1	7 500 00		12 500 00	
	30		1		3 650 00	8 850 00	
	30		1		950 00	7 900 00	
	30		2		2 000 00	5 900 00	
Dec.	1		2		2 400 00	3 500 00	
	1		2		800 00	2 700 00	
	1		2	360 00		3 060 00	
	6		2		180 00	2 880 00	
	11		2		400 00	2 480 00	
	13		3		950 00	1 530 00	
	16		3	3 100 00		4 630 00	
	20		3		900 00	3 730 00	
	21		3	650 00		4 380 00	
	23		3		1 450 00	2 930 00	
	27		3		1 200 00	1 730 00	
	31		3		310 00	1 420 00	
	31		4		225 00	1 195 00	
	31		4	2 870 00		4 065 00	
	31		4		2 000 00	2 065 00	

ACCOUNT Accounts Receivable   **ACCOUNT NO. 12**

Date		Item	Post. Ref.	Debit	Credit	Balance Debit	Balance Credit
2007 Dec.	16		3	1 750 00		1 750 00	
	21		3		650 00	1 100 00	
	31		4	1 120 00		2 220 00	
	31	Adjusting	5	500 00		2 720 00	

(continued)

EXHIBIT 6

ACCOUNT *Supplies*   **ACCOUNT NO.** *14*

Date		Item	Post. Ref.	Debit	Credit	Balance Debit	Balance Credit
2007 Nov.	10		1	1 3 5 0 00		1 3 5 0 00	
	30		1		8 0 0 00	5 5 0 00	
	23		3	1 4 5 0 00		2 0 0 0 00	
Dec.	31	Adjusting	5		1 2 4 0 00	7 6 0 00	

ACCOUNT *Prepaid Insurance*   **ACCOUNT NO.** *15*

Date		Item	Post. Ref.	Debit	Credit	Balance Debit	Balance Credit
2007 Dec.	1		2	2 4 0 0 00		2 4 0 0 00	
	31	Adjusting	5		2 0 0 00	2 2 0 0 00	

ACCOUNT *Land*   **ACCOUNT NO.** *17*

Date		Item	Post. Ref.	Debit	Credit	Balance Debit	Balance Credit
2007 Nov.	5		1	20 0 0 0 00		20 0 0 0 00	

ACCOUNT *Office Equipment*   **ACCOUNT NO.** *18*

Date		Item	Post. Ref.	Debit	Credit	Balance Debit	Balance Credit
2007 Dec.	4		2	1 8 0 0 00		1 8 0 0 00	

ACCOUNT *Accumulated Depreciation*   **ACCOUNT NO.** *19*

Date		Item	Post. Ref.	Debit	Credit	Balance Debit	Balance Credit
2007 Dec.	31	Adjusting	5		5 0 00		5 0 00

ACCOUNT *Accounts Payable*   **ACCOUNT NO.** *21*

Date		Item	Post. Ref.	Debit	Credit	Balance Debit	Balance Credit
2007 Nov.	10		1		1 3 5 0 00		1 3 5 0 00
	30		1	9 5 0 00			4 0 0 00
Dec.	4		2		1 8 0 0 00		2 2 0 0 00
	11		2	4 0 0 00			1 8 0 0 00
	20		3	9 0 0 00			9 0 0 00

(continued)

EXHIBIT 6

ACCOUNT *Wages Payable* ACCOUNT NO. *22*

Date	Item	Post. Ref.	Debit	Credit	Balance Debit	Balance Credit
2007 Dec. 31	Adjusting	5		2 5 0 00		2 5 0 00

ACCOUNT *Unearned Rent* ACCOUNT NO. *23*

Date	Item	Post. Ref.	Debit	Credit	Balance Debit	Balance Credit
2007 Dec. 1		2		3 6 0 00		3 6 0 00
31	Adjusting	5	1 2 0 00			2 4 0 00

ACCOUNT *Chris Clark, Capital* ACCOUNT NO. *31*

Date	Item	Post. Ref.	Debit	Credit	Balance Debit	Balance Credit
2007 Nov. 1		1		25 0 0 0 00		25 0 0 0 00
Dec. 31	Closing	6		7 1 0 5 00		32 1 0 5 00
31	Closing	6	4 0 0 0 00			28 1 0 5 00

ACCOUNT *Chris Clark, Drawing* ACCOUNT NO. *32*

Date	Item	Post. Ref.	Debit	Credit	Balance Debit	Balance Credit
2007 Nov. 30		2	2 0 0 0 00		2 0 0 0 00	
Dec. 31		4	2 0 0 0 00		4 0 0 0 00	
31	Closing	6		4 0 0 0 00	—	—

ACCOUNT *Income Summary* ACCOUNT NO. *33*

Date	Item	Post. Ref.	Debit	Credit	Balance Debit	Balance Credit
2007 Dec. 31	Closing	6		16 9 6 0 00		16 9 6 0 00
31	Closing	6	9 8 5 5 00			7 1 0 5 00
31	Closing	6	7 1 0 5 00		—	—

ACCOUNT *Fees Earned* ACCOUNT NO. *41*

Date	Item	Post. Ref.	Debit	Credit	Balance Debit	Balance Credit
2007 Nov. 18		1		7 5 0 0 00		7 5 0 0 00
Dec. 16		3		3 1 0 0 00		10 6 0 0 00
16		3		1 7 5 0 00		12 3 5 0 00
31		4		2 8 7 0 00		15 2 2 0 00
31		4		1 1 2 0 00		16 3 4 0 00
31	Adjusting	5		5 0 0 00		16 8 4 0 00
31	Closing	6	16 8 4 0 00		—	—

(continued)

EXHIBIT 6

ACCOUNT Rent Revenue — ACCOUNT NO. 42

Date		Item	Post. Ref.	Debit	Credit	Balance Debit	Balance Credit
2007 Dec.	31	Adjusting	5		1 2 0 00		1 2 0 00
	31	Closing	6	1 2 0 00		—	—

ACCOUNT Wages Expense — ACCOUNT NO. 51

Date		Item	Post. Ref.	Debit	Credit	Balance Debit	Balance Credit
2007 Nov.	30		1	2 1 2 5 00		2 1 2 5 00	
Dec.	13		3	9 5 0 00		3 0 7 5 00	
	27		3	1 2 0 0 00		4 2 7 5 00	
	31	Adjusting	5	2 5 0 00		4 5 2 5 00	
	31	Closing	6		4 5 2 5 00	—	—

ACCOUNT Rent Expense — ACCOUNT NO. 52

Date		Item	Post. Ref.	Debit	Credit	Balance Debit	Balance Credit
2007 Nov.	30		1	8 0 0 00		8 0 0 00	
Dec.	1		2	8 0 0 00		1 6 0 0 00	
	31	Closing	6		1 6 0 0 00	—	—

ACCOUNT Depreciation Expense — ACCOUNT NO. 53

Date		Item	Post. Ref.	Debit	Credit	Balance Debit	Balance Credit
2007 Dec.	31	Adjusting	5	5 0 00		5 0 00	
	31	Closing	6		5 0 00	—	—

ACCOUNT Utilities Expense — ACCOUNT NO. 54

Date		Item	Post. Ref.	Debit	Credit	Balance Debit	Balance Credit
2007 Nov.	30		1	4 5 0 00		4 5 0 00	
Dec.	31		3	3 1 0 00		7 6 0 00	
	31		4	2 2 5 00		9 8 5 00	
	31	Closing	6		9 8 5 00	—	—

ACCOUNT Supplies Expense — ACCOUNT NO. 55

Date		Item	Post. Ref.	Debit	Credit	Balance Debit	Balance Credit
2007 Nov.	30		1	8 0 0 00		8 0 0 00	
Dec.	31	Adjusting	5	1 2 4 0 00		2 0 4 0 00	
	31	Closing	6		2 0 4 0 00	—	—

(continued)

EXHIBIT 6

ACCOUNT *Insurance Expense*   **ACCOUNT NO.** *56*

Date		Item	Post. Ref.	Debit	Credit	Balance Debit	Balance Credit
2007 Dec.	31	Adjusting	5	2 0 0 00		2 0 0 00	
	31	Closing	6		2 0 0 00	—	—

ACCOUNT *Miscellaneous Expense*   **ACCOUNT NO.** *59*

Date		Item	Post. Ref.	Debit	Credit	Balance Debit	Balance Credit
2007 Nov.	30		1	2 7 5 00		2 7 5 00	
Dec.	6		2	1 8 0 00		4 5 5 00	
	31	Closing	6		4 5 5 00	—	—

(concluded)

EXHIBIT 7

Post-Closing Trial Balance

NetSolutions
Post-Closing Trial Balance
December 31, 2007

	Debit Balances	Credit Balances
Cash	2 0 6 5 00	
Accounts Receivable	2 7 2 0 00	
Supplies	7 6 0 00	
Prepaid Insurance	2 2 0 0 00	
Land	20 0 0 0 00	
Office Equipment	1 8 0 0 00	
Accumulated Depreciation		5 0 00
Accounts Payable		9 0 0 00
Wages Payable		2 5 0 00
Unearned Rent		2 4 0 00
Chris Clark, Capital		28 1 0 5 00
	29 5 4 5 00	29 5 4 5 00

Accounting Cycle

objective **4**

Describe the accounting cycle.

The accounting process that begins with analyzing and journalizing transactions and ends with preparing the accounting records for the next period's transactions is called the **accounting cycle**. The steps in the accounting cycle are as follows:

1. Transactions are analyzed and recorded in the journal.
2. Transactions are posted to the ledger.
3. An unadjusted trial balance is prepared.
4. Adjustment data are assembled and analyzed.
5. An optional end-of-period spreadsheet (work sheet) is prepared.
6. Adjusting entries are journalized and posted to the ledger.
7. An adjusted trial balance is prepared.
8. Financial statements are prepared.
9. Closing entries are journalized and posted to the ledger.
10. A post-closing trial balance is prepared.[2]

---

2 Some accountants include the journalizing and posting of "reversing entries" as the last step in the accounting cycle. Because reversing entries are not required, we describe and illustrate them in Appendix B at the end of the book.

Exhibit 8 illustrates the accounting cycle in graphic form. In addition, Exhibit 8 illustrates how the accounting data beginning with the source documents for a transaction flow through the accounting system and into the financial statements. In the next section, we illustrate a comprehensive example of the accounting cycle.

EXHIBIT 8 | Accounting Cycle

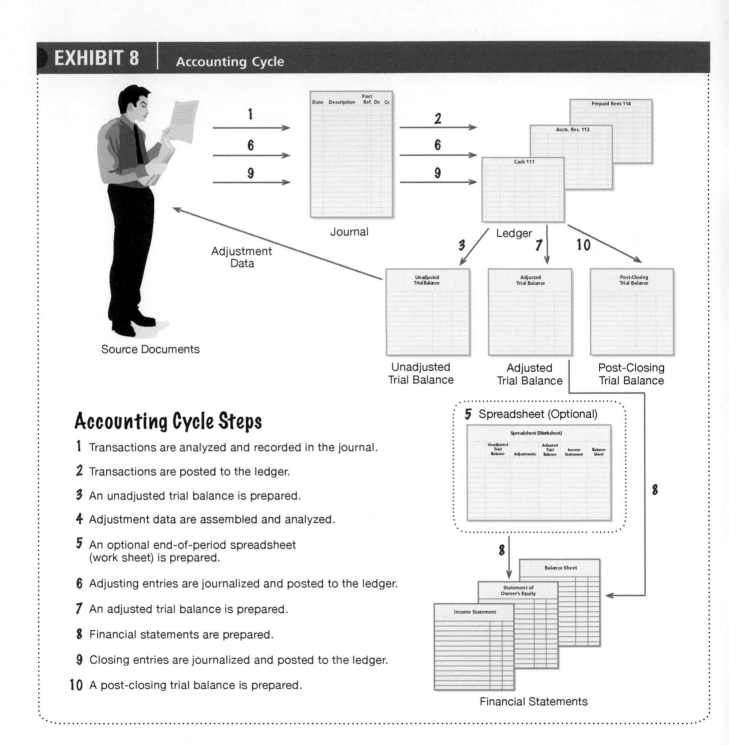

Accounting Cycle Steps

1 Transactions are analyzed and recorded in the journal.

2 Transactions are posted to the ledger.

3 An unadjusted trial balance is prepared.

4 Adjustment data are assembled and analyzed.

5 An optional end-of-period spreadsheet (work sheet) is prepared.

6 Adjusting entries are journalized and posted to the ledger.

7 An adjusted trial balance is prepared.

8 Financial statements are prepared.

9 Closing entries are journalized and posted to the ledger.

10 A post-closing trial balance is prepared.

Example Exercise 4-6

objective 4

From the following list of steps in the accounting cycle, identify what two steps are missing.

    a. Transactions are analyzed and recorded in the journal.
    b. Transactions are posted to the ledger.
    c. Adjustment data are assembled and analyzed.
    d. An optional end-of-period spreadsheet (work sheet) is prepared.
    e. Adjusting entries are journalized and posted to the ledger.
    f. Financial statements are prepared.
    g. Closing entries are journalized and posted to the ledger.
    h. A post-closing trial balance is prepared.

Follow My Example 4-6

The following two steps are missing: (1) the preparation of an unadjusted trial balance and (2) the preparation of the adjusted trial balance. The unadjusted trial balance should be prepared after step (b). The adjusted trial balance should be prepared after step (e).

For Practice: PE 4-6A, PE 4-6B

Illustration of the Accounting Cycle

objective **5**

Illustrate the accounting cycle for one period.

In this section, we will illustate the complete accounting cycle for one period. We assume that for several years Kelly Pitney has operated a part-time consulting business from her home. As of April 1, 2008, Kelly decided to move to rented quarters and to operate the business, which will be known as Kelly Consulting, on a full-time basis. Kelly Consulting entered into the following transactions during April:

Apr. 1. The following assets were received from Kelly Pitney: cash, $13,100; accounts receivable, $3,000; supplies, $1,400; and office equipment, $12,500. There were no liabilities received.
    1. Paid three months' rent on a lease rental contract, $4,800.
    2. Paid the premiums on property and casualty insurance policies, $1,800.
    4. Received cash from clients as an advance payment for services to be provided and recorded it as unearned fees, $5,000.
    5. Purchased additional office equipment on account from Office Station Co., $2,000.
    6. Received cash from clients on account, $1,800.
    10. Paid cash for a newspaper advertisement, $120.
    12. Paid Office Station Co. for part of the debt incurred on April 5, $1,200.
    12. Recorded services provided on account for the period April 1–12, $4,200.
    14. Paid part-time receptionist for two weeks' salary, $750.
    17. Recorded cash from cash clients for fees earned during the period April 1–16, $6,250.
    18. Paid cash for supplies, $800.
    20. Recorded services provided on account for the period April 13–20, $2,100.
    24. Recorded cash from cash clients for fees earned for the period April 17–24, $3,850.
    26. Received cash from clients on account, $5,600.
    27. Paid part-time receptionist for two weeks' salary, $750.
    29. Paid telephone bill for April, $130.
    30. Paid electricity bill for April, $200.
    30. Recorded cash from cash clients for fees earned for the period April 25–30, $3,050.
    30. Recorded services provided on account for the remainder of April, $1,500.
    30. Kelly withdrew $6,000 for personal use.

STEP 1. ANALYZING AND RECORDING TRANSACTIONS IN THE JOURNAL

The first step in the accounting cycle is to analyze and record transactions in the journal shown in Exhibit 9. As we illustrated in Chapter 2, the double-entry accounting system is a very powerful tool for analyzing transactions. In using this system to analyze transactions, we do the following:

1. Carefully read the description of the transaction to determine whether an asset, liability, owner's equity, revenue, expense, or drawing account is affected by the transaction.
2. For each account affected by the transaction, determine whether the account increases or decreases.
3. Determine whether each increase or decrease should be recorded as a debit or a credit following the rules of debit and credit shown in Exhibit 3 of Chapter 2.
4. Record the transaction using a journal entry.

EXHIBIT 9

Journal Entries for April, Kelly Consulting

JOURNAL   Page 1

	Date		Description	Post. Ref.	Debit	Credit	
1	2008 April	1	Cash	11	13 1 0 0 00		1
2			Accounts Receivable	12	3 0 0 0 00		2
3			Supplies	14	1 4 0 0 00		3
4			Office Equipment	18	12 5 0 0 00		4
5			Kelly Pitney, Capital	31		3 0 0 0 0 00	5
6							6
7		1	Prepaid Rent	15	4 8 0 0 00		7
8			Cash	11		4 8 0 0 00	8
9							9
10		2	Prepaid Insurance	16	1 8 0 0 00		10
11			Cash	11		1 8 0 0 00	11
12							12
13		4	Cash	11	5 0 0 0 00		13
14			Unearned Fees	23		5 0 0 0 00	14
15							15
16		5	Office Equipment	18	2 0 0 0 00		16
17			Accounts Payable	21		2 0 0 0 00	17
18							18
19		6	Cash	11	1 8 0 0 00		19
20			Accounts Receivable	12		1 8 0 0 00	20
21							21
22		10	Miscellaneous Expense	59	1 2 0 00		22
23			Cash	11		1 2 0 00	23
24							24
25		12	Accounts Payable	21	1 2 0 0 00		25
26			Cash	11		1 2 0 0 00	26
27							27
28		12	Accounts Receivable	12	4 2 0 0 00		28
29			Fees Earned	41		4 2 0 0 00	29
30							30
31		14	Salary Expense	51	7 5 0 00		31
32			Cash	11		7 5 0 00	32
33							33

(continued)

The company's chart of accounts is useful in determining which accounts are affected by the transaction. The chart of accounts for Kelly Consulting is as follows:

11	Cash		31	Kelly Pitney, Capital
12	Accounts Receivable		32	Kelly Pitney, Drawing
14	Supplies		33	Income Summary
15	Prepaid Rent		41	Fees Earned
16	Prepaid Insurance		51	Salary Expense
18	Office Equipment		52	Rent Expense
19	Accumulated Depreciation		53	Supplies Expense
21	Accounts Payable		54	Depreciation Expense
22	Salaries Payable		55	Insurance Expense
23	Unearned Fees		59	Miscellaneous Expense

After analyzing each of Kelly Consulting's transactions for April, the journal entries are recorded as shown in Exhibit 9.

EXHIBIT 9

Continued

JOURNAL Page 2

	Date	Description	Post. Ref.	Debit	Credit	
1	2008 April 17	Cash	11	6 2 5 0 00		1
2		Fees Earned	41		6 2 5 0 00	2
3						3
4	18	Supplies	14	8 0 0 00		4
5		Cash	11		8 0 0 00	5
6						6
7	20	Accounts Receivable	12	2 1 0 0 00		7
8		Fees Earned	41		2 1 0 0 00	8
9						9
10	24	Cash	11	3 8 5 0 00		10
11		Fees Earned	41		3 8 5 0 00	11
12						12
13	26	Cash	11	5 6 0 0 00		13
14		Accounts Receivable	12		5 6 0 0 00	14
15						15
16	27	Salary Expense	51	7 5 0 00		16
17		Cash	11		7 5 0 00	17
18						18
19	29	Miscellaneous Expense	59	1 3 0 00		19
20		Cash	11		1 3 0 00	20
21						21
22	30	Miscellaneous Expense	59	2 0 0 00		22
23		Cash	11		2 0 0 00	23
24						24
25	30	Cash	11	3 0 5 0 00		25
26		Fees Earned	41		3 0 5 0 00	26
27						27
28	30	Accounts Receivable	12	1 5 0 0 00		28
29		Fees Earned	41		1 5 0 0 00	29
30						30
31	30	Kelly Pitney, Drawing	32	6 0 0 0 00		31
32		Cash	11		6 0 0 0 00	32
33						33

STEP 2. POSTING TRANSACTIONS TO THE LEDGER

Periodically, the transactions recorded in the journal are posted to the accounts in the ledger. As we illustrated in Chapters 2 and 3, the posting process includes recording the date of the transaction, the debit or credit amount, and the journal reference in the account. In addition, account numbers are recorded in the Post Reference column of the journal to indicate that the entry has been posted to the accounts in the ledger. The journal entries for Kelly Consulting have been posted to the ledger shown in Exhibit 17.

STEP 3. PREPARING AN UNADJUSTED TRIAL BALANCE

In order to determine whether any errors have been made in posting the debits and credits to the ledger, an unadjusted trial balance should be prepared. The unadjusted trial balance does not provide complete proof of the accuracy of the ledger. It indicates only that the debits and the credits are equal. This proof is of value, however, because errors often affect the equality of debits and credits. If the two totals of a trial balance are not equal, an error has occurred that must be discovered and corrected.

The unadjusted trial balance for Kelly Consulting is shown in Exhibit 10. The unadjusted account balances shown in Exhibit 10 were taken from Kelly Consulting's ledger shown in Exhibit 17, on pages 170–174, before any adjusting entries were recorded.

EXHIBIT 10

Unadjusted
Trial Balance,
Kelly Consulting

Kelly Consulting
Unadjusted Trial Balance
April 30, 2008

	Debit Balances	Credit Balances
Cash	22 1 0 0 00	
Accounts Receivable	3 4 0 0 00	
Supplies	2 2 0 0 00	
Prepaid Rent	4 8 0 0 00	
Prepaid Insurance	1 8 0 0 00	
Office Equipment	14 5 0 0 00	
Accumulated Depreciation		
Accounts Payable		8 0 0 00
Salaries Payable		
Unearned Fees		5 0 0 0 00
Kelly Pitney, Capital		30 0 0 0 00
Kelly Pitney, Drawing	6 0 0 0 00	
Fees Earned		20 9 5 0 00
Salary Expense	1 5 0 0 00	
Rent Expense		
Supplies Expense		
Depreciation Expense		
Insurance Expense		
Miscellaneous Expense	4 5 0 00	
	56 7 5 0 00	56 7 5 0 00

STEP 4. ASSEMBLING AND ANALYZING ADJUSTMENT DATA

Before the financial statements can be prepared, the accounts must be updated. The four types of accounts that normally require adjustment include prepaid expenses, unearned revenue, accrued revenue, and accrued expenses. In addition, depreciation expense must be recorded for fixed assets other than land. The following data have been assembled on April 30, 2008, for analysis of possible adjustments for Kelly Consulting:

a. Insurance expired during April is $300.
b. Supplies on hand on April 30 are $1,350.
c. Depreciation of office equipment for April is $330.
d. Accrued receptionist salary on April 30 is $120.
e. Rent expired during April is $1,600.
f. Unearned fees on April 30 are $2,500.

STEP 5. PREPARING AN OPTIONAL END-OF-PERIOD SPREADSHEET (WORK SHEET)

Although an end-of-period spreadsheet (work sheet) is not required, it is useful in showing the flow of accounting information from the unadjusted trial balance to the adjusted trial balance and financial statements. In addition, an end-of-period spreadsheet (work sheet) is useful in analyzing the impact of proposed adjustments on the financial statements. The end-of-period spreadsheet (work sheet) for Kelly Consulting is shown in Exhibit 11.

EXHIBIT 11   End-of-Period Spreadsheet (Work Sheet)

	A	B	C	D	E	F	G	H	I	J	K	
					Kelly Consulting							
				End-of-Period Spreadsheet (Work Sheet)								
				For the Month Ended April 30, 2008								
		Unadjusted Trial Balance		Adjustments		Adjusted Trial Balance		Income Statement		Balance Sheet		
	Account Title	Dr.	Cr.	Dr.	Cr.	Dr.	Cr.	Dr.	Cr.	Dr.	Cr.	
1	Cash	22,100				22,100				22,100		1
2	Accounts Receivable	3,400				3,400				3,400		2
3	Supplies	2,200			(b) 850	1,350				1,350		3
4	Prepaid Rent	4,800			(e) 1,600	3,200				3,200		4
5	Prepaid Insurance	1,800			(a) 300	1,500				1,500		5
6	Office Equipment	14,500				14,500				14,500		6
7	Accum. Depreciation				(c) 330		330				330	7
8	Accounts Payable		800				800				800	8
9	Salaries Payable				(d) 120		120				120	9
10	Unearned Fees		5,000	(f) 2,500			2,500				2,500	10
11	Kelly Pitney, Capital		30,000				30,000				30,000	11
12	Kelly Pitney, Drawing	6,000				6,000				6,000		12
13	Fees Earned		20,950		(f) 2,500		23,450		23,450			13
14	Salary Expense	1,500		(d) 120		1,620		1,620				14
15	Rent Expense			(e) 1,600		1,600		1,600				15
16	Supplies Expense			(b) 850		850		850				16
17	Depreciation Expense			(c) 330		330		330				17
18	Insurance Expense			(a) 300		300		300				18
19	Miscellaneous Expense	450				450		450				19
20		56,750	56,750	5,700	5,700	57,200	57,200	5,150	23,450	52,050	33,750	20
21	Net income							18,300			18,300	21
22								23,450	23,450	52,050	52,050	22

STEP 6. JOURNALIZNG AND POSTING ADJUSTING ENTRIES

Based upon the adjustment data shown in step 4, adjusting entries for Kelly Consulting are prepared. Each adjusting entry affects at least one income statement account and one balance sheet account. Explanations for each adjustment including any computations are normally included with each adjusting entry. The adjusting entries for Kelly Consulting are shown in Exhibit 12.

Each of the adjusting entries shown in Exhibit 12 is posted to Kelly Consulting's ledger shown in Exhibit 17. The adjusting entries are identified in the ledger as "Adjusting Entry."

EXHIBIT 12

Adjusting Entries,
Kelly Consulting

			JOURNAL						Page 3	
	Date			Post. Ref.	Debit		Credit			
			Adjusting Entries							
1	2008 Apr.	30	Insurance Expense	55	3 0 0 00					1
2			Prepaid Insurance	16			3 0 0 00			2
3			Expired Insurance.							3
4										4
5		30	Supplies Expense	53	8 5 0 00					5
6			Supplies	14			8 5 0 00			6
7			Supplies used ($2,200 – $1,350).							7
8										8
9		30	Depreciation Expense	54	3 3 0 00					9
10			Accumulated Depreciation	19			3 3 0 00			10
11			Depreciation of office equipment.							11
12										12
13		30	Salary Expense	51	1 2 0 00					13
14			Salaries Payable	22			1 2 0 00			14
15			Accrued salary.							15
16										16
17		30	Rent Expense	52	1 6 0 0 00					17
18			Prepaid Rent	15			1 6 0 0 00			18
19			Rent expired during April.							19
20										20
21		30	Unearned Fees	23	2 5 0 0 00					21
22			Fees Earned	41			2 5 0 0 00			22
23			Fees earned ($5,000 – $2,500).							23

STEP 7. PREPARING AN ADJUSTED TRIAL BALANCE

After the adjustments have been journalized and posted, an adjusted trial balance is prepared to verify the equality of the total of the debit and credit balances. This is the last step before preparing the financial statements, and any errors arising from posting the adjusting entries must be found and corrected. The adjusted trial balance for Kelly Consulting as of April 30, 2008, is shown in Exhibit 13.

STEP 8. PREPARING THE FINANCIAL STATEMENTS

The most important outcome of the accounting cycle is the financial statements. The income statement is prepared first, followed by the statement of owner's equity and then the balance sheet. The statements can be prepared directly from the adjusted trial balance, the end-of-period spreadsheet, or the ledger. The net income or net loss shown on the income statement is reported on the statement of owner's equity along with any additional investments by the owner and any withdrawals. The ending owner's capi-

EXHIBIT 13

Adjusted Trial Balance, Kelly Consulting

Kelly Consulting
Adjusted Trial Balance
April 30, 2008

	Debit Balances	Credit Balances
Cash	22 1 0 0 00	
Accounts Receivable	3 4 0 0 00	
Supplies	1 3 5 0 00	
Prepaid Rent	3 2 0 0 00	
Prepaid Insurance	1 5 0 0 00	
Office Equipment	14 5 0 0 00	
Accumulated Depreciation		3 3 0 00
Accounts Payable		8 0 0 00
Salaries Payable		1 2 0 00
Unearned Fees		2 5 0 0 00
Kelly Pitney, Capital		30 0 0 0 00
Kelly Pitney, Drawing	6 0 0 0 00	
Fees Earned		23 4 5 0 00
Salary Expense	1 6 2 0 00	
Rent Expense	1 6 0 0 00	
Supplies Expense	8 5 0 00	
Depreciation Expense	3 3 0 00	
Insurance Expense	3 0 0 00	
Miscellaneous Expense	4 5 0 00	
	57 2 0 0 00	57 2 0 0 00

tal is reported on the balance sheet and is added with total liabilities to equal total assets.

The financial statements for Kelly Consulting are shown in Exhibit 14. Kelly Consulting earned net income of $18,300 for April. As of April 30, 2008, Kelly Consulting has total assets of $45,720, total liabilities of $3,420, and total owner's equity of $42,300.

EXHIBIT 14

Financial Statements, Kelly Consulting

Kelly Consulting
Income Statement
For the Month Ended April 30, 2008

Fees earned		$23 4 5 0 00
Expenses:		
Salary expense	$1 6 2 0 00	
Rent expense	1 6 0 0 00	
Supplies expense	8 5 0 00	
Depreciation expense	3 3 0 00	
Insurance expense	3 0 0 00	
Miscellaneous expense	4 5 0 00	
Total expenses		5 1 5 0 00
Net income		$18 3 0 0 00

(continued)

EXHIBIT 14

Kelly Consulting
Statement of Owner's Equity
For the Month Ended April 30, 2008

Kelly Pitney, capital, April 1, 2008		$	0
Investment during the month	$30 0 0 0 00		
Net income for the month	18 3 0 0 00		
	$48 3 0 0 00		
Less withdrawals	6 0 0 0 00		
Increase in owner's equity		42 3 0 0 00	
Kelly Pitney, capital, April 30, 2008		$42 3 0 0 00	

Kelly Consulting
Balance Sheet
April 30, 2008

Assets			Liabilities		
Current assets:			Current liabilities:		
Cash	$22 1 0 0 00		Accounts payable	$ 8 0 0 00	
Accounts receivable	3 4 0 0 00		Salaries payable	1 2 0 00	
Supplies	1 3 5 0 00		Unearned fees	2 5 0 0 00	
Prepaid rent	3 2 0 0 00		Total liabilities		$ 3 4 2 0 00
Prepaid insurance	1 5 0 0 00				
Total current assets		$31 5 5 0 00			
Property, plant, and equipment:					
Office equipment	$14 5 0 0 00				
Less accumulated depr.	3 3 0 00		**Owner's Equity**		
Total property, plant,			Kelly Pitney, capital		42 3 0 0 00
and equipment		14 1 7 0 00	Total liabilities and		
Total assets		$45 7 2 0 00	owner's equity		$45 7 2 0 00

STEP 9. JOURNALIZING AND POSTING CLOSING ENTRIES

As described earlier in this chapter, four closing entries are required at the end of an accounting period to ready the accounts for the next period. The first closing entry transfers the revenue account balances to Income Summary. The second closing entry transfers the expense account balances to Income Summary. The third entry transfers the balance of Income Summary to the owner's capital account. Finally, the fourth entry transfers any balance in the owner's drawing account to the owner's capital account. The four closing entries for Kelly Consulting are shown in Exhibit 15.

After the closing entries have been posted to the ledger, the balance in owner's capital account will agree with the amount reported on the statement of owner's equity and the balance sheet. For Kelly Consulting, the ending balance of the Kelly Pitney, Capital is $42,300, as shown in Exhibit 17. In addition, as shown in Exhibit 17, after the closing entries are posted, all the revenue, expense, and drawing accounts have zero balances. The closing entries are identified in the ledger as "Closing."

STEP 10. PREPARING A POST-CLOSING TRIAL BALANCE

The last step in the accounting cycle is to prepare a post-closing trial balance. The purpose of the post-closing trial balance is to make sure that the ledger is in balance at the

EXHIBIT 15

Closing Entries, Kelly Consulting

	Date		Description	Post. Ref.	Debit	Credit	
			Closing Entries				
1	2008 Apr.	30	Fees Earned	41	23 4 5 0 00		1
2			Income Summary	33		23 4 5 0 00	2
3							3
4		30	Income Summary	33	5 1 5 0 00		4
5			Salary Expense	51		1 6 2 0 00	5
6			Rent Expense	52		1 6 0 0 00	6
7			Supplies Expense	53		8 5 0 00	7
8			Depreciation Expense	54		3 3 0 00	8
9			Insurance Expense	55		3 0 0 00	9
10			Miscellaneous Expense	59		4 5 0 00	10
11							11
12		30	Income Summary	33	18 3 0 0 00		12
13			Kelly Pitney, Capital	31		18 3 0 0 00	13
14							14
15		30	Kelly Pitney, Capital	31	6 0 0 0 00		15
16			Kelly Pitney, Drawing	32		6 0 0 0 00	16

JOURNAL Page 4

beginning of the next period. The accounts and amounts in the post-closing trial balance should agree exactly with the accounts and amounts listed on the balance sheet at the end of the period.

The post-closing trial balance for Kelly Consulting is shown in Exhibit 16. The balances shown in the post-closing trial balance are taken from the ending balances in the ledger shown in Exhibit 17. These balances agree with the amounts shown on Kelly Consulting's balance sheet in Exhibit 14.

EXHIBIT 16

Post-Closing Trial Balance, Kelly Consulting

Kelly Consulting
Post-Closing Trial Balance
April 30, 2008

	Debit Balances	Credit Balances
Cash	22 1 0 0 00	
Accounts Receivable	3 4 0 0 00	
Supplies	1 3 5 0 00	
Prepaid Rent	3 2 0 0 00	
Prepaid Insurance	1 5 0 0 00	
Office Equipment	14 5 0 0 00	
Accumulated Depreciation		3 3 0 00
Accounts Payable		8 0 0 00
Salaries Payable		1 2 0 00
Unearned Fees		2 5 0 0 00
Kelly Pitney, Capital		42 3 0 0 00
	46 0 5 0 00	46 0 5 0 00

EXHIBIT 17

Ledger,
Kelly Consulting

LEDGER

ACCOUNT *Cash*   **ACCOUNT NO.** *11*

Date		Item	Post. Ref.	Debit	Credit	Balance Debit	Balance Credit
2008 Apr.	1		1	13 1 0 0 00		13 1 0 0 00	
	1		1		4 8 0 0 00	8 3 0 0 00	
	2		1		1 8 0 0 00	6 5 0 0 00	
	4		1	5 0 0 0 00		11 5 0 0 00	
	6		1	1 8 0 0 00		13 3 0 0 00	
	10		1		1 2 0 00	13 1 8 0 00	
	12		1		1 2 0 0 00	11 9 8 0 00	
	14		1		7 5 0 00	11 2 3 0 00	
	17		2	6 2 5 0 00		17 4 8 0 00	
	18		2		8 0 0 00	16 6 8 0 00	
	24		2	3 8 5 0 00		20 5 3 0 00	
	26		2	5 6 0 0 00		26 1 3 0 00	
	27		2		7 5 0 00	25 3 8 0 00	
	29		2		1 3 0 00	25 2 5 0 00	
	30		2		2 0 0 00	25 0 5 0 00	
	30		2	3 0 5 0 00		28 1 0 0 00	
	30		2		6 0 0 0 00	22 1 0 0 00	

ACCOUNT *Accounts Receivable*   **ACCOUNT NO.** *12*

Date		Item	Post. Ref.	Debit	Credit	Balance Debit	Balance Credit
2008 Apr.	1		1	3 0 0 0 00		3 0 0 0 00	
	6		1		1 8 0 0 00	1 2 0 0 00	
	12		1	4 2 0 0 00		5 4 0 0 00	
	20		2	2 1 0 0 00		7 5 0 0 00	
	26		2		5 6 0 0 00	1 9 0 0 00	
	30		2	1 5 0 0 00		3 4 0 0 00	

ACCOUNT *Supplies*   **ACCOUNT NO.** *14*

Date		Item	Post. Ref.	Debit	Credit	Balance Debit	Balance Credit
2008 Apr.	1		1	1 4 0 0 00		1 4 0 0 00	
	18		2	8 0 0 00		2 2 0 0 00	
	30	Adjusting	3		8 5 0 00	1 3 5 0 00	

(continued)

EXHIBIT 17

ACCOUNT *Prepaid Rent*   **ACCOUNT NO.** *15*

Date	Item	Post. Ref.	Debit	Credit	Balance Debit	Balance Credit
2008 Apr. 1		1	4 8 0 0 00		4 8 0 0 00	
30	Adjusting	3		1 6 0 0 00	3 2 0 0 00	

ACCOUNT *Prepaid Insurance*   **ACCOUNT NO.** *16*

Date	Item	Post. Ref.	Debit	Credit	Balance Debit	Balance Credit
2008 Apr. 2		1	1 8 0 0 00		1 8 0 0 00	
30	Adjusting	3		3 0 0 00	1 5 0 0 00	

ACCOUNT *Office Equipment*   **ACCOUNT NO.** *18*

Date	Item	Post. Ref.	Debit	Credit	Balance Debit	Balance Credit
2008 Apr. 1		1	12 5 0 0 00		12 5 0 0 00	
5		1	2 0 0 0 00		14 5 0 0 00	

ACCOUNT *Accumulated Depreciation*   **ACCOUNT NO.** *19*

Date	Item	Post. Ref.	Debit	Credit	Balance Debit	Balance Credit
2008 Apr. 30	Adjusting	3		3 3 0 00		3 3 0 00

ACCOUNT *Accounts Payable*   **ACCOUNT NO.** *21*

Date	Item	Post. Ref.	Debit	Credit	Balance Debit	Balance Credit
2008 Apr. 5		1		2 0 0 0 00		2 0 0 0 00
12		1	1 2 0 0 00			8 0 0 00

(continued)

EXHIBIT 17

ACCOUNT *Salaries Payable*   **ACCOUNT NO.** *22*

Date		Item	Post. Ref.	Debit	Credit	Balance	
						Debit	Credit
2008 Apr.	30	Adjusting	3		1 2 0 00		1 2 0 00

ACCOUNT *Unearned Fees*   **ACCOUNT NO.** *23*

Date		Item	Post. Ref.	Debit	Credit	Balance	
						Debit	Credit
2008 Apr.	4		1		5 0 0 0 00		5 0 0 0 00
	30	Adjusting	3	2 5 0 0 00			2 5 0 0 00

ACCOUNT *Kelly Pitney, Capital*   **ACCOUNT NO.** *31*

Date		Item	Post. Ref.	Debit	Credit	Balance	
						Debit	Credit
2008 Apr.	1		1		30 0 0 0 00		30 0 0 0 00
	30	Closing	4		18 3 0 0 00		48 3 0 0 00
	30	Closing	4	6 0 0 0 00			42 3 0 0 00

ACCOUNT *Kelly Pitney, Drawing*   **ACCOUNT NO.** *32*

Date		Item	Post. Ref.	Debit	Credit	Balance	
						Debit	Credit
2008 Apr.	30		2	6 0 0 0 00		6 0 0 0 00	
	30	Closing	4		6 0 0 0 00	—	—

ACCOUNT *Income Summary*   **ACCOUNT NO.** *33*

Date		Item	Post. Ref.	Debit	Credit	Balance	
						Debit	Credit
2008 Apr.	30	Closing	4		23 4 5 0 00		23 4 5 0 00
	30	Closing	4	5 1 5 0 00			18 3 0 0 00
	30	Closing	4	18 3 0 0 00		—	—

(continued)

EXHIBIT 17

ACCOUNT *Fees Earned*   **ACCOUNT NO.** *41*

Date		Item	Post. Ref.	Debit	Credit	Balance Debit	Balance Credit
2008 Apr.	12		1		4 2 0 0 00		4 2 0 0 00
	17		2		6 2 5 0 00		10 4 5 0 00
	20		2		2 1 0 0 00		12 5 5 0 00
	24		2		3 8 5 0 00		16 4 0 0 00
	30		2		3 0 5 0 00		19 4 5 0 00
	30		2		1 5 0 0 00		20 9 5 0 00
	30	Adjusting	3		2 5 0 0 00		23 4 5 0 00
	30	Closing	4	23 4 5 0 00		—	—

ACCOUNT *Salary Expense*   **ACCOUNT NO.** *51*

Date		Item	Post. Ref.	Debit	Credit	Balance Debit	Balance Credit
2008 Apr.	14		1	7 5 0 00		7 5 0 00	
	27		2	7 5 0 00		1 5 0 0 00	
	30	Adjusting	3	1 2 0 00		1 6 2 0 00	
	30	Closing	4		1 6 2 0 00	—	—

ACCOUNT *Rent Expense*   **ACCOUNT NO.** *52*

Date		Item	Post. Ref.	Debit	Credit	Balance Debit	Balance Credit
2008 Apr.	30	Adjusting	3	1 6 0 0 00		1 6 0 0 00	
	30	Closing	4		1 6 0 0 00	—	—

ACCOUNT *Supplies Expense*   **ACCOUNT NO.** *53*

Date		Item	Post. Ref.	Debit	Credit	Balance Debit	Balance Credit
2008 Apr.	30	Adjusting	3	8 5 0 00		8 5 0 00	
	30	Closing	4		8 5 0 00	—	—

ACCOUNT *Depreciation Expense*   **ACCOUNT NO.** *54*

Date		Item	Post. Ref.	Debit	Credit	Balance Debit	Balance Credit
2008 Apr.	30	Adjusting	3	3 3 0 00		3 3 0 00	
	30	Closing	4		3 3 0 00	—	—

(continued)

EXHIBIT 17

ACCOUNT *Insurance Expense*					ACCOUNT NO. 55	
		Post.			Balance	
Date	Item	Ref.	Debit	Credit	Debit	Credit
2008 Apr. 30	Adjusting	3	3 0 0 00		3 0 0 00	
30	Closing	4		3 0 0 00	—	—

ACCOUNT *Miscellaneous Expense*					ACCOUNT NO. 59	
		Post.			Balance	
Date	Item	Ref.	Debit	Credit	Debit	Credit
2008 Apr. 10		1	1 2 0 00		1 2 0 00	
29		2	1 3 0 00		2 5 0 00	
30		2	2 0 0 00		4 5 0 00	
30	Closing	4		4 5 0 00	—	—

(concluded)

Fiscal Year

objective 6

Explain what is meant by the fiscal year and the natural business year.

The annual accounting period adopted by a business is known as its **fiscal year**. Fiscal years begin with the first day of the month selected and end on the last day of the following twelfth month. The period most commonly used is the calendar year. Other periods are not unusual, especially for businesses organized as corporations. For example, a corporation may adopt a fiscal year that ends when business activities have reached the lowest point in its annual operating cycle. Such a fiscal year is called the **natural business year**. At the low point in its operating cycle, a business has more time to analyze the results of operations and to prepare financial statements.

Because companies with fiscal years often have highly seasonal operations, investors and others should be careful in interpreting partial-year reports for such companies. That is, you should expect the results of operations for these companies to vary significantly throughout the fiscal year.

The financial history of a business may be shown by a series of balance sheets and income statements for several fiscal years. If the life of a business is expressed by a line moving from left to right, the series of balance sheets and income statements may be graphed as follows:

REAL WORLD

Percentage of Companies with Fiscal Years Ending in:

January	5%	July	2%
February	1	August	2
March	3	September	7
April	2	October	3
May	3	November	2
June	7	December	63

Source: *Accounting Trends & Techniques,* 59th edition, 2005 (New York: American Institute of Certified Public Accountants).

Financial History of a Business

Income Statement for the year ended Dec. 31, 2006

Income Statement for the year ended Dec. 31, 2007

Income Statement for the year ended Dec. 31, 2008

Balance Sheet Dec. 31, 2006   Balance Sheet Dec. 31, 2007   Balance Sheet Dec. 31, 2008

You may think of the income statements, balance sheets, and financial history of a business as similar to the record of a college football team. The final score of each football game is similar to the net income reported on the income statement of a business. The team's season record after each game is similar to the balance sheet. At the end of the season, the final record of the team measures its success or failure. Likewise, at the end of a life of a business, its final balance sheet is a measure of its financial success or failure.

Appendix

End-of-Period Spreadsheet (Work Sheet)

Accountants often use working papers for collecting and summarizing data they need for preparing various analyses and reports. Such working papers are useful tools, but they are not considered a part of the formal accounting records. This is in contrast to the chart of accounts, the journal, and the ledger, which are essential parts of the accounting system. Working papers are usually prepared by using a spreadsheet program on a computer.

@netsolutions

The end-of-period spreadsheet (work sheet) shown in Exhibit 1 is a working paper that accountants can use to summarize adjusting entries and the account balances for the financial statements. In small companies with few accounts and adjustments, an end-of-period spreadsheet (work sheet) may not be necessary. For example, the financial statements for NetSolutions can be prepared directly from the adjusted trial balance in Exhibit 1. However, many accountants prefer to use an end-of-period spreadsheet (work sheet) as an aid to analyzing adjustment data and preparing the financial statements. We use Exhibits 18 through 21 on page 176B to describe and illustrate how to prepare this type of end-of-period spreadsheet (work sheet).

UNADJUSTED TRIAL BALANCE COLUMNS

To begin the spreadsheet (work sheet), enter at the top the name of the business, the type of working paper, and the period of time, as shown in Exhibit 18. Next, enter the unadjusted trial balance directly on the spreadsheet. The spreadsheet in Exhibit 18 shows the unadjusted trial balance for NetSolutions at December 31, 2007.

ADJUSTMENTS COLUMNS

The adjustments that we explained and illustrated for NetSolutions in Chapter 3 are entered in the Adjustments columns, as shown in Exhibit 19. Cross-referencing (by letters) the debit and credit of each adjustment is useful in reviewing the spreadsheet (work sheet). It is also helpful for identifying the adjusting entries that need to be recorded in the journal.

The order in which the adjustments are entered on the spreadsheet (work sheet) is not important. Most accountants enter the adjustments in the order in which the data are assembled. If the titles of some of the accounts to be adjusted do not appear in the trial balance, they should be entered in the Account Title column, below the trial balance totals, as needed.

To review, the entries in the Adjustments columns of the work sheet are:

(a) **Supplies.** The supplies account has a debit balance of $2,000. The cost of the supplies on hand at the end of the period is $760. Therefore, the supplies expense for December is the difference between the two amounts, or $1,240. The adjustment is entered as (1) $1,240 in the Adjustments Debit column on the same line as Supplies Expense and (2) $1,240 in the Adjustments Credit column on the same line as Supplies.

(b) **Prepaid Insurance.** The prepaid insurance account has a debit balance of $2,400, which represents the prepayment of insurance for 12 months beginning December 1. Thus, the insurance expense for December is $200 ($2,400/12). The adjustment is entered as (1) $200 in the Adjustments Debit column on the same line as Insurance Expense and (2) $200 in the Adjustments Credit column on the same line as Prepaid Insurance.

(c) **Unearned Rent.** The unearned rent account has a credit balance of $360, which represents the receipt of three months' rent, beginning with December. Thus, the rent revenue for December is $120. The adjustment is entered as (1) $120 in the Adjustments Debit column on the same line as Unearned Rent and (2) $120 in the Adjustments Credit column on the same line as Rent Revenue.

(d) **Accrued Fees.** Fees accrued at the end of December but not recorded total $500. This amount is an increase in an asset and an increase in revenue. The adjustment is entered as (1) $500 in the Adjustments Debit column on the same line as Accounts Receivable and (2) $500 in the Adjustments Credit column on the same line as Fees Earned.

(e) **Wages.** Wages accrued but not paid at the end of December total $250. This amount is an increase in expenses and an increase in liabilities. The adjustment is entered as (1) $250 in the Adjustments Debit column on the same line as Wages Expense and (2) $250 in the Adjustments Credit column on the same line as Wages Payable.

(f) **Depreciation.** Depreciation of the office equipment is $50 for December. The adjustment is entered as (1) $50 in the Adjustments Debit column on the same line as Depreciation Expense and (2) $50 in the Adjustments Credit column on the same line as Accumulated Depreciation.

Total the Adjustments columns to verify the mathematical accuracy of the adjustment data. The total of the Debit column must equal the total of the Credit column.

ADJUSTED TRIAL BALANCE COLUMNS

The adjustment data are added to or subtracted from the amounts in the Unadjusted Trial Balance columns. The adjusted amounts are then extended to (placed in) the Adjusted Trial Balance columns, as shown in Exhibit 19. For example, the cash amount of $2,065 is extended to the Adjusted Trial Balance Debit column, since no adjustments affected Cash. Accounts Receivable has an initial balance of $2,220 and a debit adjustment (increase) of $500. The amount entered in the Adjusted Trial Balance Debit column is the debit balance of $2,720. The same procedure continues until all account balances are extended to the Adjusted Trial Balance columns. Total the columns of the Adjusted Trial Balance to verify the equality of debits and credits.

INCOME STATEMENT AND BALANCE SHEET COLUMNS

The spreadsheet (work sheet) is completed by extending the adjusted trial balance amounts to the Income Statement and Balance Sheet columns. The amounts for revenues and expenses are extended to the Income Statement columns. The amounts for assets, liabilities, owner's capital, and drawing are extended to the Balance Sheet columns.[3]

In the NetSolutions spreadsheet (work sheet), the first account listed is Cash, and the balance appearing in the Adjusted Trial Balance Debit column is $2,065. Cash is an asset, is listed on the balance sheet, and has a debit balance. Therefore, $2,065 is extended to the Balance Sheet Debit column. The Fees Earned balance of $16,840 is extended to the Income Statement Credit column. The same procedure continues until all account balances have been extended to the proper columns, as shown in Exhibit 20.

---

3 The balances of the capital and drawing accounts are also extended to the Balance Sheet columns because this spreadsheet (work sheet) does not provide for separate Statement of Owner's Equity columns.

After all of the balances have been extended to the four statement columns, total each of these columns, as shown in Exhibit 21. The difference between the two Income Statement column totals is the amount of the net income or the net loss for the period. Likewise, the difference between the two Balance Sheet column totals is also the amount of the net income or net loss for the period.

If the Income Statement Credit column total (representing total revenue) is greater than the Income Statement Debit column total (representing total expenses), the difference is the net income. If the Income Statement Debit column total is greater than the Income Statement Credit column total, the difference is a net loss. For NetSolutions, the computation of net income is as follows:

Total of Credit column (revenues)	$16,960
Total of Debit column (expenses)	9,855
Net income (excess of revenues over expenses)	$ 7,105

As shown in Exhibit 21, enter the amount of the net income, $7,105, in the Income Statement Debit column and the Balance Sheet Credit column. Enter the term *Net income* in the Account Title column. If there was a net loss instead of net income, you would enter the amount in the Income Statement Credit column and the Balance Sheet Debit column and the term *Net loss* in the Account Title column. Entering the net income or net loss in the statement columns on the spreadsheet (work sheet) shows the effect of transferring the net balance of the revenue and expense accounts to the owner's capital account.

After the net income or net loss has been entered on the spreadsheet (work sheet), again total each of the four statement columns. The totals of the two Income Statement columns must now be equal. The totals of the two Balance Sheet columns must also be equal.

The spreadsheet (work sheet) is an aid in preparing the income statement, the statement of owner's equity, and the balance sheet, which are presented in Exhibit 2. The income statement is normally prepared directly from the spreadsheet (work sheet). However, the order of the expenses may be changed. As we did in Chapter 1, we list the expenses in the income statement in Exhibit 2 in order of size, beginning with the larger items. Miscellaneous expense is the last item, regardless of its amount.

The first item normally presented on the statement of owner's equity is the balance of the owner's capital account at the beginning of the period. On the spreadsheet (work sheet), however, the amount listed as capital is not always the account balance at the beginning of the period. The owner may have invested additional assets in the business during the period. Hence, for the beginning balance and any additional investments, it is necessary to refer to the capital account in the ledger. These amounts, along with the net income (or net loss) and the drawing amount shown in the spreadsheet (work sheet), are used to determine the ending capital account balance. The balance sheet can be prepared directly from the spreadsheet (work sheet) columns except for the ending balance of owner's capital, which is taken from the statement of owner's equity.

When a spreadsheet (work sheet) is used, the adjusting and closing entries are normally not journalized or posted until after the spreadsheet and financial statements have been prepared. The data for the adjusting entries are taken from the adjustments columns of the spreadsheet. The data for the first two closing entries are taken from the Income Statement columns of the spreadsheet. The amount for the closing third entry is the net income or net loss appearing at the bottom of the spreadsheet. The amount for the fourth closing entry is the drawing account balance that appears in the Balance Sheet Debit column of the spreadsheet.

EXHIBIT 18   Spreadsheet (Work Sheet) with Unadjusted Trial Balance Entered

	A	B	C	D	E	F	G	H	I	J	K	
		NetSolutions										
		End-of-Period Spreadsheet (Work Sheet)										
		For the Two Months Ended December 31, 2007										
		Unadjusted				Adjusted						
		Trial Balance		Adjustments		Trial Balance		Income Statement		Balance Sheet		
	Account Title	Dr.	Cr.	Dr.	Cr.	Dr.	Cr.	Dr.	Cr.	Dr.	Cr.	
1	Cash	2,065										1
2	Accounts Receivable	2,220										2
3	Supplies	2,000										3
4	Prepaid Insurance	2,400										4
5	Land	20,000										5
6	Office Equipment	1,800										6
7	Accounts Payable		900									7
8	Unearned Rent		360									8
9	Chris Clark, Capital		25,000									9
10	Chris Clark, Drawing	4,000										10
11	Fees Earned		16,340									11
12	Wages Expense	4,275										12
13	Rent Expense	1,600										13
14	Utilities Expense	985										14
15	Supplies Expense	800										15
16	Miscellaneous Expense	455										16
17		42,600	42,600									17
18												18
19												19
20												20
21												21
22												22
23												23
24												24
25												25

The spreadsheet (work sheet) is used for summarizing the effects of adjusting entries. It also aids in preparing financial statements.

At a Glance

1. Describe the flow of accounting information from the unadjusted trial balance into the adjusted trial balance and financial statements.

Key Points	Key Learning Outcomes	Example Exercises	Practice Exercises
Exhibit 1 illustrates the end-of-period process by which accounts are adjusted and how the adjusted accounts flow into the financial statements.	• Using an end-of-period spreadsheet (work sheet), describe how the unadjusted trial balance accounts are affected by adjustments and how the adjusted trial balance accounts flow into the income statement and balance sheet.	4-1	4-1A, 4-1B

2. Prepare financial statements from adjusted account balances.

Key Points	Key Learning Outcomes	Example Exercises	Practice Exercises
Using the end-of-period spreadsheet (work sheet) shown in Exhibit 1, the income statement and balance sheet for NetSolutions can be prepared. The statement of owner's equity is prepared by referring to transactions that have been posted to owner's capital accounts in the ledger. A classified balance sheet has sections for current assets; property, plant, and equipment; current liabilities; long-term liabilities; and owner's equity.	• Describe how the net income or net loss from the period can be determined from an end-of-period spreadsheet (work sheet).	4-2	4-2A, 4-2B
	• Prepare an income statement, statement of owner's equity, and a balance sheet.	4-3	4-3A, 4-3B
	• Indicate how accounts would be reported in a classified balance sheet.	4-4	4-4A, 4-4B

3. Prepare closing entries.

Key Points	Key Learning Outcomes	Example Exercises	Practice Exercises
Four entries are required in closing the temporary accounts. The first entry closes the revenue accounts to Income Summary. The second entry closes the expense accounts to Income Summary. The third entry closes the balance of Income Summary (net income or net loss) to the owner's capital account. The fourth entry closes the drawing account to the owner's capital account.	• Prepare the closing entry for revenues.	4-5	4-5A, 4-5B
	• Prepare the closing entry for expenses.	4-5	4-5A, 4-5B
After the closing entries have been posted to the ledger, the balance in the capital account agrees with the amount reported on the statement of owner's equity and balance sheet. In addition, the revenue, expense, and drawing accounts will have zero balances.	• Prepare the closing entry for transferring the balance of Income Summary to the owner's capital account.	4-5	4-5A, 4-5B
	• Prepare the closing entry for the owner's drawing account.	4-5	4-5A, 4-5B

(continued)

4. Describe the accounting cycle.

Key Points	Key Learning Outcomes	Example Exercises	Practice Exercises
The 10 basic steps of the accounting cycle are as follows: 1. Transactions are analyzed and recorded in the journal. 2. Transactions are posted to the ledger. 3. An unadjusted trial balance is prepared. 4. Adjustment data are assembled and analyzed. 5. An optional end-of-period spreadsheet (work sheet) is prepared. 6. Adjusting entries are journalized and posted to the ledger. 7. An adjusted trial balance is prepared. 8. Financial statements are prepared. 9. Closing entries are journalized and posted to the ledger. 10. A post-closing trial balance is prepared.	• List the 10 steps of the accounting cycle. • Determine whether any steps are out of order in a listing of accounting cycle steps. • Determine whether there are any missing steps in a listing of accounting cycle steps.	4-6	4-6A, 4-6B

5. Illustrate the accounting cycle for one period.

Key Points	Key Learning Outcomes	Example Exercises	Practice Exercises
The complete accounting for Kelly Consulting for the month of April is described and illustrated on pages 161–174.	• Complete the accounting cycle for a period from beginning to end.		

6. Explain what is meant by the fiscal year and the natural business year.

Key Points	Key Learning Outcomes	Example Exercises	Practice Exercises
The annual accounting period adopted by a business is its fiscal year. A company's fiscal year that ends when business activities have reached the lowest point in its annual operating cycle is called the natural business year.	• Explain why companies use a fiscal year that is different from the calendar year.		

Key Terms

accounting cycle (159)
clearing account (152)
closing entries (152)
closing process (152)
current assets (150)

current liabilities (150)
fiscal year (174)
fixed (plant) assets (150)
Income Summary (152)
long-term liabilities (150)

natural business year (174)
notes receivable (150)
real accounts (151)
temporary (nominal) accounts (152)

Illustrative Problem

Three years ago, T. Roderick organized Harbor Realty. At July 31, 2008, the end of the current fiscal year, the following end-of-period spreadsheet (work sheet) was prepared:

Harbor Realty
End-of-Period Spreadsheet (Work Sheet)
For the Year Ended July 31, 2008

	A	B	C	D	E	F	G	H	I	J	K	
		Unadjusted Trial Balance		Adjustments		Adjusted Trial Balance		Income Statement		Balance Sheet		
	Account Title	Dr.	Cr.	Dr.	Cr.	Dr.	Cr.	Dr.	Cr.	Dr.	Cr.	
1	Cash	3,425				3,425				3,425		1
2	Accounts Receivable	7,000		(e) 1,000		8,000				8,000		2
3	Supplies	1,270			(a) 890	380				380		3
4	Prepaid Insurance	620			(b) 315	305				305		4
5	Office Equipment	51,650				51,650				51,650		5
6	Accum. Depreciation		9,700		(c) 4,950		14,650				14,650	6
7	Accounts Payable		925				925				925	7
8	Unearned Fees		1,250	(f) 500			750				750	8
9	T. Roderick, Capital		29,000				29,000				29,000	9
10	T. Roderick, Drawing	5,200				5,200				5,200		10
11	Fees Earned		59,125		(e) 1,000		60,625		60,625			11
12					(f) 500							12
13	Wages Expense	22,415		(d) 440		22,855		22,855				13
14	Rent Expense	4,200				4,200		4,200				14
15	Utilities Expense	2,715				2,715		2,715				15
16	Miscellaneous Expense	1,505				1,505		1,505				16
17		100,000	100,000									17
18	Supplies Expense			(a) 890		890		890				18
19	Insurance Expense			(b) 315		315		315				19
20	Depreciation Expense			(c) 4,950		4,950		4,950				20
21	Wages Payable				(d) 440		440				440	21
22				8,095	8,095	106,390	106,390	37,430	60,625	68,960	45,765	22
23	Net income							23,195			23,195	23
24								60,625	60,625	68,960	68,960	24

Instructions

1. Prepare an income statement, a statement of owner's equity (no additional investments were made during the year), and a balance sheet.
2. On the basis of the data in the end-of-period spreadsheet (work sheet), journalize the closing entries.

Solution

1.

Harbor Realty
Income Statement
For the Year Ended July 31, 2008

Fees earned		$60 6 2 5 00
Expenses:		
Wages expense	$22 8 5 5 00	
Depreciation expense	4 9 5 0 00	
Rent expense	4 2 0 0 00	
Utilities expense	2 7 1 5 00	
Supplies expense	8 9 0 00	
Insurance expense	3 1 5 00	
Miscellaneous expense	1 5 0 5 00	
Total expenses		37 4 3 0 00
Net income		$23 1 9 5 00

(continued)

Harbor Realty
Statement of Owner's Equity
For the Year Ended July 31, 2008

T. Roderick, capital, August 1, 2007		$29 0 0 0 00
Net income for the year	$23 1 9 5 00	
Less withdrawals	5 2 0 0 00	
Increase in owner's equity		17 9 9 5 00
T. Roderick, capital, July 31, 2008		$46 9 9 5 00

Harbor Realty
Balance Sheet
July 31, 2008

Assets			Liabilities		
Current assets:			Current liabilities:		
Cash	$ 3 4 2 5 00		Accounts payable	$ 9 2 5 00	
Accounts receivable	8 0 0 0 00		Unearned fees	7 5 0 00	
Supplies	3 8 0 00		Wages payable	4 4 0 00	
Prepaid insurance	3 0 5 00		Total liabilities		$ 2 1 1 5 00
Total current assets		$12 1 1 0 00			
Property, plant, and equipment:					
Office equipment	$51 6 5 0 00				
Less accumulated depr.	14 6 5 0 00		**Owner's Equity**		
Total property, plant,			T. Roderick, capital		46 9 9 5 00
and equipment		37 0 0 0 00	Total liabilities and		
Total assets		$49 1 1 0 00	owner's equity		$49 1 1 0 00

2.

	JOURNAL			Page

	Date	Description	Post. Ref.	Debit	Credit	
1		Closing Entries				1
2	2008 July 31	Fees Earned		60 6 2 5 00		2
3		Income Summary			60 6 2 5 00	3
4						4
5	31	Income Summary		37 4 3 0 00		5
6		Wages Expense			22 8 5 5 00	6
7		Rent Expense			4 2 0 0 00	7
8		Utilities Expense			2 7 1 5 00	8
9		Miscellaneous Expense			1 5 0 5 00	9
10		Supplies Expense			8 9 0 00	10
11		Insurance Expense			3 1 5 00	11
12		Depreciation Expense			4 9 5 0 00	12
13						13
14	31	Income Summary		23 1 9 5 00		14
15		T. Roderick, Capital			23 1 9 5 00	15
16						16
17	31	T. Roderick, Capital		5 2 0 0 00		17
18		T. Roderick, Drawing			5 2 0 0 00	18

Self-Examination Questions

1. Which of the following accounts in the Adjusted Trial Balance columns of the end-of-period spreadsheet (work sheet) would be extended to the Balance Sheet columns?
   A. Utilities Expense
   B. Rent Revenue
   C. M. E. Jones, Drawing
   D. Miscellaneous Expense

2. Which of the following accounts would be classified as a current asset on the balance sheet?
   A. Office Equipment
   B. Land
   C. Accumulated Depreciation
   D. Accounts Receivable

3. Which of the following entries closes the owner's drawing account at the end of the period?
   A. Debit the drawing account, credit the income summary account.
   B. Debit the owner's capital account, credit the drawing account.
   C. Debit the income summary account, credit the drawing account.
   D. Debit the drawing account, credit the owner's capital account.

4. Which of the following accounts would *not* be closed to the income summary account at the end of a period?
   A. Fees Earned
   B. Wages Expense
   C. Rent Expense
   D. Accumulated Depreciation

5. Which of the following accounts would *not* be included in a post-closing trial balance?
   A. Cash
   B. Fees Earned
   C. Accumulated Depreciation
   D. J. C. Smith, Capital

Eye Openers

1. Why do some accountants prepare an end-of-period spreadsheet (work sheet)?
2. Is the end-of-period spreadsheet (work sheet) a substitute for the financial statements? Discuss.
3. In the Income Statement columns of the end-of-period spreadsheet (work sheet) for Allen Consulting Co. for the current year, the Debit column total is $262,250 and the Credit column total is $323,500 before the amount for net income or net loss has been included. In preparing the income statement from the end-of-period spreadsheet (work sheet), what is the amount of net income or net loss?
4. Describe the nature of the assets that compose the following sections of a balance sheet: (a) current assets, (b) property, plant, and equipment.
5. What is the difference between a current liability and a long-term liability?
6. What types of accounts are referred to as temporary accounts?
7. Why are closing entries required at the end of an accounting period?
8. What is the difference between adjusting entries and closing entries?
9. Describe the four entries that close the temporary accounts.
10. What is the purpose of the post-closing trial balance?
11. (a) What is the most important output of the accounting cycle? (b) Do all companies have an accounting cycle? Explain.
12. What is the natural business year?
13. Why might a department store select a fiscal year ending January 31, rather than a fiscal year ending December 31?
14. The fiscal years for several well-known companies are as follows:

Company	Fiscal Year Ending	Company	Fiscal Year Ending
Kmart	January 30	Toys "R" Us, Inc.	February 3
JCPenney	January 26	Federated Department Stores, Inc.	February 3
Target Corp.	January 28	The Limited, Inc.	February 2

What general characteristic shared by these companies explains why they do not have fiscal years ending December 31?

Practice Exercises

PE 4-1A
Flow of accounts into financial statements
obj. 1

The balances for the accounts listed below appear in the Adjusted Trial Balance columns of the end-of-period spreadsheet (work sheet). Indicate whether each balance should be extended to (a) an Income Statement column or (b) a Balance Sheet column.

1. Supplies Expense
2. Unearned Service Revenue
3. Accounts Payable
4. Rent Revenue

5. Wages Payable
6. Office Equipment
7. Depreciation Expense—Equipment
8. Brandi Gowdy, Capital

PE 4-1B
Flow of accounts into financial statements
obj. 1

The balances for the accounts listed below appear in the Adjusted Trial Balance columns of the end-of-period spreadsheet (work sheet). Indicate whether each balance should be extended to (a) an Income Statement column or (b) a Balance Sheet column.

1. Cash
2. Insurance Expense
3. Prepaid Rent
4. Supplies

5. Commissions Earned
6. Accumulated Depreciation—Equipment
7. Christina Egan, Drawing
8. Wages Expense

PE 4-2A
Determining net income from the end-of-period spreadsheet (work sheet)
obj. 2

In the Balance Sheet columns of the end-of-period spreadsheet (work sheet) for FreeLance Consulting Co. for the current year, the Debit column total is $247,690 and the Credit column total is $278,100 before the amount for net income or net loss has been included. In preparing the income statement from the end-of-period spreadsheet (work sheet), what is the amount of net income or net loss?

PE 4-2B
Determining net income from the end-of-period spreadsheet (work sheet)
obj. 2

In the Income Statement columns of the end-of-period spreadsheet (work sheet) for Irwin Consulting Co. for the current year, the Debit column total is $436,700 and the Credit column total is $523,550 before the amount for net income or net loss has been included. In preparing the income statement from the end-of-period spreadsheet (work sheet), what is the amount of net income or net loss?

PE 4-3A
Statement of owner's equity
obj. 2

Jody Padget owns and operates Padget Advertising Services. On January 1, 2007, Jody Padget, Capital had a balance of $550,600. During the year, Jody invested an additional $50,000 and withdrew $40,000. For the year ended December 31, 2007, Padget Advertising Services reported a net income of $68,150. Prepare a statement of owner's equity for the year ended December 31, 2007.

PE 4-3B
Statement of owner's equity
obj. 2

Ali Khalid owns and operates AAA Delivery Services. On January 1, 2007, Ali Khalid, Capital had a balance of $854,450. During the year, Ali made no additional investments and withdrew $38,400. For the year ended December 31, 2007, AAA Delivery Services reported a net loss of $11,875. Prepare a statement of owner's equity for the year ended December 31, 2007.

PE 4-4A
Reporting accounts on classified balance sheet
obj. 2

The following accounts appear in an adjusted trial balance of Ramrod Consulting. Indicate whether each account would be reported in the (a) current asset; (b) property, plant, and equipment; (c) current liability; (d) long-term liability; or (e) owner's equity section of the December 31, 2007, balance sheet of Ramrod Consulting.

1. Taxes Payable
2. Building
3. Supplies
4. Mortgage Payable (due in 2011)

5. Prepaid Rent
6. Salaries Payable
7. Unearned Service Fees
8. Cecily Renick, Capital

PE 4-4B
Reporting accounts on classified balance sheet
obj. 2

The following accounts appear in an adjusted trial balance of Fastback Consulting. Indicate whether each account would be reported in the (a) current asset; (b) property, plant, and equipment; (c) current liability; (d) long-term liability; or (e) owner's equity section of the December 31, 2007, balance sheet of Fastback Consulting.

1. Accounts Payable
2. Accounts Receivable
3. Glen Moore, Capital
4. Wages Payable
5. Note Payable (due in 2014)
6. Cash
7. Supplies
8. Accumulated Depreciation—Building

PE 4-5A
Closing entries with net loss
obj. 3

After the accounts have been adjusted at October 31, the end of the fiscal year, the following balances were taken from the ledger of Velocity Delivery Services Co.:

Lisa Jordon, Capital	$318,500
Lisa Jordon, Drawing	36,000
Fees Earned	475,150
Wages Expense	390,000
Rent Expense	85,000
Supplies Expense	38,350
Miscellaneous Expense	12,675

Journalize the four entries required to close the accounts.

PE 4-5B
Closing entries with net income
obj. 3

After the accounts have been adjusted at April 30, the end of the fiscal year, the following balances were taken from the ledger of Magnolia Landscaping Co.:

Jayme Carmichael, Capital	$528,900
Jayme Carmichael, Drawing	60,000
Fees Earned	690,500
Wages Expense	410,000
Rent Expense	75,000
Supplies Expense	48,650
Miscellaneous Expense	19,700

Journalize the four entries required to close the accounts.

PE 4-6A
Missing steps in the accounting cycle
obj. 4

From the following list of steps in the accounting cycle, identify what two steps are missing.

a. Transactions are analyzed and recorded in the journal.
b. An unadjusted trial balance is prepared.
c. Adjustment data are assembled and analyzed.
d. An optional end-of-period spreadsheet (work sheet) is prepared.
e. Adjusting entries are journalized and posted to the ledger.
f. An adjusted trial balance is prepared.
g. Closing entries are journalized and posted to the ledger.
h. A post-closing trial balance is prepared.

PE 4-6B
Missing steps in the accounting cycle
obj. 4

From the following list of steps in the accounting cycle, identify what two steps are missing.

a. Transactions are analyzed and recorded in the journal.
b. Transactions are posted to the ledger.
c. An unadjusted trial balance is prepared.
d. An optional end-of-period spreadsheet (work sheet) is prepared.
e. Adjusting entries are journalized and posted to the ledger.
f. An adjusted trial balance is prepared.
g. Financial statements are prepared.
h. A post-closing trial balance is prepared.

Exercises

EX 4-1
Extending account balances in an end-of-period spreadsheet (work sheet)
objs. 1, 2

The balances for the accounts listed below appear in the Adjusted Trial Balance columns of the end-of-period spreadsheet (work sheet). Indicate whether each balance should be extended to (a) an Income Statement column or (b) a Balance Sheet column.

1. Accounts Payable
2. Accounts Receivable
3. Beth Posey, Capital
4. Beth Posey, Drawing
5. Fees Earned
6. Supplies
7. Unearned Fees
8. Utilities Expense
9. Wages Expense
10. Wages Payable

EX 4-2
Classifying accounts
objs. 1, 2

Balances for each of the following accounts appear in an adjusted trial balance. Identify each as (a) asset, (b) liability, (c) revenue, or (d) expense.

1. Accounts Receivable
2. Fees Earned
3. Insurance Expense
4. Land
5. Prepaid Advertising
6. Prepaid Insurance
7. Rent Revenue
8. Salary Expense
9. Salary Payable
10. Supplies
11. Supplies Expense
12. Unearned Rent

EX 4-3
Financial statements from the end-of-period spreadsheet (work sheet)
objs. 1, 2

Sandy Bottom Consulting is a consulting firm owned and operated by Dee Schofield. The end-of-period spreadsheet (work sheet) shown below was prepared for the year ended August 31, 2008.

	A	B	C	D	E	F	G	H	I	J	K	
					Sandy Bottom Consulting							
					End-of-Period Spreadsheet (Work Sheet)							
					For the Year Ended August 31, 2008							
		Unadjusted Trial Balance		Adjustments		Adjusted Trial Balance		Income Statement		Balance Sheet		
	Account Title	Dr.	Cr.	Dr.	Cr.	Dr.	Cr.	Dr.	Cr.	Dr.	Cr.	
1	Cash	10,000				10,000				10,000		1
2	Accounts Receivable	12,500				12,500				12,500		2
3	Supplies	2,200			(a) 1,750	450				450		3
4	Office Equipment	14,500				14,500				14,500		4
5	Accumulated Depreciation		2,500		(b) 1,200		3,700				3,700	5
6	Accounts Payable		6,100				6,100				6,100	6
7	Salaries Payable				(c) 800		800				800	7
8	Dee Schofield, Capital		19,400				19,400				19,400	8
9	Dee Schofield, Drawing	2,700				2,700				2,700		9
10	Fees Earned		32,000				32,000		32,000			10
11	Salary Expense	16,250		(c) 800		17,050		17,050				11
12	Supplies Expense			(a) 1,750		1,750		1,750				12
13	Depreciation Expense			(b) 1,200		1,200		1,200				13
14	Miscellaneous Expense	1,850				1,850		1,850				14
15		60,000	60,000	3,750	3,750	62,000	62,000	21,850	32,000	40,150	30,000	15
16	Net income							10,150			10,150	16
17								32,000	32,000	40,150	40,150	17

Based upon the preceding spreadsheet, prepare an income statement, statement of owner's equity, and balance sheet for Sandy Bottom Consulting.

EX 4-4
Financial statements from the end-of-period spreadsheet (work sheet)
objs. 1, 2

Rectifier Consulting is a consulting firm owned and operated by Adam Beauchamp. The following end-of-period spreadsheet (work sheet) was prepared for the year ended June 30, 2008.

	A	B	C	D	E	F	G	H	I	J	K	
		Rectifier Consulting										
		End-of-Period Spreadsheet (Work Sheet)										
		For the Year Ended June 30, 2008										
		Unadjusted Trial Balance		Adjustments		Adjusted Trial Balance		Income Statement		Balance Sheet		
	Account Title	Dr.	Cr.	Dr.	Cr.	Dr.	Cr.	Dr.	Cr.	Dr.	Cr.	
1	Cash	8,000				8,000				8,000		1
2	Accounts Receivable	15,500				15,500				15,500		2
3	Supplies	2,500			(a) 1,850	650				650		3
4	Office Equipment	24,500				24,500				24,500		4
5	Accumulated Depreciation		4,500		(b) 900		5,400				5,400	5
6	Accounts Payable		3,300				3,300				3,300	6
7	Salaries Payable				(c) 400		400				400	7
8	Adam Beauchamp, Capital		25,200				25,200				25,200	8
9	Adam Beauchamp, Drawing	2,000				2,000				2,000		9
10	Fees Earned		51,750				51,750		51,750			10
11	Salary Expense	30,750		(c) 400		31,150		31,150				11
12	Supplies Expense			(a) 1,850		1,850		1,850				12
13	Depreciation Expense			(b) 900		900		900				13
14	Miscellaneous Expense	1,500				1,500		1,500				14
15		84,750	84,750	3,150	3,150	86,050	86,050	35,400	51,750	50,650	34,300	15
16	Net income							16,350			16,350	16
17								51,750	51,750	50,650	50,650	17

Based upon the preceding spreadsheet, prepare an income statement, statement of owner's equity, and balance sheet for Rectifier Consulting.

EX 4-5
Income statement
obj. 2

✓ *Net income, $184,500*

The following account balances were taken from the adjusted trial balance for Admiral Messenger Service, a delivery service firm, for the current fiscal year ended April 30, 2008:

Depreciation Expense	$ 5,000	Rent Expense	$ 43,400
Fees Earned	375,500	Salaries Expense	125,600
Insurance Expense	1,500	Supplies Expense	2,750
Miscellaneous Expense	1,250	Utilities Expense	11,500

Prepare an income statement.

EX 4-6
Income statement; net loss
obj. 2

✓ *Net loss, $23,300*

The following revenue and expense account balances were taken from the ledger of Cupcake Services Co. after the accounts had been adjusted on October 31, 2008, the end of the current fiscal year:

Depreciation Expense	$10,000	Service Revenue	$163,375
Insurance Expense	6,000	Supplies Expense	2,875
Miscellaneous Expense	4,750	Utilities Expense	18,750
Rent Expense	51,500	Wages Expense	92,800

Prepare an income statement.

EX 4-7
Income statement
obj. 2

Internet Project

✓ *a. Net income: $1,449*

FedEx Corporation had the following revenue and expense account balances (in millions) at its fiscal year-end of May 31, 2005:

Depreciation	$1,462	Purchased Transportation	$ 2,935
Fuel	2,317	Rentals and Landing Fees	2,314
Maintenance and Repairs	1,680	Revenues	29,363
Other Expenses	4,379	Salaries and Employee Benefits	11,963
Provision for Income Taxes	864		

a. Prepare an income statement.

b. ⟶ Compare your income statement with the related income statement that is available at the FedEx Corporation Web site, which is linked to the text's Web site at **www.thomsonedu.com/accounting/warren**. What similarities and differences do you see?

EX 4-8
Statement of owner's equity
obj. 2

✓ *Josh Winfrey, capital, Aug. 31, 2008: $652,750*

Icon Systems Co. offers its services to residents in the Pasadena area. Selected accounts from the ledger of Icon Systems Co. for the current fiscal year ended August 31, 2008, are as follows:

Josh Winfrey, Capital				Josh Winfrey, Drawing			
Aug. 31	16,000	Sept. 1 (2007)	573,750	Nov. 30	4,000	Aug. 31	16,000
		Aug. 31	95,000	Feb. 28	4,000		
				May 31	4,000		
				Aug. 31	4,000		

Income Summary			
Aug. 31	380,000	Aug. 31	475,000
31	95,000		

Prepare a statement of owner's equity for the year.

EX 4-9
Statement of owner's equity; net loss
obj. 2

✓ *Tammy Eddy, capital, June 30, 2008: $128,250*

Selected accounts from the ledger of Aspen Sports for the current fiscal year ended June 30, 2008, are as follows:

Tammy Eddy, Capital				Tammy Eddy, Drawing			
June 30	30,000	July 1 (2007)	190,800	Sept. 30	7,500	June 30	30,000
30	32,550			Dec. 31	7,500		
				May 31	7,500		
				June 30	7,500		

Income Summary			
June 30	348,150	June 30	315,600
		30	32,550

Prepare a statement of owner's equity for the year.

EX 4-10
Classifying assets
obj. 2

Identify each of the following as (a) a current asset or (b) property, plant, and equipment:

1. Accounts receivable
2. Building
3. Cash
4. Equipment
5. Prepaid insurance
6. Supplies

EX 4-11
Balance sheet classification
obj. 2

At the balance sheet date, a business owes a mortgage note payable of $750,000, the terms of which provide for monthly payments of $15,000.

Explain how the liability should be classified on the balance sheet.

EX 4-12
Balance sheet
obj. 2

✓ *Total assets: $375,000*

Healthy & Trim Co. offers personal weight reduction consulting services to individuals. After all the accounts have been closed on November 30, 2008, the end of the current fiscal year, the balances of selected accounts from the ledger of Healthy & Trim Co. are as follows:

Accounts Payable	$ 17,250	Equipment	$350,000
Accounts Receivable	41,560	Prepaid Insurance	9,600
Accumulated Depreciation—		Prepaid Rent	6,000
Equipment	51,950	Salaries Payable	6,750
Cash	?	Supplies	1,040
Cindy DeLoach, Capital	346,000	Unearned Fees	5,000

Prepare a classified balance sheet that includes the correct balance for Cash.

EX 4-13
Balance sheet
obj. 2

List the errors you find in the following balance sheet. Prepare a corrected balance sheet.

✓ Corrected balance
sheet, total assets:
$180,000

Eucalyptus Services Co.
Balance Sheet
For the Year Ended July 31, 2008

Assets			Liabilities		
Current assets:			Current liabilities:		
Cash	$ 5,280		Accounts receivable	$ 13,750	
Accounts payable	6,790		Accum. depr.—building	86,700	
Supplies	1,650		Accum. depr.—equipment	18,480	
Prepaid insurance	4,800		Net income	25,000	
Land	60,000		Total liabilities		$143,930
Total current assets		$ 78,520			
Property, plant, and					
equipment:			**Owner's Equity**		
Building	$156,700		Wages payable	$ 1,340	
Equipment	43,000		Sydney Kitchel, capital	171,870	
Total property, plant,			Total owner's equity		173,210
and equipmet		238,620	Total liabilities and		
Total assets		$317,140	owner's equity		$317,140

EX 4-14
Identifying accounts to be closed
obj. 3

From the following list, identify the accounts that should be closed to Income Summary at the end of the fiscal year:

a. Accounts Receivable
b. Accumulated Depreciation—
   Equipment
c. Depreciation Expense—Equipment
d. Equipment
e. Fees Earned
f. Keri Upshaw, Capital

g. Keri Upshaw, Drawing
h. Land
i. Supplies
j. Supplies Expense
k. Wages Expense
l. Wages Payable

EX 4-15
Closing entries
obj. 3

Prior to its closing, Income Summary had total debits of $279,615 and total credits of $392,750.

➤ Briefly explain the purpose served by the income summary account and the nature of the entries that resulted in the $279,615 and the $392,750.

EX 4-16
Closing entries with net income
obj. 3

After all revenue and expense accounts have been closed at the end of the fiscal year, Income Summary has a debit of $218,380 and a credit of $375,000. At the same date, Rachel Bray, Capital has a credit balance of $479,100, and Rachel Bray, Drawing has a balance of $18,000. (a) Journalize the entries required to complete the closing of the accounts. (b) Determine the amount of Rachel Bray, Capital at the end of the period.

EX 4-17
Closing entries with net loss
obj. 3

Firefly Services Co. offers its services to individuals desiring to improve their personal images. After the accounts have been adjusted at October 31, the end of the fiscal year, the following balances were taken from the ledger of Firefly Services Co.

Natalie Wilson, Capital	$554,500	Rent Expense	$65,000
Natalie Wilson, Drawing	20,000	Supplies Expense	3,150
Fees Earned	293,300	Miscellaneous Expense	7,100
Wages Expense	250,000		

Journalize the four entries required to close the accounts.

EX 4-18
Identifying permanent accounts
obj. 3

Which of the following accounts will usually appear in the post-closing trial balance?

a. Accounts Payable
b. Accumulated Depreciation
c. Cash
d. Depreciation Expense
e. Fees Earned
f. Office Equipment

g. Salaries Expense
h. Salaries Payable
i. Stephanie Hamm, Capital
j. Stephanie Hamm, Drawing
k. Supplies

EX 4-19
Post-closing trial balance

obj. 3

✓ *Correct column totals,*
$150,505

An accountant prepared the following post-closing trial balance:

Honest Sam's Repair Co.
Post-Closing Trial Balance
July 31, 2008

	Debit Balances	Credit Balances
Cash	12,915	
Accounts Receivable	46,620	
Supplies		2,770
Equipment		88,200
Accumulated Depreciation—Equipment	27,970	
Accounts Payable	15,750	
Salaries Payable		3,780
Unearned Rent	7,560	
Samantha Marcus, Capital	95,445	
	206,260	94,750

Prepare a corrected post-closing trial balance. Assume that all accounts have normal balances and that the amounts shown are correct.

EX 4-20
Steps in the accounting cycle

obj. 4

Rearrange the following steps in the accounting cycle in proper sequence:

a. An adjusted trial balance is prepared.
b. Financial statements are prepared.
c. A post-closing trial balance is prepared.
d. Transactions are analyzed and recorded in the journal.
e. An optional end-of-period spreadsheet (work sheet) is prepared.
f. Adjustment data are asssembled and analyzed.
g. Transactions are posted to the ledger.
h. Closing entries are journalized and posted to the ledger.
i. An unadjusted trial balance is prepared.
j. Adjusting entries are journalized and posted to the ledger.

EX 4-21
Appendix: Steps in completing an end-of-period spreadsheet (work sheet)

The steps performed in completing an end-of-period spreadsheet (work sheet) are listed below in random order.

a. Extend the adjusted trial balance amounts to the Income Statement columns and the Balance Sheet columns.
b. Enter the adjusting entries into the spreadsheet (work sheet), based upon the adjustment data.
c. Add the Debit and Credit columns of the Unadjusted Trial Balance columns of the spreadsheet (work sheet) to verify that the totals are equal.
d. Enter the amount of net income or net loss for the period in the proper Income Statement column and Balance Sheet column.
e. Add the Debit and Credit columns of the Balance Sheet and Income Statement columns of the spreadsheet (work sheet) to verify that the totals are equal.
f. Enter the unadjusted account balances from the general ledger into the Unadjusted Trial Balance columns of the spreadsheet (work sheet).
g. Add or deduct adjusting entry data to trial balance amounts, and extend amounts to the Adjusted Trial Balance columns.
h. Add the Debit and Credit columns of the Adjustments columns of the spreadsheet (work sheet) to verify that the totals are equal.
i. Add the Debit and Credit columns of the Balance Sheet and Income Statement columns of the spreadsheet (work sheet) to determine the amount of net income or net loss for the period.
j. Add the Debit and Credit columns of the Adjusted Trial Balance columns of the spreadsheet (work sheet) to verify that the totals are equal.

Indicate the order in which the preceding steps would be performed in preparing and completing a spreadsheet (work sheet).

EX 4-22
Appendix: Adjustment data on an end-of-period spreadsheet (work sheet)

✓ *Total debits of Adjustments column: $15*

Dakota Services Co. offers cleaning services to business clients. The trial balance for Dakota Services Co. has been prepared on the end-of-period spreadsheet (work sheet) for the year ended July 31, 2008, shown below.

Dakota Services Co.
End-of-Period Spreadsheet (Work Sheet)
For the Year Ended July 31, 2008

Account Title	Unadjusted Trial Balance		Adjustments		Adjusted Trial Balance	
	Dr.	Cr.	Dr.	Cr.	Dr.	Cr.
Cash	4					
Accounts Receivable	25					
Supplies	4					
Prepaid Insurance	6					
Land	25					
Equipment	16					
Accum. Depr.—Equipment		1				
Accounts Payable		13				
Wages Payable		0				
Christina Keene, Capital		56				
Christina Keene, Drawing	4					
Fees Earned		30				
Wages Expense	8					
Rent Expense	4					
Insurance Expense	0					
Utilities Expense	3					
Depreciation Expense	0					
Supplies Expense	0					
Miscellaneous Expense	1					
	100	100				

The data for year-end adjustments are as follows:

a. Fees earned, but not yet billed, $5.
b. Supplies on hand, $1.
c. Insurance premiums expired, $4.
d. Depreciation expense, $2.
e. Wages accrued, but not paid, $1.

Enter the adjustment data, and place the balances in the Adjusted Trial Balance columns.

EX 4-23
Appendix: Completing an end-of-period spreadsheet (work sheet)

✓ *Net income: $9*

Dakota Services Co. offers cleaning services to business clients. Complete the following end-of-period spreadsheet (work sheet) for Dakota Services Co.

(continued)

Dakota Services Co.
End-of-Period Spreadsheet (Work Sheet)
For the Year Ended July 31, 2008

	Adjusted Trial Balance		Income Statement		Balance Sheet	
Account Title	Dr.	Cr.	Dr.	Cr.	Dr.	Cr.
Cash	4					
Accounts Receivable	30					
Supplies	1					
Prepaid Insurance	2					
Land	25					
Equipment	16					
Accum. Depr.—Equipment		3				
Accounts Payable		13				
Wages Payable		1				
Christina Keene, Capital		56				
Christina Keene, Drawing	4					
Fees Earned		35				
Wages Expense	9					
Rent Expense	4					
Insurance Expense	4					
Utilities Expense	3					
Depreciation Expense	2					
Supplies Expense	3					
Miscellaneous Expense	1					
	108	108				
Net income (loss)						

EX 4-24
Appendix: Financial statements from an end-of-period spreadsheet (work sheet)

✓ *Christina Keene, capital, July 31, 2008: $61*

Based upon the data in Exercise 4-23, prepare an income statement, statement of owner's equity, and balance sheet for Dakota Services Co.

EX 4-25
Appendix: Adjusting entries from an end-of-period spreadsheet (work sheet)

Based upon the data in Exercise 4-22, prepare the adjusting entries for Dakota Services Co.

EX 4-26
Appendix: Closing entries from an end-of-period spreadsheet (work sheet)

Based upon the data in Exercise 4-23, prepare the closing entries for Dakota Services Co.

Problems Series A

PR 4-1A
Financial statements and closing entries
objs. 1, 2, 3

Blink-On Company maintains and repairs warning lights, such as those found on radio towers and lighthouses. Blink-On Company prepared the end-of-period spreadsheet (work sheet) at the top of the following page at March 31, 2008, the end of the current fiscal year:

	A	B	C	D	E	F	G	H	I	J	K	
	Account Title	Unadjusted Trial Balance Dr.	Cr.	Adjustments Dr.	Cr.	Adjusted Trial Balance Dr.	Cr.	Income Statement Dr.	Cr.	Balance Sheet Dr.	Cr.	

Blink-On Company
End-of-Period Spreadsheet (Work Sheet)
For the Year Ended March 31, 2008

	Account Title	UTB Dr.	UTB Cr.	Adj. Dr.	Adj. Cr.	ATB Dr.	ATB Cr.	IS Dr.	IS Cr.	BS Dr.	BS Cr.	
1	Cash	6,300				6,300				6,300		1
2	Accounts Receivable	18,900		(a) 3,500		22,400				22,400		2
3	Prepaid Insurance	4,200			(b) 2,800	1,400				1,400		3
4	Supplies	2,730			(c) 1,600	1,130				1,130		4
5	Land	98,000				98,000				98,000		5
6	Building	140,000				140,000				140,000		6
7	Acc. Depr.—Building		100,300		(d) 1,400		101,700				101,700	7
8	Equipment	100,500				100,500				100,500		8
9	Acc. Depr.—Equipment		85,100		(e) 3,200		88,300				88,300	9
10	Accounts Payable		5,700				5,700				5,700	10
11	Unearned Rent		2,100	(g) 1,200			900				900	11
12	Amanda Ayers, Capital		78,100				78,100				78,100	12
13	Amanda Ayers, Drawing	5,600				5,600				5,600		13
14	Fees Revenue		253,700		(a) 3,500		257,200		257,200			14
15	Salaries & Wages Expense	102,500		(f) 1,800		104,300		104,300				15
16	Advertising Expense	21,700				21,700		21,700				16
17	Utilities Expense	11,400				11,400		11,400				17
18	Repairs Expense	8,850				8,850		8,850				18
19	Misc. Expense	4,320				4,320		4,320				19
20		525,000	525,000									20
21	Insurance Expense			(b) 2,800		2,800		2,800				21
22	Supplies Expense			(c) 1,600		1,600		1,600				22
23	Depr. Exp.—Building			(d) 1,400		1,400		1,400				23
24	Depr. Exp.—Equipment			(e) 3,200		3,200		3,200				24
25	Salaries & Wages Payable				(f) 1,800		1,800				1,800	25
26	Rent Revenue				(g) 1,200		1,200		1,200			26
27				15,500	15,500	534,900	534,900	159,570	258,400	375,330	276,500	27
28	Net income							98,830			98,830	28
29								258,400	258,400	375,330	375,330	29

✓ 1. Net income: $98,830

Instructions

1. Prepare an income statement for the year ended March 31.
2. Prepare a statement of owner's equity for the year ended March 31. No additional investments were made during the year.
3. Prepare a balance sheet as of March 31.
4. Based upon the end-of-period spreadsheet (work sheet), journalize the closing entries.
5. Prepare a post-closing trial balance.

PR 4-2A
Financial statements and closing entries

objs. 2, 3

✓ 1. Stacey Vargas, capital, April 30: $152,800

The Nevus Company is an investigative services firm that is owned and operated by Stacey Vargas. On April 30, 2008, the end of the current fiscal year, the accountant for The Nevus Company prepared an end-of-period spreadsheet (work sheet), a part of which is shown at the top of the following page.

Instructions

1. Prepare an income statement, statement of owner's equity (no additional investments were made during the year), and a balance sheet.
2. Journalize the entries that were required to close the accounts at April 30.
3. If Stacey Vargas, Capital decreased $35,000 after the closing entries were posted, and the withdrawals remained the same, what was the amount of net income or net loss?

(continued)

	A	H	I	J	K	
	The Nevus Company					
	End-of-Period Spreadsheet (Work Sheet)					
	For the Year Ended April 30, 2008					
		Income Statement		**Balance Sheet**		
1	Cash			9,000		1
2	Accounts Receivable			37,200		2
3	Supplies			3,500		3
4	Prepaid Insurance			4,800		4
5	Equipment			169,500		5
6	Accumulated Depreciation—Equipment				55,200	6
7	Accounts Payable				10,500	7
8	Salaries Payable				2,500	8
9	Unearned Rent				3,000	9
10	Stacey Vargas, Capital				142,800	10
11	Stacey Vargas, Drawing			16,000		11
12	Service Fees		363,000			12
13	Rent Revenue		7,000			13
14	Salary Expense	270,000				14
15	Rent Expense	37,000				15
16	Supplies Expense	8,000				16
17	Depreciation Expense—Equipment	7,000				17
18	Utilities Expense	6,400				18
19	Repairs Expense	6,200				19
20	Insurance Expense	4,800				20
21	Miscellaneous Expense	4,600				21
22		344,000	370,000	240,000	214,000	22
23	Net income	26,000			26,000	23
24		370,000	370,000	240,000	240,000	24

PR 4-3A

T accounts, adjusting entries, financial statements, and closing entries; optional end-of-period spreadsheet (work sheet)

objs. 2, 3

✓*2. Net income: $13,650*

The unadjusted trial balance of Iguana Laundromat at June 30, 2008, the end of the current fiscal year, is shown below.

Iguana Laundromat
Unadjusted Trial Balance
June 30, 2008

	Debit Balances	Credit Balances
Cash	5,500	
Laundry Supplies	9,450	
Prepaid Insurance	4,300	
Laundry Equipment	142,000	
Accumulated Depreciation		75,200
Accounts Payable		4,900
Scott Mathis, Capital		53,800
Scott Mathis, Drawing	4,200	
Laundry Revenue		116,100
Wages Expense	52,000	
Rent Expense	19,650	
Utilities Expense	10,200	
Miscellaneous Expense	2,700	
	250,000	250,000

The data needed to determine year-end adjustments are as follows:

a. Laundry supplies on hand at June 30 are $1,500.
b. Insurance premiums expired during the year are $3,200.
c. Depreciation of equipment during the year is $6,000.
d. Wages accrued but not paid at June 30 are $750.

Instructions

1. For each account listed in the unadjusted trial balance, enter the balance in a T account. Identify the balance as "June 30 Bal." In addition, add T accounts for Wages Payable, Depreciation Expense, Laundry Supplies Expense, Insurance Expense, and Income Summary.
2. **Optional:** Enter the unadjusted trial balance on an end-of-period spreadsheet (work sheet) and complete the spreadsheet. Add the accounts listed in part (1) as needed.
3. Journalize and post the adjusting entries. Identify the adjustments by "Adj." and the new balances as "Adj. Bal."
4. Prepare an adjusted trial balance.
5. Prepare an income statement, a statement of owner's equity (no additional investments were made during the year), and a balance sheet.
6. Journalize and post the closing entries. Identify the closing entries by "Clos."
7. Prepare a post-closing trial balance.

PR 4-4A
*Ledger accounts,
adjusting entries,
financial statements, and
closing entries;
optional end-of-period
spreadsheet (work sheet)*

objs. 2, 3

✓*4. Net income: $24,593*

If the working papers correlating with this textbook are not used, omit Problem 4-4A.

The ledger and trial balance of Wainscot Services Co. as of March 31, 2008, the end of the first month of its current fiscal year, are presented in the working papers.
    Data needed to determine the necessary adjusting entries are as follows:

a. Service revenue accrued at March 31 is $1,750.
b. Supplies on hand at March 31 are $400.
c. Insurance premiums expired during March are $250.
d. Depreciation of the building during March is $400.
e. Depreciation of equipment during March is $200.
f. Unearned rent at March 31 is $1,000.
g. Wages accrued at March 31 are $500.

Instructions

1. **Optional:** Complete the end-of-period spreadsheet (work sheet) using the adjustment data shown above.
2. Journalize and post the adjusting entries, inserting balances in the accounts affected.
3. Prepare an adjusted trial balance.
4. Prepare an income statement, a statement of owner's equity, and a balance sheet.
5. Journalize and post the closing entries. Indicate closed accounts by inserting a line in both Balance columns opposite the closing entry. Insert the new balance of the capital account.
6. Prepare a post-closing trial balance.

PR 4-5A
*Ledger accounts,
adjusting entries,
financial statements,
and closing entries;
optional spreadsheet
(work sheet)*

objs. 2, 3

✓*5. Net income: $41,705*

The unadjusted trial balance of Quick Repairs at October 31, 2008, the end of the current year, is shown below.

	Quick Repairs Unadjusted Trial Balance October 31, 2008	Debit Balances	Credit Balances
11	Cash	2,950	
13	Supplies	12,295	
14	Prepaid Insurance	2,735	
16	Equipment	95,650	
17	Accumulated Depreciation—Equipment		21,209
18	Trucks	36,300	
19	Accumulated Depreciation—Trucks		7,400
21	Accounts Payable		4,015
31	Rhonda Salter, Capital		67,426
32	Rhonda Salter, Drawing	6,000	
41	Service Revenue		99,950
51	Wages Expense	26,925	
53	Rent Expense	9,600	
55	Truck Expense	5,350	
59	Miscellaneous Expense	2,195	
		200,000	200,000

The data needed to determine year-end adjustments are as follows:

a. Supplies on hand at October 31 are $7,120.
b. Insurance premiums expired during year are $2,000.
c. Depreciation of equipment during year is $4,200.
d. Depreciation of trucks during year is $2,200.
e. Wages accrued but not paid at October 31 are $600.

Instructions

1. For each account listed in the trial balance, enter the balance in the appropriate Balance column of a four-column account and place a check mark (✓) in the Posting Reference column.
2. **Optional:** Enter the unadjusted trial balance on an end-of-period spreadsheet (work sheet) and complete the spreadsheet. Add the accounts listed in part (3) as needed.
3. Journalize and post the adjusting entries, inserting balances in the accounts affected. The following additional accounts from Quick Repair's chart of accounts should be used: Wages Payable, 22; Supplies Expense, 52; Depreciation Expense—Equipment, 54; Depreciation Expense—Trucks, 56; Insurance Expense, 57.
4. Prepare an adjusted trial balance.
5. Prepare an income statement, a statement of owner's equity (no additional investments were made during the year), and a balance sheet.
6. Journalize and post the closing entries. (Income Summary is account #33 in the chart of accounts.) Indicate closed accounts by inserting a line in both Balance columns opposite the closing entry.
7. Prepare a post-closing trial balance.

PR 4-6A
Complete accounting cycle
objs. 4, 5, 6

✓8. Net income: $17,250

For the past several years, Dawn Lytle has operated a part-time consulting business from her home. As of October 1, 2008, Dawn decided to move to rented quarters and to operate the business, which was to be known as Sky's-The-Limit Consulting, on a full-time basis. Sky's-The-Limit Consulting entered into the following transactions during October:

Oct. 1. The following assets were received from Dawn Lytle: cash, $12,950; accounts receivable, $2,800; supplies, $1,500; and office equipment, $18,750. There were no liabilities received.
 1. Paid three months' rent on a lease rental contract, $3,600.
 2. Paid the premiums on property and casualty insurance policies, $2,400.
 4. Received cash from clients as an advance payment for services to be provided and recorded it as unearned fees, $4,150.
 5. Purchased additional office equipment on account from Office Station Co., $2,500.
 6. Received cash from clients on account, $1,900.
 10. Paid cash for a newspaper advertisement, $325.
 12. Paid Office Station Co. for part of the debt incurred on October 5, $1,250.
 12. Recorded services provided on account for the period October 1–12, $3,750.
 14. Paid part-time receptionist for two weeks' salary, $750.
 17. Recorded cash from cash clients for fees earned during the period October 1–17, $6,250.
 18. Paid cash for supplies, $600.
 20. Recorded services provided on account for the period October 13–20, $2,100.
 24. Recorded cash from cash clients for fees earned for the period October 17–24, $3,850.
 26. Received cash from clients on account, $4,450.
 27. Paid part-time receptionist for two weeks' salary, $750.
 29. Paid telephone bill for October, $250.
 31. Paid electricity bill for October, $300.
 31. Recorded cash from cash clients for fees earned for the period October 25–31, $2,975.
 31. Recorded services provided on account for the remainder of October, $1,500.
 31. Dawn withdrew $5,000 for personal use.

Instructions
1. Journalize each transaction in a two-column journal, referring to the following chart of accounts in selecting the accounts to be debited and credited. (Do not insert the account numbers in the journal at this time.)

11	Cash	31	Dawn Lytle, Capital
12	Accounts Receivable	32	Dawn Lytle, Drawing
14	Supplies	41	Fees Earned
15	Prepaid Rent	51	Salary Expense
16	Prepaid Insurance	52	Rent Expense
18	Office Equipment	53	Supplies Expense
19	Accumulated Depreciation	54	Depreciation Expense
21	Accounts Payable	55	Insurance Expense
22	Salaries Payable	59	Miscellaneous Expense
23	Unearned Fees		

2. Post the journal to a ledger of four-column accounts.
3. Prepare an unadjusted trial balance.
4. At the end of October, the following adjustment data were assembled. Analyze and use these data to complete parts (5) and (6).
   a. Insurance expired during October is $200.
   b. Supplies on hand on October 31 are $875.
   c. Depreciation of office equipment for October is $675.
   d. Accrued receptionist salary on October 31 is $150.
   e. Rent expired during October is $1,550.
   f. Unearned fees on October 31 are $1,150.
5. **Optional:** Enter the unadjusted trial balance on an end-of-period spreadsheet (work sheet) and complete the spreadsheet.
6. Journalize and post the adjusting entries.
7. Prepare an adjusted trial balance.
8. Prepare an income statement, a statement of owner's equity, and a balance sheet.
9. Prepare and post the closing entries. (Income Summary is account #33 in the chart of accounts.) Indicate closed accounts by inserting a line in both the Balance columns opposite the closing entry.
10. Prepare a post-closing trial balance.

Problems Series B

PR 4-1B
Financial statements and closing entries

objs. 1, 2, 3

✓ *1. Net loss: $10,900*

Last-Chance Company offers legal consulting advice to prison inmates. Last-Chance Company prepared the end-of-period spreadsheet (work sheet) at the top of the following page at November 30, 2008, the end of the current fiscal year.

Instructions
1. Prepare an income statement for the year ended November 30.
2. Prepare a statement of owner's equity for the year ended November 30. No additional investments were made during the year.
3. Prepare a balance sheet as of November 30.
4. On the basis of the end-of-period spreadsheet (work sheet), journalize the closing entries.
5. Prepare a post-closing trial balance.

	A	B	C	D	E	F	G	H	I	J	K	
		colspan over title										

Last-Chance Company
End-of-Period Spreadsheet (Work Sheet)
For the Year Ended November 30, 2008

	Account Title	Unadjusted Trial Balance Dr.	Cr.	Adjustments Dr.	Cr.	Adjusted Trial Balance Dr.	Cr.	Income Statement Dr.	Cr.	Balance Sheet Dr.	Cr.	
1	Cash	4,800				4,800				4,800		1
2	Accounts Receivable	15,750		(a) 4,200		19,950				19,950		2
3	Prepaid Insurance	2,700			(b) 1,450	1,250				1,250		3
4	Supplies	2,025			(c) 1,525	500				500		4
5	Land	75,000				75,000				75,000		5
6	Building	205,000				205,000				205,000		6
7	Acc. Depr.—Building		76,000		(d) 2,000		78,000				78,000	7
8	Equipment	139,000				139,000				139,000		8
9	Acc. Depr.—Equipment		54,450		(e) 5,200		59,650				59,650	9
10	Accounts Payable		9,750				9,750				9,750	10
11	Unearned Rent		4,500	(g) 2,000			2,500				2,500	11
12	Corey Evans, Capital		318,800				318,800				318,800	12
13	Corey Evans, Drawing	15,000				15,000				15,000		13
14	Fees Revenue		286,500		(a) 4,200		290,700		290,700			14
15	Salaries & Wages Expense	144,300		(f) 2,700		147,000		147,000				15
16	Advertising Expense	94,800				94,800		94,800				16
17	Utilities Expense	27,000				27,000		27,000				17
18	Travel Expense	18,750				18,750		18,750				18
19	Misc. Expense	5,875				5,875		5,875				19
20		750,000	750,000									20
21	Insurance Expense			(b) 1,450		1,450		1,450				21
22	Supplies Expense			(c) 1,525		1,525		1,525				22
23	Depr. Exp.—Building			(d) 2,000		2,000		2,000				23
24	Depr. Exp.—Equipment			(e) 5,200		5,200		5,200				24
25	Sal. & Wages Payable				(f) 2,700		2,700				2,700	25
26	Rent Revenue				(g) 2,000		2,000		2,000			26
27				19,075	19,075	764,100	764,100	303,600	292,700	460,500	471,400	27
28	Net loss								10,900	10,900		28
29								303,600	303,600	471,400	471,400	29

PR 4-2B
Financial statements and closing entries
objs. 2, 3

✓1. Chad Tillman, capital, July 31: $492,000

The Ultra Services Company is a financial planning services firm owned and operated by Chad Tillman. As of July 31, 2008, the end of the current fiscal year, the accountant for The Ultra Services Company prepared an end-of-period spreadsheet (work sheet), part of which is shown at the top of the next page.

Instructions
1. Prepare an income statement, a statement of owner's equity (no additional investments were made during the year), and a balance sheet.
2. Journalize the entries that were required to close the accounts at July 31.
3. If the balance of Chad Tillman, Capital decreased $40,000 after the closing entries were posted, and the withdrawals remained the same, what was the amount of net income or net loss?

	A		H	I	J	K	
	The Ultra Services Company						
	End-of-Period Spreadsheet (Work Sheet)						
	For the Year Ended July 31, 2008						
			Income Statement		Balance Sheet		
1	Cash				13,950		1
2	Accounts Receivable				41,880		2
3	Supplies				8,400		3
4	Prepaid Insurance				7,500		4
5	Land				180,000		5
6	Buildings				360,000		6
7	Accumulated Depreciation—Buildings					217,200	7
8	Equipment				258,270		8
9	Accumulated Depreciation—Equipment					122,700	9
10	Accounts Payable					33,300	10
11	Salaries Payable					3,300	11
12	Unearned Rent					1,500	12
13	Chad Tillman, Capital					340,500	13
14	Chad Tillman, Drawing				30,000		14
15	Service Fees			525,000			15
16	Rent Revenue			4,500			16
17	Salary Expense		219,000				17
18	Depreciation Expense—Equipment		28,500				18
19	Rent Expense		25,500				19
20	Supplies Expense		22,950				20
21	Utilities Expense		15,900				21
22	Depreciation Expense—Buildings		15,600				22
23	Repairs Expense		12,450				23
24	Insurance Expense		3,000				24
25	Miscellaneous Expense		5,100				25
26			348,000	529,500	900,000	718,500	26
27	Net income		181,500			181,500	27
28			529,500	529,500	900,000	900,000	28

PR 4-3B

T accounts, adjusting entries, financial statements, and closing entries; optional end-of-period spreadsheet (work sheet).

objs. 2, 3

✓ *2. Net income: $12,300*

The unadjusted trial balance of Best Laundry at March 31, 2008, the end of the current fiscal year, is shown below.

Best Laundry
Unadjusted Trial Balance
March 31, 2008

	Debit Balances	Credit Balances
Cash	1,450	
Laundry Supplies	3,750	
Prepaid Insurance	2,400	
Laundry Equipment	54,500	
Accumulated Depreciation		20,500
Accounts Payable		3,100
Ryan Boyle, Capital		18,900
Ryan Boyle, Drawing	1,000	
Laundry Revenue		82,500
Wages Expense	35,750	
Rent Expense	18,000	
Utilities Expense	6,800	
Miscellaneous Expense	1,350	
	125,000	125,000

The data needed to determine year-end adjustments are as follows:

a. Laundry supplies on hand at March 31 are $950.
b. Insurance premiums expired during the year are $2,000.
c. Depreciation of equipment during the year is $2,900.
d. Wages accrued but not paid at March 31 are $600.

Instructions

1. For each account listed in the unadjusted trial balance, enter the balance in a T account. Identify the balance as "Mar. 31 Bal." In addition, add T accounts for Wages Payable, Depreciation Expense, Laundry Supplies Expense, Insurance Expense, and Income Summary.
2. **Optional:** Enter the unadjusted trial balance on an end-of-period spreadsheet (work sheet) and complete the spreadsheet. Add the accounts listed in Part (1) as needed.
3. Journalize and post the adjusting entries. Identify the adjustments by "Adj." and the new balances as "Adj. Bal."
4. Prepare an adjusted trial balance.
5. Prepare an income statement, a statement of owner's equity (no additional investments were made during the year), and a balance sheet.
6. Journalize and post the closing entries. Identify the closing entries by "Clos."
7. Prepare a post-closing trial balance.

PR 4-4B
Ledger accounts, adjusting entries, financial statements, and closing entries; optional end-of-period spreadsheet (work sheet)

objs. 2, 3

✓ *4. Net income: $23,818*

If the working papers correlating with this textbook are not used, omit Problem 4-4B.

The ledger and trial balance of Wainscot Services Co. as of March 31, 2008, the end of the first month of its current fiscal year, are presented in the working papers.

Data needed to determine the necessary adjusting entries are as follows:

a. Service revenue accrued at March 31 is $2,000.
b. Supplies on hand at March 31 are $400.
c. Insurance premiums expired during March are $150.
d. Depreciation of the building during March is $625.
e. Depreciation of equipment during March is $200.
f. Unearned rent at March 31 is $1,800.
g. Wages accrued but not paid at March 31 are $600.

Instructions

1. **Optional:** Complete the end-of-period spreadsheet (work sheet) using the adjustment data shown above.
2. Journalize and post the adjusting entries, inserting balances in the accounts affected.
3. Prepare an adjusted trial balance.
4. Prepare an income statement, a statement of owner's equity, and a balance sheet.
5. Journalize and post the closing entries. Indicate closed accounts by inserting a line in both Balance columns opposite the closing entry. Insert the new balance of the capital account.
6. Prepare a post-closing trial balance.

PR 4-5B
Ledger accounts, adjusting entries, financial statements, and closing entries; optional end-of-period spreadsheet (work sheet).

objs. 2, 3

✓ *5. Net income: $30,175*

The unadjusted trial balance of Reliable Repairs at December 31, 2008, the end of the current year, is shown at the top of the next page. The data needed to determine year-end adjustments are as follows:

a. Supplies on hand at December 31 are $6,500.
b. Insurance premiums expired during the year are $2,500.
c. Depreciation of equipment during the year is $4,800.
d. Depreciation of trucks during the year is $3,500.
e. Wages accrued but not paid at December 31 are $1,000.

Reliable Repairs
Unadjusted Trial Balance
December 31, 2008

		Debit Balances	Credit Balances
11	Cash	2,825	
13	Supplies	10,820	
14	Prepaid Insurance	7,500	
16	Equipment	54,200	
17	Accumulated Depreciation—Equipment		12,050
18	Trucks	50,000	
19	Accumulated Depreciation—Trucks		27,100
21	Accounts Payable		12,015
31	Lee Mendoza, Capital		32,885
32	Lee Mendoza, Drawing	5,000	
41	Service Revenue		90,950
51	Wages Expense	28,010	
53	Rent Expense	8,100	
55	Truck Expense	6,350	
59	Miscellaneous Expense	2,195	
		175,000	175,000

Instructions

1. For each account listed in the unadjusted trial balance, enter the balance in the appropriate Balance column of a four-column account and place a check mark (✔) in the Posting Reference column.

2. **Optional:** Enter the unadjusted trial balance on an end-of-period spreadsheet (work sheet) and complete the spreadsheet. Add the accounts listed in part (3) as needed.

3. Journalize and post the adjusting entries, inserting balances in the accounts affected. The following additional accounts from Reliable's chart of accounts should be used: Wages Payable, 22; Supplies Expense, 52; Depreciation Expense—Equipment, 54; Depreciation Expense—Trucks, 56; Insurance Expense, 57.

4. Prepare an adjusted trial balance.

5. Prepare an income statement, a statement of owner's equity (no additional investments were made during the year), and a balance sheet.

6. Journalize and post the closing entries. (Income Summary is account #33 in the chart of accounts.) Indicate closed accounts by inserting a line in both Balance columns opposite the closing entry.

7. Prepare a post-closing trial balance.

PR 4-6B
Complete accounting cycle
objs. 4, 5, 6

✔8. Net income: $10,980

For the past several years, Derrick Epstein has operated a part-time consulting business from his home. As of June 1, 2008, Derrick decided to move to rented quarters and to operate the business, which was to be known as Luminary Consulting, on a full-time basis. Luminary Consulting entered into the following transactions during June:

June 1. The following assets were received from Derrick Epstein: cash, $26,200; accounts receivable, $6,000; supplies, $2,800; and office equipment, $25,000. There were no liabilities received.

1. Paid three months' rent on a lease rental contract, $5,250.

2. Paid the premiums on property and casualty insurance policies, $2,100.

4. Received cash from clients as an advance payment for services to be provided and recorded it as unearned fees, $2,700.

5. Purchased additional office equipment on account from Office Station Co., $5,000.

6. Received cash from clients on account, $3,000.

10. Paid cash for a newspaper advertisement, $200.

12. Paid Office Station Co. for part of the debt incurred on June 5, $1,000.

12. Recorded services provided on account for the period June 1–12, $5,100.

14. Paid part-time receptionist for two weeks' salary, $800.

17. Recorded cash from cash clients for fees earned during the period June 1–16, $3,500.

(continued)

June 18. Paid cash for supplies, $750.
20. Recorded services provided on account for the period June 13–20, $1,100.
24. Recorded cash from cash clients for fees earned for the period June 17–24, $4,150.
26. Received cash from clients on account, $4,900.
27. Paid part-time receptionist for two weeks' salary, $800.
29. Paid telephone bill for June, $150.
30. Paid electricity bill for June, $400.
30. Recorded cash from cash clients for fees earned for the period June 25–30, $1,500.
30. Recorded services provided on account for the remainder of June, $1,000.
30. Derrick withdrew $8,000 for personal use.

Instructions

1. Journalize each transaction in a two-column journal, referring to the following chart of accounts in selecting the accounts to be debited and credited. (Do not insert the account numbers in the journal at this time.)

11	Cash	31	Derrick Epstein, Capital
12	Accounts Receivable	32	Derrick Epstein, Drawing
14	Supplies	41	Fees Earned
15	Prepaid Rent	51	Salary Expense
16	Prepaid Insurance	52	Rent Expense
18	Office Equipment	53	Supplies Expense
19	Accumulated Depreciation	54	Depreciation Expense
21	Accounts Payable	55	Insurance Expense
22	Salaries Payable	59	Miscellaneous Expense
23	Unearned Fees		

2. Post the journal to a ledger of four-column accounts.
3. Prepare an unadjusted trial balance.
4. At the end of June, the following adjustment data were assembled. Analyze and use these data to complete parts (5) and (6).
   a. Insurance expired during June is $175.
   b. Supplies on hand on June 30 are $2,000.
   c. Depreciation of office equipment for June is $500.
   d. Accrued receptionist salary on June 30 is $120.
   e. Rent expired during June is $1,500.
   f. Unearned fees on June 30 are $1,875.
5. **Optional:** Enter the unadjusted trial balance on an end-of-period spreadsheet (work sheet) and complete the spreadsheet.
6. Journalize and post the adjusting entries.
7. Prepare an adjusted trial balance.
8. Prepare an income statement, a statement of owner's equity, and a balance sheet.
9. Prepare and post the closing entries. (Income Summary is account #33 in the chart of accounts.) Indicate closed accounts by inserting a line in both the Balance columns opposite the closing entry.
10. Prepare a post-closing trial balance.

Continuing Problem

The unadjusted trial balance of Dancin Music as of May 31, 2008, along with the adjustment data for the two months ended May 31, 2008, are shown in Chapter 3.

Based upon the adjustment data, the adjusted trial balance shown at the top of the following page was prepared.

Instructions

1. **Optional.** Using the data from Chapter 3, prepare an end-of-period spreadsheet (work sheet).
2. Prepare an income statement, a statement of owner's equity, and a balance sheet. (*Note:* Kris Payne made investments in Dancin Music on April 1 and May 1, 2008.)

✓ *2. Net income: $4,925*

Dancin Music
Adjusted Trial Balance
May 31, 2008

	Debit Balances	Credit Balances
Cash	12,085	
Accounts Receivable	4,250	
Supplies	160	
Prepaid Insurance	3,080	
Office Equipment	5,000	
Accumulated Depreciation—Office Equipment		100
Accounts Payable		5,750
Wages Payable		200
Unearned Revenue		2,400
Kris Payne, Capital		12,500
Kris Payne, Drawing	1,300	
Fees Earned		18,550
Wages Expense	2,600	
Office Rent Expense	2,600	
Equipment Rent Expense	1,300	
Utilities Expense	910	
Music Expense	2,565	
Advertising Expense	1,730	
Supplies Expense	940	
Insurance Expense	280	
Depreciation Expense	100	
Miscellaneous Expense	600	
	39,500	39,500

3. Journalize and post the closing entries. The income summary account is #33 in the ledger of Dancin Music. Indicate closed accounts by inserting a line in both Balance columns opposite the closing entry.
4. Prepare a post-closing trial balance.

Comprehensive Problem 1

✓ 8. Net income, $22,160

Kelly Pitney began her consulting business, Kelly Consulting, on April 1, 2008. The accounting cycle for Kelly Consulting for April, including financial statements, was illustrated on pages 161–174. During May, Kelly Consulting entered into the following transactions:

May 3. Received cash from clients as an advance payment for services to be provided and recorded it as unearned fees, $1,550.
5. Received cash from clients on account, $1,750.
9. Paid cash for a newspaper advertisement, $100.
13. Paid Office Station Co. for part of the debt incurred on April 5, $400.
15. Recorded services provided on account for the period May 1–15, $5,100.
16. Paid part-time receptionist for two weeks' salary including the amount owed on April 30, $750.
17. Recorded cash from cash clients for fees earned during the period May 1–16, $7,380.
20. Purchased supplies on account, $500.
21. Recorded services provided on account for the period May 16–20, $2,900.
25. Recorded cash from cash clients for fees earned for the period May 17–23, $4,200.
27. Received cash from clients on account, $6,600.
28. Paid part-time receptionist for two weeks' salary, $750.
30. Paid telephone bill for May, $150.
31. Paid electricity bill for May, $225.
31. Recorded cash from cash clients for fees earned for the period May 26–31, $2,875.
31. Recorded services provided on account for the remainder of May, $2,200.
31. Kelly withdrew $7,500 for personal use.

Instructions

1. The chart of accounts for Kelly Consulting is shown on page 163, and the post-closing trial balance as of April 30, 2008, is shown on page 169. For each account in the post-closing trial balance, enter the balance in the appropriate Balance column of a four-column account. Date the balances May 1, 2008, and place a check mark (✓) in the Post Reference column. Journalize each of the May transactions in a two-column journal using Kelly Consulting's chart of accounts. (Do not insert the account numbers in the journal at this time.)
2. Post the journal to a ledger of four-column accounts.
3. Prepare an unadjusted trial balance.
4. At the end of May, the following adjustment data were assembled. Analyze and use these data to complete parts (5) and (6).
   a. Insurance expired during May is $300.
   b. Supplies on hand on May 31 are $950.
   c. Depreciation of office equipment for May is $330.
   d. Accrued receptionist salary on May 31 is $260.
   e. Rent expired during May is $1,600.
   f. Unearned fees on May 31 are $1,300.
5. **Optional:** Enter the unadjusted trial balance on an end-of-period spreadsheet (work sheet) and complete the spreadsheet.
6. Journalize and post the adjusting entries.
7. Prepare an adjusted trial balance.
8. Prepare an income statement, a statement of owner's equity, and a balance sheet.
9. Prepare and post the closing entries. (Income Summary is account #33 in the chart of accounts.) Indicate closed accounts by inserting a line in both the Balance columns opposite the closing entry.
10. Prepare a post-closing trial balance.

Special Activities

SA 4-1
Ethics and professional conduct in business

ETHICS

Fantasy Graphics is a graphics arts design consulting firm. Terri Bierman, its treasurer and vice president of finance, has prepared a classified balance sheet as of January 31, 2008, the end of its fiscal year. This balance sheet will be submitted with Fantasy Graphics' loan application to Booneville Trust & Savings Bank.

In the Current Assets section of the balance sheet, Terri reported a $100,000 receivable from Kent Miles, the president of Fantasy Graphics, as a trade account receivable. Kent borrowed the money from Fantasy Graphics in November 2006 for a down payment on a new home. He has orally assured Terri that he will pay off the account receivable within the next year. Terri reported the $100,000 in the same manner on the preceding year's balance sheet.

Evaluate whether it is acceptable for Terri Bierman to prepare the January 31, 2008, balance sheet in the manner indicated above.

SA 4-2
Financial statements

The following is an excerpt from a telephone conversation between Jan Young, president of Cupboard Supplies Co., and Steve Nisbet, owner of Nisbet Employment Co.

Jan: Steve, you're going to have to do a better job of finding me a new computer programmer. That last guy was great at programming, but he didn't have any common sense.

Steve: What do you mean? The guy had a master's degree with straight A's.

Jan: Yes, well, last month he developed a new financial reporting system. He said we could do away with manually preparing an end-of-period spreadsheet (work sheet) and financial statements. The computer would automatically generate our financial statements with "a push of a button."

Steve: So what's the big deal? Sounds to me like it would save you time and effort.

Jan: Right! The balance sheet showed a minus for supplies!

Steve: Minus supplies? How can that be?

Jan: That's what I asked.

Steve: So, what did he say?

Jan: Well, after he checked the program, he said that it must be right. The minuses were greater than the pluses. . . .

Steve: Didn't he know that Supplies can't have a credit balance—it must have a debit balance?

Jan: He asked me what a debit and credit were.

Steve: I see your point.

1. ▭▭▶ Comment on (a) the desirability of computerizing Cupboard Supplies Co.'s financial reporting system, (b) the elimination of the end-of-period spreadsheet (work sheet) in a computerized accounting system, and (c) the computer programmer's lack of accounting knowledge.

2. ▭▭▶ Explain to the programmer why Supplies could not have a credit balance.

SA 4-3
Financial statements

Assume that you recently accepted a position with the First Security Bank as an assistant loan officer. As one of your first duties, you have been assigned the responsibility of evaluating a loan request for $80,000 from DiamondJewelry.com, a small proprietorship. In support of the loan application, Marion Zastrow, owner, submitted a "Statement of Accounts" (trial balance) for the first year of operations ended December 31, 2008.

DiamondJewelry.com
Statement of Accounts
December 31, 2008

Cash	2,050	
Billings Due from Others	15,070	
Supplies (chemicals, etc.)	7,470	
Trucks	26,370	
Equipment	8,090	
Amounts Owed to Others		2,850
Investment in Business		23,500
Service Revenue		73,650
Wages Expense	30,050	
Utilities Expense	7,330	
Rent Expense	2,400	
Insurance Expense	700	
Other Expenses	470	
	100,000	100,000

1. ▭▭▶ Explain to Marion Zastrow why a set of financial statements (income statement, statement of owner's equity, and balance sheet) would be useful to you in evaluating the loan request.

2. In discussing the "Statement of Accounts" with Marion Zastrow, you discovered that the accounts had not been adjusted at December 31. Analyze the "Statement of Accounts" and indicate possible adjusting entries that might be necessary before an accurate set of financial statements could be prepared.

3. ▭▭▶ Assuming that an accurate set of financial statements will be submitted by Marion Zastrow in a few days, what other considerations or information would you require before making a decision on the loan request?

SA 4-4
Compare balance sheets

Group Project

Internet Project

In groups of three or four, compare the balance sheets of two different companies, and present to the class a summary of the similarities and differences of the two companies. You may obtain the balance sheets you need from one of the following sources:

1. Your school or local library.
2. The investor relations department of each company.
3. The company's Web site on the Internet.
4. EDGAR (Electronic Data Gathering, Analysis, and Retrieval), the electronic archives of financial statements filed with the Securities and Exchange Commission.

SEC documents can be retrieved using the EdgarScan™ service from Pricewaterhouse-Coopers at **http://edgarscan.pwcglobal.com**. To obtain annual report information, key in a company name in the appropriate space. EdgarScan will list the reports available to you for the company you've selected. Select the most recent annual report filing, identified as a 10-K or 10-K405. EdgarScan provides an outline of the report, including the separate financial statements, which can also be selected in an Excel® spreadsheet.

Answers to Self-Examination Questions

1. **C** The drawing account, M. E. Jones, Drawing (answer C), would be extended to the Balance Sheet columns of the work sheet. Utilities Expense (answer A), Rent Revenue (answer B), and Miscellaneous Expense (answer D) would all be extended to the Income Statement columns of the work sheet.

2. **D** Cash or other assets that are expected to be converted to cash or sold or used up within one year or less, through the normal operations of the business, are classified as current assets on the balance sheet. Accounts Receivable (answer D) is a current asset, since it will normally be converted to cash within one year. Office Equipment (answer A), Land (answer B), and Accumulated Depreciation (answer C) are all reported in the property, plant, and equipment section of the balance sheet.

3. **B** The entry to close the owner's drawing account is to debit the owner's capital account and credit the drawing account (answer B).

4. **D** Since all revenue and expense accounts are closed at the end of the period, Fees Earned (answer A), Wages Expense (answer B), and Rent Expense (answer C) would all be closed to Income Summary. Accumulated Depreciation (answer D) is a contra asset account that is not closed.

5. **B** Since the post-closing trial balance includes only balance sheet accounts (all of the revenue, expense, and drawing accounts are closed), Cash (answer A), Accumulated Depreciation (answer C), and J. C. Smith, Capital (answer D) would appear on the post-closing trial balance. Fees Earned (answer B) is a temporary account that is closed prior to preparing the post-closing trial balance.

Accounting for Merchandising Businesses

© JOSE JUAREZ/ASSOCIATED PRESS

objectives

After studying this chapter, you should be able to:

1 *Distinguish between the activities and financial statements of service and merchandising businesses.*

2 *Describe and illustrate the financial statements of a merchandising business.*

3 *Describe and illustrate the accounting for merchandise transactions including:*
   • *sale of merchandise*
   • *purchase of merchandise*
   • *transportation costs, sales taxes, and trade discounts*
   • *dual nature of merchandising transactions*

4 *Describe the adjusting and closing process for a merchandising business.*

Whole Foods Market

When you buy groceries, textbooks, school supplies, or an automobile, you are doing business with either a retail or a merchandising business. One such merchandising business is Whole Foods Market, the world's leading retailer of natural and organic foods. Whole Foods obtains its products locally and around the world, with a unique commitment to sustainable agriculture. In addition, Whole Foods has distinguished itself by placing 15th on the Fortune ®100 Best Companies to Work For.

Assume you bought groceries at Whole Foods Market and received the receipt such as shown below.

```
              WHOLE
              FOODS
              M A R K E T

*     365  FRENCH ROAST 2      9.99 B
****  TAX   .39   BAL          10.38

      Cash                     20.00

      CHANGE                    9.62

TOTAL NUMBER OF ITEMS SOLD = 1
2/24/06   3:32 PM 0713 10 0064 706

      Your cashier today is MAX
      Thank You For Shopping at
 Whole Foods Buckhead 404-324-4100
```

This receipt indicates that one item was purchased totaling $9.99, the sales tax was $0.39 (4%), the total due was $10.38, the clerk was given $20.00, and change of $9.62 was given back to the customer. The receipt also indicates that the sale was made by Buckhead Store of the Whole Foods Market chain, located in Atlanta, Georgia. The date and time of the sale and other data used internally by the store are also indicated.

As you may have guessed from the preceding receipt, the accounting for a merchandising business is more complex than that for a service business. For example, the accounting system for a merchandiser must be designed to record the receipt of goods for resale, keep track of the goods available for sale, and record the sale and cost of the merchandise sold.

In this chapter, we will focus on the accounting principles and concepts for merchandising businesses. We begin our discussion by highlighting the basic differences between the activities of merchandise and service businesses. We then describe and illustrate financial statements for merchandising businesses and purchases and sales transactions.

Nature of Merchandising Businesses

objective 1

Distinguish between the activities and financial statements of service and merchandising businesses.

@netsolutions

How do the activities of NetSolutions, an attorney, and an architect, which are service businesses, differ from those of Wal-Mart or Best Buy, which are merchandising businesses? These differences are best illustrated by focusing on the revenues and expenses in the following condensed income statements:

Service Business		Merchandising Business	
Fees earned	$XXX	Sales	$XXX
Operating expenses	−XXX	Cost of merchandise sold	−XXX
Net income	$XXX	Gross profit	$XXX
		Operating expenses	−XXX
		Net income	$XXX

The revenue activities of a service business involve providing services to customers. On the income statement for a service business, the revenues from services are reported as *fees earned*. The operating expenses incurred in providing the services are subtracted from the fees earned to arrive at *net income*.

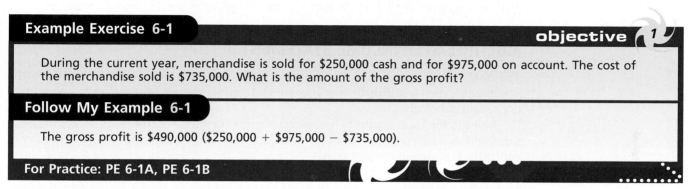

Sales − Cost of Merchandise Sold = Gross Profit

Gross Profit − Operating Expenses = Net Income

In contrast, the revenue activities of a merchandising business involve the buying and selling of merchandise. A merchandising business must first purchase merchandise to sell to its customers. When this merchandise is sold, the revenue is reported as sales, and its cost is recognized as an expense called the **cost of merchandise sold**. The cost of merchandise sold is subtracted from sales to arrive at gross profit. This amount is called **gross profit** because it is the profit *before* deducting operating expenses.

Merchandise on hand (not sold) at the end of an accounting period is called **merchandise inventory**. Merchandise inventory is reported as a current asset on the balance sheet.

In the remainder of this chapter, we illustrate merchandiser financial statements and transactions that affect the income statement (sales, cost of merchandise sold, and gross profit) and the balance sheet (merchandise inventory).

Example Exercise 6-1
objective 1

During the current year, merchandise is sold for $250,000 cash and for $975,000 on account. The cost of the merchandise sold is $735,000. What is the amount of the gross profit?

Follow My Example 6-1

The gross profit is $490,000 ($250,000 + $975,000 − $735,000).

For Practice: PE 6-1A, PE 6-1B

THE OPERATING CYCLE

The operations of a merchandising business involve the purchase of merchandise for sale (purchasing activity), the sale and distribution of the products to customers (sales activity), and the receipt of cash from customers (collection activity). This overall process is referred to as the *operating cycle*. Thus, the operating cycle begins with spending cash, and it ends with receiving cash from customers. The operating cycle for a merchandising business is shown below.

Operating cycles differ, depending upon the nature of the business and its operations. For example, the operating cycles for tobacco, distillery, and lumber industries are much longer than the operating cycles of the automobile, consumer electronics, and home furnishings industries. Likewise, the operating cycles for retailers are usually shorter than for manufacturers because retailers purchase goods in a form ready for sale to the customer. Of course, some retailers will have shorter operating cycles than others because of the nature of their products. For example, a jewelry store or an automobile dealer normally has a longer operating cycle than a consumer electronics store or a grocery store.

Businesses with longer operating cycles normally have higher profit margins on their products than businesses with shorter operating cycles. For example, it is not unusual for jewelry stores to price their jewelry at 30%–50% above cost. In contrast, grocery stores operate on very small profit margins, often below 5%. Grocery stores make up the difference by selling their products more quickly.

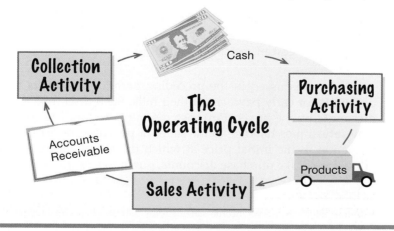

The Operating Cycle

Collection Activity — Cash — Purchasing Activity — Products — Sales Activity — Accounts Receivable

Financial Statements for a Merchandising Business

objective **2**

Describe and illustrate the financial statements of a merchandising business.

@netsolutions

In this section, we illustrate the financial statements for NetSolutions after it becomes a retailer of computer hardware and software. During 2007, we assume that Chris Clark implemented the second phase of NetSolutions' business plan. Accordingly, Chris notified clients that beginning July 1, 2008, NetSolutions would be terminating its consulting services. Instead, it would become a personalized retailer.

NetSolutions' business strategy is to focus on offering personalized service to individuals and small businesses who are upgrading or purchasing new computer systems. NetSolutions' personal service before the sale will include a no-obligation, on-site assessment of the customer's computer needs. By providing tailor-made solutions, personalized service, and follow-up, Chris feels that NetSolutions can compete effectively against larger retailers, such as Best Buy or Office Depot, Inc.

MULTIPLE-STEP INCOME STATEMENT

The 2009 income statement for NetSolutions is shown in Exhibit 1.[1] This form of income statement, called a **multiple-step income statement**, contains several sections, subsections, and subtotals.

Sales is the total amount charged customers for merchandise sold, including cash sales and sales on account. Both sales returns and allowances and sales discounts are subtracted in arriving at net sales.

Sales returns and allowances are granted by the seller to customers for damaged or defective merchandise. For example, rather than have a buyer return merchandise, a seller may offer a $500 allowance to the customer as compensation for damaged merchandise. Sales returns and allowances are recorded when the merchandise is returned or when the allowance is granted by the seller.

Sales discounts are granted by the seller to customers for early payment of amounts owed. For example, a seller may offer a customer a 2% discount on a sale of $10,000 if the customer pays within 10 days. If the customer pays within the 10-day period, the seller receives cash of $9,800 and the buyer receives a discount of $200 ($10,000 × 2%). Sales discounts are recorded when the customer pays the bill.

Net sales is determined by subtracting sales returns and allowances and sales discounts from sales. Rather than reporting sales, sales returns and allowances, and sales discounts as shown in Exhibit 1, many companies report only net sales.

Cost of merchandise sold is the cost of the merchandise sold to customers. To illustrate the determination of the cost of merchandise sold, assume that NetSolutions purchased $340,000 of merchandise during the last half of 2008. If the inventory at December 31, 2008, the end of the year, is $59,700, the cost of the merchandise sold during 2007 is $280,300.

For many merchandising businesses, the cost of merchandise sold is usually the largest expense. For example, the approximate percentage of cost of merchandise sold to sales is 61% for JCPenney and 67% for The Home Depot.

Purchases	$340,000
Less merchandise inventory, December 31, 2008	59,700
Cost of merchandise sold	$280,300

As we discussed in the preceding paragraphs, sellers may offer customers sales discounts for early payment of their bills. Such discounts are referred to as **purchases discounts** by the buyer. Purchase discounts reduce the cost of merchandise. A buyer may return merchandise to the seller (a **purchase return**), or the buyer may receive a reduction in the initial price at which the merchandise was purchased (a **purchase allowance**). Like purchase discounts, purchases returns and allowances reduce the cost

---

1 We use the NetSolutions income statement for 2009 as a basis for illustration because, as will be shown, it allows us to better illustrate the computation of the cost of merchandise sold.

> **EXHIBIT 1**   Multiple-Step Income Statement

NetSolutions
Income Statement
For the Year Ended December 31, 2009

Revenue from sales:			
Sales		$720 185 00	
Less: Sales returns and allowances	$ 6 140 00		
Sales discounts	5 790 00	11 930 00	
Net sales			$708 255 00
Cost of merchandise sold			525 305 00
Gross profit			$182 950 00
Operating expenses:			
Selling expenses:			
Sales salaries expense	$53 430 00		
Advertising expense	10 860 00		
Depr. expense—store equipment	3 100 00		
Delivery expense	2 800 00		
Miscellaneous selling expense	630 00		
Total selling expenses		$ 70 820 00	
Administrative expenses:			
Office salaries expense	$21 020 00		
Rent expense	8 100 00		
Depr. expense—office equipment	2 490 00		
Insurance expense	1 910 00		
Office supplies expense	610 00		
Misc. administrative expense	760 00		
Total administrative expenses		34 890 00	
Total operating expenses			105 710 00
Income from operations			$ 77 240 00
Other income and expense:			
Rent revenue		$ 600 00	
Interest expense		(2 440 00)	(1 840 00)
Net income			$ 75 400 00

of merchandise purchased during a period. In addition, transportation costs paid by the buyer for merchandise also increase the cost of merchandise purchased.

To continue the illustration, assume that during 2009 NetSolutions purchased additional merchandise of $521,980. It received credit for purchases returns and allowances of $9,100, took purchases discounts of $2,525, and paid transportation costs of $17,400. The purchases returns and allowances and the purchases discounts are deducted from the total purchases to yield the **net purchases**. The transportation costs, termed **transportation in**, are added to the net purchases to yield the **cost of merchandise purchased** of $527,755, as shown below.

Purchases		$521,980
Less: Purchases returns and allowances	$9,100	
Purchases discounts	2,525	11,625
Net purchases		$510,355
Add transportation in		17,400
Cost of merchandise purchased		$527,755

The ending inventory of NetSolutions on December 31, 2008, $59,700, becomes the beginning inventory for 2009. This beginning inventory is added to the cost of merchandise purchased to yield **merchandise available for sale**. The ending inventory, which is assumed to be $62,150, is then subtracted from the merchandise available for sale to yield the cost of merchandise sold of $525,305, as shown in Exhibit 2.

EXHIBIT 2   Cost of Merchandise Sold

Merchandise inventory, January 1, 2009			$ 59,700
Purchases		$521,980	
Less: Purchases returns and allowances	$9,100		
Purchases discounts	2,525	11,625	
Net purchases		$510,355	
Add transportation in		17,400	
Cost of merchandise purchased			527,755
Merchandise available for sale			$587,455
Less merchandise inventory, December 31, 2009 . .			62,150
Cost of merchandise sold			$525,305

The cost of merchandise sold was determined by deducting the merchandise on hand at the end of the period from the merchandise available for sale during the period. The merchandise on hand at the end of the period is determined by taking a physical count of inventory on hand. This method of determining the cost of merchandise sold and the amount of merchandise on hand is called the **periodic system** of accounting for merchandise inventory. Under the periodic system, the inventory records do not show the amount available for sale or the amount sold during the period. In contrast, under the **perpetual system** of accounting for merchandise inventory, each purchase and sale of merchandise is recorded in the inventory and the cost of merchandise sold accounts. As a result, the amount of merchandise available for sale and the amount sold are continuously (perpetually) disclosed in the inventory records.

Most large retailers and many small merchandising businesses use computerized perpetual inventory systems. Such systems normally use bar codes, such as the one on the back of this textbook. An optical scanner reads the bar code to record merchandise purchased and sold. Merchandise businesses using a perpetual inventory system report the cost of merchandise sold as a single line on the income statement, as shown in Exhibit 1 for NetSolutions. Merchandise businesses using the periodic inventory system report the cost of merchandise sold by using the format shown in Exhibit 2. Because of its wide use, we will use the perpetual inventory system throughout the remainder of this chapter. The periodic inventory system is described and illustrated in Appendix 2 of this chapter.

Gross profit is determined by subtracting the cost of merchandise sold from net sales. Exhibit 1 shows that NetSolutions reported gross profit of $182,950 in 2009. *Operating income*, sometimes called **income from operations**, is determined by subtracting operating expenses from gross profit. Most merchandising businesses classify operating expenses as either selling expenses or administrative expenses. Expenses that are incurred directly in the selling of merchandise are **selling expenses**. They include such expenses as salespersons' salaries, store supplies used, depreciation of store equipment, delivery expense, and advertising. Expenses incurred in the administration or general operations of the business are **administrative expenses** or *general expenses*. Examples of these expenses are office salaries, depreciation of office equipment, and office supplies used. Credit card expense is also normally classified as an administrative expense. Although selling and administrative expenses may be reported separately, many companies report operating expenses as a single item.

Retailers, such as Best Buy, Sears Holding Corporation, and Wal-Mart, and grocery store chains, such as Winn-Dixie Stores, Inc. and Kroger, use bar codes and optical scanners as part of their computerized inventory systems.

Other income and expense is reported on NetSolutions' income statement in Exhibit 1. Revenue from sources other than the primary operating activity of a business is classified as **other income**. In a merchandising business, these items include income from interest, rent, and gains resulting from the sale of fixed assets.

Expenses that cannot be traced directly to operations are identified as **other expense**. Interest expense that results from financing activities and losses incurred in the disposal of fixed assets are examples of these items.

Other income and other expense are offset against each other on the income statement, as shown in Exhibit 1. If the total of other income exceeds the total of other expense, the difference is added to income from operations to determine net income. If the reverse is true, the difference is subtracted from income from operations.

Example Exercise 6-2

objective 2

Based upon the following data, determine the cost of merchandise sold for May. Follow the format used in Exhibit 2.

Merchandise inventory, May 1	$121,200
Merchandise inventory, May 31	142,000
Purchases	985,000
Purchases returns and allowances	23,500
Purchases discounts	21,000
Transportation in	11,300

Follow My Example 6-2

Cost of merchandise sold:

Merchandise inventory, May 1			$ 121,200
Purchases		$985,000	
Less: Purchases returns and allowances	$23,500		
Purchases discounts	21,000	44,500	
Net purchases		$940,500	
Add transportation in		11,300	
Cost of merchandise purchased			951,800
Merchandise available for sale			$1,073,000
Less merchandise inventory, May 31			142,000
Cost of merchandise sold			$ 931,000

For Practice: PE 6-2A, PE 6-2B

SINGLE-STEP INCOME STATEMENT

An alternate form of income statement is the **single-step income statement**. As shown in Exhibit 3, the income statement for NetSolutions deducts the total of all expenses *in one step* from the total of all revenues.

The single-step form emphasizes total revenues and total expenses as the factors that determine net income. A criticism of the single-step form is that such amounts as gross profit and income from operations are not readily available for analysis.

STATEMENT OF OWNER'S EQUITY

The statement of owner's equity for NetSolutions is shown in Exhibit 4. This statement is prepared in the same manner that we described previously for a service business.

BALANCE SHEET

As we discussed and illustrated in previous chapters, the balance sheet may be presented with assets on the left-hand side and the liabilities and owner's equity on the

EXHIBIT 3

Single-Step Income Statement

NetSolutions
Income Statement
For the Year Ended December 31, 2009

Revenues:		
Net sales		$708 2 5 5 00
Rent revenue		6 0 0 00
Total revenues		$708 8 5 5 00
Expenses:		
Cost of merchandise sold	$525 3 0 5 00	
Selling expenses	70 8 2 0 00	
Administrative expenses	34 8 9 0 00	
Interest expense	2 4 4 0 00	
Total expenses		633 4 5 5 00
Net income		$ 75 4 0 0 00

EXHIBIT 4

Statement of Owner's Equity for Merchandising Business

NetSolutions
Statement of Owner's Equity
For the Year Ended December 31, 2009

Chris Clark, capital, January 1, 2009		$153 8 0 0 00
Net income for year	$75 4 0 0 00	
Less withdrawals	18 0 0 0 00	
Increase in owner's equity		57 4 0 0 00
Chris Clark, capital, December 31, 2009		$211 2 0 0 00

Business Connections

REAL WORLD

H&R BLOCK VERSUS THE HOME DEPOT

H&R Block is a service business that primarily offers tax planning and preparation to its customers. The Home Depot is the world's largest home improvement retailer and the second largest merchandise business in the United States. The differences in the operations of a service and merchandise business are illustrated in their income statements, as shown below.

As will be discussed in a later chapter, corporations are subject to income taxes. Thus, the income statements of H&R Block and Home Depot report "income taxes" as a deduction from "income before income taxes" in arriving at net income. This is in contrast to a proprietorship such as NetSolutions, which is not subject to income taxes.

H&R Block
Condensed Income Statement
For the Year Ending April 30, 2005
(in millions)

Revenue	$4,420
Operating expenses	3,368
Operating income	$1,052
Other income (expense)	(34)
Income before taxes	$1,018
Income taxes	382
Net income	$ 636

The Home Depot
Condensed Income Statement
For the Year Ending January 30, 2005
(in millions)

Net sales	$73,094
Cost of merchandise sold	48,664
Gross profit	$24,430
Operating expenses	16,504
Operating income	$ 7,926
Other income (expense)	(14)
Income before taxes	$ 7,912
Income taxes	2,911
Net income	$ 5,001

right-hand side. This form of the balance sheet is called the **account form**. The balance sheet may also be presented in a downward sequence in three sections. This form of balance sheet is called the **report form**. The report form of balance sheet for NetSolutions is shown in Exhibit 5. In this balance sheet, note that merchandise inventory at the end of the period is reported as a current asset and that the current portion of the note payable is $5,000.

EXHIBIT 5

Report Form of
Balance Sheet

NetSolutions Balance Sheet December 31, 2009				
Assets				
Current assets:				
Cash			$52 9 5 0 00	
Accounts receivable			91 0 8 0 00	
Merchandise inventory			62 1 5 0 00	
Office supplies			4 8 0 00	
Prepaid insurance			2 6 5 0 00	
Total current assets				$209 3 1 0 00
Property, plant, and equipment:				
Land			$20 0 0 0 00	
Store equipment	$27 1 0 0 00			
Less accumulated depreciation	5 7 0 0 00	21 4 0 0 00		
Office equipment	$15 5 7 0 00			
Less accumulated depreciation	4 7 2 0 00	10 8 5 0 00		
Total property, plant, and equipment				52 2 5 0 00
Total assets				$261 5 6 0 00
Liabilities				
Current liabilities:				
Accounts payable			$22 4 2 0 00	
Note payable (current portion)			5 0 0 0 00	
Salaries payable			1 1 4 0 00	
Unearned rent			1 8 0 0 00	
Total current liabilities				$ 30 3 6 0 00
Long-term liabilities:				
Note payable (final payment due 2019)				20 0 0 0 00
Total liabilities				$ 50 3 6 0 00
Owner's Equity				
Chris Clark, capital				211 2 0 0 00
Total liabilities and owner's equity				$261 5 6 0 00

objective **3**

Describe and illustrate the accounting for merchandise transactions including:
- *sale of merchandise*
- *purchase of merchandise*
- *transportation costs, sales taxes, and trade discounts*
- *dual nature of merchandising transactions*

Merchandising Transactions

In the preceding section, we described and illustrated the financial statements of a merchandising business, NetSolutions. In this section, we describe and illustrate the recording of merchandise transactions including sales, purchases, transportation costs, and sales taxes. We also discuss trade discounts and the dual nature of merchandising transactions. As a basis for recording merchandise transactions, we begin by describing the chart of accounts for a merchandising business.

CHART OF ACCOUNTS FOR A MERCHANDISING BUSINESS

The chart of accounts for a merchandising business should reflect the elements of the financial statements we described and illustrated in the preceding section. The chart of

EXHIBIT 6

Chart of Accounts
for NetSolutions
Merchandising
Business

Balance Sheet Accounts		Income Statement Accounts	
	100 Assets		400 Revenues
110	Cash	410	Sales
112	Accounts Receivable	411	Sales Returns and Allowances
115	Merchandise Inventory	412	Sales Discounts
116	Office Supplies		
117	Prepaid Insurance		500 Costs and Expenses
120	Land	510	Cost of Merchandise Sold
123	Store Equipment	520	Sales Salaries Expense
124	Accumulated Depreciation—	521	Advertising Expense
	Store Equipment	522	Depreciation Expense—Store
125	Office Equipment		Equipment
126	Accumulated Depreciation—	523	Delivery Expense
	Office Equipment	529	Miscellaneous Selling Expense
		530	Office Salaries Expense
	200 Liabilities	531	Rent Expense
210	Accounts Payable	532	Depreciation Expense—Office
211	Salaries Payable		Equipment
212	Unearned Rent	533	Insurance Expense
215	Notes Payable	534	Office Supplies Expense
		539	Misc. Administrative Expense
	300 Owner's Equity		
310	Chris Clark, Capital		600 Other Income
311	Chris Clark, Drawing	610	Rent Revenue
312	Income Summary		
			700 Other Expense
		710	Interest Expense

@netsolutions

accounts for NetSolutions is shown in Exhibit 6. The accounts related to merchandising transactions are shown in color.

NetSolutions is now using three-digit account numbers, which permits it to add new accounts as they are needed. The first digit indicates the major financial statement classification (1 for assets, 2 for liabilities, and so on). The second digit indicates the subclassification (e.g., 11 for current assets, 12 for noncurrent assets). The third digit identifies the specific account (e.g., 110 for Cash, 123 for Store Equipment).

NetSolutions is using a more complex numbering system because it has a greater variety of transactions. In addition, its growth creates a need for more detailed information for use in managing it. For example, a wages expense account was adequate for NetSolutions when it was a small service business with few employees. However, as a merchandising business, NetSolutions now uses two payroll accounts, one for Sales Salaries Expense and one for Office Salaries Expense. In the following paragraphs, we use the accounts appearing in Exhibit 6 to record various merchandising transactions of NetSolutions.

SALES TRANSACTIONS

Merchandise transactions are recorded in the accounts, using the rules of debit and credit that we described and illustrated in earlier chapters. Special journals may be used, or transactions may be entered, recorded, and posted to the accounts electronically. Although journal entries may not be manually prepared, we will use a two-column general journal format in this chapter in order to simplify the discussion.[2]

Cash Sales A business may sell merchandise for cash. Cash sales are normally rung up (entered) on a cash register and recorded in the accounts. To illustrate, assume that

---

2 Special journals and computerized accounting systems for merchandising businesses are described in Appendix 1 at the end of this chapter.

on January 3, NetSolutions sells merchandise for $1,800. These cash sales can be recorded as follows:

				JOURNAL			Page 25	
Date			Description		Post. Ref.	Debit	Credit	
2009 Jan.	3	Cash				1 8 0 0 00		
		Sales					1 8 0 0 00	
		To record cash sales.						

Under the perpetual inventory system, the cost of merchandise sold and the reduction in merchandise inventory should also be recorded. In this way, the merchandise inventory account will indicate the amount of merchandise on hand (not sold). To illustrate, assume that the cost of merchandise sold on January 3 was $1,200. The entry to record the cost of merchandise sold and the reduction in the merchandise inventory is as follows:

Jan.	3	Cost of Merchandise Sold			1 2 0 0 00		
		Merchandise Inventory				1 2 0 0 00	
		To record the cost of merch. sold.					

In recent years, a large percentage of retail sales have been made to customers who use credit cards such as MasterCard or VISA. How do retailers record sales made with the use of credit cards? Such sales are recorded as cash sales. This is because the retailer normally receives payment within a few days of making the sale. Specifically, such sales are normally processed by a clearing-house that contacts the bank that issued the card. The issuing bank then electronically transfers cash directly to the retailer's bank account.[3] Thus, if the customers in the preceding sales had used MasterCards to pay for their purchases, the sales would be recorded exactly as shown above. Any processing fees charged by the clearing-house or issuing bank are periodically recorded as an expense as shown below.

Jan.	31	Credit Card Expense			4 8 00		
		Cash				4 8 00	
		To record service charges on credit					
		card sales for the month.					

Instead of using MasterCard or VISA, a customer may use a credit card that is not issued by a bank, such as American Express or Discover. If the seller uses a clearing-house, the clearing-house will collect the receivable and transfer the cash to the retailer's bank account similar to the way it would have if the customer had used MasterCard or VISA. Large businesses, however, may not use a clearing-house. In such cases, nonbank credit card sales must first be reported to the card company before cash is received. Thus, a receivable is created with the nonbank credit card company.

---

3 CyberSource is one of the major credit card clearing-houses. For a more detailed description of how credit card sales are processed, see the following CyberSource web page: http://www.cybersource.com/products_and_services/electronic_payments/credit_card_processing/howitworks.xml.

However, since most retailers use clearing-houses to process both bank and nonbank credit cards, we will record all credit card sales as cash sales.

Sales on Account   A business may sell merchandise on account. The seller records such sales as a debit to Accounts Receivable and a credit to Sales. An example of an entry for a NetSolutions sale on account of $510 follows. The cost of merchandise sold was $280.

Jan.	12	Accounts Receivable—Sims Co.	5 1 0 00	
		Sales		5 1 0 00
		Invoice No. 7172.		
	12	Cost of Merchandise Sold	2 8 0 00	
		Merchandise Inventory		2 8 0 00
		Cost of merch. sold on Invoice No. 7172.		

Sales Discounts   The terms of a sale are normally indicated on the **invoice** or bill that the seller sends to the buyer. An example of a sales invoice for NetSolutions is shown in Exhibit 7.

EXHIBIT 7   Invoice

106-8

@netsolutions
Invoice

**5101 Washington Ave.
Cincinnati, OH 45227-5101**

Made in U.S.A.

SOLD TO
Omega Technologies
1000 Matrix Blvd.
San Jose, CA. 95116–1000

CUSTOMER'S ORDER NO. & DATE
412 Jan. 10, 2009

DATE SHIPPED Jan. 12, 2009	**HOW SHIPPED AND ROUTE** US Express Trucking Co.	**TERMS** 2/10, n/30	**INVOICE DATE** Jan. 12, 2009
FROM Cincinnati	**F.O.B.** Cincinnati		

QUANTITY	**DESCRIPTION**	**UNIT PRICE**	**AMOUNT**
10	3COM Megahertz 10/100 Lan PC Card	150.00	1,500.00

The terms for when payments for merchandise are to be made, agreed on by the buyer and the seller, are called the **credit terms**. If payment is required on delivery, the terms are *cash* or *net cash*. Otherwise, the buyer is allowed an amount of time, known as the **credit period**, in which to pay.

The credit period usually begins with the date of the sale as shown on the invoice. If payment is due within a stated number of days after the date of the invoice, such as 30 days, the terms are *net 30 days*. These terms may be written as *n/30*.[4] If payment is due by the end of the month in which the sale was made, the terms are written as *n/eom*.

---

4 The word *net* as used here does not have the usual meaning of a number after deductions have been subtracted, as in *net income*.

As a means of encouraging the buyer to pay before the end of the credit period, the seller may offer a discount. For example, a seller may offer a 2% discount if the buyer pays within 10 days of the invoice date. If the buyer does not take the discount, the total amount is due within 30 days. These terms are expressed as *2/10, n/30* and are read as *2% discount if paid within 10 days, net amount due within 30 days*. The credit terms of 2/10, n/30 are summarized in Exhibit 8, using the information from the invoice in Exhibit 7.

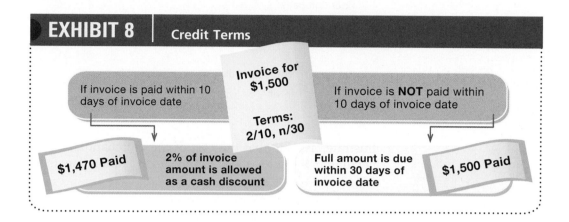

EXHIBIT 8 | **Credit Terms**

Invoice for $1,500
Terms: 2/10, n/30

If invoice is paid within 10 days of invoice date → $1,470 Paid / 2% of invoice amount is allowed as a cash discount

If invoice is **NOT** paid within 10 days of invoice date → Full amount is due within 30 days of invoice date / $1,500 Paid

Discounts taken by the buyer for early payment are recorded as sales discounts by the seller. Since managers may want to know the amount of the sales discounts for a period, the seller normally records the sales discounts in a separate account. The sales discounts account is a *contra* (or *offsetting*) account to Sales. To illustrate, assume that cash is received within the discount period (10 days) from the credit sale of $1,500, shown on the invoice in Exhibit 7. NetSolutions would record the receipt of the cash as follows:

Jan.	22	Cash	1 4 7 0 00	
		Sales Discounts	3 0 00	
		Accounts Receivable—Omega Tech.		1 5 0 0 00
		Collection on Invoice No. 106-8, less		
		2% discount.		

Sales Returns and Allowances   Merchandise sold may be returned to the seller (**sales return**). In addition, because of defects or for other reasons, the seller may reduce the initial price at which the goods were sold (**sales allowance**). If the return or allowance is for a sale on account, the seller usually issues the buyer a **credit memorandum**. This memorandum shows the amount of and the reason for the seller's credit to an account receivable. A credit memorandum issued by NetSolutions is illustrated in Exhibit 9.

Like sales discounts, sales returns and allowances reduce sales revenue. They also result in additional shipping and other expenses. Since managers often want to know the amount of returns and allowances for a period, the seller records sales returns and allowances in a separate account. Sales Returns and Allowances is a *contra* (or *offsetting*) account to Sales.

The seller debits Sales Returns and Allowances for the amount of the return or allowance. If the original sale was on account, the seller credits Accounts Receivable. Since the merchandise inventory is kept up to date in a perpetual system, the seller adds the cost of the returned merchandise to the merchandise inventory account. The seller must also credit the cost of returned merchandise to the cost of merchandise sold account, since this account was debited when the original sale was recorded. To

> **EXHIBIT 9**
>
> Credit Memorandum

@netsolutions	No. 32
5101 Washington Ave.	
Cincinnati, OH 45227–5101	

CREDIT MEMORANDUM

TO	DATE
Krier Company	January 13, 2009
7608 Melton Avenue	
Los Angeles, CA 90025-3942	

WE CREDIT YOUR ACCOUNT AS FOLLOWS

1 Controller Kit	225.00

illustrate, assume that the cost of the merchandise returned in Exhibit 9 was $140. NetSolutions records the credit memo in Exhibit 9 as follows:

Jan.	13	Sales Returns and Allowances	2 2 5 00	
		Accounts Receivable—Krier Company		2 2 5 00
		Credit Memo No. 32.		

Jan.	13	Merchandise Inventory	1 4 0 00	
		Cost of Merchandise Sold		1 4 0 00
		Cost of merchandise returned, Credit		
		Memo No. 32.		

What if the buyer pays for the merchandise and the merchandise is later returned? In this case, the seller may issue a credit and apply it against other accounts receivable owed by the buyer, or the cash may be refunded. If the credit is applied against the buyer's other receivables, the seller records entries similar to those preceding. If cash is refunded for merchandise returned or for an allowance, the seller debits Sales Returns and Allowances and credits Cash.

Example Exercise 6-3   •   objective 3

Journalize the following merchandise transactions:

a. Sold merchandise on account, $7,500 with terms 2/10, n/30. The cost of the merchandise sold was $5,625.
b. Received payment less the discount.

Follow My Example 6-3

a.	Accounts Receivable	7,500	
	Sales		7,500
	Cost of Merchandise Sold	5,625	
	Merchandise Inventory		5,625
b.	Cash	7,350	
	Sales Discounts	150	
	Accounts Receivable		7,500

For Practice: PE 6-3A, PE 6-3B

Integrity, Objectivity, and Ethics in Business

ETHICS

THE CASE OF THE FRAUDULENT PRICE TAGS

One of the challenges for a retailer is policing its sales return policy. There are many ways in which customers can unethically or illegally abuse such policies. In one case, a couple was accused of attaching Marshalls' store price tags to cheaper merchandise bought or obtained else- where. The couple then returned the cheaper goods and received the substantially higher refund amount. Company security officials discovered the fraud and had the couple arrested after they had allegedly bilked the company for over $1 million.

PURCHASE TRANSACTIONS

As we indicated earlier in this chapter, most large retailers and many small merchandising businesses use computerized perpetual inventory systems. Under the perpetual inventory system, cash purchases of merchandise are recorded as follows:

	JOURNAL			Page 24
Date	**Description**	**Post. Ref.**	**Debit**	**Credit**
2009 Jan. 3	Merchandise Inventory		2 5 1 0 00	
	Cash			2 5 1 0 00
	Purchased inventory from Bowen Co.			

Purchases of merchandise on account are recorded as follows:

Jan. 4	Merchandise Inventory		9 2 5 0 00	
	Accounts Payable—Thomas Corporation			9 2 5 0 00
	Purchased inventory on account.			

Purchases Discounts Purchases discounts taken by the buyer for early payment of an invoice reduce the cost of the merchandise purchased. Most businesses design their accounting systems so that all available discounts are taken. Even if the buyer has to borrow to make the payment within a discount period, it is normally to the buyer's advantage to do so. To illustrate, assume that Alpha Technologies issues an invoice for $3,000 to NetSolutions, dated March 12, with terms 2/10, n/30. The last day of the discount period in which the $60 discount can be taken is March 22. Assume that in order to pay the invoice on March 22, NetSolutions borrows the money for the remaining 20 days of the credit period. If we assume an annual interest rate of 6% and a 360-day year, the interest on the loan of $2,940 ($3,000 − $60) is $9.80 ($2,940 × 6% × 20/360). The net savings to NetSolutions is $50.20, computed as follows:

Discount of 2% on $3,000	$60.00
Interest for 20 days at rate of 6% on $2,940	−9.80
Savings from borrowing	$50.20

The savings can also be seen by comparing the interest rate on the money *saved* by taking the discount and the interest rate on the money *borrowed* to take the discount. For NetSolutions, the interest rate on the money saved in this example is estimated by converting 2% for 20 days to a yearly rate, as follows:

$$2\% \times \frac{360 \text{ days}}{20 \text{ days}} = 2\% \times 18 = 36\%$$

If NetSolutions borrows the money to take the discount, it *pays* interest of 6%. If NetSolutions does not take the discount, it *pays* estimated interest of 36% for using the $2,940 for an additional 20 days.

Under the perpetual inventory system, the buyer initially debits the merchandise inventory account for the amount of the invoice. When paying the invoice, the buyer credits the merchandise inventory account for the amount of the discount. In this way, the merchandise inventory shows the *net* cost to the buyer. For example, NetSolutions would record the Alpha Technologies invoice and its payment at the end of the discount period as follows:

Mar.	12	Merchandise Inventory	3 0 0 0 00	
		Accounts Payable—Alpha Technologies		3 0 0 0 00
	22	Accounts Payable—Alpha Technologies	3 0 0 0 00	
		Cash		2 9 4 0 00
		Merchandise Inventory		6 0 00

If NetSolutions does not take the discount because it does not pay the invoice until April 11, it would record the payment as follows:

Apr.	11	Accounts Payable—Alpha Technologies	3 0 0 0 00	
		Cash		3 0 0 0 00

Purchases Returns and Allowances   When merchandise is returned (**purchases return**) or a price adjustment is requested (**purchases allowance**), the buyer (debtor) usually sends the seller a letter or a debit memorandum. A **debit memorandum**, shown in Exhibit 10, informs the seller of the amount the buyer proposes to *debit* to the account payable due the seller. It also states the reasons for the return or the request for a price reduction.

The buyer may use a copy of the debit memorandum as the basis for recording the return or allowance or wait for approval from the seller (creditor). In either case, the buyer must debit Accounts Payable and credit Merchandise Inventory. To illustrate,

EXHIBIT 10

Debit Memorandum

@netsolutions   **No. 18**
5101 Washington Ave.
Cincinnati, OH 45227–5101

DEBIT MEMORANDUM

TO	**DATE**
Maxim Systems	March 7, 2009
7519 East Willson Ave.	
Seattle, WA 98101–7519	

WE DEBIT YOUR ACCOUNT AS FOLLOWS

10 Server Network Interface Cards, your Invoice No. 7291, are being returned via parcel post. Our order specified No. 825X.	@ 90.00	900.00

NetSolutions records the return of the merchandise indicated in the debit memo in Exhibit 10 as follows:

Mar.	7	Accounts Payable—Maxim Systems		9 00 00	
		Merchandise Inventory			9 00 00
		Debit Memo No. 18.			

When a buyer returns merchandise or has been granted an allowance prior to paying the invoice, the amount of the debit memorandum is deducted from the invoice amount. The amount is deducted before the purchase discount is computed. For example, assume that on May 2, NetSolutions purchases $5,000 of merchandise from Delta Data Link, subject to terms 2/10, n/30. On May 4, NetSolutions returns $3,000 of the merchandise, and on May 12, NetSolutions pays the original invoice less the return. NetSolutions would record these transactions as follows:

May	2	Merchandise Inventory		5 000 00	
		Accounts Payable—Delta Data Link			5 000 00
		Purchased merchandise.			
	4	Accounts Payable—Delta Data Link		3 000 00	
		Merchandise Inventory			3 000 00
		Returned portion of merch. purchased.			
	12	Accounts Payable—Delta Data Link		2 000 00	
		Cash			1 960 00
		Merchandise Inventory			40 00
		Paid invoice [($5,000 − $3,000) × 2%			
		= $40; $2,000 − $40 = $1,960].			

Example Exercise 6-4

objective 3

Rofles Company purchased merchandise on account from a supplier for $11,500, terms 2/10, n/30. Rofles Company returned $3,000 of the merchandise and received full credit.

a. If Rofles Company pays the invoice within the discount period, what is the amount of cash required for the payment?
b. Under a perpetual inventory system, what account is credited by Rofles Company to record the return?

Follow My Example 6-4

a. $8,330. Purchase of $11,500 less the return of $3,000 less the discount of $170 [($11,500 − $3,000) × 2%].
b. Merchandise Inventory

For Practice: PE 6-4A, PE 6-4B

TRANSPORTATION COSTS, SALES TAXES, AND TRADE DISCOUNTS

In the preceding two sections, we described and illustrated merchandise transactions involving sales and purchases. In this section, we discuss merchandise transactions involving transportation costs, sales taxes, and trade discounts.

The buyer bears the transportation costs if the shipping terms are FOB shipping point.

Sometimes FOB shipping point and FOB destination are expressed in terms of the location at which the title to the merchandise passes to the buyer. For example, if Toyota Motor Corporation's assembly plant in Osaka, Japan, sells automobiles to a dealer in Chicago, FOB shipping point could be expressed as FOB Osaka. Likewise, FOB destination could be expressed as FOB Chicago.

Transportation Costs   The terms of a sale should indicate when the ownership (title) of the merchandise passes to the buyer. This point determines which party, the buyer or the seller, must pay the transportation costs.[5]

The ownership of the merchandise may pass to the buyer when the seller delivers the merchandise to the transportation company or freight carrier. For example, DaimlerChrysler records the sale and the transfer of ownership of its vehicles to dealers when the vehicles are shipped from the factory. In this case, the terms are said to be **FOB (free on board) shipping point**. This term means that the dealer pays the transportation costs from the shipping point (factory) to the final destination. Such costs are part of the dealer's total cost of purchasing inventory and should be added to the cost of the inventory by debiting Merchandise Inventory.

To illustrate, assume that on June 10, NetSolutions buys merchandise from Magna Data on account, $900, terms FOB shipping point, and pays the transportation cost of $50. NetSolutions records these two transactions as follows:

June	10	Merchandise Inventory		900 00	
		Accounts Payable—Magna Data			900 00
		Purchased merchandise, terms FOB			
		shipping point.			
	10	Merchandise Inventory		50 00	
		Cash			50 00
		Paid shipping cost on merchandise			
		purchased.			

The ownership of the merchandise may pass to the buyer when the buyer receives the merchandise. In this case, the terms are said to be **FOB (free on board) destination**. This term means that the seller delivers the merchandise to the buyer's final destination, free of transportation charges to the buyer. The seller thus pays the transportation costs to the final destination. The seller debits Delivery Expense or Transportation Out, which is reported on the seller's income statement as an expense.

To illustrate, assume that on June 15, NetSolutions sells merchandise to Kranz Company on account, $700, terms FOB destination. The cost of the merchandise sold is $480, and NetSolutions pays the transportation cost of $40. NetSolutions records the sale, the cost of the sale, and the transportation cost as follows:

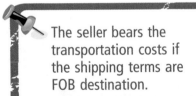

The seller bears the transportation costs if the shipping terms are FOB destination.

June	15	Accounts Receivable—Kranz Company		700 00	
		Sales			700 00
		Sold merchandise, terms FOB			
		destination.			
	15	Cost of Merchandise Sold		480 00	
		Merchandise Inventory			480 00
		Recorded cost of merchandise sold to			
		Kranz Company.			
	15	Delivery Expense		40 00	
		Cash			40 00
		Paid shipping cost on merch. sold.			

---

5 The passage of title also determines whether the buyer or seller must pay other costs, such as the cost of insurance, while the merchandise is in transit.

As a convenience to the buyer, the seller may prepay the transportation costs, even though the terms are FOB shipping point. The seller will then add the transportation costs to the invoice. The buyer will debit Merchandise Inventory for the total amount of the invoice, including the transportation costs. Any discount terms would not apply to the prepaid transportation costs.

To illustrate, assume that on June 20, NetSolutions sells merchandise to Planter Company on account, $800, terms FOB shipping point. NetSolutions pays the transportation cost of $45 and adds it to the invoice. The cost of the merchandise sold is $360. NetSolutions records these transactions as follows:

June	20	Accounts Receivable—Planter Company	800 00	
		Sales		800 00
		Sold merch., terms FOB shipping point.		
	20	Cost of Merchandise Sold	360 00	
		Merchandise Inventory		360 00
		Recorded cost of merchandise sold to		
		Planter Company.		
	20	Accounts Receivable—Planter Company	45 00	
		Cash		45 00
		Prepaid shipping cost on merch. sold.		

Shipping terms, the passage of title, and whether the buyer or seller is to pay the transportation costs are summarized in Exhibit 11.

Example Exercise 6-5

objective 3

Determine the amount to be paid in full settlement of each of invoices (a) and (b), assuming that credit for returns and allowances was received prior to payment and that all invoices were paid within the discount period.

	Merchandise	Transportation Paid by Seller	Transportation Terms	Returns and Allowances
a.	$4,500	$200	FOB shipping point, 1/10, n/30	$ 800
b.	5,000	60	FOB destination, 2/10, n/30	2,500

Follow My Example 6-5

a. $3,863. Purchase of $4,500 less return of $800 less the discount of $37 [($4,500 − $800) × 1%] plus $200 of shipping.
b. $2,450. Purchase of $5,000 less return of $2,500 less the discount of $50 [($5,000 − $2,500) × 2%].

For Practice: PE 6-5A, PE 6-5B

Sales Taxes   Almost all states and many other taxing units levy a tax on sales of merchandise.[6] The liability for the sales tax is incurred when the sale is made.

At the time of a cash sale, the seller collects the sales tax. When a sale is made on account, the seller charges the tax to the buyer by debiting Accounts Receivable. The seller credits the sales account for the amount of the sale and credits the tax to Sales

_____

6 Businesses that purchase merchandise for resale to others are normally exempt from paying sales taxes on their purchases. Only final buyers of merchandise normally pay sales taxes.

EXHIBIT 11 | **Transportation Terms**

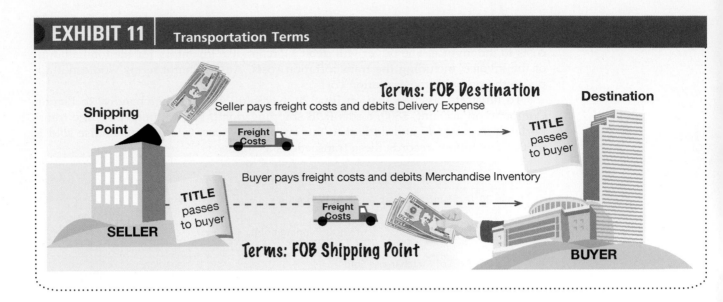

The six states with the highest sales tax are Mississippi, Rhode Island, Tennessee, Minnesota, Nevada, and Washington. Some states have no sales tax, including Alaska, Delaware, Montana, New Hampshire, and Oregon.

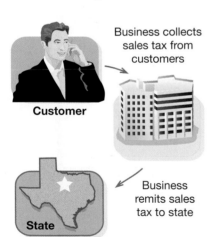

Tax Payable. For example, the seller would record a sale of $100 on account, subject to a tax of 6%, as follows:

Aug.	12	Accounts Receivable—Lemon Co.	1 0 6 00	
		Sales		1 0 0 00
		Sales Tax Payable		6 00
		Invoice No. 339.		

Normally on a regular basis, the seller pays to the taxing unit the amount of the sales tax collected. The seller records such a payment as follows:

Sept.	15	Sales Tax Payable	2 9 0 0 00	
		Cash		2 9 0 0 00
		Payment for sales taxes collected		
		during August.		

Trade Discounts Wholesalers are businesses that sell merchandise to other businesses rather than to the general public. Many wholesalers publish catalogs. Rather than updating their catalogs frequently, wholesalers often publish price updates, which may involve large discounts from the list prices in their catalogs. In addition, wholesalers may offer special discounts to certain classes of buyers, such as government agencies or businesses that order large quantities. Such discounts are called **trade discounts**.

Sellers and buyers do not normally record the list prices of merchandise and the related trade discounts in their accounts. For example, assume that an item has a list price of $1,000 and a 40% trade discount. The seller records the sale of the item at $600 [$1,000 less the trade discount of $400 ($1,000 × 40%)]. Likewise, the buyer records the purchase at $600.

DUAL NATURE OF MERCHANDISE TRANSACTIONS

Each merchandising transaction affects a buyer and a seller. In the illustration on the next page, we show how the same transactions would be recorded by both the seller and the buyer. In this example, the seller is Scully Company and the buyer is Burton Co.

Transaction	Scully Company (Seller)			Burton Co. (Buyer)		

July 1. Scully Company sold merchandise on account to Burton Co., $7,500, terms FOB shipping point, n/45. The cost of the merchandise sold was $4,500.	Accounts Receivable—Burton Co.
	  Sales
	
	Cost of Merchandise Sold
	  Merchandise Inventory
		7,500
		
		4,500
			7,500
			
			4,500
				Merchandise Inventory
				  Accounts Payable—Scully Co.
					7,500	7,500

July 2. Burton Co. paid transportation charges of $150 on July 1 purchase from Scully Company.	No entry.			Merchandise Inventory Cash	150	150

July 5. Scully Company sold merchandise on account to Burton Co., $5,000, terms FOB destination, n/30. The cost of the merchandise sold was $3,500.	Accounts Receivable—Burton Co.
	  Sales
	
	Cost of Merchandise Sold
	  Merchandise Inventory
		5,000
		
		3,500
			5,000
			
			3,500
				Merchandise Inventory
				  Accounts Payable—Scully Co.
					5,000	5,000

July 7. Scully Company paid transportation costs of $250 for delivery of merchandise sold to Burton Co. on July 5.	Delivery Expense Cash	250	250	No entry.		

July 13. Scully Company issued Burton Co. a credit memorandum for merchandise returned, $1,000. The merchandise had been purchased by Burton Co. on account on July 5. The cost of the merchandise returned was $700.	Sales Returns and Allowances
	  Accounts Receivable—Burton Co.
	
	Merchandise Inventory
	  Cost of Merchandise Sold
		1,000
		
		700
			1,000
			
			700
				Accounts Payable—Scully Co.
				  Merchandise Inventory
					1,000	1,000

July 15. Scully Company received payment from Burton Co. for purchase of July 5.	Cash
	  Accounts Receivable—Burton Co.
		4,000	4,000	Accounts Payable—Scully Co.
				  Cash
					4,000	4,000

July 18. Scully Company sold merchandise on account to Burton Co., $12,000, terms FOB shipping point, 2/10, n/eom. Scully Company prepaid transportation costs of $500, which were added to the invoice. The cost of the merchandise sold was $7,200.	Accounts Receivable—Burton Co.
	  Sales
	
	Accounts Receivable—Burton Co.
	  Cash
	
	Cost of Merchandise Sold
	  Merchandise Inventory
		12,000
		
		500
		
		7,200
			12,000
			
			500
			
			7,200
				Merchandise Inventory
				  Accounts Payable—Scully Co.
					12,500	12,500

July 28. Scully Company received payment from Burton Co. for purchase of July 18, less discount (2% × $12,000).	Cash
	Sales Discounts
	  Accounts Receivable—Burton Co.
		12,260
		240
			12,500	Accounts Payable—Scully Co.
				  Merchandise Inventory
				  Cash
					12,500	240
						12,260

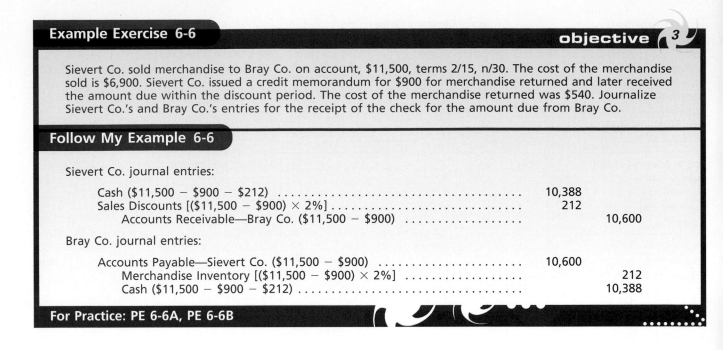

Example Exercise 6-6

objective **3**

Sievert Co. sold merchandise to Bray Co. on account, $11,500, terms 2/15, n/30. The cost of the merchandise sold is $6,900. Sievert Co. issued a credit memorandum for $900 for merchandise returned and later received the amount due within the discount period. The cost of the merchandise returned was $540. Journalize Sievert Co.'s and Bray Co.'s entries for the receipt of the check for the amount due from Bray Co.

Follow My Example 6-6

Sievert Co. journal entries:

Cash ($11,500 − $900 − $212)	10,388	
Sales Discounts [($11,500 − $900) × 2%]	212	
Accounts Receivable—Bray Co. ($11,500 − $900)		10,600

Bray Co. journal entries:

Accounts Payable—Sievert Co. ($11,500 − $900)	10,600	
Merchandise Inventory [($11,500 − $900) × 2%]		212
Cash ($11,500 − $900 − $212)		10,388

For Practice: PE 6-6A, PE 6-6B

The Adjusting and Closing Process

objective **4**

Describe the adjusting and closing process for a merchandising business.

We have described and illustrated the chart of accounts and the analysis and recording of transactions for a merchandising business. We have also illustrated the preparation of financial statements for a merchandiser, NetSolutions. In the remainder of this chapter, we describe the adjusting and closing process for a merchandising business. In this discussion, we will focus primarily on the elements of the accounting cycle that are likely to differ from those of a service business.

@netsolutions

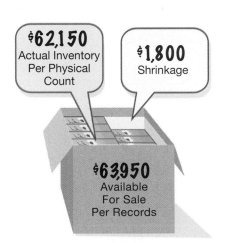

$62,150
Actual Inventory Per Physical Count

$1,800
Shrinkage

$63,950
Available For Sale Per Records

ADJUSTING ENTRY FOR INVENTORY SHRINKAGE

Under the perpetual inventory system, a separate merchandise inventory account is maintained in the ledger. During the accounting period, this account shows the amount of merchandise for sale at any time. However, merchandising businesses may experience some loss of inventory due to shoplifting, employee theft, or errors in recording or counting inventory. As a result, the physical inventory taken at the end of the accounting period may differ from the amount of inventory shown in the inventory records. Normally, the amount of merchandise for sale, as indicated by the balance of the merchandise inventory account, is larger than the total amount of merchandise counted during the physical inventory. For this reason, the difference is often called **inventory shrinkage** or *inventory shortage*.

To illustrate, NetSolutions' inventory records indicate that $63,950 of merchandise should be available for sale on December 31, 2009. The physical inventory taken on December 31, 2009, however, indicates that only $62,150 of merchandise is actually available. Thus, the inventory shrinkage for the year ending December 31, 2009, is $1,800 ($63,950 − $62,150), as shown at the left. This amount is recorded by the following adjusting entry:

		Adjusting Entry		
Dec.	31	Cost of Merchandise Sold	1 8 0 0 00	
		Merchandise Inventory		1 8 0 0 00
		Inv. shrinkage ($63,950 − $62,150).		

Retailers lose an estimated $30 billion to inventory shrinkage. The primary causes of the shrinkage are employee theft and shoplifting.

After this entry has been recorded, the accounting records agree with the actual physical inventory at the end of the period. Since no system of procedures and safeguards can totally eliminate it, inventory shrinkage is often considered a normal cost of operations. If the amount of the shrinkage is abnormally large, it may be disclosed separately on the income statement. In such cases, the shrinkage may be recorded in a separate account, such as Loss from Merchandise Inventory Shrinkage.[7]

CLOSING ENTRIES

The closing entries for a merchandising business are similar to those for a service business. The first entry closes the temporary accounts with credit balances, such as Sales, to the income summary account. The second entry closes the temporary accounts with debit balances, including Sales Returns and Allowances, Sales Discounts, and Cost of Merchandise Sold, to the income summary account. The third entry closes the balance of the income summary account to the owner's capital account. The fourth entry closes the owner's drawing account to the owner's capital account. The closing entries for NetSolutions are shown below.

	JOURNAL			Page 29	
Date	Item	Post. Ref.	Debit	Credit	
2009	Closing Entries				1
Dec. 31	Sales	410	720 185 00		2
	Rent Revenue	610	600 00		3
	Income Summary	312		720 785 00	4
					5
31	Income Summary	312	645 385 00		6
	Sales Returns and Allowances	411		6 140 00	7
	Sales Discounts	412		5 790 00	8
	Cost of Merchandise Sold	510		525 305 00	9
	Sales Salaries Expense	520		53 430 00	10
	Advertising Expense	521		10 860 00	11
	Depr. Expense—Store Equipment	522		3 100 00	12
	Delivery Expense	523		2 800 00	13
	Miscellaneous Selling Expense	529		630 00	14
	Office Salaries Expense	530		21 020 00	15
	Rent Expense	531		8 100 00	16
	Depr. Expense—Office Equipment	532		2 490 00	17
	Insurance Expense	533		1 910 00	18
	Office Supplies Expense	534		610 00	19
	Misc. Administrative Expense	539		760 00	20
	Interest Expense	710		2 440 00	21
					22
31	Income Summary	312	75 400 00		23
	Chris Clark, Capital	310		75 400 00	24
					25
31	Chris Clark, Capital	310	18 000 00		26
	Chris Clark, Drawing	311		18 000 00	27

The balance of Income Summary, after the first two closing entries have been posted, is the net income or net loss for the period. The third closing entry transfers

---

7 The adjusting process for a merchandising business may be aided by preparing an end-of-period spreadsheet (work sheet). An end-of-period spreadsheet (work sheet) for a merchandising business is described and illustrated in Appendix C.

this balance to the owner's capital account. NetSolutions' income summary account after the closing entries have been posted is as follows:

ACCOUNT *Income Summary*					ACCOUNT NO. *312*	
		Post.			**Balance**	
Date	**Item**	**Ref.**	**Debit**	**Credit**	**Debit**	**Credit**
2009 Dec. 31	Revenues	29		720 7 8 5 00		720 7 8 5 00
31	Expenses	29	645 3 8 5 00			75 4 0 0 00
31	Net income	29	75 4 0 0 00		—	—

After the closing entries have been prepared and posted to the accounts, a post-closing trial balance may be prepared to verify the debit-credit equality. The only accounts that should appear on the post-closing trial balance are the asset, contra asset, liability, and owner's capital accounts with balances. These are the same accounts that appear on the end-of-period balance sheet.

Example Exercise 6-7

  4

Pulmonary Company's perpetual inventory records indicate that $382,800 of merchandise should be on hand on March 31, 2008. The physical inventory indicates that $371,250 of merchandise is actually on hand. Journalize the adjusting entry for the inventory shrinkage for Pulmonary Company for the year ended March 31, 2008.

Follow My Example 6-7

Mar. 31	Cost of Merchandise Sold	11,550	
	Merchandise Inventory		11,550
	Inventory shrinkage ($382,800 − $371,250).		

For Practice: PE 6-7A, PE 6-7B

FINANCIAL ANALYSIS AND INTERPRETATION

The ratio of net sales to assets measures how effectively a business is using its assets to generate sales. A high ratio indicates an effective use of assets. The assets used in computing the ratio may be the total assets at the end of the year, the average of the total assets at the beginning and end of the year, or the average of the monthly assets. For our purposes, we will use the average of the total assets at the beginning and end of the year. The ratio is computed as follows:

$$\text{Ratio of Net Sales to Assets} = \frac{\text{Net Sales}}{\text{Average Total Assets}}$$

To illustrate the use of this ratio, the following data (in millions) are taken from annual reports of Sears Holding Corporation and JCPenney:

	Sears	JCPenney
Total revenues (net sales)	$19,701	$18,424
Total assets:		
Beginning of year	6,074	18,300
End of year	8,651	14,127

The ratio of net sales to assets for each company is as follows:

	Sears	JCPenney
Ratio of net sales to assets	2.68*	1.14**

*$19,701/[($6,074 + $8,651)/2]
**$18,424/[($18,300 + $14,127)/2]

Based on these ratios, Sears appears better than JCPenney in utilizing its assets to generate sales. Comparing this ratio over time for both Sears and JCPenney, as well as comparing it with industry averages, would provide a better basis for interpreting the financial performance of each company.

At a Glance

1. Distinguish between the activities and financial statements of service and merchandising businesses.

Key Points	Key Learning Outcomes	Example Exercises	Practice Exercises
The primary differences between a service business and a merchandising business relate to revenue activities. Merchandising businesses purchase merchandise for selling to customers. On a merchandising business's income statement, revenue from selling merchandise is reported as sales. The cost of the merchandise sold is subtracted from sales to arrive at gross profit. The operating expenses are subtracted from gross profit to arrive at net income. Merchandise inventory, which is merchandise not sold, is reported as a current asset on the balance sheet.	• Describe how the activities of a service and a merchandising business differ. • Describe the differences between the income statements of a service and a merchandising business. • Compute gross profit. • Describe how merchandise inventory is reported on the balance sheet.	6-1	6-1A, 6-1B

2. Describe and illustrate the financial statements of a merchandising business.

Key Points	Key Learning Outcomes	Example Exercises	Practice Exercises
The multiple-step income statement of a merchandiser reports sales, sales returns and allowances, sales discounts, and net sales. The cost of the merchandise sold is subtracted from net sales to determine the gross profit. The cost of merchandise sold is determined by using either the periodic or perpetual system. Operating income is determined by subtracting operating expenses from gross profit. Operating expenses are normally classified as selling or administrative expenses. Net income is determined by adding or subtracting the net of other income and expense. The income statement may also be reported in a single-step form. The statement of owner's equity is similar to that for a service business. The balance sheet reports merchandise inventory at the end of the period as a current asset.	• Prepare a multiple-step income statement for a merchandising business. • Describe how cost of merchandise sold is determined under a periodic inventory system. • Compute cost of merchandise sold under a periodic inventory system as shown in Exhibit 2. • Prepare a single-step income statement. • Prepare a statement of owner's equity for a merchandising business. • Prepare a balance sheet for a merchandising business.	6-2	6-2A, 6-2B

3. Describe and illustrate the accounting for merchandise transactions including:
- **sale of merchandise**
- **purchase of merchandise**
- **transportation costs, sales taxes, and trade discounts**
- **dual nature of merchandising transactions**

Key Points	Key Learning Outcomes	Example Exercises	Practice Exercises
Sales of merchandise for cash or on account are recorded by crediting Sales. Under the perpetual inventory system, the cost of merchandise sold and the reduction in merchandise inventory are also recorded for the sale. For sales of merchandise on account, the credit terms may allow discounts for early payment. Such discounts are recorded by the seller as a debit to Sales Discounts. Sales discounts are reported as a deduction from the amount initially recorded in Sales. Likewise, when merchandise is returned or a price adjustment is granted, the seller debits Sales Returns and Allowances.	• Prepare journal entries to record sales of merchandise for cash or using a credit card.		
	• Prepare journal entries to record sales of merchandise on account.	6-3	6-3A, 6-3B
	• Prepare journal entries to record sales discounts and sales returns and allowances.	6-3	6-3A, 6-3B
Purchases of merchandise for cash or on account are recorded by debiting Merchandise Inventory. For purchases of merchandise on account, the credit terms may allow cash discounts for early payment. Such purchases discounts are viewed as a reduction in the cost of the merchandise purchased. When merchandise is returned or a price adjustment is granted, the buyer credits Merchandise Inventory.	• Prepare journal entries to record the purchase of merchandise for cash.		
	• Prepare journal entries to record the purchase of merchandise on account.	6-4	6-4A, 6-4B
	• Prepare journal entries to record purchases discounts and purchases returns and allowances.	6-4	6-4A, 6-4B
When merchandise is shipped FOB shipping point, the buyer pays the transportation costs and debits Merchandise Inventory. When merchandise is shipped FOB destination, the seller pays the transportation costs and debits Transportation Out or Delivery Expense. If the seller prepays transportation costs as a convenience to the buyer, the seller debits Accounts Receivable for the costs.	• Prepare journal entries for transportation costs from the point of view of the buyer and seller.		
	• Determine the total cost of the purchase of merchandise under differing transportation terms.	6-5	6-5A, 6-5B
The liability for sales tax is incurred when the sale is made and is recorded by the seller as a credit to the sales tax payable account. When the amount of the sales tax is paid to the taxing unit, Sales Tax Payable is debited and Cash is credited.	• Prepare journal entries for the collection and payment of sales taxes by the seller.		
Many wholesalers offer trade discounts, which are discounts off the list prices of merchandise. Normally, neither the seller nor the buyer records the list price and the related trade discount in the accounts.	• Determine the cost of merchandise purchased when a trade discount is offered by the seller.		
Each merchandising transaction affects a buyer and a seller. The illustration in this chapter shows how the same transactions would be recorded by both.	• Record the same merchandise transactions for the buyer and seller.	6-6	6-6A, 6-6B

4. Describe the adjusting and closing process for a merchandising business.			
Key Points	**Key Learning Outcomes**	**Example Exercises**	**Practice Exercises**
The accounting cycle for a merchandising business is similar to that of a service business. However, a merchandiser is likely to experience inventory shrinkage, which must be recorded. The normal adjusting entry is to debit Cost of Merchandise Sold and credit Merchandise Inventory for the amount of the shrinkage.	• Prepare the adjusting journal entry for inventory shrinkage.	6-7	6-7A, 6-7B
The closing entries for a merchandise business are similar to those for a service business. The first entry closes sales and other revenue to Income Summary. The second entry closes cost of merchandise sold, sales discounts, sales returns and allowances, and other expenses to Income Summary. The third entry closes the balance of Income Summary (the net income or net loss) to the owner's capital account. The fourth entry closes the owner's drawing account to the owner's capital account.	• Prepare the closing entries for a merchandise business.		

Key Terms

account form (257)
administrative expenses (general expenses) (254)
cost of merchandise purchased (253)
cost of merchandise sold (251)
credit memorandum (261)
credit period (260)
credit terms (260)
debit memorandum (264)
FOB (free on board) destination (266)
FOB (free on board) shipping point (266)

gross profit (251)
income from operations (operating income) (254)
inventory shrinkage (270)
invoice (260)
merchandise available for sale (254)
merchandise inventory (251)
multiple-step income statement (252)
net purchases (253)
net sales (252)
other expense (255)
other income (255)

periodic system (254)
perpetual system (254)
purchase return or allowance (252)
purchases discounts (252)
report form (257)
sales (252)
sales discounts (252)
sales returns and allowances (252)
selling expenses (254)
single-step income statement (255)
trade discounts (268)
transportation in (253)

Illustrative Problem

The following transactions were completed by Montrose Company during May of the current year. Montrose Company uses a perpetual inventory system.

May 3. Purchased merchandise on account from Floyd Co., $4,000, terms FOB shipping point, 2/10, n/30, with prepaid transportation costs of $120 added to the invoice.

5. Purchased merchandise on account from Kramer Co., $8,500, terms FOB destination, 1/10, n/30.

6. Sold merchandise on account to C. F. Howell Co., list price $4,000, trade discount 30%, terms 2/10, n/30. The cost of the merchandise sold was $1,125.

May 8. Purchased office supplies for cash, $150.

10. Returned merchandise purchased on May 5 from Kramer Co., $1,300.

13. Paid Floyd Co. on account for purchase of May 3, less discount.

14. Purchased merchandise for cash, $10,500.

15. Paid Kramer Co. on account for purchase of May 5, less return of May 10 and discount.

16. Received cash on account from sale of May 6 to C. F. Howell Co., less discount.

19. Sold merchandise on MasterCard credit cards, $2,450. The cost of the merchandise sold was $980.

22. Sold merchandise on account to Comer Co., $3,480, terms 2/10, n/30. The cost of the merchandise sold was $1,400.

24. Sold merchandise for cash, $4,350. The cost of the merchandise sold was $1,750.

25. Received merchandise returned by Comer Co. from sale on May 22, $1,480. The cost of the returned merchandise was $600.

31. Paid a service processing fee of $140 for MasterCard sales.

Instructions

1. Journalize the preceding transactions.
2. Journalize the adjusting entry for merchandise inventory shrinkage, $3,750.

Solution

1.

May	3	Merchandise Inventory		4,120	
		Accounts Payable—Floyd Co.			4,120
	5	Merchandise Inventory		8,500	
		Accounts Payable—Kramer Co.			8,500
	6	Accounts Receivable—C. F. Howell Co.		2,800	
		Sales			2,800
		[$4,000 − (30% × $4,000)].			
	6	Cost of Merchandise Sold		1,125	
		Merchandise Inventory			1,125
	8	Office Supplies		150	
		Cash			150
	10	Accounts Payable—Kramer Co.		1,300	
		Merchandise Inventory			1,300
	13	Accounts Payable—Floyd Co.		4,120	
		Merchandise Inventory			80
		Cash			4,040
		[$4,000 − (2% × $4,000) + $120].			
	14	Merchandise Inventory		10,500	
		Cash			10,500
	15	Accounts Payable—Kramer Co.		7,200	
		Merchandise Inventory			72
		Cash			7,128
		[($8,500 − $1,300) × 1% = $72;			
		$8,500 − $1,300 − $72 = $7,128].			
	16	Cash		2,744	
		Sales Discounts		56	
		Accounts Receivable—C. F. Howell Co.			2,800
	19	Cash		2,450	
		Sales			2,450
	19	Cost of Merchandise Sold		980	
		Merchandise Inventory			980
	22	Accounts Receivable—Comer Co.		3,480	
		Sales			3,480
	22	Cost of Merchandise Sold		1,400	
		Merchandise Inventory			1,400
	24	Cash		4,350	
		Sales			4,350
	24	Cost of Merchandise Sold		1,750	
		Merchandise Inventory			1,750

	May 25	Sales Returns and Allowances	1,480	
		Accounts Receivable—Comer Co.		1,480
	25	Merchandise Inventory	600	
		Cost of Merchandise Sold		600
	31	Credit Card Expense	140	
		Cash		140
2.	May 31	Cost of Merchandise Sold	3,750	
		Merchandise Inventory		3,750
		Inventory shrinkage.		

Self-Examination Questions

(Answers at End of Chapter)

1. If merchandise purchased on account is returned, the buyer may inform the seller of the details by issuing a(n):
   A. debit memorandum.
   B. credit memorandum.
   C. invoice.
   D. bill.

2. If merchandise is sold on account to a customer for $1,000, terms FOB shipping point, 1/10, n/30, and the seller prepays $50 in transportation costs, the amount of the discount for early payment would be:
   A. $0.   C. $10.00.
   B. $5.00.   D. $10.50.

3. The income statement in which the total of all expenses is deducted from the total of all revenues is termed the:
   A. multiple-step form.   C. account form.
   B. single-step form.   D. report form.

4. On a multiple-step income statement, the excess of net sales over the cost of merchandise sold is called:
   A. operating income.
   B. income from operations.
   C. gross profit.
   D. net income.

5. Which of the following expenses would normally be classified as other expense on a multiple-step income statement?
   A. Depreciation expense—office equipment
   B. Sales salaries expense
   C. Insurance expense
   D. Interest expense

Eye Openers

1. What distinguishes a merchandising business from a service business?
2. Can a business earn a gross profit but incur a net loss? Explain.
3. In computing the cost of merchandise sold, does each of the following items increase or decrease that cost? (a) transportation costs, (b) beginning merchandise inventory, (c) purchase discounts, (d) ending merchandise inventory.
4. Describe how the periodic system differs from the perpetual system of accounting for merchandise inventory.
5. Differentiate between the multiple-step and the single-step forms of the income statement.
6. What are the major advantages and disadvantages of the single-step form of income statement compared to the multiple-step statement?
7. What type of revenue is reported in the other income section of the multiple-step income statement?
8. Name at least three accounts that would normally appear in the chart of accounts of a merchandising business but would not appear in the chart of accounts of a service business.
9. How are sales to customers using MasterCard and VISA recorded?
10. The credit period during which the buyer of merchandise is allowed to pay usually begins with what date?
11. What is the meaning of (a) 2/10, n/60; (b) n/30; (c) n/eom?
12. What is the nature of (a) a credit memorandum issued by the seller of merchandise, (b) a debit memorandum issued by the buyer of merchandise?

13. Who bears the transportation costs when the terms of sale are (a) FOB shipping point, (b) FOB destination?
14. Pembroke Office Equipment, which uses a perpetual inventory system, experienced a normal inventory shrinkage of $13,762. What accounts would be debited and credited to record the adjustment for the inventory shrinkage at the end of the accounting period?
15. Assume that Pembroke Office Equipment in Eye Opener 14 experienced an abnormal inventory shrinkage of $215,650. Pembroke Office Equipment has decided to record the abnormal inventory shrinkage so that it would be separately disclosed on the income statement. What account would be debited for the abnormal inventory shrinkage?

Practice Exercises

PE 6-1A
Determine gross profit
obj. 1

During the current year, merchandise is sold for $127,500 cash and $435,600 on account. The cost of the merchandise sold is $422,325. What is the amount of the gross profit?

PE 6-1B
Determine gross profit
obj. 1

During the current year, merchandise is sold for $17,500 cash and $141,750 on account. The cost of the merchandise sold is $127,400. What is the amount of the gross profit?

PE 6-2A
Computing cost of merchandise sold
obj. 2

Based upon the following data, determine the cost of merchandise sold for July:

Merchandise inventory, July 1	$ 88,370
Merchandise inventory, July 31	92,120
Purchases	681,400
Purchases returns and allowances	9,250
Purchases discounts	7,000
Transportation in	3,180

PE 6-2B
Computing cost of merchandise sold
obj. 2

Based upon the following data, determine the cost of merchandise sold for April:

Merchandise inventory, April 1	$128,120
Merchandise inventory, April 30	140,500
Purchases	983,400
Purchases returns and allowances	10,250
Purchases discounts	8,000
Transportation in	5,680

PE 6-3A
Entries for sales transactions
obj. 3

Journalize the following merchandise transactions:

a. Sold merchandise on account, $12,250 with terms 2/10, n/30. The cost of the merchandise sold was $7,400.
b. Received payment less the discount.

PE 6-3B
Entries for sales transactions
obj. 3

Journalize the following merchandise transactions:

a. Sold merchandise on account, $22,500 with terms 1/10, n/30. The cost of the merchandise sold was $14,150.
b. Received payment less the discount.

PE 6-4A
Purchase transactions
obj. 3

Wilder Company purchased merchandise on account from a supplier for $7,500, terms 2/10, n/30. Wilder Company returned $1,500 of the merchandise and received full credit.

a. If Wilder Company pays the invoice within the discount period, what is the amount of cash required for the payment?
b. Under a perpetual inventory system, what account is credited by Wilder Company to record the return?

PE 6-4B
Purchase transactions
obj. 3

Gupta Company purchased merchandise on account from a supplier for $13,200, terms 1/10, n/30. Gupta Company returned $1,700 of the merchandise and received full credit.

a. If Gupta Company pays the invoice within the discount period, what is the amount of cash required for the payment?
b. Under a perpetual inventory system, what account is debited by Gupta Company to record the return?

PE 6-5A
Payments under different transportation terms
obj. 3

Determine the amount to be paid in full settlement of each of invoices (a) and (b), assuming that credit for returns and allowances was received prior to payment and that all invoices were paid within the discount period.

	Merchandise	Transportation Paid by Seller	Transportation Terms	Returns and Allowances
a.	$6,000	$400	FOB shipping point, 1/10, n/30	$1,000
b.	2,500	150	FOB destination, 2/10, n/30	900

PE 6-5B
Payments under different transportation terms
obj. 3

Determine the amount to be paid in full settlement of each of invoices (a) and (b), assuming that credit for returns and allowances was received prior to payment and that all invoices were paid within the discount period.

	Merchandise	Transportation Paid by Seller	Transportation Terms	Returns and Allowances
a.	$ 8,150	$200	FOB destination, 2/10, n/30	$1,300
b.	12,750	625	FOB shipping point, 2/10, n/30	3,000

PE 6-6A
Recording transactions for buyer and seller
obj. 3

Stuckey Co. sold merchandise to Bullock Co. on account, $5,250, terms 2/15, n/30. The cost of the merchandise sold is $3,150. Stuckey Co. issued a credit memorandum for $650 for merchandise returned and later received the amount due within the discount period. The cost of the merchandise returned was $390. Journalize Stuckey Co.'s and Bullock Co.'s entries for the receipt of the check for the amount due from Bullock Co.

PE 6-6B
Recording transactions for buyer and seller
obj. 3

Sparks Co. sold merchandise to Boyt Co. on account, $8,500, terms FOB shipping point, 2/10, n/30. The cost of the merchandise sold is $5,100. Sparks Co. paid transportation charges of $225 and later received the amount due within the discount period. Journalize Sparks Co.'s and Boyt Co.'s entries for the receipt of the check for the amount due from Boyt Co.

PE 6-7A
Entry for inventory shrinkage
obj. 4

Triangle Company's perpetual inventory records indicate that $111,500 of merchandise should be on hand on September 30, 2008. The physical inventory indicates that $107,400 of merchandise is actually on hand. Journalize the adjusting entry for the inventory shrinkage for Triangle Company for the year ended September 30, 2008.

PE 6-7B
Entry for inventory shrinkage
obj. 4

Three Turtles Company's perpetual inventory records indicate that $543,735 of merchandise should be on hand on August 31, 2008. The physical inventory indicates that $520,250 of merchandise is actually on hand. Journalize the adjusting entry for the inventory shrinkage for Three Turtles Company for the year ended August 31, 2008.

Exercises

EX 6-1
Determining gross profit
obj. 1

During the current year, merchandise is sold for $2,850,750. The cost of the merchandise sold is $1,995,525.

a. What is the amount of the gross profit?
b. Compute the gross profit percentage (gross profit divided by sales).
c. ━━━ Will the income statement necessarily report a net income? Explain.

EX 6-2
Determining cost of merchandise sold
obj. 1

In 2005, Best Buy reported revenue of $27,433 million. Its gross profit was $6,495 million. What was the amount of Best Buy's cost of merchandise sold?

EX 6-3
Identify items missing in determining cost of merchandise sold
obj. 2

For (a) through (d), identify the items designated by "X" and "Y."

a. Purchases − (X + Y) = Net purchases.
b. Net purchases + X = Cost of merchandise purchased.
c. Merchandise inventory (beginning) + Cost of merchandise purchased = X.
d. Merchandise available for sale − X = Cost of merchandise sold.

EX 6-4
Cost of merchandise sold and related items
obj. 2

✓a. Cost of merchandise sold, $1,218,300

The following data were extracted from the accounting records of Meniscus Company for the year ended June 30, 2008:

Merchandise inventory, July 1, 2007	$ 183,250
Merchandise inventory, June 30, 2008	200,100
Purchases	1,279,600
Purchases returns and allowances	41,200
Purchases discounts	20,500
Sales	1,800,000
Transportation in	17,250

a. Prepare the cost of merchandise sold section of the income statement for the year ended June 30, 2008, using the periodic inventory system.
b. Determine the gross profit to be reported on the income statement for the year ended June 30, 2008.

EX 6-5
Cost of merchandise sold
obj. 2

✓ Correct cost of merchandise sold, $820,500

Identify the errors in the following schedule of cost of merchandise sold for the current year ended March 31, 2008:

Cost of merchandise sold:			
Merchandise inventory, March 31, 2008			$135,750
Purchases		$852,100	
Plus: Purchases returns and allowances	$10,500		
Purchases discounts	8,000	18,500	
Gross purchases		$870,600	
Less transportation in		7,500	
Cost of merchandise purchased			863,100
Merchandise available for sale			$998,850
Less merchandise inventory, April 1, 2007			115,150
Cost of merchandise sold			$883,700

EX 6-6
Income statement for merchandiser
obj. 2

For the fiscal year, sales were $4,125,800, sales discounts were $380,000, sales returns and allowances were $186,750, and the cost of merchandise sold was $2,475,500.

a. What was the amount of net sales?
b. What was the amount of gross profit?

EX 6-7
Income statement for merchandiser
obj. 2

The following expenses were incurred by a merchandising business during the year. In which expense section of the income statement should each be reported: (a) selling, (b) administrative, or (c) other?

1. Advertising expense.
2. Depreciation expense on store equipment.
3. Insurance expense on office equipment.
4. Interest expense on notes payable.
5. Rent expense on office building.
6. Salaries of office personnel.
7. Salary of sales manager.
8. Sales supplies used.

EX 6-8
Single-step income statement
obj. 2
✓ *Net income: $451,450*

Summary operating data for The Voodoo Company during the current year ended November 30, 2008, are as follows: cost of merchandise sold, $2,175,350; administrative expenses, $500,000; interest expense, $23,200; rent revenue, $30,000; net sales, $4,000,000; and selling expenses, $880,000. Prepare a single-step income statement.

EX 6-9
Multiple-step income statement
obj. 2

Identify the errors in the following income statement:

The Euclidian Company
Income Statement
For the Year Ended March 31, 2008

Revenue from sales:			
Sales		$7,127,500	
Add: Sales returns and allowances	$112,300		
Sales discounts	60,000	172,300	
Gross sales			$7,299,800
Cost of merchandise sold			4,175,100
Income from operations			$3,124,700
Expenses:			
Selling expenses		$ 710,000	
Administrative expenses		525,000	
Delivery expense		18,100	
Total expenses			1,253,100
			$1,871,600
Other expense:			
Interest revenue			80,000
Gross profit			$1,791,600

EX 6-10
Determining amounts for items omitted from income statement
obj. 2
✓ *a. $30,000*
✓ *h. $690,000*

Two items are omitted in each of the following four lists of income statement data. Determine the amounts of the missing items, identifying them by letter.

Sales	$400,000	$500,000	$1,000,000	$ (g)
Sales returns and allowances	(a)	15,000	(e)	30,500
Sales discounts	20,000	8,000	40,000	37,000
Net sales	350,000	(c)	910,000	(h)
Cost of merchandise sold	(b)	285,000	(f)	540,000
Gross profit	200,000	(d)	286,500	150,000

EX 6-11
Multiple-step income statement
obj. 2

✓ *a. Net income: $137,500*

On August 31, 2008, the balances of the accounts appearing in the ledger of The Bent Needle Company, a furniture wholesaler, are as follows:

Administrative Expenses	$125,000	Notes Payable	$ 25,000
Building	512,500	Office Supplies	10,600
Cash	48,500	Salaries Payable	3,220
Cost of Merchandise Sold	700,000	Sales	1,275,000
Interest Expense	7,500	Sales Discounts	20,000
Jason Ritchie, Capital	568,580	Sales Returns and Allowances	80,000
Jason Ritchie, Drawing	25,000	Selling Expenses	205,000
Merchandise Inventory	130,000	Store Supplies	7,700

a. Prepare a multiple-step income statement for the year ended August 31, 2008.
b. Compare the major advantages and disadvantages of the multiple-step and single-step forms of income statements.

EX 6-12
Chart of accounts
obj. 3

Gemini Co. is a newly organized business with a list of accounts arranged in alphabetical order below.

Accounts Payable	Miscellaneous Administrative Expense
Accounts Receivable	Miscellaneous Selling Expense
Accumulated Depreciation—Office Equipment	Notes Payable
Accumulated Depreciation—Store Equipment	Office Equipment
Advertising Expense	Office Salaries Expense
Cash	Office Supplies
Cost of Merchandise Sold	Office Supplies Expense
Delivery Expense	Prepaid Insurance
Depreciation Expense—Office Equipment	Rent Expense
Depreciation Expense—Store Equipment	Salaries Payable
Income Summary	Sales
Insurance Expense	Sales Discounts
Interest Expense	Sales Returns and Allowances
Jung Qiang, Capital	Sales Salaries Expense
Jung Qiang, Drawing	Store Equipment
Land	Store Supplies
Merchandise Inventory	Store Supplies Expense

Construct a chart of accounts, assigning account numbers and arranging the accounts in balance sheet and income statement order, as illustrated in Exhibit 6. Each account number is three digits: the first digit is to indicate the major classification ("1" for assets, and so on); the second digit is to indicate the subclassification ("11" for current assets, and so on); and the third digit is to identify the specific account ("110" for Cash, and so on).

EX 6-13
Sales-related transactions, including the use of credit cards
obj. 3

Journalize the entries for the following transactions:

a. Sold merchandise for cash, $12,150. The cost of the merchandise sold was $9,100.
b. Sold merchandise on account, $6,000. The cost of the merchandise sold was $4,000.
c. Sold merchandise to customers who used MasterCard and VISA, $30,780. The cost of the merchandise sold was $20,000.
d. Sold merchandise to customers who used American Express, $17,650. The cost of the merchandise sold was $10,500.
e. Received an invoice from National Credit Co. for $1,900, representing a service fee paid for processing MasterCard, VISA, and American Express sales.

EX 6-14
Sales returns and allowances
obj. 3

During the year, sales returns and allowances totaled $172,100. The cost of the merchandise returned was $100,300. The accountant recorded all the returns and allowances by debiting the sales account and crediting Cost of Merchandise Sold for $172,100.

━━━▶ Was the accountant's method of recording returns acceptable? Explain. In your explanation, include the advantages of using a sales returns and allowances account.

EX 6-15
Sales-related transactions
obj. 3

After the amount due on a sale of $18,500, terms 2/10, n/eom, is received from a customer within the discount period, the seller consents to the return of the entire shipment. The cost of the merchandise returned was $11,100. (a) What is the amount of the refund owed to the customer? (b) Journalize the entries made by the seller to record the return and the refund.

EX 6-16
Sales-related transactions
obj. 3

The debits and credits for three related transactions are presented in the following T accounts. Describe each transaction.

Cash				Sales		
(5)	9,310				(1)	11,750

Accounts Receivable				Sales Discounts		
(1)	11,750	(3)	2,250	(5)	190	
		(5)	9,500			

Merchandise Inventory				Sales Returns and Allowances		
(4)	1,350	(2)	6,900	(3)	2,250	

Cost of Merchandise Sold			
(2)	6,900	(4)	1,350

EX 6-17
Sales-related transactions
obj. 3
✓d. $9,654

Merchandise is sold on account to a customer for $9,200, terms FOB shipping point, 2/10, n/30. The seller paid the transportation costs of $638. Determine the following: (a) amount of the sale, (b) amount debited to Accounts Receivable, (c) amount of the discount for early payment, and (d) amount due within the discount period.

EX 6-18
Purchase-related transaction
obj. 3

Hushpuppy Company purchased merchandise on account from a supplier for $6,750, terms 2/10, n/30. Hushpuppy Company returned $1,500 of the merchandise and received full credit.

a. If Hushpuppy Company pays the invoice within the discount period, what is the amount of cash required for the payment?
b. Under a perpetual inventory system, what account is credited by Hushpuppy Company to record the return?

EX 6-19
Purchase-related transactions
obj. 3

A retailer is considering the purchase of 100 units of a specific item from either of two suppliers. Their offers are as follows:

A: $375 a unit, total of $37,500, 2/10, n/30, plus transportation costs of $1,050.
B: $380 a unit, total of $38,000, 1/10, n/30, no charge for transportation.

Which of the two offers, A or B, yields the lower price?

EX 6-20
Purchase-related transactions
obj. 3

The debits and credits from four related transactions are presented in the following T accounts. Describe each transaction.

Cash				Accounts Payable		
		(2)	450	(3)	500	(1)	11,500
		(4)	10,780	(4)	11,000		

Merchandise Inventory			
(1)	11,500	(3)	500
(2)	450	(4)	220

EX 6-21
Purchase-related transactions
obj. 3
✓ (c) Cash, cr. $7,350

Madamé Co., a women's clothing store, purchased $10,000 of merchandise from a supplier on account, terms FOB destination, 2/10, n/30. Madamé Co. returned $2,500 of the merchandise, receiving a credit memorandum, and then paid the amount due within the discount period. Journalize Madamé Co.'s entries to record (a) the purchase, (b) the merchandise return, and (c) the payment.

EX 6-22
Purchase-related transactions
obj. 3
✓ (e) Cash, dr. $1,410

Journalize entries for the following related transactions of La Paz Company:

a. Purchased $18,400 of merchandise from Harbin Co. on account, terms 2/10, n/30.
b. Paid the amount owed on the invoice within the discount period.
c. Discovered that $4,500 of the merchandise was defective and returned items, receiving credit.
d. Purchased $3,000 of merchandise from Harbin Co. on account, terms n/30.
e. Received a check for the balance owed from the return in (c), after deducting for the purchase in (d).

EX 6-23
Determining amounts to be paid on invoices
obj. 3
✓ a. $6,435

Determine the amount to be paid in full settlement of each of the following invoices, assuming that credit for returns and allowances was received prior to payment and that all invoices were paid within the discount period.

	Merchandise	Transportation Paid by Seller		Returns and Allowances
a.	$ 8,000	—	FOB shipping point, 1/10, n/30	$1,500
b.	2,900	$125	FOB shipping point, 2/10, n/30	400
c.	3,850	—	FOB destination, 2/10, n/30	—
d.	15,000	—	FOB destination, n/30	2,500
e.	5,000	275	FOB shipping point, 2/10, n/30	1,000

EX 6-24
Sales tax
obj. 3
✓ c. $12,932

A sale of merchandise on account for $12,200 is subject to a 6% sales tax. (a) Should the sales tax be recorded at the time of sale or when payment is received? (b) What is the amount of the sale? (c) What is the amount debited to Accounts Receivable? (d) What is the title of the account to which the $732 ($12,200 × 6%) is credited?

EX 6-25
Sales tax transactions
obj. 3

Journalize the entries to record the following selected transactions:

a. Sold $15,750 of merchandise on account, subject to a sales tax of 8%. The cost of the merchandise sold was $9,450.
b. Paid $29,183 to the state sales tax department for taxes collected.

EX 6-26
Sale related transactions
obj. 3

Sellers Co., a furniture wholesaler, sells merchandise to Beyer Co. on account, $14,500, terms 2/10, n/30. The cost of the merchandise sold is $8,800. Sellers Co. issues a credit memorandum for $3,750 for merchandise returned and subsequently receives the amount due within the discount period. The cost of the merchandise returned is $2,100. Journalize Sellers Co.'s entries for (a) the sale, including the cost of the merchandise sold, (b) the credit memorandum, including the cost of the returned merchandise, and (c) the receipt of the check for the amount due from Beyer Co.

EX 6-27
Purchase-related transactions
obj. 3

Based on the data presented in Exercise 6-26, journalize Beyer Co.'s entries for (a) the purchase, (b) the return of the merchandise for credit, and (c) the payment of the invoice within the discount period.

EX 6-28
Normal balances of merchandise accounts
obj. 3

What is the normal balance of the following accounts: (a) Sales, (b) Sales Discounts, (c) Sales Returns and Allowances, (d) Cost of Merchandise Sold, (e) Delivery Expense, (f) Merchandise Inventory, (g) Sales Tax Payable?

EX 6-29
Adjusting entry for merchandise inventory shrinkage
obj. 4

Teramycin Inc.'s perpetual inventory records indicate that $715,275 of merchandise should be on hand on January 31, 2008. The physical inventory indicates that $698,150 of merchandise is actually on hand. Journalize the adjusting entry for the inventory shrinkage for Teramycin Inc. for the year ended January 31, 2008.

EX 6-30
Closing the accounts of a merchandiser
obj. 4

From the following list, identify the accounts that should be closed to Income Summary at the end of the fiscal year under a perpetual inventory system: (a) Accounts Payable, (b) Advertising Expense, (c) Cost of Merchandise Sold, (d) Merchandise Inventory, (e) Sales, (f) Sales Discounts, (g) Sales Returns and Allowances, (h) Supplies, (i) Supplies Expense, (j) Terry Weaver, Drawing, (k) Wages Payable.

EX 6-31
Closing entries; net income
obj. 4

Based on the data presented in Exercise 6-11, journalize the closing entries.

EX 6-32
Closing entries
obj. 4

On October 31, 2008, the balances of the accounts appearing in the ledger of Kavanaugh Company, a furniture wholesaler, are as follows:

Accumulated Dep.—Building	$152,300	Notes Payable	$ 120,000
Administrative Expenses	326,500	Salaries Payable	3,400
Building	278,400	Sales	1,567,700
Cash	44,200	Sales Discounts	90,000
Cost of Merchandise Sold	940,000	Sales Returns and Allow.	60,000
Interest Expense	9,600	Sales Tax Payable	24,500
Lillian Kavanaugh, Capital	705,775	Selling Expenses	620,000
Lillian Kavanaugh, Drawing	39,750	Store Supplies	22,900
Merchandise Inventory	130,000	Store Supplies Exp.	12,325

Prepare the October 31, 2008, closing entries for Kavanaugh Company.

EX 6-33
Ratio of net sales to total assets

The Home Depot reported the following data (in millions) in its financial statements for 2005 and 2004:

	2005	2004
Net sales	$73,094	$64,816
Total assets at the end of the year	38,907	34,437
Total assets at the beginning of the year	34,437	30,011

a. Determine the ratio of net sales to average total assets for The Home Depot for 2005 and 2004. Round to two decimal places.
b. What conclusions can be drawn from these ratios concerning the trend in the ability of The Home Depot to effectively use its assets to generate sales?

EX 6-34
Ratio of net sales to total assets

Kroger, a national supermarket chain, reported the following data (in millions) in its financial statements for 2005:

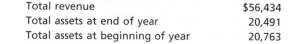

Total revenue	$56,434
Total assets at end of year	20,491
Total assets at beginning of year	20,763

a. Compute the ratio of net sales to assets for 2005. Round to two decimal places.

b. ⬛━━▶ Would you expect the ratio of net sales to assets for Kroger to be similar to or different from that of Tiffany & Co.? Tiffany is the large North American retailer of jewelry, with a ratio of net sales to average total assets of 0.87.

APPENDIX 1
EX 6-35
Merchandising special journals

✓d. $62,500

Patel Rug Company had the following credit sales transactions during March 2008:

Date	Customer	Quantity	Rug Style	Sales
Mar. 3	Samantha McGill	1	10 by 8 Chinese	$14,750
8	L. Smith	1	8 by 12 Persian	10,000
19	Paula Larkin	1	8 by 10 Indian	11,500
26	Amy Pugh	1	10 by 12 Persian	21,000

The March 1 inventory was $26,000, consisting of:

Quantity	Style	Cost per Rug	Total Cost
2	10 by 8 Chinese	$7,500	$15,000
2	8 by 12 Persian	5,500	11,000

During March, Patel Rug Company purchased the following rugs from Lee Rug Importers:

Date	Quantity	Rug Style	Cost per Rug	Amount
Mar. 10	2	8 by 10 Indian	$ 6,000	$12,000
12	1	10 by 8 Chinese	10,500	10,500
21	3	10 by 12 Persian	16,500	49,500

The general ledger includes the following accounts:

Account Number	Account
11	Accounts Receivable
12	Merchandise Inventory
21	Accounts Payable
41	Sales
51	Cost of Merchandise Sold

a. Record the sales in a two-column sales journal. Use the sales journal form shown in Appendix 1 at the end of this chapter. Begin with Invoice No. 80.

b. Record the purchases in a purchases journal. Use the purchases journal form shown in Appendix 1 at the end of this chapter.

c. Assume that you have posted the journal entries to the appropriate ledgers. Insert the correct posting references in the sales and purchases journals.

d. Determine the March 31 balance of Merchandise Inventory.

APPENDIX 2
EX 6-36
Accounts for periodic and perpetual inventory systems

Indicate which of the following accounts would be included in the chart of accounts of a merchandising company using either the (a) periodic inventory system or (b) perpetual inventory system. If the account would be included in the chart of accounts of a company using the periodic and perpetual systems, indicate (c) for both.

(1) Cost of Merchandise Sold

(2) Purchases Discounts

(3) Sales

(4) Merchandise Inventory

(5) Sales Discounts

(6) Purchases Returns and Allowances

(7) Delivery Expense

(8) Sales Returns and Allowances

(9) Transportation In

(10) Purchases

APPENDIX 2
EX 6-37
Rules of debit and credit for periodic inventory accounts

Complete the following table by indicating for (a) through (g) whether the proper answer is debit or credit.

Account	Increase	Decrease	Normal Balance
Purchases	(a)	credit	(b)
Purchases Discounts	credit	debit	(c)
Purchases Returns and Allowances	(d)	(e)	credit
Transportation In	(f)	credit	(g)

APPENDIX 2
EX 6-38
Journal entries using the periodic inventory system

The following selected transactions were completed by Lorimer Company during August of the current year. Lorimer Company uses the periodic inventory system.

Aug. 3. Purchased $24,500 of merchandise on account, FOB shipping point, terms 2/10, n/30.
4. Paid transportation costs of $475 on the August 3 purchase.
7. Returned $4,000 of the merchandise purchased on August 3.
11. Sold merchandise on account, $12,700, FOB destination, 2/15, n/30. The cost of merchandise sold was $7,600.
12. Paid transportation costs of $300 for the merchandise sold on August 11.
13. Paid for the purchase of August 3 less the return and discount.
26. Received payment on account for the sale of August 11 less the discount.

Journalize the entries to record the transactions of Lorimer Company.

APPENDIX 2
EX 6-39
Journal entries using perpetual inventory system

Using the data shown in Exercise 6-38, journalize the entries for the transactions assuming that Lorimer Company uses the perpetual inventory system.

APPENDIX 2
EX 6-40
Closing entries using periodic inventory system

Greenway Company is a small rug retailer owned and operated by Lorene Greenway. After the accounts have been adjusted on March 31, the following account balances were taken from the ledger:

Advertising Expense	$ 25,800
Depreciation Expense	5,100
Lorene Greenway, Drawing	50,000
Merchandise Inventory, March 1	34,500
Merchandise Inventory, March 31	42,150
Miscellaneous Expense	6,350
Purchases	480,000
Purchases Discounts	2,000
Purchases Returns and Allowances	9,000
Sales	925,000
Sales Discounts	4,000
Sales Returns and Allowances	8,000
Salaries Expense	76,300
Transportation In	15,400

Journalize the closing entries on March 31.

Problems Series A

PR 6-1A
Multiple-step income statement and report form of balance sheet
obj. 2

✓ *1. Net income:*
$120,000

The following selected accounts and their current balances appear in the ledger of Magic Vinyl Co. for the fiscal year ended March 31, 2008:

Cash	$ 184,500	Sales Returns and Allowances	$ 27,720
Accounts Receivable	145,200	Sales Discounts	26,280
Merchandise Inventory	210,000	Cost of Merchandise Sold	930,000
Office Supplies	6,720	Sales Salaries Expense	207,840
Prepaid Insurance	4,080	Advertising Expense	52,560
Office Equipment	102,000	Depreciation Expense—	
Accumulated Depreciation—		Store Equipment	7,680
Office Equipment	15,360	Miscellaneous Selling Expense	1,920
Store Equipment	183,600	Office Salaries Expense	100,980
Accumulated Depreciation—		Rent Expense	37,620
Store Equipment	41,040	Depreciation Expense—	
Accounts Payable	66,720	Office Equipment	15,240
Salaries Payable	2,880	Insurance Expense	4,680
Note Payable		Office Supplies Expense	1,560
(final payment due 2018)	67,200	Miscellaneous Administrative	
Tiffany Garland, Capital	564,900	Expense	1,920
Tiffany Garland, Drawing	42,000	Interest Expense	6,000
Sales	1,542,000		

Instructions
1. Prepare a multiple-step income statement.
2. Prepare a statement of owner's equity.
3. Prepare a report form of balance sheet, assuming that the current portion of the note payable is $9,000.
4. Briefly explain (a) how multiple-step and single-step income statements differ and (b) how report-form and account-form balance sheets differ.

PR 6-2A
Single-step income statement and account form of balance sheet
objs. 2, 4

✓ *3. Total assets: $779,700*

Selected accounts and related amounts for Magic Vinyl Co. for the fiscal year ended March 31, 2008, are presented in Problem 6-1A.

Instructions
1. Prepare a single-step income statement in the format shown in Exhibit 3.
2. Prepare a statement of owner's equity.
3. Prepare an account form of balance sheet, assuming that the current portion of the note payable is $9,000.
4. Prepare closing entries as of March 31, 2008.

PR 6-3A
Sales-related transactions
obj. 3

The following selected transactions were completed by Cardroom Supply Co., which sells office supplies primarily to wholesalers and occasionally to retail customers.

Jan. 2. Sold merchandise on account to Kibler Co., $10,000, terms FOB destination, 1/10, n/30. The cost of the merchandise sold was $6,500.
3. Sold merchandise for $12,000 plus 8% sales tax to cash customers. The cost of merchandise sold was $9,000.
4. Sold merchandise on account to Glickman Co., $5,600, terms FOB shipping point, n/eom. The cost of merchandise sold was $3,100.
5. Sold merchandise for $8,000 plus 8% sales tax to customers who used Master-Card. The cost of merchandise sold was $6,000.
12. Received check for amount due from Kibler Co. for sale on January 2.
14. Sold merchandise to customers who used American Express cards, $15,000. The cost of merchandise sold was $9,200.
16. Sold merchandise on account to Bryan Co., $12,000, terms FOB shipping point, 1/10, n/30. The cost of merchandise sold was $7,200.

Jan. 18. Issued credit memorandum for $3,000 to Bryan Co. for merchandise returned from sale on January 16. The cost of the merchandise returned was $1,800.

19. Sold merchandise on account to Cooney Co., $15,750, terms FOB shipping point, 2/10, n/30. Added $400 to the invoice for transportation costs prepaid. The cost of merchandise sold was $9,500.

26. Received check for amount due from Bryan Co. for sale on January 16 less credit memorandum of January 18 and discount.

28. Received check for amount due from Cooney Co. for sale of January 19.

31. Received check for amount due from Glickman Co. for sale of January 4.

31. Paid Speedy Delivery Service $1,875 for merchandise delivered during January to customers under shipping terms of FOB destination.

Feb. 3. Paid First State Bank $1,150 for service fees for handling MasterCard and American Express sales during January.

15. Paid $1,600 to state sales tax division for taxes owed on sales.

Instructions

Journalize the entries to record the transactions of Cardroom Supply Co.

PR 6-4A
Purchase-related transactions

obj. 3

The following selected transactions were completed by Scat Trak Company during July of the current year:

July 1. Purchased merchandise from Kermit Co., $18,750, terms FOB destination, n/30.

3. Purchased merchandise from Basaway Co., $12,150, terms FOB shipping point, 2/10, n/eom. Prepaid transportation costs of $180 were added to the invoice.

4. Purchased merchandise from Phillips Co., $13,800, terms FOB destination, 2/10, n/30.

6. Issued debit memorandum to Phillips Co. for $1,900 of merchandise returned from purchase on July 4.

13. Paid Basaway Co. for invoice of July 3, less discount.

14. Paid Phillips Co. for invoice of July 4, less debit memorandum of July 6 and discount.

19. Purchased merchandise from Cleghorne Co., $18,000, terms FOB shipping point, n/eom.

19. Paid transportation charges of $500 on July 19 purchase from Cleghorne Co.

20. Purchased merchandise from Graham Co., $9,000, terms FOB destination, 1/10, n/30.

30. Paid Graham Co. for invoice of July 20, less discount.

31. Paid Kermit Co. for invoice of July 1.

31. Paid Cleghorne Co. for invoice of July 19.

Instructions

Journalize the entries to record the transactions of Scat Trak Company for July.

PR 6-5A
Sales-related and purchase-related transactions

obj. 3

The following were selected from among the transactions completed by Southmont Company during April of the current year:

Apr. 3. Purchased merchandise on account from Mandell Co., list price $30,000, trade discount 40%, terms FOB destination, 2/10, n/30.

4. Sold merchandise for cash, $12,800. The cost of the merchandise sold was $7,600.

5. Purchased merchandise on account from Quinn Co., $18,750, terms FOB shipping point, 2/10, n/30, with prepaid transportation costs of $715 added to the invoice.

6. Returned $3,500 of merchandise purchased on April 3 from Mandell Co.

11. Sold merchandise on account to Campo Co., list price $6,000, trade discount 20%, terms 1/10, n/30. The cost of the merchandise sold was $3,200.

13. Paid Mandell Co. on account for purchase of April 3, less return of April 6 and discount.

14. Sold merchandise on VISA, $52,700. The cost of the merchandise sold was $31,500.

15. Paid Quinn Co. on account for purchase of April 5, less discount.

Apr. 21. Received cash on account from sale of April 11 to Campo Co., less discount.
24. Sold merchandise on account to Elkins Co., $8,150, terms 1/10, n/30. The cost of the merchandise sold was $4,500.
28. Paid VISA service fee of $1,500.
30. Received merchandise returned by Elkins Co. from sale on April 24, $1,200. The cost of the returned merchandise was $900.

Instructions
Journalize the transactions.

PR 6-6A
Sales-related and purchase-related transactions for seller and buyer

obj. 3

The following selected transactions were completed during August between Sellars Company and Beyer Co.:

Aug. 1. Sellars Company sold merchandise on account to Beyer Co., $17,850, terms FOB destination, 2/15, n/eom. The cost of the merchandise sold was $10,700.
2. Sellars Company paid transportation costs of $140 for delivery of merchandise sold to Beyer Co. on August 1.
5. Sellars Company sold merchandise on account to Beyer Co., $27,550, terms FOB shipping point, n/eom. The cost of the merchandise sold was $16,500.
6. Beyer Co. returned $1,800 of merchandise purchased on account on August 1 from Sellars Company. The cost of the merchandise returned was $1,050.
9. Beyer Co. paid transportation charges of $165 on August 5 purchase from Sellars Company.
15. Sellars Company sold merchandise on account to Beyer Co., $32,000, terms FOB shipping point, 1/10, n/30. Sellars Company paid transportation costs of $1,243, which were added to the invoice. The cost of the merchandise sold was $19,200.
16. Beyer Co. paid Sellars Company for purchase of August 1, less discount and less return of August 6.
25. Beyer Co. paid Sellars Company on account for purchase of August 15, less discount.
31. Beyer Co. paid Sellars Company on account for purchase of August 5.

Instructions
Journalize the August transactions for (1) Sellars Company and (2) Beyer Co.

APPENDIX 2
PR 6-7A
Purchase-related transactions using periodic inventory system

Selected transactions for Scat Trak Company during July of the current year are listed in Problem 6-4A.

Instructions
Journalize the entries to record the transactions of Scat Trak Company for July using the periodic inventory system.

APPENDIX 2
PR 6-8A
Sales-related and purchase-related transactions using periodic inventory system

Selected transactions for Southmont Company during April of the current year are listed in Problem 6-5A.

Instructions
Journalize the entries to record the transactions of Southmont Company for April using the periodic inventory system.

APPENDIX 2
PR 6-9A
Sales-related and purchase-related transactions for buyer and seller using periodic inventory system

Selected transactions during August between Sellars Company and Beyer Co. are listed in Problem 6-6A.

Instructions
Journalize the entries to record the transactions for (1) Sellars Company and (2) Beyers Co. assuming that both companies use the periodic inventory system.

APPENDIX 2
PR 6-10A
Periodic inventory accounts, multiple-step income statement, closing entries

✓2. *Net income, $725,200*

On July 31, 2008, the balances of the accounts appearing in the ledger of Odell Company are as follows:

Cash	$ 73,200	Sales Discounts	$ 37,500
Accounts Receivable	288,500	Purchases	2,146,000
Merchandise Inventory, Aug. 1, 2007	350,900	Purchases Returns and Allowances	24,000
Office Supplies	12,100	Purchases Discounts	18,000
Prepaid Insurance	18,000	Transportation In	43,600
Land	140,000	Sales Salaries Expense	625,000
Store Equipment	683,100	Advertising Expense	220,000
Accumulated Depreciation—		Delivery Expense	36,000
Store Equipment	223,600	Depreciation Expense—Store	
Office Equipment	314,000	Equipment	23,600
Accumulated Depreciation—		Miscellaneous Selling Expense	42,800
Office Equipment	65,000	Office Salaries Expense	400,000
Accounts Payable	111,300	Rent Expense	125,000
Salaries Payable	11,800	Insurance Expense	12,000
Unearned Rent	33,200	Office Supplies Expense	9,200
Notes Payable	50,000	Depreciation Expense—	
Marcus Odell, Capital	760,200	Office Equipment	6,000
Marcus Odell, Drawing	75,000	Miscellaneous Administrative Expense	23,400
Sales	4,425,800	Rent Revenue	25,000
Sales Returns and Allowances	40,000	Interest Expense	3,000

Instructions
1. Does Odell Company use the periodic or perpetual inventory system? Explain.
2. Prepare a multiple-step income statement for Odell Company for the year ended July 31, 2008. The merchandise inventory as of July 31, 2008, was $376,400.
3. Prepare the closing entries for Odell Company as of July 31, 2008.

Problems Series B

PR 6-1B
Multiple-step income statement and report form of balance sheet

obj. 2

✓1. *Net income: $61,200*

The following selected accounts and their current balances appear in the ledger of Hobbs' Co. for the fiscal year ended June 30, 2008:

Cash	$ 68,850	Sales Returns and Allowances	$ 18,900
Accounts Receivable	55,800	Sales Discounts	9,900
Merchandise Inventory	90,000	Cost of Merchandise Sold	963,000
Office Supplies	2,340	Sales Salaries Expense	189,000
Prepaid Insurance	6,120	Advertising Expense	25,470
Office Equipment	57,600	Depreciation Expense—	
Accumulated Depreciation—		Store Equipment	4,140
Office Equipment	9,720	Miscellaneous Selling Expense	990
Store Equipment	105,750	Office Salaries Expense	36,900
Accumulated Depreciation—		Rent Expense	19,935
Store Equipment	43,740	Insurance Expense	11,475
Accounts Payable	24,300	Depreciation Expense—	
Salaries Payable	1,800	Office Equipment	8,100
Note Payable		Office Supplies Expense	810
(final payment due 2018)	27,000	Miscellaneous Administrative	
Jeremiah Hobbs, Capital	241,200	Expense	1,080
Jeremiah Hobbs, Drawing	22,500	Interest Expense	900
Sales	1,351,800		

Instructions
1. Prepare a multiple-step income statement.
2. Prepare a statement of owner's equity.
3. Prepare a report form of balance sheet, assuming that the current portion of the note payable is $2,250.
4. Briefly explain (a) how multiple-step and single-step income statements differ and (b) how report-form and account-form balance sheets differ.

PR 6-2B

Single-step income statement and account form of balance sheet

objs. 2, 4

✓ 3. Total assets: $333,000

Selected accounts and related amounts for Hobbs' Co. for the fiscal year ended June 30, 2008, are presented in Problem 6-1B.

Instructions

1. Prepare a single-step income statement in the format shown in Exhibit 3.
2. Prepare a statement of owner's equity.
3. Prepare an account form of balance sheet, assuming that the current portion of the note payable is $2,250.
4. Prepare closing entries as of June 30, 2008.

PR 6-3B

Sales-related transactions

obj. 3

The following selected transactions were completed by Water Tech Supplies Co., which sells irrigation supplies primarily to wholesalers and occasionally to retail customers.

July 1. Sold merchandise on account to Upshaw Co., $8,000, terms FOB shipping point, n/eom. The cost of merchandise sold was $4,800.
2. Sold merchandise for $15,000 plus 7% sales tax to cash customers. The cost of merchandise sold was $8,800.
5. Sold merchandise on account to Westone Company, $16,000, terms FOB destination, 1/10, n/30. The cost of merchandise sold was $10,500.
8. Sold merchandise for $11,500 plus 7% sales tax to customers who used VISA cards. The cost of merchandise sold was $7,000.
13. Sold merchandise to customers who used MasterCard cards, $8,000. The cost of merchandise sold was $4,750.
14. Sold merchandise on account to Tyler Co., $7,500, terms FOB shipping point, 1/10, n/30. The cost of merchandise sold was $4,000.
15. Received check for amount due from Westone Company for sale on July 5.
16. Issued credit memorandum for $800 to Tyler Co. for merchandise returned from sale on July 14. The cost of the merchandise returned was $360.
18. Sold merchandise on account to Horton Company, $6,850, terms FOB shipping point, 2/10, n/30. Paid $210 for transportation costs and added them to the invoice. The cost of merchandise sold was $4,100.
24. Received check for amount due from Tyler Co. for sale on July 14 less credit memorandum of July 16 and discount.
28. Received check for amount due from Horton Company for sale of July 18.
31. Paid Uptown Delivery Service $3,100 for merchandise delivered during July to customers under shipping terms of FOB destination.
31. Received check for amount due from Upshaw Co. for sale of July 1.
Aug. 3. Paid First National Bank $780 for service fees for handling MasterCard and VISA sales during July.
10. Paid $1,855 to state sales tax division for taxes owed on sales.

Instructions

Journalize the entries to record the transactions of Water Tech Supplies Co.

PR 6-4B

Purchase-related transactions

obj. 3

The following selected transactions were completed by Bodyworks Co. during October of the current year:

Oct. 1. Purchased merchandise from Mantooth Co., $11,800, terms FOB shipping point, 2/10, n/eom. Prepaid transportation costs of $325 were added to the invoice.
5. Purchased merchandise from Hauck Co., $17,500, terms FOB destination, n/30.
10. Paid Mantooth Co. for invoice of October 1, less discount.
13. Purchased merchandise from Lieu Co., $7,500, terms FOB destination, 1/10, n/30.
14. Issued debit memorandum to Lieu Co. for $2,500 of merchandise returned from purchase on October 13.
18. Purchased merchandise from Fowler Company, $9,600, terms FOB shipping point, n/eom.

Oct. 18. Paid transportation charges of $150 on October 18 purchase from Fowler Company.
   19. Purchased merchandise from Hatcher Co., $9,750, terms FOB destination, 2/10, n/30.
   23. Paid Lieu Co. for invoice of October 13, less debit memorandum of October 14 and discount.
   29. Paid Hatcher Co. for invoice of October 19, less discount.
   31. Paid Fowler Company for invoice of October 18.
   31. Paid Hauck Co. for invoice of October 5.

Instructions
Journalize the entries to record the transactions of Bodyworks Co. for October.

PR 6-5B
Sales-related and purchase-related transactions

obj. 3

The following were selected from among the transactions completed by Theisen Company during December of the current year:

Dec. 3. Purchased merchandise on account from Shipley Co., list price $24,000, trade discount 25%, terms FOB shipping point, 2/10, n/30, with prepaid transportation costs of $615 added to the invoice.
   5. Purchased merchandise on account from Kirch Co., $10,250, terms FOB destination, 2/10, n/30.
   6. Sold merchandise on account to Murdock Co., list price $18,000, trade discount 35%, terms 2/10, n/30. The cost of the merchandise sold was $8,250.
   7. Returned $1,800 of merchandise purchased on December 5 from Kirch Co.
   13. Paid Shipley Co. on account for purchase of December 3, less discount.
   15. Paid Kirch Co. on account for purchase of December 5, less return of December 7 and discount.
   16. Received cash on account from sale of December 6 to Murdock Co., less discount.
   19. Sold merchandise on MasterCard, $39,500. The cost of the merchandise sold was $23,700.
   22. Sold merchandise on account to Milk River Co., $11,300, terms 2/10, n/30. The cost of the merchandise sold was $6,700.
   23. Sold merchandise for cash, $17,680. The cost of the merchandise sold was $9,100.
   28. Received merchandise returned by Milk River Co. from sale on December 22, $2,000. The cost of the returned merchandise was $1,100.
   31. Paid MasterCard service fee of $1,050.

Instructions
Journalize the transactions.

PR 6-6B
Sales-related and purchase-related transactions for seller and buyer

obj. 3

The following selected transactions were completed during November between Sallis Company and Byce Company:

Nov. 2. Sallis Company sold merchandise on account to Byce Company, $12,500, terms FOB shipping point, 2/10, n/30. Sallis Company paid transportation costs of $425, which were added to the invoice. The cost of the merchandise sold was $7,500.
   8. Sallis Company sold merchandise on account to Byce Company, $21,600, terms FOB destination, 1/15, n/eom. The cost of the merchandise sold was $13,000.
   8. Sallis Company paid transportation costs of $879 for delivery of merchandise sold to Byce Company on November 8.
   12. Byce Company returned $5,000 of merchandise purchased on account on November 8 from Sallis Company. The cost of the merchandise returned was $2,900.
   12. Byce Company paid Sallis Company for purchase of November 2, less discount.
   23. Byce Company paid Sallis Company for purchase of November 8, less discount and less return of November 12.

Nov. 24. Sallis Company sold merchandise on account to Byce Company, $15,000, terms FOB shipping point, n/eom. The cost of the merchandise sold was $9,000.

26. Byce Company paid transportation charges of $400 on November 24 purchase from Sallis Company.

30. Byce Company paid Sallis Company on account for purchase of November 24.

Instructions

Journalize the November transactions for (1) Sallis Company and (2) Byce Company.

APPENDIX 2
PR 6-7B
Purchase-related transactions using periodic inventory system

Selected transactions for Bodyworks Co. during October of the current year are listed in Problem 6-4B.

Instructions

Journalize the entries to record the transactions of Bodyworks Co. for October using the periodic inventory system.

APPENDIX 2
PR 6-8B
Sales-related and purchase-related transactions using periodic inventory system

Selected transactions for Theisen Company during December of the current year are listed in Problem 6-5B.

Instructions

Journalize the entries to record the transactions of Theisen Company for December using the periodic inventory system.

APPENDIX 2
PR 6-9B
Sales-related and purchase-related transactions for buyer and seller using periodic inventory system

Selected transactions during November between Sallis Company and Byce Company are listed in Problem 6-6B.

Instructions

Journalize the entries to record the transactions for (1) Sallis Company and (2) Byce Company assuming that both companies use the periodic inventory system.

APPENDIX 2
PR 6-10B
Periodic inventory accounts, multiple-step income statement, closing entries

✔ *2. Net income, $181,300*

On April 30, 2008, the balances of the accounts appearing in the ledger of Headwinds Company are as follows:

Cash	$ 18,300	Sales Discounts	$ 9,375
Accounts Receivable	72,125	Purchases	536,500
Merchandise Inventory, May 1, 2007	87,725	Purchases Returns and Allowances	6,000
Office Supplies	3,025	Purchases Discounts	4,500
Prepaid Insurance	4,500	Transportation In	10,900
Land	35,000	Sales Salaries Expense	156,250
Store Equipment	170,775	Advertising Expense	55,000
Accumulated Depreciation—		Delivery Expense	9,000
Store Equipment	55,900	Depreciation Expense—	
Office Equipment	78,500	Store Equipment	5,900
Accumulated Depreciation—		Miscellaneous Selling Expense	10,700
Office Equipment	16,250	Office Salaries Expense	100,000
Accounts Payable	27,825	Rent Expense	31,250
Salaries Payable	2,950	Insurance Expense	3,000
Unearned Rent	8,300	Office Supplies Expense	2,300
Notes Payable	12,500	Depreciation Expense—	
Kasey Kurtz, Capital	190,050	Office Equipment	1,500
Kasey Kurtz, Drawing	18,750	Miscellaneous Administrative Expense	5,850
Sales	1,106,450	Rent Revenue	6,250
Sales Returns and Allowances	10,000	Interest Expense	750

Instructions

1. Does Headwinds Company use a periodic or perpetual inventory system? Explain.
2. Prepare a multiple-step income statement for Headwinds Company for the year ended April 30, 2008. The merchandise inventory as of April 30, 2008, was $94,100.
3. Prepare the closing entries for Headwinds Company as of April 30, 2008.

Comprehensive Problem 2

✓8. Net income: $231,962

World Boards Co. is a merchandising business. The account balances for World Boards Co. as of March 1, 2008 (unless otherwise indicated), are as follows:

110	Cash	$ 21,200
112	Accounts Receivable	51,300
115	Merchandise Inventory	200,800
116	Prepaid Insurance	5,600
117	Store Supplies	3,800
123	Store Equipment	156,500
124	Accumulated Depreciation—Store Equipment	18,900
210	Accounts Payable	32,200
211	Salaries Payable	—
310	Evan Raskind, Capital, April 1, 2007	185,100
311	Evan Raskind, Drawing	45,000
312	Income Summary	—
410	Sales	1,073,700
411	Sales Returns and Allowances	30,900
412	Sales Discounts	19,800
510	Cost of Merchandise Sold	541,000
520	Sales Salaries Expense	111,600
521	Advertising Expense	27,000
522	Depreciation Expense	—
523	Store Supplies Expense	—
529	Miscellaneous Selling Expense	4,200
530	Office Salaries Expense	60,700
531	Rent Expense	27,900
532	Insurance Expense	—
539	Miscellaneous Administrative Expense	2,600

During March, the last month of the fiscal year, the following transactions were completed:

Mar. 1. Paid rent for March, $2,400.
3. Purchased merchandise on account from Huisman Co., terms 2/10, n/30, FOB shipping point, $21,600.
4. Paid transportation charges on purchase of March 3, $500.
6. Sold merchandise on account to Hillcrest Co., terms 2/10, n/30, FOB shipping point, $8,500. The cost of the merchandise sold was $5,000.
7. Received $8,900 cash from Foley Co. on account, no discount.
10. Sold merchandise for cash, $27,200. The cost of the merchandise sold was $16,000.
13. Paid for merchandise purchased on March 3, less discount.
14. Received merchandise returned on sale of March 6, $1,500. The cost of the merchandise returned was $900.
15. Paid advertising expense for last half of March, $2,600.
16. Received cash from sale of March 6, less return of March 14 and discount.
19. Purchased merchandise for cash, $11,800.
19. Paid $9,000 to Bakke Co. on account, no discount.
20. Sold merchandise on account to Wilts Co., terms 1/10, n/30, FOB shipping point, $22,300. The cost of the merchandise sold was $13,200.

Mar. 21. For the convenience of the customer, paid shipping charges on sale of March 20, $1,100.

21. Received $17,600 cash from Owen Co. on account, no discount.

21. Purchased merchandise on account from Nye Co., terms 1/10, n/30, FOB destination, $19,900.

24. Returned $2,000 of damaged merchandise purchased on March 21, receiving credit from the seller.

26. Refunded cash on sales made for cash, $1,200. The cost of the merchandise returned was $700.

28. Paid sales salaries of $7,600 and office salaries of $4,800.

29. Purchased store supplies for cash, $800.

30. Sold merchandise on account to Whitetail Co., terms 2/10, n/30, FOB shipping point, $18,750. The cost of the merchandise sold was $11,250.

30. Received cash from sale of March 20, less discount, plus transportation paid on March 21.

31. Paid for purchase of March 21, less return of March 24 and discount.

Instructions

1. Enter the balances of each of the accounts in the appropriate balance column of a four-column account. Write *Balance* in the item section, and place a check mark (✔) in the Posting Reference column. Journalize the transactions for March.

2. Post the journal to the general ledger, extending the month-end balances to the appropriate balance columns after all posting is completed. In this problem, you are not required to update or post to the accounts receivable and accounts payable subsidiary ledgers.

3. Prepare an unadjusted trial balance.

4. At the end of March, the following adjustment data were assembled. Analyze and use these data to complete (5) and (6).

a.	Merchandise inventory on March 31		$196,139
b.	Insurance expired during the year		1,875
c.	Store supplies on hand on March 31		1,500
d.	Depreciation for the current year		9,500
e.	Accrued salaries on March 31:		
	Sales salaries	$1,200	
	Office salaries	800	2,000

5. **Optional:** Enter the unadjusted trial balance on a 10-column end-of-period spreadsheet (work sheet), and complete the spreadsheet. See Appendix C for how to prepare an end-of-period spreadsheet (work sheet) for a merchandising business.

6. Journalize and post the adjusting entries.

7. Prepare an adjusted trial balance.

8. Prepare an income statement, a statement of owner's equity, and a balance sheet.

9. Prepare and post the closing entries. Indicate closed accounts by inserting a line in both the Balance columns opposite the closing entry. Insert the new balance in the owner's capital account.

10. Prepare a post-closing trial balance.

Special Activities

SA 6-1
*Ethics and professional
conduct in business*

ETHICS

On February 24, 2008, Lawn Ranger Company, a garden retailer, purchased $40,000 of corn seed, terms 2/10, n/30, from Nebraska Farm Co. Even though the discount period had expired, Corey Gilbert subtracted the discount of $800 when he processed the documents for payment on March 25, 2008.

➤ Discuss whether Corey Gilbert behaved in a professional manner by subtracting the discount, even though the discount period had expired.

SA 6-2
Purchases discounts and accounts payable

The Eclipse Video Store Co. is owned and operated by Jared Helms. The following is an excerpt from a conversation between Jared Helms and Allison Fain, the chief accountant for The Eclipse Video Store.

Jared: Allison, I've got a question about this recent balance sheet.
Allison: Sure, what's your question?
Jared: Well, as you know, I'm applying for a bank loan to finance our new store in Winterville, and I noticed that the accounts payable are listed as $85,000.
Allison: That's right. Approximately $78,000 of that represents amounts due our suppliers, and the remainder is miscellaneous payables to creditors for utilities, office equipment, supplies, etc.
Jared: That's what I thought. But as you know, we normally receive a 2% discount from our suppliers for earlier payment, and we always try to take the discount.
Allison: That's right. I can't remember the last time we missed a discount.
Jared: Well, in that case, it seems to me the accounts payable should be listed minus the 2% discount. Let's list the accounts payable due suppliers as $76,440, rather than $78,000. Every little bit helps. You never know. It might make the difference between getting the loan and not.

How would you respond to Jared Helms' request?

SA 6-3
Determining cost of purchase

The following is an excerpt from a conversation between Kate Fleming and Bob Dent. Kate is debating whether to buy a stereo system from Design Sound, a locally owned electronics store, or Big Sound Electronics, an online electronics company.

Kate: Bob, I don't know what to do about buying my new stereo.
Bob: What's the problem?
Kate: Well, I can buy it locally at Design Sound for $580.00. However, Big Sound Electronics has the same system listed for $599.99.
Bob: So what's the big deal? Buy it from Design Sound.
Kate: It's not quite that simple. Big Sound said something about not having to pay sales tax, since I was out-of-state.
Bob: Yes, that's a good point. If you buy it at Design Sound, they'll charge you 8% sales tax.
Kate: But Big Sound Electronics charges $18.99 for shipping and handling. If I have them send it next-day air, it'll cost $24.99 for shipping and handling.
Bob: I guess it is a little confusing.
Kate: That's not all. Design Sound will give an additional 1% discount if I pay cash. Otherwise, they will let me use my VISA, or I can pay it off in three monthly installments.
Bob: Anything else???
Kate: Well . . . Big Sound says I have to charge it on my VISA. They don't accept checks.
Bob: I am not surprised. Many online stores don't accept checks.
Kate: I give up. What would you do?

1. Assuming that Big Sound Electronics doesn't charge sales tax on the sale to Kate, which company is offering the best buy?
2. What might be some considerations other than price that might influence Kate's decision on where to buy the stereo system?

SA 6-4
Sales discounts

Your sister operates Emigrant Parts Company, an online boat parts distributorship that is in its third year of operation. The income statement is shown at the top of the following page and was recently prepared for the year ended July 31, 2008.

Your sister is considering a proposal to increase net income by offering sales discounts of 2/15, n/30, and by shipping all merchandise FOB shipping point. Currently, no sales discounts are allowed and merchandise is shipped FOB destination. It is estimated that these credit terms will increase net sales by 15%. The ratio of the cost of merchandise sold to net sales is expected to be 65%. All selling and administrative expenses are expected to remain unchanged, except for store supplies, miscellaneous selling, office supplies, and miscellaneous administrative expenses, which are expected to increase proportionately with

Emigrant Parts Company
Income Statement
For the Year Ended July 31, 2008

Revenues:		
Net sales		$800,000
Interest revenue		10,000
Total revenues		$810,000
Expenses:		
Cost of merchandise sold	$520,000	
Selling expenses	90,000	
Administrative expenses	48,550	
Interest expense	15,000	
Total expenses		673,550
Net income		$136,450

increased net sales. The amounts of these preceding items for the year ended July 31, 2008, were as follows:

Store supplies expense	$12,000
Miscellaneous selling expense	3,000
Office supplies expense	2,000
Miscellaneous administrative expense	1,000

The other income and other expense items will remain unchanged. The shipment of all merchandise FOB shipping point will eliminate all delivery expense, which for the year ended July 31, 2008, were $18,750.

1. Prepare a projected single-step income statement for the year ending July 31, 2009, based on the proposal. Assume all sales are collected within the discount period.
2. a. ➤ Based on the projected income statement in (1), would you recommend the implementation of the proposed changes?
   b. Describe any possible concerns you may have related to the proposed changes described in (1).

SA 6-5
Shopping for a television

Group Project

Assume that you are planning to purchase a 50-inch Plasma television. In groups of three or four, determine the lowest cost for the television, considering the available alternatives and the advantages and disadvantages of each alternative. For example, you could purchase locally, through mail order, or through an Internet shopping service. Consider such factors as delivery charges, interest-free financing, discounts, coupons, and availability of warranty services. Prepare a report for presentation to the class.

Answers to Self-Examination Questions

1. **A** A debit memorandum (answer A), issued by the buyer, indicates the amount the buyer proposes to debit to the accounts payable account. A credit memorandum (answer B), issued by the seller, indicates the amount the seller proposes to credit to the accounts receivable account. An invoice (answer C) or a bill (answer D), issued by the seller, indicates the amount and terms of the sale.
2. **C** The amount of discount for early payment is $10 (answer C), or 1% of $1,000. Although the $50 of transportation costs paid by the seller is debited to the customer's account, the customer is not entitled to a discount on that amount.
3. **B** The single-step form of income statement (answer B) is so named because the total of all expenses is deducted in one step from the total of all revenues. The multiple-step form (answer A) includes numerous sections and subsections with several subtotals. The ac-

count form (answer C) and the report form (answer D) are two common forms of the balance sheet.
4. **C** Gross profit (answer C) is the excess of net sales over the cost of merchandise sold. Operating income (answer A) or income from operations (answer B) is the excess of gross profit over operating expenses. Net income (answer D) is the final figure on the income statement after all revenues and expenses have been reported.
5. **D** Expenses such as interest expense (answer D) that cannot be associated directly with operations are identified as *other expense* or *nonoperating expense*. Depreciation expense—office equipment (answer A) is an administrative expense. Sales salaries expense (answer B) is a selling expense. Insurance expense (answer C) is a mixed expense with elements of both selling expense and administrative expense. For small businesses, insurance expense is usually reported as an administrative expense.

Inventories

objectives

After studying this chapter, you should be able to:

1 *Describe the importance of control over inventory.*

2 *Describe three inventory cost flow assumptions and how they impact the income statement and balance sheet.*

3 *Determine the cost of inventory under the perpetual inventory system, using the FIFO, LIFO, and average cost methods.*

4 *Determine the cost of inventory under the periodic inventory system, using the FIFO, LIFO, and average cost methods.*

5 *Compare and contrast the use of the three inventory costing methods.*

6 *Describe and illustrate the reporting of merchandise inventory in the financial statements.*

7 *Estimate the cost of inventory, using the retail method and the gross profit method.*

Best Buy

ssume that in September you purchased a Philips HDTV plasma television from Best Buy. At the same time, you purchased a Sony surround sound system for $299.99. You liked your surround sound so well that in November you purchased an identical Sony system on sale for $249.99 for your bedroom TV. Over the holidays, you moved to a new apartment and in the process of unpacking discovered that one of the Sony surround sound systems was missing. Luckily, your renters/homeowners insurance policy will cover the theft, but the insurance company needs to know the cost of the system that was stolen.

The Sony systems were identical. However, to respond to the insurance company, you will need to identify which system was stolen. Was it the first system, which cost $299.99, or was it the second system, which cost $249.99? Whichever assumption you make may determine the amount that you receive from the insurance company.

Merchandising businesses such as Best Buy make similar assumptions when identical merchandise is purchased at different costs. For example, Best Buy may have purchased thousands of Sony surround sound systems over the past year at different costs. At the end of a period, some of the Sony systems will still be in inventory, and some will have been sold. But which costs relate to the sold systems, and which costs relate to the Sony systems still in inventory? Best Buy's assumption about inventory costs can involve large dollar amounts and, thus, can have a significant impact on the financial statements. For example, Best Buy reported $2,851,000,000 of inventory and net income of $984,000,000 for the year ending February 26, 2005.

In this chapter, we will discuss such issues as how to determine the cost of merchandise in inventory and the cost of merchandise sold. However, we begin this chapter by discussing the importance of control over inventory.

Control of Inventory

objective   *1*

Describe the importance of control over inventory.

For companies such as Best Buy, good control over inventory must be maintained. Two primary objectives of control over inventory are safeguarding the inventory and properly reporting it in the financial statements.[1]

Control over inventory should begin as soon as the inventory is received. A *receiving report* should be completed by the company's receiving department in order to establish initial accountability for the inventory. To make sure the inventory received is what was ordered, the receiving report should agree with the company's original *purchase order* for the merchandise. A purchase order authorizes the purchase of an item from a vendor. Likewise, the price at which the inventory was ordered, as shown on the purchase order, should be compared to the price at which the vendor billed the company, as shown on the *vendor's invoice*. After the receiving report, purchase order, and vendor's invoice have been reconciled, the company should record the inventory and related account payable in the accounting records.

Controls for safeguarding inventory include developing and using security measures to prevent inventory damage or customer or employee theft. For example, inventory should be stored in a warehouse or other area to which access is restricted to authorized employees. When shopping, you may have noticed how retail stores protect inventory from customer theft. Retail stores often use such devices as two-way mirrors, cameras, and security guards. High-priced items are often displayed in locked cabinets. Retail clothing stores often place plastic alarm tags on valuable items such as leather coats. Sensors at the exit doors set off alarms if the tags have not been removed by the clerk. These controls are designed to prevent customers from shoplifting.

---

1 Additional controls used by businesses are described and illustrated in Chapter 8, "Sarbanes-Oxley, Internal Controls, and Cash."

Using a perpetual inventory system for merchandise also provides an effective means of control over inventory. The amount of each type of merchandise is always readily available in a subsidiary *inventory ledger*. In addition, the subsidiary ledger can be an aid in maintaining inventory quantities at proper levels. Frequently, comparing balances with predetermined maximum and minimum levels allows for the timely re-ordering of merchandise and prevents the ordering of excess inventory.

To ensure the accuracy of the amount of inventory reported in the financial statements, a merchandising business should take a **physical inventory** (i.e., count the merchandise). In a perpetual inventory system, the physical inventory is compared to the recorded inventory in order to determine the amount of shrinkage or shortage. If the inventory shrinkage is unusually large, management can investigate further and take any necessary corrective action. Knowing that a physical inventory will be taken also helps prevent employee thefts or misuses of inventory.

Most companies take their physical inventories when their inventory levels are the lowest. For example, most retailers take their physical inventories in late January or early February, which is after the holiday selling season but before restocking for spring.

Inventory Cost Flow Assumptions

Describe three inventory cost flow assumptions and how they impact the income statement and balance sheet.

A major accounting issue arises when identical units of merchandise are acquired at different unit costs during a period. In such cases, when an item is sold, it is necessary to determine its unit cost using a cost flow assumption so that the proper accounting entry can be recorded. There are three common cost flow assumptions used in business. Each of these assumptions is identified with an inventory costing method, as shown below.

Cost Flow Assumption

1. Cost flow is in the order in which the costs were incurred.	2. Cost flow is in the reverse order in which the costs were incurred.	3. Cost flow is an average of the costs.

Inventory Costing Method

First-in, First-out (FIFO)	**Last-in, First-out (LIFO)**	**Average Cost**

To illustrate, assume that three identical units of Item X are purchased during May, as shown at the top of page 310. Assume that one unit is sold on May 30 for $20. If this unit can be identified with a specific purchase, the *specific identification method* can be used to determine the cost of the unit sold. For example, if the unit sold was purchased on May 18, the cost assigned to the unit is $13 and the gross profit is $7 ($20 − $13). If, however, the unit sold was purchased on May 10, the cost assigned to the unit is $9 and the gross profit is $11 ($20 − $9).

	Item X	Units	Cost
May 10	Purchase	1	$ 9
18	Purchase	1	13
24	Purchase	1	14
Total		3	$36
Average cost per unit			$12

The specific identification method is normally used by automobile dealerships, jewelry stores, and art galleries.

The specific identification method is not practical unless each unit can be identified accurately. An automobile dealer, for example, may be able to use this method, since each automobile has a unique serial number. For many businesses, however, identical units cannot be separately identified, and a cost flow must be assumed. That is, which units have been sold and which units are still in inventory must be assumed using the first-in, first-out; last-in, first-out; or average cost method.

When the **first-in, first-out (FIFO) method** is used, the ending inventory is made up of the most recent costs. When the **last-in, first-out (LIFO) method** is used, the ending inventory is made up of the earliest costs. When the **average cost method** is used, the cost of the units in inventory is an average of the purchase costs.

To illustrate, we use the preceding example to prepare the income statement for May and the balance sheet as of May 31 for each of the cost flow methods, again assuming that one unit is sold. These financial statements are shown in Exhibit 1.

EXHIBIT 1 | Effect of Inventory Costing Methods on Financial Statements

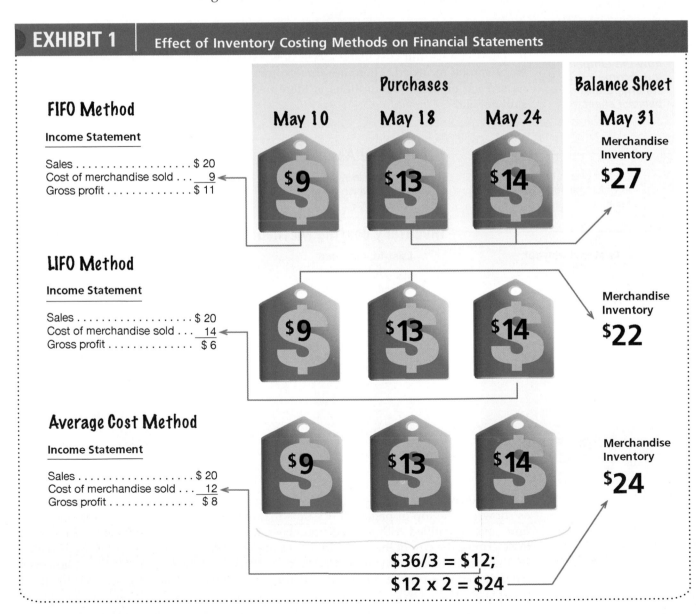

As you can see, the selection of an inventory costing method can have a significant impact on the financial statements. For this reason, the selection has important implications for managers and others in analyzing and interpreting the financial statements. The chart in Exhibit 2 shows the frequency with which FIFO, LIFO, and the average methods are used in practice.

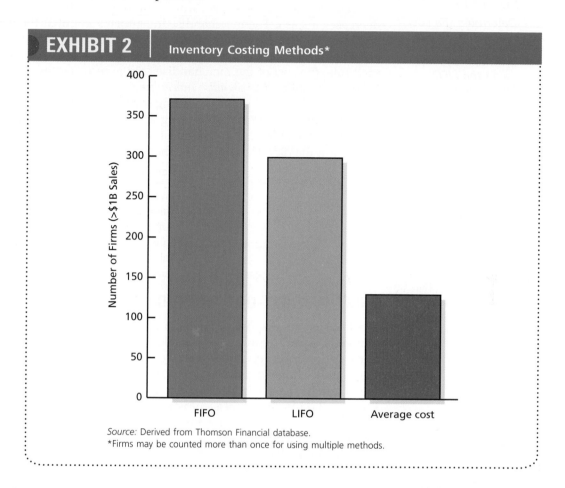

EXHIBIT 2 | Inventory Costing Methods*

Source: Derived from Thomson Financial database.
*Firms may be counted more than once for using multiple methods.

Example Exercise 7-1

objective 2

Three identical units of Item QBM are purchased during February, as shown below.

	Item QBM	Units	Cost
Feb. 8	Purchase	1	$ 45
15	Purchase	1	48
26	Purchase	1	51
Total		3	$144
Average cost per unit			$ 48 ($144/3 units)

Assume that one unit is sold on February 27 for $70.

Determine the gross profit for February and ending inventory on February 28 using the (a) first-in, first-out (FIFO); (b) last-in, first-out (LIFO); and (c) average cost methods.

Follow My Example 7-1

		Gross Profit	Ending Inventory
a.	First-in, first-out (FIFO)	$25 ($70 − $45)	$99 ($48 + $51)
b.	Last-in, first-out (LIFO)	$19 ($70 − $51)	$93 ($45 + $48)
c.	Average cost	$22 ($70 − $48)	$96 ($48 × 2)

For Practice: PE 7-1A, PE 7-1B

Inventory Costing Methods Under a Perpetual Inventory System

objective   **3**

Determine the cost of inventory under the perpetual inventory system, using the FIFO, LIFO, and average cost methods.

In a perpetual inventory system, as we discussed in Chapter 6, all merchandise increases and decreases are recorded in a manner similar to recording increases and decreases in cash. The merchandise inventory account at the beginning of an accounting period indicates the merchandise in stock on that date. Purchases are recorded by debiting *Merchandise Inventory* and crediting *Cash* or *Accounts Payable*. On the date of each sale, the cost of the merchandise sold is recorded by debiting *Cost of Merchandise Sold* and crediting *Merchandise Inventory*.

As we illustrated in the preceding section, when identical units of an item are purchased at different unit costs during a period, a cost flow must be assumed. In such cases, the FIFO, LIFO, or average cost method is used. We illustrate each of these methods, using the data for Item 127B, shown below.

Item 127B		Units	Cost
Jan. 1	Inventory	100	$20
4	Sale	70	
10	Purchase	80	21
22	Sale	40	
28	Sale	20	
30	Purchase	100	22

FIRST-IN, FIRST-OUT METHOD

Most businesses dispose of goods in the order in which the goods are purchased. This would be especially true of perishables and goods whose styles or models often change. For example, grocery stores shelve their milk products by expiration dates. Likewise, men's and women's clothing stores display clothes by season. At the end of a season, they often have sales to clear their stores of off-season or out-of-style clothing. Thus, the FIFO method is often consistent with the *physical flow* or movement of merchandise. To the extent that this is the case, the FIFO method provides results that are about the same as those obtained by identifying the specific costs of each item sold and in inventory.

When the FIFO method of costing inventory is used, costs are included in the cost of merchandise sold in the order in which they were incurred. To illustrate, Exhibit 3

EXHIBIT 3

Entries and Perpetual Inventory Account (FIFO)

Jan. 4	Accounts Receivable	2,100	
	Sales		2,100
4	Cost of Merchandise Sold	1,400	
	Merchandise Inventory		1,400

10	Merchandise Inventory	1,680	
	Accounts Payable		1,680

22	Accounts Receivable	1,200	
	Sales		1,200
22	Cost of Merchandise Sold	810	
	Merchandise Inventory		810

28	Accounts Receivable	600	
	Sales		600
28	Cost of Merchandise Sold	420	
	Merchandise Inventory		420

30	Merchandise Inventory	2,200	
	Accounts Payable		2,200

Item 127B

	Purchases			Cost of Merchandise Sold			Inventory		
Date	Quantity	Unit Cost	Total Cost	Quantity	Unit Cost	Total Cost	Quantity	Unit Cost	Total Cost
Jan. 1							100	20	2,000
4				70	20	1,400	30	20	600
10	80	21	1,680				30	20	600
							80	21	1,680
22				30	20	600			
				10	21	210	70	21	1,470
28				20	21	420	50	21	1,050
30	100	22	2,200				50	21	1,050
							100	22	2,200
31	Balances					2,630			3,250

Cost of merchandise sold

January 31, inventory

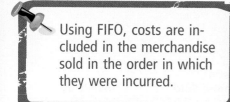

Using FIFO, costs are included in the merchandise sold in the order in which they were incurred.

shows the journal entries for purchases and sales and the inventory subsidiary ledger account for Item 127B. The number of units in inventory after each transaction, together with total costs and unit costs, are shown in the account. We assume that the units are sold on account for $30 each.

You should note that after the 70 units were sold on January 4, there was an inventory of 30 units at $20 each. The 80 units purchased on January 10 were acquired at a unit cost of $21, instead of $20. Therefore, the inventory after the January 10 purchase is reported on two lines, 30 units at $20 each and 80 units at $21 each. Next, note that the $810 cost of the 40 units sold on January 22 is made up of the remaining 30 units at $20 each and 10 unit at $21. At this point, 70 units are in inventory at a cost of $21 per unit. The remainder of the illustration is explained in a similar manner.

Example Exercise 7-2

objective 3

Beginning inventory, purchases, and sales for Item ER27 are as follows:

Nov.	1	Inventory	40 units at $5
	5	Sale	32 units
	11	Purchase	60 units at $7
	21	Sale	45 units

Assuming a perpetual inventory system and using the first-in, first-out (FIFO) method, determine (a) the cost of merchandise sold on November 21 and (b) the inventory on November 30.

Follow My Example 7-2

a. Cost of merchandise sold (November 21):

8 units at $5	$ 40
37 units at $7	259
45 units	$299

b. Inventory, November 30:

$161 = (23 units × $7)

For Practice: PE 7-2A, PE 7-2B

LAST-IN, FIRST-OUT METHOD

When the LIFO method is used in a perpetual inventory system, the cost of the units sold is the cost of the most recent purchases. To illustrate, Exhibit 4 shows the journal entries for purchases and sales and the subsidiary ledger account for Item 127B, prepared on a LIFO basis.

Using LIFO, the cost of units sold is the cost of the most recent purchases.

If you compare the ledger accounts for the FIFO perpetual system and the LIFO perpetual system, you should discover that the accounts are the same through the January 10 purchase. Using LIFO, however, the cost of the 40 units sold on January 22 is the cost of the units from the January 10 purchase ($21 per unit). The cost of the 70 units in inventory after the sale on January 22 is the cost of the 30 units remaining from the beginning inventory and the cost of the 40 units remaining from the January 10 purchase. The remainder of the LIFO illustration is explained in a similar manner.

When the LIFO method is used, the inventory ledger is sometimes maintained in units only. The units are converted to dollars when the financial statements are prepared at the end of the period.

The use of the LIFO method was originally limited to rare situations in which the units sold were taken from the most recently acquired goods. For tax reasons, which we will discuss later, its use has greatly increased during the past few decades. LIFO is now often used even when it does not represent the physical flow of goods.

EXHIBIT 4   Entries and Perpetual Inventory Account (LIFO)

Jan. 4	Accounts Receivable	2,100	
	Sales		2,100
4	Cost of Merchandise Sold	1,400	
	Merchandise Inventory		1,400

| 10 | Merchandise Inventory | 1,680 | |
| | Accounts Payable | | 1,680 |

22	Accounts Receivable	1,200	
	Sales		1,200
22	Cost of Merchandise Sold	840	
	Merchandise Inventory		840

28	Accounts Receivable	600	
	Sales		600
28	Cost of Merchandise Sold	420	
	Merchandise Inventory		420

| 30 | Merchandise Inventory | 2,200 | |
| | Accounts Payable | | 2,200 |

Item 127B

		Purchases			Cost of Merchandise Sold			Inventory		
Date	Quantity	Unit Cost	Total Cost	Quantity	Unit Cost	Total Cost	Quantity	Unit Cost	Total Cost
Jan. 1							100	20	2,000
4				70	20	1,400	30	20	600
10	80	21	1,680				30	20	600
							80	21	1,680
22				40	21	840	30	20	600
							40	21	840
28				20	21	420	30	20	600
							20	21	420
30	100	22	2,200				30	20	600
							20	21	420
							100	22	2,200
31	Balances					2,660			3,220

↑ Cost of merchandise sold   ↑ January 31, inventory

Example Exercise 7-3   objective ③

Beginning inventory, purchases, and sales for Item ER27 are as follows:

Nov. 1	Inventory	40 units at $5
5	Sale	32 units
11	Purchase	60 units at $7
21	Sale	45 units

Assuming a perpetual inventory system and using the last-in, first-out (LIFO) method, determine (a) the cost of the merchandise sold on November 21 and (b) the inventory on November 30.

Follow My Example 7-3

a. Cost of merchandise sold (November 21):

$315 = (45 units × $7)

b. Inventory, November 30:

8 units at $5	$ 40
15 units at $7	105
23 units	$145

For Practice: PE 7-3A, PE 7-3B

The FIFO, LIFO, and average cost flow assumptions also apply to other areas of business. For example, individuals and businesses often purchase marketable securities at different costs per share. When such investments are sold, the investor must either specifically identify which shares are sold or use the FIFO cost flow assumption.

AVERAGE COST METHOD

When the average cost method is used in a perpetual inventory system, an average unit cost for each type of item is computed each time a purchase is made. This unit cost is then used to determine the cost of each sale until another purchase is made and a new average is computed. This averaging technique is called a *moving average*. Since the average cost method is rarely used in a perpetual inventory system, we do not illustrate it in this chapter.

COMPUTERIZED PERPETUAL INVENTORY SYSTEMS

The records for a perpetual inventory system may be maintained manually. However, such a system is costly and time consuming for businesses with a large number of inventory items with many purchase and sales transactions. In most cases, the record keeping for perpetual inventory systems is computerized.

An example of using computers in maintaining perpetual inventory records for retail stores follows.

1. The relevant details for each inventory item, such as a description, quantity, and unit size, are stored in an inventory record. The individual inventory records make up the computerized inventory file, the total of which agrees with the balance of the inventory ledger account.
2. Each time an item is purchased or returned by a customer, the inventory data are entered into the computer's inventory records and files.
3. Each time an item is sold, a salesclerk scans the item's bar code with an optical scanner. The scanner reads the magnetic code and rings up the sale on the cash register. The inventory records and files are then updated for the cost of goods sold.
4. After a physical inventory is taken, the inventory count data are entered into the computer. These data are compared with the current balances, and a listing of the overages and shortages is printed. The inventory balances are then adjusted to the quantities determined by the physical count.

Such systems can be extended to aid managers in controlling and managing inventory quantities. For example, items that are selling fast can be reordered before the stock is depleted. Past sales patterns can be analyzed to determine when to mark down merchandise for sales and when to restock seasonal merchandise. In addition, such systems can provide managers with data for developing and fine-tuning their marketing strategies. For example, such data can be used to evaluate the effectiveness of advertising campaigns and sales promotions.

REAL WORLD

Wal-Mart, Target, and other retailers use bar code scanners as part of their perpetual inventory systems.

Inventory Costing Methods Under a Periodic Inventory System

objective 4

Determine the cost of inventory under the periodic inventory system, using the FIFO, LIFO, and average cost methods.

When the periodic inventory system is used, only revenue is recorded each time a sale is made. No entry is made at the time of the sale to record the cost of the merchandise sold. At the end of the accounting period, a physical inventory is taken to determine the cost of the inventory and the cost of the merchandise sold.[2]

Like the perpetual inventory system, a cost flow assumption must be made when identical units are acquired at different unit costs during a period. In such cases, the FIFO, LIFO, or average cost method is used.

FIRST-IN, FIRST-OUT METHOD

To illustrate the use of the FIFO method in a periodic inventory system, we use the same data for Item 127B as in the perpetual inventory example. The beginning inventory entry and purchases of Item 127B in January are as follows:

Jan. 1	Inventory:	100 units at	$20	$2,000
10	Purchase:	80 units at	21	1,680
30	Purchase:	100 units at	22	2,200
Available for sale during month		280		$5,880

---

2 Determining the cost of merchandise sold using the periodic system was illustrated in Chapter 6.

The physical count on January 31 shows that 150 units are on hand. Using the FIFO method, the cost of the merchandise on hand at the end of the period is made up of the most recent costs. The cost of the 150 units in ending inventory on January 31 is determined as follows:

Most recent costs, January 30 purchase	100 units at	$22	$2,200
Next most recent costs, January 10 purchase	50 units at	$21	1,050
Inventory, January 31	150 units		$3,250

Deducting the cost of the January 31 inventory of $3,250 from the cost of merchandise available for sale of $5,880 yields the cost of merchandise sold of $2,630, as shown below.

Beginning inventory, January 1	$2,000
Purchases ($1,680 + $2,200)	3,880
Cost of merchandise available for sale in January	$5,880
Ending inventory, January 31	3,250
Cost of merchandise sold	$2,630

The $3,250 cost of the ending merchandise inventory on January 31 is made up of the most recent costs. The $2,630 cost of merchandise sold is made up of the beginning inventory and the earliest costs. Exhibit 5 shows the relationship of the cost of merchandise sold for January and the ending inventory on January 31.

EXHIBIT 5 | First-In, First-Out Flow of Costs

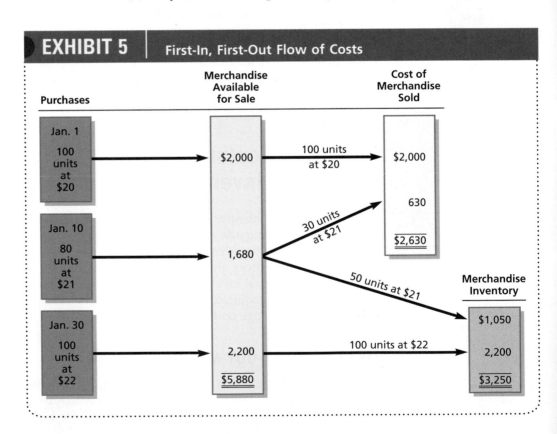

LAST-IN, FIRST-OUT METHOD

When the LIFO method is used, the cost of merchandise on hand at the end of the period is made up of the earliest costs. Based upon the same data as in the FIFO example, the cost of the 150 units in ending inventory on January 31 is determined as follows:

Beginning inventory, January 1	100 units at	$20	$2,000
Next earliest costs, January 10	50 units at	$21	1,050
Inventory, January 31	150 units		$3,050

Deducting the cost of the January 31 inventory of $3,050 from the cost of merchandise available for sale of $5,880 yields the cost of merchandise sold of $2,830, as shown below.

Beginning inventory, January 1	$2,000
Purchases ($1,680 + $2,200)	3,880
Cost of merchandise available for sale in January	$5,880
Ending inventory, January 31	3,050
Cost of merchandise sold	$2,830

The $3,050 cost of the ending merchandise inventory on January 31 is made up of the earliest costs. The $2,830 cost of merchandise sold is made up of the most recent costs. Exhibit 6 shows the relationship of the cost of merchandise sold for January and the ending inventory on January 31.

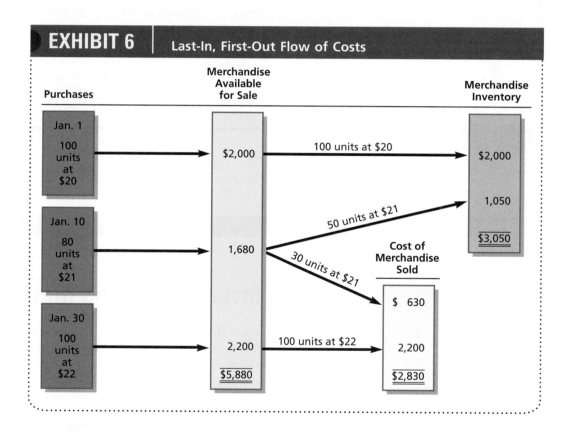

EXHIBIT 6 | Last-In, First-Out Flow of Costs

AVERAGE COST METHOD

The average cost method is sometimes called the *weighted average method*. When this method is used, costs are matched against revenue according to an average of the unit costs of the goods sold. The same weighted average unit costs are used in determining the cost of the merchandise inventory at the end of the period. For businesses in which merchandise sales may be made up of various purchases of identical units, the average cost method approximates the physical flow of goods.

The weighted average unit cost is determined by dividing the total cost of the units of each item available for sale during the period by the related number of units of that item. Using the same cost data as in the FIFO and LIFO examples, the average cost of the 280 units, $21, and the cost of 150 units in ending inventory, are determined as follows:

Average unit cost: $5,880/280 units = $21
Inventory, January 31: 150 units at $21 = $3,150

Deducting the cost of the January 31 inventory of $3,150 from the cost of merchandise available for sale of $5,880 yields the cost of merchandise sold of $2,730, as shown below.

Beginning inventory, January 1	$2,000
Purchases ($1,680 + $2,200)	3,880
Cost of merchandise available for sale in January	$5,880
Ending inventory, January 31	3,150
Cost of merchandise sold	$2,730

Example Exercise 7-4   objective 4

The units of an item available for sale during the year were as follows:

Jan.	1	Inventory	6 units at $50	$ 300
Mar.	20	Purchase	14 units at $55	770
Oct.	30	Purchase	20 units at $62	1,240
		Available for sale	40 units	$2,310

There are 16 units of the item in the physical inventory at December 31. The periodic inventory system is used. Determine the inventory cost using (a) the first-in, first-out (FIFO) method, (b) the last-in, first-out (LIFO) method, and (c) the average cost method.

Follow My Example 7-4

a. First-in, first-out (FIFO) method: $992 = (16 units × $62)
b. Last-in, first-out (LIFO) method: $850 = (6 units × $50) + (10 units × $55)
c. Average cost method: $924 (16 units × $57.75), where average cost = $57.75 = $2,310/40 units

For Practice: PE 7-4A, PE 7-4B

Comparing Inventory Costing Methods

objective 5

Compare and contrast the use of the three inventory costing methods.

As we have illustrated, a different cost flow is assumed for each of the three alternative methods of costing inventories. You should note that if the cost of units had remained stable, all three methods would have yielded the same results. Since prices do change, however, the three methods will normally yield different amounts for (1) the cost of the merchandise sold for the period, (2) the gross profit (and net income) for the period, and (3) the ending inventory. Using the preceding examples for the periodic inventory system and sales of $3,900 (130 units × $30), the partial income statements, shown on page 319, indicate the effects of each method when prices are rising.[3]

As shown in the partial income statements, the FIFO method yielded the lowest amount for the cost of merchandise sold and the highest amount for gross profit (and net income). It also yielded the highest amount for the ending inventory. On the other hand, the LIFO method yielded the highest amount for the cost of merchandise sold, the lowest amount for gross profit (and net income), and the lowest amount for ending inventory. The average cost method yielded results that were between those of FIFO and LIFO.

---

3 Similar results would also occur when comparing inventory costing methods under a perpetual inventory system.

Partial Income Statements

	First-In, First-Out		Average Cost		Last-In, First-Out	
Net sales		$3,900		$3,900		$3,900
Cost of merchandise sold:						
Beginning inventory	$2,000		$2,000		$2,000	
Purchases	3,880		3,880		3,880	
Merchandise available for sale	$5,880		$5,880		$5,880	
Less ending inventory	3,250		3,150		3,050	
Cost of merchandise sold		2,630		2,730		2,830
Gross profit		$1,270		$1,170		$1,070

USE OF THE FIRST-IN, FIRST-OUT METHOD

When the FIFO method is used during a period of inflation or rising prices, the earlier unit costs are lower than the more recent unit costs, as shown in the preceding FIFO example. Thus, FIFO will show a larger gross profit. However, the inventory must be replaced at prices higher than indicated by the cost of merchandise sold. In fact, the balance sheet will report the ending merchandise inventory at an amount that is about the same as its current replacement cost. When the rate of inflation reaches double digits, as it did during the 1970s, the larger gross profits that result from the FIFO method are often called *inventory profits* or *illusory profits*. You should note that in a period of deflation or declining prices, the effect is just the opposite.

USE OF THE LAST-IN, FIRST-OUT METHOD

When the LIFO method is used during a period of inflation or rising prices, the results are opposite those of the other two methods. As shown in the preceding example, the LIFO method will yield a higher amount of cost of merchandise sold, a lower amount of gross profit, and a lower amount of inventory at the end of the period than the other two methods. The reason for these effects is that the cost of the most recently acquired units is about the same as the cost of their replacement. In a period of inflation, the more recent unit costs are higher than the earlier unit costs. Thus, it can be argued that the LIFO method more nearly matches current costs with current revenues.

During periods of rising prices, using LIFO offers an income tax savings. The income tax savings results because LIFO reports the lowest amount of net income of the three methods. During the double-digit inflationary period of the 1970s, many businesses changed from FIFO to LIFO for the tax savings. However, the ending inventory on the balance sheet may be quite different from its current replacement cost. In such cases, the financial statements normally include a note that states the estimated difference between the LIFO inventory and the inventory if FIFO had been used. Again, you should note that in a period of deflation or falling price levels, the effects are just the opposite.

USE OF THE AVERAGE COST METHOD

As you might have already reasoned, the average cost method of inventory costing is, in a sense, a compromise between FIFO and LIFO. The effect of price trends is averaged in determining the cost of merchandise sold and the ending inventory. For a series of purchases, the average cost will be the same, regardless of the direction of price trends. For example, a complete reversal of the sequence of unit costs presented in the preceding illustration would not affect the reported cost of merchandise sold, gross profit, or ending inventory.

Integrity, Objectivity, and Ethics in Business

WHERE'S THE BONUS?

Managers are often given bonuses based on reported earnings numbers. This can create a conflict. LIFO can improve the value of the company through lower taxes. However, LIFO also produces a lower earnings number and, therefore, lower management bonuses. Ethically, managers should select accounting procedures that will maximize the value of the firm, rather than their own compensation. Compensation specialists can help avoid this ethical dilemma by adjusting the bonus plan for the accounting procedure differences.

Reporting Merchandise Inventory in the Financial Statements

objective **6**

Describe and illustrate the reporting of merchandise inventory in the financial statements.

Dell Inc. recorded over $39.3 million of charges (expenses) in writing down its inventory of notebook computers. The remaining inventories of computers were then sold at significantly reduced prices.

As we indicated earlier, cost is the primary basis for valuing inventories. In some cases, however, inventory is valued at other than cost. Two such cases arise when (1) the cost of replacing items in inventory is below the recorded cost and (2) the inventory is not salable at normal sales prices. This latter case may be due to imperfections, shop wear, style changes, or other causes.

VALUATION AT LOWER OF COST OR MARKET

If the cost of replacing an item in inventory is lower than the original purchase cost, the **lower-of-cost-or-market (LCM) method** is used to value the inventory. *Market*, as used in *lower of cost or market*, is the cost to replace the merchandise on the inventory date. This market value is based on quantities normally purchased from the usual source of supply. In businesses where inflation is the norm, market prices rarely decline. In businesses where technology changes rapidly (e.g., microcomputers and televisions), market declines are common. The primary advantage of the lower-of-cost-or-market method is that gross profit (and net income) is reduced in the period in which the market decline occurred.

In applying the lower-of-cost-or-market method, the cost and replacement cost can be determined in one of three ways. Cost and replacement cost can be determined for (1) each item in the inventory, (2) major classes or categories of inventory, or (3) the inventory as a whole. In practice, the cost and replacement cost of each item are usually determined.

To illustrate, assume that there are 400 identical units of Item A in inventory, acquired at a unit cost of $10.25 each. If at the inventory date the item would cost $10.50 to replace, the cost price of $10.25 would be multiplied by 400 to determine the inventory value. On the other hand, if the item could be replaced at $9.50 a unit, the replacement cost of $9.50 would be used for valuation purposes.

Exhibit 7 illustrates a method of organizing inventory data and applying the lower-of-cost-or-market method to each inventory item. The amount of the market decline, $450 ($15,520 − $15,070), may be reported as a separate item on the income statement

EXHIBIT 7

Determining Inventory at Lower of Cost or Market

	A	B	C	D	E	F	G	
			Unit	Unit		Total		
		Inventory	Cost	Market			Lower	
	Commodity	Quantity	Price	Price	Cost	Market	of C or M	
1	A	400	$10.25	$ 9.50	$ 4,100	$ 3,800	$ 3,800	1
2	B	120	22.50	24.10	2,700	2,892	2,700	2
3	C	600	8.00	7.75	4,800	4,650	4,650	3
4	D	280	14.00	14.75	3,920	4,130	3,920	4
5	Total				$15,520	$15,472	$15,070	5

or included in the cost of merchandise sold. Regardless, net income will be reduced by the amount of the market decline.

Example Exercise 7-5

objective 6

On the basis of the following data, determine the value of the inventory at the lower of cost or market. Apply lower of cost or market to each inventory item as shown in Exhibit 7.

Commodity	Inventory Quantity	Unit Cost Price	Unit Market Price
C17Y	10	$ 39	$40
B563	7	110	98

Follow My Example 7-5

	A	B	C	D	E	F	G	
			Unit Cost	Unit Market		Total		
	Commodity	Inventory Quantity	Price	Price	Cost	Market	Lower of C or M	
1	C17Y	10	$ 39	$ 40	$ 390	$ 400	$ 390	1
2	B563	7	110	98	770	686	686	2
3	Total				$1,160	$1,086	$1,076	3

For Practice: PE 7-5A, PE 7-5B

VALUATION AT NET REALIZABLE VALUE

Out-of-date merchandise is a major problem for many types of retailers. For example, you may have noticed the shelf-life dates of grocery products, such as milk, eggs, canned goods, and meat. Grocery stores often mark down the prices of products nearing the end of their shelf life to avoid having to dispose of the products as waste.

As you would expect, merchandise that is out of date, spoiled, or damaged or that can be sold only at prices below cost should be written down. Such merchandise should be valued at net realizable value. **Net realizable value** is the estimated selling price less any direct cost of disposal, such as sales commissions. For example, assume that damaged merchandise costing $1,000 can be sold for only $800, and direct selling expenses are estimated to be $150. This inventory should be valued at $650 ($800 − $150), which is its net realizable value.

For example, Digital Theater Systems Inc. provides digital entertainment technologies, products, and services to the motion picture, consumer electronics, and professional audio industries. In the notes to its recent financial statements, Digital Theater reported the following write-downs of its monochrome projector inventory:

Inventories are stated at the lower of cost or market. Cost is determined using the first-in, first-out method. The Company evaluates its ending inventories for estimated excess quantities and obsolescence. The Company's evaluation includes the analysis of future sales demand by product, within specific time horizons. Inventories in excess of projected future demand are written down to net realizable value. In addition, the Company assesses the impact of changing technology on inventory balances and writes down inventories that are considered obsolete. The Company recorded an inventory write-down of $3,871 (thousands) related to its monochrome projector inventory during the year ended December 31, 2004 due to declines in future demand and technological obsolescence.

MERCHANDISE INVENTORY ON THE BALANCE SHEET

General Motors Corporation uses the last-in, first-out (LIFO) method to account for all U.S. inventories other than those of Saturn Corporation. The cost of non-U.S., Saturn inventories is determined by using either first-in, first-out (FIFO) or average cost.

Merchandise inventory is usually presented in the Current Assets section of the balance sheet, following receivables. Both the method of determining the cost of the inventory (FIFO, LIFO, or average) and the method of valuing the inventory (cost or the lower of cost or market) should be shown. It is not unusual for large businesses with varied activities to use different costing methods for different segments of their inventories.

The details may be disclosed in parentheses on the balance sheet or in a note to the financial statements. Exhibit 8 shows how parentheses may be used.

A company may change its inventory costing methods for a valid reason. In such cases, the effect of the change and the reason for the change should be disclosed in the financial statements for the period in which the change occurred.

EXHIBIT 8   Merchandise Inventory on the Balance Sheet

Metro Arts
Balance Sheet
December 31, 2008

Assets			
Current assets:			
Cash			$ 19 4 0 0 00
Accounts receivable	$80 0 0 0 00		
Less allowance for doubtful accounts	3 0 0 0 00	77 0 0 0 00	
Merchandise inventory—at lower of cost (first-in,			
first-out method) or market		216 3 0 0 00	

EFFECT OF INVENTORY ERRORS ON THE FINANCIAL STATEMENTS

Any errors in the merchandise inventory will affect both the balance sheet and the income statement. For example, an error in the physical inventory will misstate the ending inventory, current assets, and total assets on the balance sheet. In addition, an error in inventory will also affect the cost of merchandise sold and gross profit on the income statement.

To illustrate the effect of inventory errors on the financial statements, we use the following partial income statement of SysExpress Company. We will illustrate the effect of inventory errors using the periodic system. This is because it is easier to see the impact of inventory errors on the income statement using the periodic system.[4]

SysExpress Company
Income Statement
For the Year Ended December 31, 2008

Net sales		$980,000
Merchandise inventory, January 1, 2008	$ 55,000	
Purchases	650,000	
Merchandise available for sale	$705,000	
Less merchandise inventory, December 31, 2008	60,000	
Cost of merchandise sold		645,000
Gross profit		$335,000

Assume that in taking the physical inventory on December 31, 2008, SysExpress incorrectly records its physical inventory as $57,500 instead of the correct amount of $60,000. As a result, the merchandise inventory, current assets, and total assets reported on the December 31, 2008, balance sheet would be understated by $2,500 ($60,000 − $57,500). Because the ending physical inventory is understated, the cost of merchandise sold will be overstated by $2,500. Thus, the gross profit and the net income for the year will be understated by $2,500. Since the net income is closed to owner's equity (capital) at the end of the period, the owner's equity on the December 31, 2008, balance sheet will also be understated by $2,500. These effects on SysExpress's financial statements are summarized as follows:

---

4 The effect of inventory errors would be the same under the perpetual inventory system.

	Amount of Misstatement
Balance Sheet:	
Merchandise inventory understated	$(2,500)
Current assets understated	(2,500)
Total assets understated	(2,500)
Owner's equity understated	(2,500)
Income Statement:	
Cost of merchandise sold overstated	$ 2,500
Gross profit understated	(2,500)
Net income understated	(2,500)

Now assume that in the preceding example the physical inventory had been overstated on December 31, 2008, by $2,500. That is, SysExpress erroneously recorded its inventory as $62,500. In this case, the effects on the balance sheet and income statement would be just the opposite of those indicated above.

Inventory errors often arise from shipping terms and inventory held on consignment. As we discussed in Chapter 6, shipping terms determine when the title to merchandise passes. When goods are purchased or sold *FOB shipping point*, title passes to the buyer when the goods are shipped. When the terms are *FOB destination*, title passes to the buyer when the goods are delivered.

To illustrate inventory errors arising from shipping terms, assume that SysExpress orders $8,300 of merchandise FOB shipping point on December 27. Assume also that the supplier ships the merchandise on December 30. When SysExpress counts its physical inventory on December 31, the merchandise is still in transit. In such cases, it would be easy for SysExpress to overlook the inventory in transit and not include it in the December 31 physical inventory. Likewise, merchandise *sold* by SysExpress FOB destination is still SysExpress's inventory even if it is still in transit to the buyer on December 31.

Inventory errors also arise frequently from consigned inventory. Manufacturers sometimes ship merchandise to retailers who act as the manufacturer's agent when selling the merchandise. The manufacturer, called the *consignor*, retains title until the goods are sold. Such merchandise is said to be shipped on consignment to the retailer, called the *consignee*. The unsold merchandise is a part of the manufacturer's (consignor's) inventory, even though the merchandise is in the hands of the retailer (consignee). In taking its year-end physical inventory, the retailer (consignee) must be careful to not include any consigned inventory on hand as part of its physical inventory. Likewise, the manufacturer (consignor) must be careful to include consigned inventory in its physical inventory even though the inventory is not on hand.

Example Exercise 7-6

objective **6**

Zula Repair Shop incorrectly counted its December 31, 2008, inventory as $250,000 instead of the correct amount of $220,000. Indicate the effect of the misstatement on Zula's December 31, 2008, balance sheet and income statement for the year ended December 31, 2008.

Follow My Example 7-6

	Amount of Misstatement Overstatement (Understatement)
Balance Sheet:	
Merchandise inventory overstated	$ 30,000
Current assets overstated	30,000
Total assets overstated	30,000
Owner's equity overstated	30,000
Income Statement:	
Cost of merchandise sold understated	$(30,000)
Gross profit overstated	30,000
Net income overstated	30,000

For Practice: PE 7-6A, PE 7-6B

Estimating Inventory Cost

objective **7**

Estimate the cost of inventory, using the retail method and the gross profit method.

It may be necessary for a business to know the amount of inventory when perpetual inventory records are not maintained and it is impractical to take a physical inventory. For example, a business that uses a periodic inventory system may need monthly income statements, but taking a physical inventory each month may be too costly. Moreover, when a disaster such as a fire has destroyed the inventory, the amount of the loss must be determined. In this case, taking a physical inventory is impossible, and even if perpetual inventory records have been kept, the accounting records may also have been destroyed. In such cases, the inventory cost can be estimated by using (1) the retail method or (2) the gross profit method.

RETAIL METHOD OF INVENTORY COSTING

The **retail inventory method** of estimating inventory cost is based on the relationship of the cost of merchandise available for sale to the retail price of the same merchandise. To use this method, the retail prices of all merchandise are maintained and totaled. Next, the inventory at retail is determined by deducting sales for the period from the retail price of the goods that were available for sale during the period. The estimated inventory cost is then computed by multiplying the inventory at retail by the ratio of cost to selling (retail) price for the merchandise available for sale, as illustrated in Exhibit 9.

EXHIBIT 9

Determining Inventory by the Retail Method

	A	B	C	
		Cost	**Retail**	
1	Merchandise inventory, January 1	$19,400	$ 36,000	1
2	Purchases in January (net)	42,600	64,000	2
3	Merchandise available for sale	$62,000	$100,000	3
4	Ratio of cost to retail price: $\frac{\$62,000}{\$100,000} = 62\%$			4
5	Sales for January (net)		70,000	5
6	Merchandise inventory, January 31, at retail		$ 30,000	6
7	Merchandise inventory, January 31, at estimated cost			7
8	($30,000 × 62%)		$ 18,600	8

When estimating the percent of cost to selling price, we assume that the mix of the items in the ending inventory is the same as the entire stock of merchandise available for sale. In Exhibit 9, for example, it is unlikely that the retail price of every item was made up of exactly 62% cost and 38% gross profit. We assume, however, that the weighted average of the cost percentages of the merchandise in the inventory ($30,000) is the same as in the merchandise available for sale ($100,000).

When the inventory is made up of different classes of merchandise with very different gross profit rates, the cost percentages and the inventory should be developed for each class of inventory.

One of the major advantages of the retail method is that it provides inventory figures for preparing monthly or quarterly statements when the periodic system is used. Department stores and similar merchandisers like to determine gross profit and operating income each month but may take a physical inventory only once or twice a year. In addition, comparing the estimated ending inventory with the physical ending inventory, both at retail prices, will help identify inventory shortages resulting from shoplifting and other causes. Management can then take appropriate actions.

The retail method may also be used as an aid in taking a physical inventory. In this case, the items counted are recorded on the inventory sheets at their retail (selling) prices instead of their cost prices. The physical inventory at selling price is then converted to cost by applying the ratio of cost to selling (retail) price for the merchandise available for sale.

To illustrate, assume that the data in Exhibit 9 are for an entire fiscal year rather than for only January. If the physical inventory taken at the end of the year totaled $29,000, priced at retail, this amount rather than the $30,000 would be converted to cost. Thus, the inventory at cost would be $17,980 ($29,000 × 62%) instead of $18,600 ($30,000 × 62%). The $17,980 would be used for the year-end financial statements and for income tax purposes.

Example Exercise 7-7

objective 7

A business using the retail method of inventory costing determines that merchandise inventory at retail is $900,000. If the ratio of cost to retail price is 70%, what is the amount of inventory to be reported on the financial statements?

Follow My Example 7-7

$630,000 ($900,000 × 70%)

For Practice: PE 7-7A, PE 7-7B

GROSS PROFIT METHOD OF ESTIMATING INVENTORIES

The **gross profit method** uses the estimated gross profit for the period to estimate the inventory at the end of the period. The gross profit is usually estimated from the actual rate for the preceding year, adjusted for any changes made in the cost and sales prices during the current period. By using the gross profit rate, the dollar amount of sales for a period can be divided into its two components: (1) gross profit and (2) cost of merchandise sold. The latter amount may then be deducted from the cost of merchandise available for sale to yield the estimated cost of the inventory.

Exhibit 10 illustrates the gross profit method for estimating a company's inventory on January 31. In this example, the inventory on January 1 is assumed to be $57,000, the net purchases during the month are $180,000, and the net sales during the month are $250,000. In addition, the historical gross profit was 30% of net sales.

EXHIBIT 10

Estimating Inventory by Gross Profit Method

	A	B	C	
		Cost	Retail	
1	Merchandise inventory, January 1		$ 57,000	1
2	Purchases in January (net)		180,000	2
3	Merchandise available for sale		$237,000	3
4	Sales for January (net)	$250,000		4
5	Less estimated gross profit ($250,000 × 30%)	75,000		5
6	Estimated cost of merchandise sold		175,000	6
7	Estimated merchandise inventory, January 31		$ 62,000	7

The gross profit method is useful for estimating inventories for monthly or quarterly financial statements in a periodic inventory system. It is also useful in estimating the cost of merchandise destroyed by fire or other disasters.

Example Exercise 7-8

objective 7

Based upon the following data, estimate the cost of ending merchandise inventory:

Sales (net)	$1,250,000
Estimated gross profit rate	40%
Beginning merchandise inventory	$100,000
Purchases (net)	800,000
Merchandise available for sale	$900,000

Follow My Example 7-8

Merchandise available for sale	$900,000
Less cost of merchandise sold [$1,250,000 × (100% − 40%)]	750,000
Estimated ending merchandise inventory	$150,000

For Practice: PE 7-8A, PE 7-8B

Financial Analysis and Interpretation

A merchandising business should keep enough inventory on hand to meet the needs of its customers. A failure to do so may result in lost sales. At the same time, too much inventory reduces solvency by tying up funds that could be better used to expand or improve operations. In addition, excess inventory increases expenses such as storage, insurance, and property taxes. Finally, excess inventory increases the risk of losses due to price declines, damage, or changes in customers' buying patterns.

As with many types of financial analyses, it is possible to use more than one measure to analyze the efficiency and effectiveness by which a business manages its inventory. Two such measures are the inventory turnover and the number of days' sales in inventory.

Inventory turnover measures the relationship between the volume of goods (merchandise) sold and the amount of inventory carried during the period. It is computed as follows:

$$\text{Inventory Turnover} = \frac{\text{Cost of Merchandise Sold}}{\text{Average Inventory}}$$

To illustrate, the following data have been taken from recent annual reports for SUPERVALU Inc. and Zale Corporation:

	SUPERVALU	Zale
Cost of merchandise sold	$16,681,472,000	$1,157,226,000
Inventories:		
Beginning of year	$1,078,343,000	$826,824,000
End of year	$1,032,034,000	$853,580,000
Average	$1,055,188,500	$840,202,000
Inventory turnover	15.8	1.4

The inventory turnover is 15.8 for SUPERVALU and 1.4 for Zale. Generally, the larger the inventory turnover, the more efficient and effective the management of inventory. However, differences in companies and industries may be too great to allow specific statements as to what is a good inventory turnover. For example, SUPERVALU is a leading food distributor and the tenth largest food retailer in the United States. Because SUPERVALU's inventory is perishable, we would expect it to have a high inventory turnover. In contrast, Zale Corporation is the largest speciality retailer of fine jewelry in the United States. Thus, we would expect Zale to have a lower inventory turnover than SUPERVALU.

The **number of days' sales in inventory** is a rough measure of the length of time it takes to acquire, sell, and replace the inventory. It is computed as follows:

$$\text{Number of Days' Sales in Inventory} = \frac{\text{Average Inventory}}{\text{Average Daily Cost of Merchandise Sold}}$$

The average daily cost of merchandise sold is determined by dividing the cost of merchandise sold by 365. The number of days' sales in inventory for SUPERVALU and Zale is computed as shown below.

	SUPERVALU	Zale
Average daily cost of merchandise sold:		
$16,681,472,000/365	$45,702,663	
$1,157,226,000/365		$3,170,482
Average inventory	$1,055,188,500	$840,202,000
Number of days' sales in inventory	23.1 days	265.0 days

Generally, the lower the number of days' sales in inventory, the better. As with inventory turnover, we should expect differences among industries, such as those for SUPERVALU and Zale.

Business Connections

REAL WORLD

RAPID INVENTORY AT COSTCO

Costco Wholesale Corporation operates over 300 membership warehouses that offer members low prices on a limited selection of nationally branded and selected private label products. Costco emphasizes generating high sales volumes and rapid inventory turnover. This enables Costco to operate profitably at significantly lower gross margins than traditional wholesalers, discount retailers, and supermarkets. In addition, Costco's rapid turnover provides it the opportunity to conserve on its cash, as described below.

Because of its high sales volume and rapid inventory turnover, Costco generally has the opportunity to receive cash from the sale of a substantial portion of its inventory at mature warehouse operations before it is required to pay all its merchandise vendors, even though Costco takes advantage of early payment terms to obtain payment dis-

counts. As sales in a given warehouse increase and inventory turnover becomes more rapid, a greater percentage of the inventory is financed through payment terms provided by vendors rather than by working capital (cash).

© DON RYAN/ASSOCIATED PRESS

At a Glance

1. Describe the importance of control over inventory.

Key Points	Key Learning Outcomes	Example Exercises	Practice Exercises
Two primary objectives of control over inventory are safeguarding the inventory and properly reporting it in the financial statements. The perpetual inventory system enhances control over inventory. In addition, a physical inventory count should be taken periodically to detect shortages as well as to deter employee thefts.	• Describe controls for safeguarding inventory. • Describe how a perpetual inventory system enhances control over inventory. • Describe why taking a physical inventory enhances control over inventory.		

2. Describe three inventory cost flow assumptions and how they impact the income statement and balance sheet.

Key Points	Key Learning Outcomes	Example Exercises	Practice Exercises
The three common cost flow assumptions used in business are the (1) first-in, first-out method (FIFO); (2) last-in, first-out method (LIFO); and (3) average cost method. The choice of a cost flow assumption directly affects the income statement and balance sheet.	• Describe the FIFO, LIFO, and average cost flow methods. • Describe how choice of a cost flow method affects the income statement and balance sheet.	7-1	7-1A, 7-1B

3. Determine the cost of inventory under the perpetual inventory system, using the FIFO, LIFO, and average cost methods.

Key Points	Key Learning Outcomes	Example Exercises	Practice Exercises
In a perpetual inventory system, the number of units and the cost of each type of merchandise are recorded in a subsidiary inventory ledger, with a separate account for each type of merchandise.	• Determine the cost of inventory and cost of merchandise sold using a perpetual inventory system under the FIFO method.	7-2	7-2A, 7-2B
	• Determine the cost of inventory and cost of merchandise sold using a perpetual inventory system under the LIFO method.	7-3	7-3A, 7-3B

4. Determine the cost of inventory under the periodic inventory system, using the FIFO, LIFO, and average cost methods.

Key Points	Key Learning Outcomes	Example Exercises	Practice Exercises
In a periodic inventory system, a physical inventory is taken to determine the cost of the inventory and the cost of merchandise sold.	• Determine the cost of inventory and cost of merchandise sold using a periodic inventory system under the FIFO method.	7-4	7-4A, 7-4B
	• Determine the cost of inventory and cost of merchandise sold using a periodic inventory system under the LIFO method.	7-4	7-4A, 7-4B
	• Determine the cost of inventory and cost of merchandise sold using a periodic inventory system under the average cost method.	7-4	7-4A, 7-4B

5. Compare and contrast the use of the three inventory costing methods.

Key Points	Key Learning Outcomes	Example Exercises	Practice Exercises
The three inventory costing methods will normally yield different amounts for (1) the ending inventory, (2) the cost of merchandise sold for the period, and (3) the gross profit (and net income) for the period.	• Indicate which inventory cost flow method will yield the highest and lowest ending inventory and net income under periods of increasing prices. • Indicate which inventory cost flow method will yield the highest and lowest ending inventory and net income under periods of decreasing prices.		

6. Describe and illustrate the reporting of merchandise inventory in the financial statements.

Key Points	Key Learning Outcomes	Example Exercises	Practice Exercises
The lower of cost or market is used to value inventory. Inventory that is out of date, spoiled, or damaged is valued at its net realizable value. Merchandise inventory is usually presented in the Current Assets section of the balance sheet, following receivables. The method of determining the cost and valuing the inventory is reported. Errors in reporting inventory based upon the physical inventory will affect the balance sheet and income statement.	• Determine inventory using lower of cost or market. • Illustrate the use of net realizable value for spoiled or damaged inventory. • Prepare the Current Assets section of the balance sheet that includes inventory. • Determine the effect of inventory errors on the balance sheet and income statement.	7-5 7-6	7-5A, 7-5B 7-6A, 7-6B

7. Estimate the cost of inventory, using the retail method and the gross profit method.

Key Points	Key Learning Outcomes	Example Exercises	Practice Exercises
The retail method of estimating inventory determines inventory at retail prices and then converts it to cost using the ratio of cost to selling (retail) price. The gross profit method of estimating inventory deducts gross profit from the sales to determine the cost of merchandise sold. This amount is then deducted from the cost of merchandise available for sale to determine the ending inventory.	• Estimate ending inventory using the retail method. • Estimate ending inventory using the gross profit method.	7-7 7-8	7-7A, 7-7B 7-8A, 7-8B

Key Terms

average cost method (310)
first-in, first-out (FIFO) method
  (310)
gross profit method (325)
inventory turnover (326)

last-in, first-out (LIFO) method
  (310)
lower-of-cost-or-market (LCM)
  method (320)
net realizable value (321)

number of days' sales in
  inventory (326)
physical inventory (309)
retail inventory method (324)

Illustrative Problem

Stewart Co.'s beginning inventory and purchases during the year ended December 31, 2008, were as follows:

		Units	Unit Cost	Total Cost
January 1	Inventory	1,000	$50.00	$ 50,000
March 10	Purchase	1,200	52.50	63,000
June 25	Sold 800 units			
August 30	Purchase	800	55.00	44,000
October 5	Sold 1,500 units			
November 26	Purchase	2,000	56.00	112,000
December 31	Sold 1,000 units			
Total		5,000		$269,000

Instructions

1. Determine the cost of inventory on December 31, 2008, using the perpetual inventory system and each of the following inventory costing methods:
   a. first-in, first-out
   b. last-in, first-out
2. Determine the cost of inventory on December 31, 2008, using the periodic inventory system and each of the following inventory costing methods:
   a. first-in, first-out
   b. last-in, first-out
   c. average cost
3. Assume that during the fiscal year ended December 31, 2008, sales were $290,000 and the estimated gross profit rate was 40%. Estimate the ending inventory at December 31, 2008, using the gross profit method.

Solution

1. a. First-in, first-out method: $95,200 (shown on page 331)
   b. Last-in, first-out method: $91,000 ($35,000 + $56,000) (shown on page 331)
2. a. First-in, first-out method:
      1,700 units at $56 = $95,200
   b. Last-in, first-out method:

1,000 units at $50.00	$50,000
700 units at $52.50	36,750
1,700 units	$86,750

1. a. First-in, first-out method: $95,200

Date	Purchases			Cost of Merchandise Sold			Inventory		
	Quantity	Unit Cost	Total Cost	Quantity	Unit Cost	Total Cost	Quantity	Unit Cost	Total Cost
2008 Jan. 1							1,000	50.00	50,000
Mar. 10	1,200	52.50	63,000				1,000	50.00	50,000
							1,200	52.50	63,000
June 25				800	50.00	40,000	200	50.00	10,000
							1,200	52.50	63,000
Aug. 30	800	55.00	44,000				200	50.00	10,000
							1,200	52.50	63,000
							800	55.00	44,000
Oct. 5				200	50.00	10,000	700	55.00	38,500
				1,200	52.50	63,000			
				100	55.00	5,500			
Nov. 26	2,000	56.00	112,000				700	55.00	38,500
							2,000	56.00	112,000
Dec. 31				700	55.00	38,500	1,700	56.00	95,200
				300	56.00	16,800			
Balances						173,800			95,200

b. Last-in, first-out method: $91,000 ($35,000 + $56,000)

Date	Purchases			Cost of Merchandise Sold			Inventory		
	Quantity	Unit Cost	Total Cost	Quantity	Unit Cost	Total Cost	Quantity	Unit Cost	Total Cost
2008 Jan. 1							1,000	50.00	50,000
Mar. 10	1,200	52.50	63,000				1,000	50.00	50,000
							1,200	52.50	63,000
June 25				800	52.50	42,000	1,000	50.00	50,000
							400	52.50	21,000
Aug. 30	800	55.00	44,000				1,000	50.00	50,000
							400	52.50	21,000
							800	55.00	44,000
Oct. 5				800	55.00	44,000	700	50.00	35,000
				400	52.50	21,000			
				300	50.00	15,000			
Nov. 26	2,000	56.00	112,000				700	50.00	35,000
							2,000	56.00	112,000
Dec. 31				1,000	56.00	56,000	700	50.00	35,000
							1,000	56.00	56,000
Balances						178,000			91,000

c. Average cost method:

Average cost per unit: $269,000/5,000 units = $53.80
Inventory, December 31, 2008: 1,700 units at $53.80 = $91,460

3.

Merchandise inventory, January 1, 2008		$ 50,000
Purchases (net)		219,000
Merchandise available for sale		$269,000
Sales (net)	$290,000	
Less estimated gross profit ($290,000 × 40%)	116,000	
Estimated cost of merchandise sold		174,000
Estimated merchandise inventory, December 31, 2008		$ 95,000

Self-Examination Questions

1. The inventory costing method that is based on the assumption that costs should be charged against revenue in the order in which they were incurred is:
   A. FIFO.
   B. LIFO.
   C. average cost.
   D. perpetual inventory.

2. The following units of a particular item were purchased and sold during the period:

Beginning inventory	40 units at $20
First purchase	50 units at $21
Second purchase	50 units at $22
First sale	110 units
Third purchase	50 units at $23
Second sale	45 units

   What is the cost of the 35 units on hand at the end of the period as determined under the perpetual inventory system by the LIFO costing method?
   A. $715
   B. $705
   C. $700
   D. $805

3. The following units of a particular item were available for sale during the period:

Beginning inventory	40 units at $20
First purchase	50 units at $21
Second purchase	50 units at $22
Third purchase	50 units at $23

   What is the unit cost of the 35 units on hand at the end of the period as determined under the periodic inventory system by the FIFO costing method?
   A. $20   B. $21   C. $22   D. $23

4. If merchandise inventory is being valued at cost and the price level is steadily rising, the method of costing that will yield the highest net income is:
   A. LIFO.
   B. FIFO.
   C. average.
   D. periodic.

5. If the inventory at the end of the year is understated by $7,500, the error will cause an:
   A. understatement of cost of merchandise sold for the year by $7,500.
   B. overstatement of gross profit for the year by $7,500.
   C. overstatement of merchandise inventory for the year by $7,500.
   D. understatement of net income for the year by $7,500.

Eye Openers

1. Before inventory purchases are recorded, the receiving report should be reconciled to what documents?
2. What security measures may be used by retailers to protect merchandise inventory from customer theft?
3. Which inventory system provides the more effective means of controlling inventories (perpetual or periodic)? Why?
4. Why is it important to periodically take a physical inventory if the perpetual system is used?
5. Do the terms *FIFO* and *LIFO* refer to techniques used in determining quantities of the various classes of merchandise on hand? Explain.
6. Does the term *last-in* in the LIFO method mean that the items in the inventory are assumed to be the most recent (last) acquisitions? Explain.
7. If merchandise inventory is being valued at cost and the price level is steadily rising, which of the three methods of costing—FIFO, LIFO, or average cost—will yield (a) the highest inventory cost, (b) the lowest inventory cost, (c) the highest gross profit, and (d) the lowest gross profit?
8. Which of the three methods of inventory costing—FIFO, LIFO, or average cost—will in general yield an inventory cost most nearly approximating current replacement cost?
9. If inventory is being valued at cost and the price level is steadily rising, which of the three methods of costing—FIFO, LIFO, or average cost—will yield the lowest annual income tax expense? Explain.
10. Can a company change its method of costing inventory? Explain.
11. Because of imperfections, an item of merchandise cannot be sold at its normal selling price. How should this item be valued for financial statement purposes?
12. How is the method of determining the cost of the inventory and the method of valuing it disclosed in the financial statements?

13. The inventory at the end of the year was understated by $8,750. (a) Did the error cause an overstatement or an understatement of the gross profit for the year? (b) Which items on the balance sheet at the end of the year were overstated or understated as a result of the error?

14. Fargo Co. sold merchandise to Keepsakes Company on December 31, FOB shipping point. If the merchandise is in transit on December 31, the end of the fiscal year, which company would report it in its financial statements? Explain.

15. A manufacturer shipped merchandise to a retailer on a consignment basis. If the merchandise is unsold at the end of the period, in whose inventory should the merchandise be included?

16. What uses can be made of the estimate of the cost of inventory determined by the gross profit method?

Practice Exercises

PE 7-1A
Cost flow methods, gross profit, and ending inventory

obj. 2

Three identical units of Item T4W are purchased during July, as shown below.

Item T4W		Units	Cost
July 6	Purchase	1	$115
19	Purchase	1	118
24	Purchase	1	121
Total		3	$354
Average cost per unit			$118 ($354/3 units)

Assume that one unit is sold on July 28 for $150.

Determine the gross profit for July and ending inventory on July 31 using the (a) first-in, first-out (FIFO); (b) last-in, first-out (LIFO); and (c) average cost methods.

PE 7-1B
Cost flow methods, gross profit, and ending inventory

obj. 2

Three identical units of Item S77 are purchased during October, as shown below.

Item S77		Units	Cost
Oct. 6	Purchase	1	$ 88
19	Purchase	1	85
24	Purchase	1	82
Total		3	$255
Average cost per unit			$ 85 ($255/3 units)

Assume that one unit is sold on October 26 for $100.

Determine the gross profit for October and ending inventory on October 31 using the (a) first-in, first-out (FIFO); (b) last-in, first-out (LIFO); and (c) average cost methods.

PE 7-2A
Perpetual inventory using FIFO method

obj. 3

Beginning inventory, purchases, and sales for Item SJ68 are as follows:

Aug. 1	Inventory	28 units at $34
8	Sale	15 units
15	Purchase	22 units at $38
30	Sale	20 units

Assuming a perpetual inventory system and using the first-in, first-out (FIFO) method, determine (a) the cost of merchandise sold on August 30 and (b) the inventory on August 31.

PE 7-2B
Perpetual inventory using FIFO method
obj. 3

Beginning inventory, purchases, and sales for Item FC33 are as follows:

Mar.	1	Inventory	23 units at $10
	8	Sale	18 units
	15	Purchase	57 units at $14
	29	Sale	40 units

Assuming a perpetual inventory system and using the first-in, first-out (FIFO) method, determine (a) the cost of merchandise sold on March 29 and (b) the inventory on March 31.

PE 7-3A
Perpetual inventory using LIFO method
obj. 3

Beginning inventory, purchases, and sales for Item SJ68 are as follows:

Aug.	1	Inventory	28 units at $34
	8	Sale	15 units
	15	Purchase	22 units at $38
	30	Sale	20 units

Assuming a perpetual inventory system and using the last-in, first-out (LIFO) method, determine (a) the cost of merchandise sold on August 30 and (b) the inventory on August 31.

PE 7-3B
Perpetual inventory using LIFO method
obj. 3

Beginning inventory, purchases, and sales for Item FC33 are as follows:

Mar.	1	Inventory	23 units at $10
	8	Sale	18 units
	15	Purchase	57 units at $14
	29	Sale	40 units

Assuming a perpetual inventory system and using the last-in, first-out (LIFO) method, determine (a) the cost of merchandise sold on March 29 and (b) the inventory on March 31.

PE 7-4A
Periodic inventory using FIFO, LIFO, average cost methods
obj. 4

The units of an item available for sale during the year were as follows:

Jan.	1	Inventory	12 units at $25	$ 300
Apr.	20	Purchase	28 units at $30	840
Nov.	30	Purchase	40 units at $36	1,440
		Available for sale	80 units	$2,580

There are 20 units of the item in the physical inventory at December 31. The periodic inventory system is used. Determine the inventory cost using (a) the first-in, first-out (FIFO) method; (b) the last-in, first-out (LIFO) method; and (c) the average cost method.

PE 7-4B
Periodic inventory using FIFO, LIFO, average cost methods
obj. 4

The units of an item available for sale during the year were as follows:

Jan.	1	Inventory	18 units at $300	$ 5,400
Apr.	20	Purchase	46 units at $275	12,650
Nov.	30	Purchase	36 units at $250	9,000
		Available for sale	100 units	$27,050

There are 38 units of the item in the physical inventory at December 31. The periodic inventory system is used. Determine the inventory cost using (a) the first-in, first-out (FIFO) method; (b) the last-in, first-out (LIFO) method; and (c) the average cost method.

PE 7-5A
Lower of cost or market
obj. 6

On the basis of the following data, determine the value of the inventory at the lower of cost or market. Apply lower of cost or market to each inventory item as shown in Exhibit 7.

Commodity	Inventory Quantity	Unit Cost Price	Unit Market Price
TRP4	96	$29	$18
V555	200	13	14

PE 7-5B
Lower of cost or market
obj. 6

On the basis of the following data, determine the value of the inventory at the lower of cost or market. Apply lower of cost or market to each inventory item as shown in Exhibit 7.

Commodity	Inventory Quantity	Unit Cost Price	Unit Market Price
E662	215	$30	$28
C11R	741	22	26

PE 7-6A
Effect of inventory errors
obj. 6

During the taking of its physical inventory on December 31, 2008, Genesis Company incorrectly counted its inventory as $126,000 instead of the correct amount of $135,000. Indicate the effect of the misstatement on Genesis's December 31, 2008, balance sheet and income statement for the year ended December 31, 2008.

PE 7-6B
Effect of inventory errors
obj. 6

During the taking of its physical inventory on December 31, 2008, Poindexter Company incorrectly counted its inventory as $769,000 instead of the correct amount of $740,000. Indicate the effect of the misstatement on Poindexter's December 31, 2008, balance sheet and income statement for the year ended December 31, 2008.

PE 7-7A
Retail inventory method
obj. 7

A business using the retail method of inventory costing determines that merchandise inventory at retail is $675,000. If the ratio of cost to retail price is 80%, what is the amount of inventory to be reported on the financial statements?

PE 7-7B
Retail inventory method
obj. 7

A business using the retail method of inventory costing determines that merchandise inventory at retail is $280,000. If the ratio of cost to retail price is 65%, what is the amount of inventory to be reported on the financial statements?

PE 7-8A
Gross profit method
obj. 7

Based upon the following data, estimate the cost of ending merchandise inventory:

Sales (net)	$1,500,000
Estimated gross profit rate	35%
Beginning merchandise inventory	$ 180,000
Purchases (net)	1,200,000
Merchandise available for sale	$1,380,000

PE 7-8B
Gross profit method
obj. 7

Based upon the following data, estimate the cost of ending merchandise inventory:

Sales (net)	$800,000
Estimated gross profit rate	36%
Beginning merchandise inventory	$ 75,000
Purchases (net)	625,000
Merchandise available for sale	$700,000

Exercises

EX 7-1
Control of inventories
obj. 1

Handy Hardware Store currently uses a periodic inventory system. Peggy Yang, the owner, is considering the purchase of a computer system that would make it feasible to switch to a perpetual inventory system.

Peggy is unhappy with the periodic inventory system because it does not provide timely information on inventory levels. Peggy has noticed on several occasions that the store runs out of good-selling items, while too many poor-selling items are on hand.

Peggy is also concerned about lost sales while a physical inventory is being taken. Handy Hardware currently takes a physical inventory twice a year. To minimize distractions, the store is closed on the day inventory is taken. Peggy believes that closing the store is the only way to get an accurate inventory count.

▬▬▶ Will switching to a perpetual inventory system strengthen Handy Hardware's control over inventory items? Will switching to a perpetual inventory system eliminate the need for a physical inventory count? Explain.

EX 7-2
Control of inventories
obj. 1

PacTec Luggage Shop is a small retail establishment located in a large shopping mall. This shop has implemented the following procedures regarding inventory items:

a. Since the display area of the store is limited, only a sample of each piece of luggage is kept on the selling floor. Whenever a customer selects a piece of luggage, the salesclerk gets the appropriate piece from the store's stockroom. Since all salesclerks need access to the stockroom, it is not locked. The stockroom is adjacent to the break room used by all mall employees.
b. Whenever PacTec receives a shipment of new inventory, the items are taken directly to the stockroom. PacTec's accountant uses the vendor's invoice to record the amount of inventory received.
c. Since the shop carries mostly high-quality, designer luggage, all inventory items are tagged with a control device that activates an alarm if a tagged item is removed from the store.

▬▬▶ State whether each of these procedures is appropriate or inappropriate. If it is inappropriate, state why.

EX 7-3
Perpetual inventory using FIFO
objs. 2, 3

✓ *Inventory balance, November 30, $1,302*

Beginning inventory, purchases, and sales data for portable MP3 players are as follows:

Nov.	1	Inventory	70 units at $40
	5	Sale	52 units
	16	Purchase	30 units at $42
	21	Sale	24 units
	24	Sale	8 units
	30	Purchase	14 units at $45

The business maintains a perpetual inventory system, costing by the first-in, first-out method. Determine the cost of the merchandise sold for each sale and the inventory balance after each sale, presenting the data in the form illustrated in Exhibit 3.

EX 7-4
Perpetual inventory using LIFO
objs. 2, 3

✓ *Inventory balance, November 30, $1,270*

Assume that the business in Exercise 7-3 maintains a perpetual inventory system, costing by the last-in, first-out method. Determine the cost of merchandise sold for each sale and the inventory balance after each sale, presenting the data in the form illustrated in Exhibit 4.

EX 7-5
Perpetual inventory using LIFO
objs. 2, 3

✓ *Inventory balance, July 31, $1,764*

Beginning inventory, purchases, and sales data for cell phones for July are as follows:

Inventory		Purchases		Sales	
July 1	100 units at $30	July 3	80 units at $32	July 7	72 units
		21	60 units at $33	13	80 units
				31	32 units

Assuming that the perpetual inventory system is used, costing by the LIFO method, determine the cost of merchandise sold for each sale and the inventory balance after each sale, presenting the data in the form illustrated in Exhibit 4.

EX 7-6
Perpetual inventory using FIFO
objs. 2, 3

✓ *Inventory balance, July 31, $1,848*

Assume that the business in Exercise 7-5 maintains a perpetual inventory system, costing by the first-in, first-out method. Determine the cost of merchandise sold for each sale and the inventory balance after each sale, presenting the data in the form illustrated in Exhibit 3.

EX 7-7
FIFO, LIFO costs under perpetual inventory system
objs. 2, 3
✓ *a. $5,040*

The following units of a particular item were available for sale during the year:

Beginning inventory	100 units at $60
Sale	75 units at $112
First purchase	155 units at $65
Sale	135 units at $112
Second purchase	200 units at $72
Sale	175 units at $112

The firm uses the perpetual inventory system, and there are 70 units of the item on hand at the end of the year. What is the total cost of the ending inventory according to (a) FIFO, (b) LIFO?

EX 7-8
Periodic inventory by three methods
objs. 2, 4
✓ *b. $1,410*

The units of an item available for sale during the year were as follows:

Jan. 1	Inventory	18 units at $40
Feb. 26	Purchase	36 units at $46
June 18	Purchase	42 units at $52
Dec. 29	Purchase	24 units at $55

There are 33 units of the item in the physical inventory at December 31. The periodic inventory system is used. Determine the inventory cost by (a) the first-in, first-out method, (b) the last-in, first-out method, and (c) the average cost method.

EX 7-9
Periodic inventory by three methods; cost of merchandise sold
objs. 2, 4

✓ *a. Inventory, $9,760*

The units of an item available for sale during the year were as follows:

Jan. 1	Inventory	168 units at $60
Apr. 15	Purchase	232 units at $65
Sept. 3	Purchase	80 units at $68
Nov. 23	Purchase	120 units at $70

There are 140 units of the item in the physical inventory at December 31. The periodic inventory system is used. Determine the inventory cost and the cost of merchandise sold by three methods, presenting your answers in the following form:

	Cost	
Inventory Method	**Merchandise Inventory**	**Merchandise Sold**
a. First-in, first-out	$	$
b. Last-in, first-out		
c. Average cost		

EX 7-10
Comparing inventory methods
obj. 5

Assume that a firm separately determined inventory under FIFO and LIFO and then compared the results.

1. In each space below, place the correct sign [less than (<), greater than (>), or equal (=)] for each comparison, assuming periods of rising prices.

a. FIFO inventory	_____	LIFO inventory
b. FIFO cost of goods sold	_____	LIFO cost of goods sold
c. FIFO net income	_____	LIFO net income
d. FIFO income tax	_____	LIFO income tax

2. Why would management prefer to use LIFO over FIFO in periods of rising prices?

EX 7-11

Lower-of-cost-or-market inventory

obj. 6

✓ *LCM: $10,473*

On the basis of the following data, determine the value of the inventory at the lower of cost or market. Assemble the data in the form illustrated in Exhibit 7.

Commodity	Inventory Quantity	Unit Cost Price	Unit Market Price
62CF3	10	$120	$131
41DH2	35	80	75
O3MQ3	10	275	260
23FH6	16	40	28
10KT4	40	90	94

EX 7-12

Merchandise inventory on the balance sheet

obj. 6

Based on the data in Exercise 7-11 and assuming that cost was determined by the FIFO method, show how the merchandise inventory would appear on the balance sheet.

EX 7-13

Effect of errors in physical inventory

obj. 6

Morena White Water Co. sells canoes, kayaks, whitewater rafts, and other boating supplies. During the taking of its physical inventory on December 31, 2008, Morena White Water incorrectly counted its inventory as $279,150 instead of the correct amount of $285,780.

a. State the effect of the error on the December 31, 2008, balance sheet of Morena White Water.
b. State the effect of the error on the income statement of Morena White Water for the year ended December 31, 2008.

EX 7-14

Effect of errors in physical inventory

obj. 6

Megan's Motorcycle Shop sells motorcycles, jet skis, and other related supplies and accessories. During the taking of its physical inventory on December 31, 2008, Megan's Motorcycle Shop incorrectly counted its inventory as $315,200 instead of the correct amount of $300,750.

a. State the effect of the error on the December 31, 2008, balance sheet of Megan's Motorcycle Shop.
b. State the effect of the error on the income statement of Megan's Motorcycle Shop for the year ended December 31, 2008.

EX 7-15

Error in inventory

obj. 6

During 2008, the accountant discovered that the physical inventory at the end of 2007 had been understated by $8,175. Instead of correcting the error, however, the accountant assumed that an $8,175 overstatement of the physical inventory in 2008 would balance out the error.

 Are there any flaws in the accountant's assumption? Explain.

EX 7-16

Retail inventory method

obj. 7

A business using the retail method of inventory costing determines that merchandise inventory at retail is $1,260,000. If the ratio of cost to retail price is 74%, what is the amount of inventory to be reported on the financial statements?

EX 7-17

Retail inventory method

obj. 7

✓ *Inventory, September 30: $173,400*

On the basis of the following data, estimate the cost of the merchandise inventory at September 30 by the retail method:

		Cost	Retail
September 1	Merchandise inventory	$ 220,000	$ 320,000
September 1–30	Purchases (net)	1,718,000	2,530,000
September 1–30	Sales (net)		2,595,000

EX 7-18
Gross profit inventory method

obj. 7

The merchandise inventory was destroyed by fire on August 19. The following data were obtained from the accounting records:

Jan. 1	Merchandise inventory	$ 360,000	
Jan. 1–Aug. 19	Purchases (net)	3,200,000	
	Sales (net)	5,200,000	
	Estimated gross profit rate	36%	

a. Estimate the cost of the merchandise destroyed.
b. Briefly describe the situations in which the gross profit method is useful.

EX 7-19
Inventory turnover

The following data were taken from recent annual reports of Apple Computer, Inc., a manufacturer of personal computers and related products, and American Greetings Corporation, a manufacturer and distributor of greeting cards and related products:

	Apple	American Greetings
Cost of goods sold	$9,888,000,000	$905,201,000
Inventory, end of year	165,000,000	222,874,000
Inventory, beginning of the year	101,000,000	246,171,000

a. Determine the inventory turnover for Apple and American Greetings. Round to one decimal place.
b. Would you expect American Greetings' inventory turnover to be higher or lower than Apple's? Why?

EX 7-20
Inventory turnover and number of days' sales in inventory

✓a. Albertson's, 40 days' sales in inventory

Kroger, Albertson's, Inc., and Safeway Inc. are the three largest grocery chains in the United States. Inventory management is an important aspect of the grocery retail business. Recent balance sheets for these three companies indicated the following merchandise inventory information:

	Merchandise Inventory	
	End of Year (in millions)	Beginning of Year (in millions)
Albertson's	$3,162	$3,104
Kroger	4,356	4,169
Safeway	2,741	2,642

The cost of goods sold for each company were:

	Cost of Goods Sold (in millions)
Albertson's	$28,711
Kroger	42,140
Safeway	25,228

a. Determine the number of days' sales in inventory and inventory turnover for the three companies. Round to the nearest day and one decimal place.
b. Interpret your results in (a).
c. If Albertson's had Kroger's number of days' sales in inventory, how much additional cash flow would have been generated from the smaller inventory relative to its actual average inventory position?

Problems Series A

PR 7-1A
FIFO perpetual inventory

The beginning inventory at Continental Office Supplies and data on purchases and sales for a three-month period are as follows:

objs. 2, 3

✓ *3. $11,420*

Date	Transaction	Number of Units	Per Unit	Total
Jan. 1	Inventory	50	$20.00	$1,000
7	Purchase	200	22.00	4,400
20	Sale	90	40.00	3,600
30	Sale	110	40.00	4,400
Feb. 8	Sale	20	44.00	880
10	Purchase	130	23.00	2,990
27	Sale	90	42.00	3,780
28	Sale	50	45.00	2,250
Mar. 5	Purchase	180	24.00	4,320
13	Sale	90	50.00	4,500
23	Purchase	100	26.00	2,600
30	Sale	80	50.00	4,000

Instructions

1. Record the inventory, purchases, and cost of merchandise sold data in a perpetual inventory record similar to the one illustrated in Exhibit 3, using the first-in, first-out method.
2. Determine the total sales and the total cost of merchandise sold for the period. Journalize the entries in the sales and cost of merchandise sold accounts. Assume that all sales were on account.
3. Determine the gross profit from sales for the period.
4. Determine the ending inventory cost.

PR 7-2A
LIFO perpetual inventory

objs. 2, 3

✓ *2. Gross profit, $11,180*

The beginning inventory at Continental Office Supplies and data on purchases and sales for a three-month period are shown in Problem 7-1A.

Instructions

1. Record the inventory, purchases, and cost of merchandise sold data in a perpetual inventory record similar to the one illustrated in Exhibit 4, using the last-in, first-out method.
2. Determine the total sales, the total cost of merchandise sold, and the gross profit from sales for the period.
3. Determine the ending inventory cost.

PR 7-3A
Periodic inventory by three methods

objs. 2, 4

✓ *1. $6,863*

Del Mar Appliances uses the periodic inventory system. Details regarding the inventory of appliances at August 1, 2007, purchases invoices during the year, and the inventory count at July 31, 2008, are summarized as follows:

Model	Inventory, August 1	Purchases Invoices 1st	2nd	3rd	Inventory Count, July 31
T742	2 at $125	2 at $130	4 at $135	2 at $140	5
PM18	7 at 242	6 at 250	5 at 260	10 at 259	9
K21G	6 at 80	5 at 82	8 at 89	8 at 90	6
H60W	2 at 108	2 at 110	3 at 128	3 at 130	5
B153Z	8 at 88	4 at 79	3 at 85	6 at 92	8
J600T	5 at 160	4 at 170	4 at 175	7 at 180	8
C273W	—	4 at 75	4 at 100	4 at 101	5

Instructions

1. Determine the cost of the inventory on July 31, 2008, by the first-in, first-out method. Present data in columnar form, using the following headings:

Model	Quantity	Unit Cost	Total Cost

   If the inventory of a particular model comprises one entire purchase plus a portion of another purchase acquired at a different unit cost, use a separate line for each purchase.
2. Determine the cost of the inventory on July 31, 2008, by the last-in, first-out method, following the procedures indicated in (1).

3. Determine the cost of the inventory on July 31, 2008, by the average cost method, using the columnar headings indicated in (1).
4. ▬▬▶ Discuss which method (FIFO or LIFO) would be preferred for income tax purposes in periods of (a) rising prices and (b) declining prices.

PR 7-4A
Lower-of-cost-or-market inventory
obj. 6
✓ Total LCM, $43,703

If the working papers correlating with this textbook are not used, omit Problem 7-4A.

Data on the physical inventory of Exchange Company as of December 31, 2008, are presented in the working papers. The quantity of each commodity on hand has been determined and recorded on the inventory sheet. Unit market prices have also been determined as of December 31 and recorded on the sheet. The inventory is to be determined at cost and also at the lower of cost or market, using the first-in, first-out method. Quantity and cost data from the last purchases invoice of the year and the next-to-the-last purchases invoice are summarized as follows:

	Last Purchases Invoice		Next-to-the-Last Purchases Invoice	
Description	Quantity Purchased	Unit Cost	Quantity Purchased	Unit Cost
AC172	25	$ 60	30	$ 58
BE43	35	175	20	180
CJ9	18	130	25	128
E34	150	25	100	24
F17	10	565	10	560
G68	100	15	100	14
K41	10	385	5	384
Q79	500	6	500	6
RZ13	80	22	50	21
S60	5	250	4	260
W21	100	20	75	19
XR90	9	750	9	740

Instructions
Record the appropriate unit costs on the inventory sheet, and complete the pricing of the inventory. When there are two different unit costs applicable to an item, proceed as follows:

1. Draw a line through the quantity, and insert the quantity and unit cost of the last purchase.
2. On the following line, insert the quantity and unit cost of the next-to-the-last purchase.
3. Total the cost and market columns and insert the lower of the two totals in the Lower of C or M column. The first item on the inventory sheet has been completed as an example.

PR 7-5A
Retail method; gross profit method
obj. 7
✓ 1. $306,000

Selected data on merchandise inventory, purchases, and sales for Hacienda Co. and San Lucas Co. are as follows:

	Cost	Retail
Hacienda Co.		
Merchandise inventory, June 1	$ 200,000	$ 290,000
Transactions during June:		
Purchases (net)	2,086,000	2,885,000
Sales		2,780,000
Sales returns and allowances		30,000
San Lucas Co.		
Merchandise inventory, November 1	$ 225,000	
Transactions during November and December:		
Purchases (net)	1,685,000	
Sales	2,815,000	
Sales returns and allowances	85,000	
Estimated gross profit rate	40%	

Instructions
1. Determine the estimated cost of the merchandise inventory of Hacienda Co. on June 30 by the retail method, presenting details of the computations.
2. a. Estimate the cost of the merchandise inventory of San Lucas Co. on December 31 by the gross profit method, presenting details of the computations.
   b. Assume that San Lucas Co. took a physical inventory on December 31 and discovered that $269,250 of merchandise was on hand. What was the estimated loss of inventory due to theft or damage during November and December?

Problems Series B

PR 7-1B
FIFO perpetual inventory
objs. 2, 3

✓ *3. $1,560,000*

The beginning inventory of merchandise at Citrine Co. and data on purchases and sales for a three-month period are as follows:

Date		Transaction	Number of Units	Per Unit	Total
March	1	Inventory	132	$1,500	$198,000
	8	Purchase	108	2,000	216,000
	11	Sale	72	4,800	345,600
	22	Sale	66	4,800	316,800
April	3	Purchase	96	2,300	220,800
	10	Sale	60	5,000	300,000
	21	Sale	30	5,000	150,000
	30	Purchase	120	2,350	282,000
May	5	Sale	120	5,250	630,000
	13	Sale	72	5,250	378,000
	21	Purchase	180	2,400	432,000
	28	Sale	90	5,400	486,000

Instructions
1. Record the inventory, purchases, and cost of merchandise sold data in a perpetual inventory record similar to the one illustrated in Exhibit 3, using the first-in, first-out method.
2. Determine the total sales and the total cost of merchandise sold for the period. Journalize the entries in the sales and cost of merchandise sold accounts. Assume that all sales were on account.
3. Determine the gross profit from sales for the period.
4. Determine the ending inventory cost.

PR 7-2B
LIFO perpetual inventory
objs. 2, 3

✓ *2. Gross profit, $1,527,600*

The beginning inventory and data on purchases and sales for a three-month period are shown in Problem 7-1B.

Instructions
1. Record the inventory, purchases, and cost of merchandise sold data in a perpetual inventory record similar to the one illustrated in Exhibit 4, using the last-in, first-out method.
2. Determine the total sales, the total cost of merchandise sold, and the gross profit from sales for the period.
3. Determine the ending inventory cost.

PR 7-3B
Periodic inventory by three methods

Concord Appliances uses the periodic inventory system. Details regarding the inventory of appliances at January 1, 2008, purchases invoices during the year, and the inventory count at December 31, 2008, are summarized as follows:

objs. 2, 4

✓1. $11,108

| Model | Inventory, January 1 | Purchases Invoices ||| Inventory Count, December 31 |
		1st	2nd	3rd	
F10	5 at $ 60	6 at $ 65	2 at $ 65	2 at $ 70	3
J64	6 at 305	3 at 310	3 at 316	4 at 317	4
M13	2 at 520	2 at 527	2 at 530	2 at 535	4
Q73	6 at 520	8 at 531	4 at 549	6 at 542	7
144Z	9 at 213	7 at 215	6 at 222	6 at 225	11
Z120	—	4 at 222	4 at 232	—	2
W941	4 at 140	6 at 144	8 at 148	7 at 156	5

Instructions

1. Determine the cost of the inventory on December 31, 2008, by the first-in, first-out method. Present data in columnar form, using the following headings:

    Model   Quantity   Unit Cost   Total Cost

    If the inventory of a particular model comprises one entire purchase plus a portion of another purchase acquired at a different unit cost, use a separate line for each purchase.
2. Determine the cost of the inventory on December 31, 2008, by the last-in, first-out method, following the procedures indicated in (1).
3. Determine the cost of the inventory on December 31, 2008, by the average cost method, using the columnar headings indicated in (1).
4. ▬▬▶ Discuss which method (FIFO or LIFO) would be preferred for income tax purposes in periods of (a) rising prices and (b) declining prices.

PR 7-4B
Lower-of-cost-or-market inventory
obj. 6
✓Total LCM, $43,548

If the working papers correlating with this textbook are not used, omit Problem 7-4B.

Data on the physical inventory of Satchell Co. as of December 31, 2008, are presented in the working papers. The quantity of each commodity on hand has been determined and recorded on the inventory sheet. Unit market prices have also been determined as of December 31 and recorded on the sheet. The inventory is to be determined at cost and also at the lower of cost or market, using the first-in, first-out method. Quantity and cost data from the last purchases invoice of the year and the next-to-the-last purchases invoice are summarized as follows:

| | Last Purchases Invoice | | Next-to-the-Last Purchases Invoice | |
Description	Quantity Purchased	Unit Cost	Quantity Purchased	Unit Cost
AC172	30	$ 60	40	$ 59
BE43	25	175	15	180
CJ9	20	130	15	128
E34	150	25	100	27
F17	6	550	15	540
G68	75	14	100	13
K41	8	400	4	398
Q79	500	6	500	7
RZ13	65	22	50	21
S60	5	250	4	260
W21	120	20	115	17
XR90	10	750	8	740

Instructions

Record the appropriate unit costs on the inventory sheet, and complete the pricing of the inventory. When there are two different unit costs applicable to an item:

1. Draw a line through the quantity, and insert the quantity and unit cost of the last purchase.
2. On the following line, insert the quantity and unit cost of the next-to-the-last purchase.
3. Total the cost and market columns and insert the lower of the two totals in the Lower of C or M column. The first item on the inventory sheet has been completed as an example.

PR 7-5B
Retail method; gross profit method

obj. 7

✓ 1. $187,000

Selected data on merchandise inventory, purchases, and sales for Miramar Co. and Boyar's Co. are as follows:

	Cost	Retail
Miramar Co.		
Merchandise inventory, March 1	$ 185,000	$ 280,000
Transactions during March:		
Purchases (net)	2,246,000	3,295,000
Sales		3,360,000
Sales returns and allowances		60,000
Boyar's Co.		
Merchandise inventory, August 1	$ 425,000	
Transactions during August and September:		
Purchases (net)	2,980,000	
Sales	5,075,000	
Sales returns and allowances	75,000	
Estimated gross profit rate	40%	

Instructions

1. Determine the estimated cost of the merchandise inventory of Miramar Co. on March 31 by the retail method, presenting details of the computations.
2. a. Estimate the cost of the merchandise inventory of Boyar's Co. on September 30 by the gross profit method, presenting details of the computations.
   b. Assume that Boyar's Co. took a physical inventory on September 30 and discovered that $398,250 of merchandise was on hand. What was the estimated loss of inventory due to theft or damage during August and September?

Special Activities

SA 7-1
Ethics and professional conduct in business

ETHICS

Beeson Co. is experiencing a decrease in sales and operating income for the fiscal year ending December 31, 2008. Julia Faure, controller of Beeson Co., has suggested that all orders received before the end of the fiscal year be shipped by midnight, December 31, 2008, even if the shipping department must work overtime. Since Beeson Co. ships all merchandise FOB shipping point, it would record all such shipments as sales for the year ending December 31, 2008, thereby offsetting some of the decreases in sales and operating income.
➤ Discuss whether Julia Faure is behaving in a professional manner.

SA 7-2
LIFO and inventory flow

The following is an excerpt from a conversation between Jack O'Brien, the warehouse manager for Murrieta Wholesale Co., and its accountant, Carole Timmons. Murrieta Wholesale operates a large regional warehouse that supplies produce and other grocery products to grocery stores in smaller communities.

Jack: Carole, can you explain what's going on here with these monthly statements?
Carole: Sure, Jack. How can I help you?
Jack: I don't understand this last-in, first-out inventory procedure. It just doesn't make sense.
Carole: Well, what it means is that we assume that the last goods we receive are the first ones sold. So the inventory is made up of the items we purchased first.
Jack: Yes, but that's my problem. It doesn't work that way! We always distribute the oldest produce first. Some of that produce is perishable! We can't keep any of it very long or it'll spoil.
Carole: Jack, you don't understand. We only *assume* that the products we distribute are the last ones received. We don't actually have to distribute the goods in this way.
Jack: I always thought that accounting was supposed to show what really happened. It all sounds like "make believe" to me! Why not report what really happens?

➤ Respond to Jack's concerns.

SA 7-3
Costing inventory

Kowalski Company began operations in 2007 by selling a single product. Data on purchases and sales for the year were as follows:

Purchases:

Date	Units Purchased	Unit Cost	Total Cost
April 6	3,875	$12.20	$ 47,275
May 18	4,125	13.00	53,625
June 6	5,000	13.20	66,000
July 10	5,000	14.00	70,000
August 10	3,400	14.25	48,450
October 25	1,600	14.50	23,200
November 4	1,000	14.95	14,950
December 10	1,000	16.00	16,000
	25,000		$339,500

Sales:

April	2,000 units
May	2,000
June	2,500
July	3,000
August	3,500
September	3,500
October	2,250
November	1,250
December	1,000
Total units	21,000
Total sales	$325,000

On January 6, 2008, the president of the company, Jolly Zondra, asked for your advice on costing the 4,000-unit physical inventory that was taken on December 31, 2007. Moreover, since the firm plans to expand its product line, she asked for your advice on the use of a perpetual inventory system in the future.

1. Determine the cost of the December 31, 2007, inventory under the periodic system, using the (a) first-in, first-out method, (b) last-in, first-out method, and (c) average cost method.
2. Determine the gross profit for the year under each of the three methods in (1).
3. a. Explain varying viewpoints why each of the three inventory costing methods may best reflect the results of operations for 2007.
   b. Which of the three inventory costing methods may best reflect the replacement cost of the inventory on the balance sheet as of December 31, 2007?
   c. Which inventory costing method would you choose to use for income tax purposes? Why?
   d. Discuss the advantages and disadvantages of using a perpetual inventory system. From the data presented in this case, is there any indication of the adequacy of inventory levels during the year?

SA 7-4
Inventory ratios for Dell and HP

Dell Inc. and Hewlett-Packard Development Company, L.P. (HP) are both manufacturers of computer equipment and peripherals. However, the two companies follow two different strategies. Dell follows a build-to-order strategy, where the consumer orders the computer from a Web page. The order is then manufactured and shipped to the customer within days of the order. In contrast, HP follows a build-to-stock strategy, where the computer is first built for inventory, then sold from inventory to retailers, such as Best Buy. The two strategies can be seen in the difference between the inventory turnover and number of days' sales in inventory ratios for the two companies. The following financial statement information is provided for Dell and HP for a recent fiscal year (in millions):

	Dell	HP
Inventory, beginning of period	$ 327	$ 7,071
Inventory, end of period	459	6,877
Cost of goods sold	40,190	66,224

a. Determine the inventory turnover ratio and number of days' sales in inventory ratio for each company. Round to one decimal place.
b. Interpret the difference between the ratios for the two companies.

SA 7-5
Comparing inventory ratios for two companies

The Neiman Marcus Group, Inc., is a high-end specialty retailer, while Amazon.com uses its e-commerce services, features, and technologies to sell its products through the Internet. Recent balance sheet inventory disclosures for Neiman Marcus and Amazon.com are as follows:

	End-of-Period Inventory	Beginning-of-Period Inventory
Neiman Marcus Group, Inc.	$720,277,000	$687,062,000
Amazon.com	479,709,000	293,917,000

The cost of merchandise sold reported by each company was as follows:

	Neiman Marcus Group, Inc.	Amazon.com
Cost of merchandise sold	$2,321,110,000	$5,319,127,000

a. Determine the inventory turnover and number of days' sales in inventory for Neiman Marcus and Amazon.com.
b. ◖▬▬▬▶ Interpret your results.

SA 7-6
Comparing inventory ratios for three companies

The general merchandise retail industry has a number of segments represented by the following companies:

Company Name	Merchandise Concept
Costco Wholesale Corporation	Membership warehouse
Wal-Mart	Discount general merchandise
JCPenney	Department store

For a recent year, the following cost of merchandise sold and beginning and ending inventories have been provided from corporate annual reports for these three companies:

	Costco	Wal-Mart	JCPenney
Cost of merchandise sold	$42,092	$219,793	$11,285
Merchandise inventory, beginning	3,339	26,612	3,156
Merchandise inventory, ending	3,644	29,447	3,169

a. Determine the inventory turnover ratio for all three companies. Round to one decimal place.
b. Determine the number of days' sales in inventory for all three companies. Round to one decimal place.
c. ◖▬▬▬▶ Interpret these results based upon each company's merchandise concept.

Answers to Self-Examination Questions

1. **A** The FIFO method (answer A) is based on the assumption that costs are charged against revenue in the order in which they were incurred. The LIFO method (answer B) charges the most recent costs incurred against revenue, and the average cost method (answer C) charges a weighted average of unit costs of items sold against revenue. The perpetual inventory system (answer D) is a system and not a method of costing.

2. **A** The LIFO method of costing is based on the assumption that costs should be charged against revenue in the reverse order in which costs were incurred. Thus, the oldest costs are assigned to inventory. Thirty of the 35 units would be assigned a unit cost of $20 (since 10 of the beginning inventory units were sold on the first sale), and the remaining 5 units would be assigned a cost of $23, for a total of $715 (answer A).

3. **D** The FIFO method of costing is based on the assumption that costs should be charged against revenue in the order in which they were incurred (first-in, first-out). Thus, the most recent costs are assigned to inventory. The 35 units would be assigned a unit cost of $23 (answer D).

4. **B** When the price level is steadily rising, the earlier unit costs are lower than recent unit costs. Under the FIFO method (answer B), these earlier costs are matched against revenue to yield the highest possible net income. The periodic inventory system (answer D) is a system and not a method of costing.

5. **D** The understatement of inventory by $7,500 at the end of the year will cause the cost of merchandise sold for the year to be overstated by $7,500, the gross profit for the year to be understated by $7,500, the merchandise inventory to be understated by $7,500, and the net income for the year to be understated by $7,500 (answer D).